Unrest in the Roman Empire

Lisa Pilar Eberle is Assistant Professor in the Institute for Ancient History at the University of Tübingen. *Myles Lavan* is Professor of Classics at the University of St. Andrews.

Lisa Pilar Eberle, Myles Lavan (eds.)

Unrest in the Roman Empire

A Discursive History

Campus Verlag
Frankfurt/New York

Funded with the kind support of the Fritz Thyssen Stiftung, the Universitätsbund Tübingen e. V., and the Forum Spätantike at the Universität Tübingen.

Fritz Thyssen Stiftung
für Wissenschaftsförderung

Universitätsbund
Tübingen e. V.

ISBN 978-3-593-51932-6 Print
ISBN 978-3-593-45850-2 E-Book (PDF)
ISBN 978-3-593-45851-9 E-Book (EPUB)

All rights reserved. No part of this book may be reproduced or transmitted in any form or by any means, electronic or mechanical, including photocopying, recording, or by any information storage and retrieval system, without permission in writing from the publishers.
Despite careful control of the content Campus Verlag GmbH cannot be held liable for the content of external links. The content of the linked pages is the sole responsibility of their operators.
© 2024. Campus Verlag in the Beltz publishing group
Werderstr. 10, 69469 Weinheim, info@campus.de
Cover design: Beltz publishing group.
Cover illustration: © Ivory relief, 'The Stoning of Saint Stephen'. The Walters Art Gallery, Baltimore: https://art.thewalters.org/detail/27619/the-stoning-of-st-stephen/, Creative Commons License.
Typesetting: le-tex xerif
Printed in the United States of America

www.campus.de

Contents

Acknowledgements 7

1. Unrest in the Roman Empire: Discourse and Politics 9
   Lisa Pilar Eberle and Myles Lavan

2. Tell Me How I Conquered You: Theorizing Accommodation and
   Unrest in the *Book of Daniel* 33
   Dan-el Padilla Peralta

3. The Roman Language of Civil War: From Internal War and *Stasis* to
   Bellum Civile 55
   Carsten Hjort Lange

4. Struggles to Define and Counter-Define Unrest in the Cities of the
   Early Roman East 75
   Benjamin Gray

5. Josephus's Multilayered Discourse on the Judean Revolt against
   Rome 103
   Katell Berthelot

6. Narrating Mutiny: Towards a Discursive History of Military Unrest 123
   Hans Kopp

7. Aporetic Unrest: Reimagining Materialism and Empire in Appian . 151
   Lisa Pilar Eberle

8. From War to Criminality: The Roman Discourse of Provincial
   Revolt 173
   Myles Lavan

9. Usurpers, Bandits and Barbarians: Narratives of Provincial Unrest in the Fourth Century 193
   Bruno Pottier

10. Towards a Discursive History of Christian Persecution 219
    James Corke-Webster

11. Violent Histories: Women and Unrest from Roman to Late Roman Historiography 255
    Ulriika Vihervalli

12. Roman War, Rabbinic Law, and Provincial Sovereigntism 275
    Natalie B. Dohrmann

Index 301

Contributors 311

Acknowledgements

In a way, this volume owes its existence to Jonathan Prag, who invited us both to a workshop on an entirely unrelated topic. That was where we first discussed our respective work on revolt and resistance, and where we conceived the idea for this collaboration. The project was made possible through the generosity of the Thyssen Stiftung, which funded the workshop in Tübingen in June 2019 that was the crucible from which this volume emerged. Not everyone who attended that workshop ended up contributing to the final volume, but those who did not still shaped our thinking and that of our contributors. We are indebted to Henning Börm, Damián Fernández, Gil Gambash, Nicole Giannella, Victoria Leonard, Michèle Lowrie, Peter Morton, John Weisweiler and Greg Woolf for their generous and stimulating participation; and to Antonia Lakner and Philipp Schäfer for helping the workshop run so smoothly.

Two major events intervened between that workshop and the publication of this volume. The Covid pandemic derailed our initial plans for publication. We are deeply grateful to our contributors for their commitment and forbearance through what proved an unexpectedly protracted process. The second event played out at the US Capitol on January 6th 2021. Those scenes, and their contested aftermath, hammered home the importance of the kind of sense-making that our volume explores.

The Schools of Classics and History at St Andrews generously funded a visiting fellowship for Lisa in spring 2023, which enabled us to co-write the introduction. Thanks too to the Thyssen Stiftung (again) for covering the printing costs of the volume and to the Universitätsbund Tübingen e. V. and the Forum Spätantike at the University of Tübingen for providing additional funding that allowed us to make the volume open access (twelve months after publication). The program 'Mehr Zeit' of the Gleichstellungskommission at the Philosophische Fakultät in Tübingen funded Leopold Luz' careful work copy editing and typesetting this volume, for which we are very grateful.

1. Unrest in the Roman Empire: Discourse and Politics

Lisa Pilar Eberle and Myles Lavan

On January 6th 2021 millions of people around the world looked on as a group of mostly white men entered the US Capitol by force. What happened that day in Washington, DC? March, protest, siege; coup d'état, putsch, insurrection; attack, armed invasion; conspiracy; legitimate political discourse; or white race riot? These are just some of the terms that have since been used to describe the events of January 6th (Lepore 2023). The choice of label is anything but trivial. The various terms encapsulate radically different understandings of what happened and its implications. Was it legitimate? What caused it? What response does it require? Might such events be prevented in the future? The different terms imply different answers to these questions, often eliding some while foregrounding others. As such, they each constitute a distinct attitude, a distinct politics, vis-à-vis these events, often intertwined with larger political frameworks and struggles.

The events of January 6th 2021 were hardly fathomable at the time of the conference from which this volume originated, in May 2019; and yet, these events and their aftermath vividly illustrate the central concern of our project: the far-reaching significance of how historical actors identify and explain instances of unrest (a term to which we will return). How such events come to be understood is in no way self-evident. The discursive construction of unrest is contested precisely because it is so consequential. Discourses of unrest prescribe not only attitudes but actions, sometimes long after the events they describe. The contributions to this volume analyse discursive constructions of unrest in the Roman empire with the aim of widening our understanding of the politics that pervaded this imperial formation.

Unrest

The claim that Roman rule had brought peace (*pax*) to the world was central to imperial ideology.[1] To later historians too, stability and longevity have often seemed clear and distinctive characteristics of the empire that demanded explanation.[2] Yet imperial society was arguably less calm and stable than these perspectives suggest. Various sets of evidence hint that at least some of the men and women that lived in the empire did not accept the circumstances in which they found themselves. Indeed, the empire itself provided important avenues for challenging the status quo. By petitioning Roman officials and the emperor himself, imperial subjects continually sought to alter their current place in the social order.[3] Crucially, this practice was not limited to social elites living in towns. Village- and mountain-dwellers in Egypt and Anatolia demonstrably appealed not just to Roman officials but also to the emperor (often to shield themselves against the depredations of those very officials) and some slaves had recourse to the refuge that the emperor promised them against the power of their master.[4] At different moments, however, people engaged in forms of collective action that aimed to change their allotted circumstances in life. Examples include assembled townspeople menacing Roman office-holders and local elites with turnips, stones or fire, plundering bands in the countryside seeking anything from higher wages at harvest season to the establishment of a new polity, slave rebellions, army mutinies and other uprisings – categories that in practice could readily blend into each other.[5] This volume's focus on 'unrest' is directed at this second group of strategies, involving collective action to contest the social constellations in which people were embedded.

---

[1] Woolf 1993 remains foundational. For a more detailed treatment see now Cornwell 2017.
[2] de Ste Croix 1981, Lendon 1997, Ando 2000, Noreña 2011 are key contributions to the debate.
[3] For this perspective on petitioning see Bryen 2013: 126–64, 200–2. Ma 1999 develops similar ideas in the context of the Seleucid empire.
[4] Kelly 2011: 123–67 discusses the social make-up of petitioners in Roman Egypt. For the evidence from Anatolia see Hermann 1990. Gaius, *Inst*. 1.53 as well as the various entries in *Dig*. 1.6 illuminate the special place of the emperor's jurisdiction vis-à-vis slaves and their masters.
[5] Strabo 17.1.53, Suet. *Vesp*. 4.3 (turnips); Philostr. *V A* 1.15 (fire and stones); Joseph. *AJ* 17.278–84, *BJ* 2.60–65, Tac. *Hist*. 2.61 (rural bands with high aspirations); Tac. *Ann*. 4.27 (runaway soldiers recruiting runaway slaves). Aldrete 2013 analyses the evidence for rioting in Rome. Shaw 2013 discusses social conflict during harvesting season. Morton 2012 examines the tension between slave revolt and provincial rebellion in second-century BCE Sicily.

Just how often did such forms of unrest occur? In an attempt to question Rome's success at bringing peace to the world, Thomas Pékary catalogued all attested instances of such unrest between 31/30 BCE and 189/90 CE and found a total of 138 separate events.[6] It remains hard to know what to do with this number. It is clear that these instances only represent the tip of an iceberg. The evidence we have is incidental and in no way complete. The ancient historians of the period considered many of these events unworthy of inclusion in their works; many were also invested in silencing and trivialising their occurrence.[7] In his *Histories* Tacitus dramatised the succession crisis of 68–69 CE by narrating seemingly unrelated instances of slave uprisings, mutinies, provincial rebellions and civic discord in Achaea, Asia, Pontus, northern Africa and various parts of Gaul.[8] Did he know of a similar range of events for other years in the first century? And how many other instances of unrest in 68–69 were unknown to Tacitus, or neglected by him? Our inability to answer these questions makes it impossible to meaningfully assess the incidence of unrest in the empire, let alone compare it with other periods and places. Yet contemporary authors do not appear to presume that their readers would be surprised to learn about such events. On balance, it seems likely that various forms of unrest – from banditry and urban protest to anti-Roman uprisings and rebellious slaves and soldiers – were pervasive features of the Roman world. Grasping their causes, unfolding and consequences is important to our understanding of social and political life in the empire.[9]

Yet the surviving evidence makes these questions hard to answer. The narrative sources for unrest are problematic on more than one level. Besides the issue of the unknown number of events which they overlooked or chose

---

6 Pékary 1989. For a similar inventory in the city of Rome between 200 BCE and 375 CE see Aldrete 2013: 425, counting 154 instances.
7 Cf. Cass. Dio 51.20.5. For the ideological and pragmatic background to the silencing see Woolf 1993, Gambash 2015: 124–43.
8 Pékary 1989: 140 gathers the relevant passages. Lavan 2017: 34 analyses Tacitus's goals in featuring these events.
9 Beyond analyses of individual revolts and regions, see Dyson 1971, 1975 and Gambash 2015 on provincial revolts; Shaw 1984, Riess 2001 and Grünewald 2004 on banditry; MacMullen 1985 and Flaig 1992 on usurpation; Kelly 2007, Aldrete 2013 and Magalhães de Oliveira 2012, 2020 on urban protest; Urbainczyk 2008 and Bradley 2011 on slave revolts; Thonemann 2013 on non-state spaces. A lot of these works focus on the west; for a survey of unrest from the Greek-speaking East see Brélaz 2005. MacMullen 1966 and Shaw 2000 provide helpful, if more pointillistic overviews. On resistance in forms other than unrest see, most recently, the contributions in Jolowicz and Elsner 2023.

to suppress, there is the brusque brevity with which they treat those they do mention. With the singular exception of the rebellion in Judaea between 66 and 73 CE, few instances of unrest receive more than a sentence or two. More importantly, research on revolt and resistance in other periods and places should make Roman historians suspicious of how the elite authors of these texts recount these events. In 1381, Ricardian England witnessed a large-scale peasant rebellion, attested by numerous contemporary authors of high literature like Chaucer. Yet Stephen Justice has shown, by contrasting their accounts with six enigmatic texts that originated among the rebels, that Chaucer and his peers were simply incapable of comprehending the rebels' motivations and strategies. Justice brilliantly reconstructs 'a political culture in the countryside that the lords and chroniclers and poets barely knew *of* before the events of 1381 exploded it in their faces, and which, even then, they could not *know*' (1994: 5).

Ranajit Guha developed and systematised similar ideas in his work on peasant revolts in British India (1983, 1999). His influential studies showed that the authors of many accounts of peasant rebellion in India, from colonial administrators to historians working in the twentieth century, pay no heed to the worlds of the peasant rebels. While some deny the rebels' actions legitimacy by deploying the tropes of barbarism, immorality and criminality; others deny them rationality and even agency by resorting to notions of spontaneity and attempting to explain their actions as quasi-automatic responses to external stimuli.[10] For Guha all these authors, including liberal and radical historians critical of British rule, partake in 'the prose of counter-insurgency'; in refusing to centre the consciousness of the rebels, they all side with colonialism against its potential and projected alternatives (1983: 58–9).

Taken together, these ideas have important consequences for attempts to study unrest in the Roman empire. For one, we need to reckon with our own language and its politics. 'Unrest' is our gloss on the Latin noun *motus* ('movement', 'disturbance', 'unrest'), which, together with a network of related words and imagery, appears as the most capacious of the various categories Roman authors used to gesture at the events that interest us, capable of encompassing anything from the revolt of a provincial governor to incursions from beyond the frontiers of the empire (Lavan 2017: 22–23). The term is obviously characteristic of the 'prose of counter-insurgency,' ancient and

---

[10] Thompson 1971 articulates an analogous critique of then prevailing understandings of peasant rebellions in eighteenth-century England.

modern. It implies a static order, in which motion is a pathology. Its connotations of agentless movement tend to deny the actions and events to which it is applied a sense of purpose and direction. By understanding these actions and events solely with reference to an assumed order, the concept both disavows and delegitimises whatever politics underpinned them. This calls for some remarks on our choice of language and analytical lens.

Our choice of 'unrest' as a reference point seeks to harness the historical blindness that results from its complicity in counter-insurgency. A term that refuses to know has methodological potential for historians, who, in many instances, simply cannot know and are careful not to presume. We take 'unrest' as emblematic of our epistemological starting point: a guarded scepticism vis-à-vis the possibilities of knowledge about the frequency, patterns and logics of collective action through which inhabitants of the Roman empire sought to change the life circumstances in which they found themselves. At the same time, we distance ourselves from the boundary-work that the language of unrest tends to perform: reifying one set of people, actions, institutions into an order while externalising others. Patrick Lantschner has shown that urban unrest in medieval cities should be understood as forms of communication that were integral to the political system (2014). One can see various forms of unrest, from urban protest to provincial revolts, as similarly essential to Roman rule. They provided Roman authorities an opportunity to intervene, showcasing Rome's dreadful and redemptive qualities in equal measure: both the spectacular and randomised violence that the Roman state could wield and the realisation of its one big promise, (the restoration of) peace (Eberle 2018: 185–89).

Beyond refusing to treat the boundaries inherent in the language of unrest as meaningful for historical analysis, we also vehemently reject the way in which this language denies the participants in unrest their status as historical actors with complex beliefs and motivations. In fact, for all the scepticism that animates this volume, we are not completely ignorant about the kinds of politics that could and did inform instances of unrest in the Roman empire.[11] Indeed, the arguments of Justice and Guha give new importance to the scanty, but by no means non-existent, evidence for the politics that characterised unrest in the empire. Details that are usually viewed apart, in the context of the individual instances of unrest in which they are attested, can

---

11 See, for instance, Magalhães de Oliveira 2012. Some of the 'cultures of resistance' in Kosmin and Moyer 2022 also amount to precisely such politics.

when assembled in a more synoptic, empire-wide perspective reveal some recurring patterns.

For instance, ambitions of creating an alternative polity were pervasive. Past polities, from Persian and Hellenistic empires to more locally specific ones such as Israel, were readily invoked.[12] The goal of creating a new and better Rome also recurred and might have intensified over time.[13] In at least one case, imperial subjects seem to have aspired to create something that for all we know had not existed before: in the late second century BCE at least some of Aristonikos' followers might have aspired to become *Heliopolitai*, the members of a polity connected with the sun-god (Strabo 14.1.38). For all the abstract hopes that may have animated instances of unrest in the empire, many of them were also anchored in one of the most universal and visceral experiences of well-being: foodstuffs and how they were obtained. The price and production of bread and elite manipulations thereof were a continual focal point for urban protest all throughout the empire.[14] Increased agrarian prosperity numbered among the promises of both revolting slaves and rebellious provincial elites.[15]

Ultimately, of course, the politics of unrest could have highly particular, often local, inflections. In his campaigns against Roman rule the Pontic king Mithridates seems to have exploited stereotypes of Roman greed that had a long history in the Greek East.[16] In early first-century CE Ephesos a group of silversmiths managed to rally a crowd around the looming threat to Artemis' importance (*Acts* 19:23–32). In the late second-century CE Nile delta a group of self-styled *boukoloi* (shepherds) drew on tales of pastoralist resistance with a long history in the region as they faced off against Roman legions under the leadership of a priest named Isidoros.[17] The distinctly Jewish politics of the three rebellions that engulfed Judaea and the Eastern Mediterranean in the

---

12 Joseph. *AJ* 17.278–84, *BJ* 2.60–65 (Persian); Diod. Sic. 34/35.2.24 (Hellenistic); Mildenberg 1984: 29–31 (Israel).
13 Eberle 2018: 196–99 gathers examples and evidence, from the Pseudo-Neros in the first-century CE Greek East to the polities taking shape in third-century Gaul and Syria. For possible intensification in the second and third centuries CE see MacMullen 1985 and Flaig 1992.
14 For examples see Tac. *Ann.* 12.34, Suet. *Claud.* 18.2, Zos. 6.1.1–2 (Rome), *IEph.* 215 (Ephesos), Lib. *Or.* 1.230, Amm. Marc. 14.7.2–6 with Magalhães de Oliveira 2022: 261–6 (Antiocheia).
15 Manganaro 1990, pl. 86 figs. 3–5 (slave rebels on Sicily); Schäfer 1981: 66 (provincial elites in Judaea).
16 Erskine 1999 outlines the history, McGing 1986: 105–8 its Mithridatic inflection.
17 Cass. Dio 71.4, SHA *Marc.* 21. For a possible cultural background see Rutherford 2000; Blouin 2014: ch. 9 provides a socio-environmental analysis of the events.

late first and early second centuries CE are the best documented and studied in the empire.[18]

Discourses

While we think it is important and possible to make some progress in recuperating the politics of unrest, the multiplicity of social worlds in which they originated, and the imaginaries of resistance on which they drew, the aims of this volume are more modest.[19] We focus on how people throughout the empire conceptualised and explained unrest, of necessity concentrating on the texts that have survived from antiquity, which were mostly written by the literate social and political elite. These accounts of unrest in many ways conform to Guha's model of the 'prose of counter-insurgency'.[20]

For instance, close readings have elucidated how Tacitus and his contemporaries could and did think about what historians today have come to think of as provincial revolts.[21] Unlike modern historians, they did not compartmentalise these revolts in a distinct category that set them apart from all other forms of unrest. Terms like *defectio*, *tumultus* and *rebellio* readily intermingled in how they understood these events. *Rebellio* is particularly interesting since it shows the imperial elite ready to recognise provincial unrest as forms of war, as attempts to fight back. The Roman elite also thought about why some people might choose to fight back. In their imagination the outrages and vices of Roman officials were common motives and causes. Other widespread scripts included the unruly nature of some provincial populations and the discord and lack of self-control that was pervasive among them. As should be clear, these thought patterns readily side with the empire against the participants in provincial revolts. They tend to deny agency to imperial subjects. Revolts are quasi-automatic reflexes, immediate reactions to the actions of Roman officials or manifestations of

---

18 McLaren and Goodman 2016, Rajak 2016, and Schwartz 2016 provide helpful entry points to the vast bibliography.
19 The papers collected in Courrier and Magalhães de Oliveira 2022 illustrate this multiplicity beautifully. For imaginaries of resistance see Goldhill 2023 and Padilla Peralta in this volume.
20 For the prose of counter-insurgency in a different ancient polity see Richardson 2010, who examines discourses of unrest in Assyrian official documents.
21 The following sketch is based on the observations of Woolf 2011: 33–44 and Lavan 2017.

essential qualities that are incompatible with the demands of Roman rule. While these accounts do not systematically deny the politics of revolts, they allow for at most a limited version thereof: *re-bellio*, fighting back, often understood as fighting for freedom (*libertas*).

Yet there is more to say about these narratives than just recognising their instantiation of the 'prose of counter-insurgency'. They also reveal conceptions of, and attitudes to, unrest that are historically and culturally contingent. The first aim of this volume is to analyse these conceptions and attitudes as they are preserved in the written record of the Roman imperial world. For this purpose we examine the operations by which ancient authors sought to make sense of, and respond to, instances of unrest. If ancient narratives are the imperfect lenses through which we can glimpse unrest in the empire, this volume aims to study the structure and shape of the lens, rather than the vista it may reveal. We are particularly interested in the operations of categorisation, explanation and framing.

Categorisation matters because the lexicon of unrest in any given language constitutes an implicit typology. The mere act of labelling an instance of unrest as one thing rather than another is an act of sense-making, an attempt to make the world legible by reducing its complexity and making it familiar.[22] Particular terms often carry with them assumptions about the people undertaking these actions and their goals and motivations, as well as about the nature of these events more generally: their origins, possible outcomes and their relationship to the surrounding social world.

For example, Latin lacked a specific term for the disobedience of soldiers (what today we term 'mutiny') but rather conflated it with the wider phenomenon of civic disobedience (*seditio*). As Hans Kopp shows in his contribution to this volume, this categorisation meant that for ancient authors unrest among soldiers was inextricably linked to understandings of unrest in the republican city, with important implications for how they thought about the potential legitimacy of such actions. More generally, the Latin vocabulary of unrest, as we find it in the republican period, was predicated on a distinction between internal and external forms of unrest – with *seditio* and criminality on the one hand and *bellum* and *rebellio* on the other. The invention of the category of *bellum civile*, which forms the subject of Carsten Hjort Lange's paper

---

22 On legibility, see especially Scott 1998.

in this volume, purposefully collapsed and blurred this distinction to great rhetorical and historical effect.[23] The meaning of these categories and the realms of their application also changed across time. The contributions of Myles Lavan and Bruno Pottier trace a gradual shift in the usage of the term *rebellio* from its republican sense of the renewal of war by a foreign people to a much more generic term for an armed uprising, such that even the actions of a rival to imperial power could be labelled *rebellio*. On the Greek side, Katell Berthelot outlines a shift in the usage of *stasis*, from the classical sense of complete breakdown in the political community, with many parallels to the later Roman concept of *bellum civile*, to a statist term for insurrection against the established power, like Latin *seditio*. We might, then, think of the Greek and Latin lexica of unrest as providing the malleable but resilient building blocks around which discourses of unrest in the Roman empire were structured.

One area in which ancient authors repeatedly went beyond these building blocks was in *explanation*, in positing causation for instances of unrest. Whatever the value of ancient explanations of the origins and course of unrest in revealing the dynamics of unrest (often very limited), explanations constitute a form of theorising about society. It is here, in the attempt to link causes and effects that we can observe implicit 'sociologies' of unrest – and thus also social order. Models invoking character – at times essentialising whole peoples, at times more focused on individuals – were remarkably widespread. At the more essentialising end, the minimalist trope of representing unrest as the eruption of an unmotivated, quasi-natural force, innate in some people or places, can be found not just in Tacitus but also among Roman jurists.[24] As Katell Berthelot's contribution on Flavius Josephus shows, the more elaborate (but not necessarily better informed) schema of understanding provincial revolts as reactions to the depredations of immoral governors or their agents and/or enacted by an ethnic group rising organically to secure its freedom, also provided important explanatory templates that appealed beyond the Latin-writing elites of the empire. Some civic elites in the Greek East also developed their very own pathologising accounts of unrest in the cities that they inhabited. These accounts, so Benjamin Gray demon-

---

23 The idea of *bellum civile* has had such a resonance, both in antiquity and in the more recent past, that the bibliography on the concept and its implications is vast. For recent studies of *bellum civile* in ancient literature see Ginsberg 2016, Ginsberg and Krasne 2018, and Lowrie and Vinken 2022.
24 Bryen 2023 discusses the jurists' notion of *mali homines* in the provinces.

strates, were inextricably intertwined with a new understanding of political life: in a normative universe in which peaceful co-existence and mutual understanding were the hallmark of *polis* life, unrest could only be the result of ethical failure and perversion.

The social and political elites of the empire were also able to think the origins of unrest in ways that lay beyond these widespread tropes and their moralising tendencies. As Lisa Pilar Eberle shows, Appian imagined that people throughout the empire fielded armies against Roman legions because a lack of land was forcing them to do so. Myles Lavan notes Cassius Dio's tendency to ascribe unrest to fiscal pressures. Bruno Pottier draws attention to the fourth-century CE *De Rebus Bellicis*, an anonymous pamphlet addressed to an unknown emperor, whose author located the origins of unrest in the empire's monetary and fiscal policy and how it inspired hatred of the *potentes*. On Natalie Dohrmann's analysis, the rabbis writing in the aftermath of the three Jewish revolts had a culturally specific understanding of what had brought about those revolts: potentially disruptive pressure points in Jewish society such as sectarianism and idolatry, which they sought to keep in check through their own legalist writings. In principle the rabbis were not wrong – or so Dan-el Padilla Peralta argues in his reading of the *Book of Daniel* as a playbook for cultural survival in the face of the epistemic violence that imperial rule entailed. As Padilla Peralta suggests, the strategies he excavates provided the parameters, including explanations and justifications, within which violent opposition to imperial rule could take place.

Framing is important because discourses of unrest and the explanatory models that they invoked gained their persuasive force from their connections with larger, pre-existing modes of thought and knowledge. Different cultures throughout the empire offered a number of different intellectual paradigms – discourses in a narrow sense – through which unrest could be comprehended. The chapters that follow reveal some of the most important, including political thought, ethnography, jurisprudence and rhetoric. Historiography – perhaps the most important frame for our encounter with ancient unrest – both drew on (and influenced) those other fields, and itself provided resources for making sense of unrest. Ulriika Vihervalli's account of how women figure in accounts of unrest in the historiographical tradition highlights an often-overlooked aspect of the strategies of meaning-making that this tradition invoked. Pottier's suggestion that the moral sentiments that the author of *De Rebus Bellicis* articulated in their explanation of unrest had some echoes in contemporary Christian writings adds yet another possible framework to the list.

Within the context of framing, the overarching divide between Greek and Latin lexica and traditions, their mutual influences, and subtle differences also need to be mentioned. For example, Carsten Lange's chapter in this volume shows how the Roman discourse on internal conflict in the late republic was shaped by inherited Greek models and also how Greek historiography of the imperial period was in turn influenced by Roman concepts of *seditio* and *bellum civile*. Katell Berthelot reveals how Josephus, a Hellenised Jewish aristocrat, narrated the Jewish War using long-established Greek terms and concepts – *polemos, stasis, lēsteia* – but used them in novel ways, reflecting his exposure to Roman norms, values and discourses on unrest. Myles Lavan demonstrates how Cassius Dio, a Greek-speaking Roman senator, innovated within the Greek historiographical tradition in order to incorporate the Roman concept of *rebellio* – the renewal of resistance by a defeated foreign people – into the Greek lexicon of unrest.

Politics

Discourses of unrest are always political. The various examples we have sketched vary in the legitimacy they accord to instances of unrest, articulate different understandings of its origins and causes, and in so doing, also prescribe differing attitudes and responses. Hence, we do not see the analysis of discourses of unrest as an end in itself. Instead, we aim to interrogate their politics, both as structures and as they are articulated and deployed in particular texts. We are particularly interested in the variety of relationships and attitudes to unrest that they instantiate, in the multiplicity of subject positions relative to the empire from which they emerge, and in their connection to other, often more general, forms of politics. Regarding attitudes to unrest, one can sketch a crude spectrum along which particular narratives fall depending on whether they conceive of the unrest as normal or pathological, inevitable or preventable, something that can be managed or an existential threat – and hence participation in unrest as calling for leniency or the harshest reprisals.

To illustrate this dynamic we might return to Tacitus and the imperial elite of the early empire.[25] The version of the 'prose of counter-insurgency' that this elite shared suggests that they felt remarkably unthreatened by provincial revolts. These men could see such revolts as acts of war, often in response to legitimate grievances. Arguably, this way of understanding revolts was predicated on a fatalistic account of their origins. For them revolts were inevitable. All the attempts at explanation we have surveyed ultimately harken back to well-known and unalterable character traits of human beings, especially to their vices. As a result, these revolts could not threaten Roman rule and its legitimacy. More particularly, this way of understanding revolts also prescribed a particular (re)action – fighting back in turn to establish, once again, the fragile peace that the emperor had promised the world – while precluding others, including attempts at institutional reform. It is striking that these are the precise forms of (re)action that we know this elite took vis-à-vis provincial revolts at the time.

One apparent paradox in the distribution of attitudes to unrest that the contributions to this volume reveal is that the most vituperative condemnation of unrest and clearest rejection of its politics tends to emerge not from the metropolitan elite but from the provinces, specifically from groups that aspired to leading positions in local society there. As Katell Berthelot shows, it is Josephus, not for example Tacitus, who systematically indicts the agents of unrest in Judea as criminous murderers (*sikarioi*) and bandits (*lēstai*). It is the rabbis, not Roman commentators, who seem most threatened by the prospect of the renewal of unrest in the second and third centuries – or so Natalie Dohrmann's contribution would suggest. In the cities of the Greek East, it is their fellow-citizens, not the Roman elite, who present challenging the status quo as a moral failure and a threat to the wellbeing of the polis. In doing so, Benjamin Gray shows, they sought to close down the politics of rival interest groups by denigrating various aspects of their actions as unrest not politics, thus breaking with a centuries-long tradition of Greek political thought and practice. Gray's analysis of this development together with Berthelot on Josephus demonstrate how the concept of *stasis* was transformed as part of this process.

It is widely acknowledged that the Roman empire relied on the cooperation of local elites. Demonstrably, this cooperation did not end with the collection of taxes and the reference to and reinforcement of imperial ideology.

---

25 Again, the following sketch is based on the observations of Woolf 2011: 33–44 and Lavan 2017.

Based on the contributions in this volume, we should imagine that local elites throughout the empire harnessed and retooled local tradition to patrol, delegitimise and suppress various forms of unrest in their respective communities. Dan-el Padilla Peralta's analysis of the *Book of Daniel* is a salutary reminder that these same elites could also rework and textualise such tradition in ways that created a place for them both within and beyond the purview of imperial power, thus maintaining a space from which violent opposition to the empire could unfold.

The contributions to this volume reveal the wide variety of subject positions from which narratives of unrest were produced. Yet the contributions to this volume also highlight the infinitely larger number of discourses and perspectives that our sources do not allow us to grasp. For instance, what about individuals and communities that were neither Greek-speaking nor Jewish? We might readily wonder how people in Gaul or among the semi-Nomadic populations of North Africa made sense of unrest in their midst. Moreover, as Ulriika Vihervalli's examination of the ways in which authors in the Latin historiographical tradition portrayed the involvement of women in instances of unrest, the surviving accounts of unrest are all male-authored. Women might not necessarily have thought differently about unrest; still, the fact that women rarely fought, combined with the existence of martial rape, made their experience of warfare deeply gendered, which might have given rise to additional and different ways of knowing unrest throughout the empire.[26] James Corke-Webster's analysis of the emergence of a uniquely Christian lexicon for the violence (*diogmos*) that members of this group suffered throughout the empire further increases the plausibility of such different traditions.

Lastly, discourses of unrest tend to be embedded in larger politics that are not directly related to the experience and metabolisation of unrest itself. At times, these connections with larger politics were the result of purposeful decisions on the part of individual authors and groups; often, however, they also reveal those articulating them as situated in their time and place and participating in wider developments in the history of the empire.

Regarding individual authors and works, Lisa Pilar Eberle's analysis of Appian's *Romaika* reveals his apologetic account of unrest to be connected with mid-second-century efforts to level the empire's geography of power: if provincials had fought against Rome because circumstances in the past had

---

26 On martial rape see Gaca 2014.

forced them to do so, there was less need to keep reiterating their subject status in the present. James Corke-Webster's account of how Christian writers understood the violence experienced by their community argues that a growing conviction that the emperor's virtues or failings were the ultimate determinants of the wellbeing of his subjects led second- and third-century Christians to re-imagine violence that their predecessors had ascribed to Jewish and, at times, local Gentile agency as having been instigated by particular emperors. Ulriika Vihervalli shows how Orosius, in an effort to mark the arrival of a new era, manipulated the conventions of Latin historiography by which the portrayal of female suffering in contexts of unrest signalled their heightened severity and tragedy: since the arrival of Christ only anonymous masses died in the context of unrest.

We may also note longer-term trends that reach beyond individual authors and their works. Classical models provided important templates for thinking about unrest, but it seems that the new imperial contexts of the Hellenistic and Roman periods complicated inherited distinctions between 'internal' and 'external' conflict. Carsten Lange's chapter sketches the early stages of this process, noting for example how the regulation of the award of triumphs began to police a distinction between wars that were external and those that were not. He also illustrates how Polybius wrestled with the question of whether third-century conflicts like Carthage's Mercenary Revolt or the revolt of Falerii against Rome were internal or external in nature. The chapters of Myles Lavan and Bruno Pottier follow the same thread through the imperial period and into Late Antiquity, suggesting that 'externalising' models of explaining unrest in the provinces were gradually displaced by 'internalising' models. Instead of being conceived as arising in subject populations that were seen as discrete foreign peoples, unrest came to be seen as arising from 'within' – as a form of criminality, the result of the (misguided) ambitions of members of the lower classes, or the justified acts of resistance against a tyrannical ruler. Arguably, this shift reflected wider developments, including the rise of jurisprudence as a prestigious tradition of thought and knowledge, larger changes in the conception of the empire among the metropolitan elite and the increasing frequency of (attempts at) usurpation in the third and fourth centuries with which this elite now had to contend.

But this impression of broad trends overlaps with a more punctuated picture of idiosyncratic experimentation and the pointed redeployment of traditional models. The chapters in this volume reveal a number of texts with quite singular understandings of unrest. One might think of *De Rebus Bellicis* with its unusual focus on fiscal and monetary politics or Appian's apologetic account of centuries of military opposition to Roman rule. The history of discourses of unrest in the empire remains to be written; the contributions in this volume suggest that any such history would have to combine longer-term trends with the start-and-stop of abortive developments. The present volume, as it stands, expands our understanding of the varied politics that pervaded the Roman empire. It foregrounds the intellectual labour at every level of society that went into (re)making this imperial formation throughout its long history.

The volume

The eleven chapters that follow present case studies in the discourse of unrest. They variously focus on particular contexts of unrest (Lange on civil war, Kopp on mutiny, Lavan and Pottier on provincial revolt), particular authors or corpora (Berthelot on Josephus, Eberle on Appian, Gray on Greek civic discourse), particular themes (Vihervalli on the gendering of unrest) or particular subject positions (Padilla Peralta on local elites struggling for epistemic survival, Corke-Webster on Christian accounts of violence against Christians, Dohrmann on the early rabbis). They share a focus on the discursive construction of unrest, its politics and its history. The order of presentation is roughly chronological, to reveal the plural histories we sketched above, while also illustrating the diversity of subject positions and diverse politics towards unrest that can be found in the surviving material.

We open with Dan-el Padilla Peralta's case study of how minoritarian groups theorised strategies of accommodation and resistance in the late Hellenistic period. He reads the *Book of Daniel*, a composite text that acquired its present form over a period from the fourth to the second centuries BCE, as theorising the scope for accommodation and resistance in the face of imperial domination. *Daniel*, he argues, tells its readers that minoritarian cultural experts could parlay their expertise, particularly in divination, into imperial recognition of the value of their culture (not to mention personal success) – though this would often require them to trump the claims of other minoritised communities. *Daniel* not only promises that this strategy offers a way to resist the claims of the imperial culture and still survive, but also memorialises reasons for why forms of resistance beyond the cultural sphere may be warranted. Read in this way, *Daniel* can thus be seen as expressing a theory of the possibilities for 'survivance', for preserving and furthering a minoritised community's cultural commitments in the face of imperial violence, developed in the context of the disintegration of the Hellenistic communities and the rise of Rome.

Carsten Lange reconstructs the emergence in the republican period of the concept of 'civil war', *bellum civile*. His chapter traces Roman responses to a series of conflicts that were clearly internal in some sense, from the revolt of 'allied' Falerii ca 241 BCE to the civil wars of the first century BCE. He argues that the Roman concept of *bellum civile* was related to, but distinct from, Greek ideas of conflict within the political community, both in privileging citizenship (as opposed to other modes of commonality) as the essence of the community that was being torn apart and in bearing with it a notion of escalation from other, less destructive forms of internal conflict. Lange argues that the particular concept of *bellum civile* emerged relatively late in the history of efforts by Roman statesmen and writers to make distinctions across a broad spectrum of internal and external conflict; he suggests it was popularised by Sulla.

Benjamin Gray examines how the citizens and communities of the Greek East narrated the outbreak and settlement of civic conflicts in the Roman period. He traces the emergence in this period of a rival new framework for understanding civic order, how it breaks down and how it might be restored. Where the classical model of political life saw struggles between antagonistic interest groups (so long as they were contained within political institutions) as the essence of politics, a competing new model privileged peaceful co-existence, personal sympathy and mutual understanding – and re-imagined certain forms of traditional political activism as a pathology. The chapter provides a particularly clear illustration of how understandings of unrest are bound up with understandings of a well-functioning society. Gray also shows that the development of these new ideas was itself political, as a class that prospered under Roman rule sought to shut down the politics of fellow citizens who argued for different values, such as autonomy, democracy or equality.

Katell Berthelot examines the account of the first Jewish revolt in Josephus' *Jewish War*, a narrative whose complexities have fed a vast literature on the causes of the revolt. She shows that the narrative interweaves at least three explanatory models that represent the war variously as a revolt against

Rome, an insurrection against the legitimate order and a rebellion against the God of Israel. She shows that these represent choices on Josephus' part, drawing on a repertoire of different ways of conceptualising unrest in order to make the revolt legible to his intended audience and deflect responsibility for it onto a criminal minority. She also highlights the account's complex politics, reflecting Josephus interstitial position as a Jew under Roman domination but also a member of an aristocratic class whose position was threatened by instability.

Hans Kopp focuses attention on the phenomenon we term mutiny, ranging over the works of Livy, Tacitus and the jurists. Unrest in the army provides a valuable case study in elite efforts to make sense of plebeian agency. Kopp illustrates the presence in historiography and jurisprudence of two different ways of understanding the course of mutinies, one of which sees such unrest as the co-ordinated action of a rational, self-organising community; the other sees it as irrational, frenzied and chaotic. Kopp's close reading of the Latin historians, particularly Livy and Tacitus, also illustrates how these sophisticated texts sometimes problematise conventional distinctions, such as that between the sedition of soldiers and *defectio* by allies, or between frenzied and coordinated action.

Lisa Pilar Eberle analyses a recurring feature of how Appian framed and accounted for unrest in his *Romaika*: by pointing to the rebels' *aporia gēs*, a concept that readily conflates the dearth of a particular resource, land, with the lack of alternative actions. As she shows, this explanatory model was most likely unique to Appian and inextricably intertwined with his view of human action and motivation more generally. Its intellectual roots might lie in the rhetorical strategies of conciliatory political rhetoric as evidenced in the Graeco-Roman historiographical tradition. Its traction in the Hadrianic empire most likely stemmed from its resonance with contemporary attempts to level the imperial geography of power across Rome, Italy and the provinces. If imperial subjects had opposed Roman rule because they could not help it, they could also be treated as something other than subjects. Arguably, Appian's commitment to this view of the empire and 'aporetic unrest' as explanation of unrest to match it was not only a political and intellectual choice; it was also intertwined with his personal identity.

Myles Lavan investigates Roman accounts of the outbreak of violence in the provinces in the light of a distinction between 'externalising' and 'internalising' models of unrest, depending on whether they conceive of unrest as occurring outside or within a political community. Models of the former type tend to conflate unrest with warfare with foreign peoples; the latter tend to see it as a form of criminality. Lavan argues that outbreaks of violence in the provinces continued to be viewed through an externalising lens surprisingly late in the imperial period. It is only in the later second century that we can see the proliferation of internalising models that see unrest as the work of criminous subjects, typically bandits (*latrones*). Lavan argues that this development reflects broader changes in elite conceptions of what the empire was and also the growing cultural power of the jurists. It is no coincidence that the spread of externalising accounts of provincial revolt is roughly contemporaneous with the extension of the activity of the jurists into public law and their increasing involvement in administration.

Bruno Pottier continues the history of how Roman historians made sense of major outbreaks of violence in the provinces, finding further changes as the nature of the empire evolved in Late Antiquity. Where historians of the early empire had tended to understand such conflict as the work of peoples who were ethnically distinct, imperfectly integrated into the empire and motivated to recover their independence, he argues, late antique historiography relies on a more varied but still highly schematic repertoire of explanatory models. One mode continued to associate conflict with ethnic difference, othering the populations of less urbanised areas. But a new mode conceived of rebellion in the provinces as a pathology of imperial politics, seeing it as the work of opportunists of low status who took advantage of moments of disruption to seek to set themselves up as rivals to the Roman state. A third mode similarly embedded provincial revolt in imperial politics, but understood it as a legitimate defence of Republican principles against the depredations of a tyrant. Pottier highlights the inadequacy of all three models and explores the challenge this poses for historians who seek to understand the dynamics of the events described. He also highlights a striking omission common to all three models, specifically their reluctance to attribute to these rebellions to socio-economic causes, with a single notable exception (the fourth-century *De Rebus Bellicis*, with its original and complex analysis of fiscal and monetary policy as the ultimate cause of provincial unrest) proving the rule.

James Corke-Webster analyses unrest involving early Christians as it was understood by Christians themselves. From this perspective, phenomena that local or imperial elites would have seen in terms of unrest or even criminality appear as persecution (*diogmos*). But this perspective too needed models to make sense of the outbreak and development of conflict, and those models were historically situated. In the earliest Christian texts, Corke-Webster shows, the marginalisation and violence that Christians suffer played out within a local frame: the wider Jewish community they inhabited, sometimes mediated through local political authorities. Only in the late second and third centuries do Christian texts begin to identify the emperors and the Roman state as agents of persecution. Corke-Webster argues that this reflects the influence of imperial ideology of the period, which encouraged provincials to see their welfare as dependent upon the emperor's personal virtues: virtuous emperors brought their subjects prosperity, inadequate emperors brought disaster. Corke-Webster traces a further change in perspective in the fourth century, whereby an increasingly self-confident Christian elite reimagined what previous generations had seen as persecution by the state's judicial apparatus as warfare (*polemos*) between Christianity and the state, with Christianity imagined as acting at the same level as the state, rather than being subject to it.

Ulriika Vihervalli examines the politics of narratives of unrest from a different and often neglected angle – that of gender. It is a reasonable assumption that women were particularly vulnerable in times of unrest, but that was not a preoccupation of ancient authors, nor is it Vihervalli's concern here. Instead, she investigates the role of gender in the narratives of unrest we find in ancient historians, specifically the early-imperial historians Livy and Tacitus and their late-antique, Christian successors Eusebius and Orosius. She shows that the appearance of women in their narratives is selective, stylised and deeply embedded in contemporary gender politics. One through-line is the use of representations of female suffering to accentuate the pathos of revolt narratives, a trope that can be traced through the four authors, with the single, notable exception of Orosius' description of his own times, when the absence of female suffering serves to illustrate the felicity of a new Christian era. More complex is the issue of female agency in the course of unrest. Both Livy and Tacitus repeatedly trace the ultimate cause of unrest back to women, or relations with women. By contrast, Eusebius's narrative stands out for the relative invisibility of female actors, suggesting that his understanding of historical causation had no place for female agency.

Natalie Dohrmann's study of the early rabbis opens up another perspective on unrest that originated among a marginalised group within the empire. She focuses on rabbinic discussion of culturally controversial topics such as sectarianism and priestly and prophetic authority. These discussions are not overtly about unrest, yet she shows they were informed by profound anxiety about unrest, given the long-standing tradition in Jewish culture of resistance to imperial powers. She reveals the components of a discourse that aimed at preventing unrest by marginalising potentially disruptive topics. The chapter illustrates the potency of silence as a response to unrest and shows that the strategy is not limited to hegemonic discourses. Dohrmann is particularly acute on the complexity of the rabbis' politics. Their anxiety about the spectre of recurring unrest was not just a pragmatic survival strategy aimed at preventing another destructive war, as it might have been for Josephus and his aristocratic peers a century earlier, but also a reflection of the rabbinic movement's particular commitment to legalism as the basis of their cultural authority.

The wide variety of events we loosely term unrest form the murky centre around which this volume is structured. Our goal has been to highlight the contestations over their origins, course and consequences as our sources allow them to come into view. We have also foregrounded our own subject positions as historians of the Roman world. As Ranajit Guha so perceptively established, the history of unrest does not end with the concrete events themselves. Onlookers were also participants in insurgency and unrest; observers, both contemporary and retrospective, have through their understandings of such events continually perpetuated and occasionally (re)shaped their historical import and consequences.[27] Ultimately, of course, this process extends to the present and to the ways in which historians working today categorise, explain and frame the different forms of collective action by which individuals sought to change the life circumstances in which they found themselves. By focusing on such participant-observers, from antiquity to the present, and the different ways in which they could and did understand unrest, this volume thus seeks to not only reject but also undo some of the boundary work between empire and its others that terms like resistance, rebellion and unrest are so often made to perform.

---

27 Guha 1983: 48. Price 2001: 30–39 outlines some aspects of this dynamic in regard to the concept of *stasis* and its application.

Works cited

Aldrete, Gregory S. 2013. 'Riots', in Paul Erdkamp, ed., *The Cambridge Companion to Rome*. Cambridge, 425–40.

Ando, Clifford. 2000. *Imperial Ideology and Provincial Loyalty in the Roman Empire*. Berkeley, CA.

Blouin, Katherine. 2014. *Triangular Landscapes: Environment, Society, and the State in the Nile Delta under Roman Rule*. Oxford.

Brélaz, Cédric. 2005. *La sécurité publique en Asie Mineure sous le Principat (Ier-IIIe s. ap. J.-C.). Institutions municipales et institutions impériales dans l'Orient romain*. Basel.

Bryen, Ari. 2013. *Violence in Roman Egypt*. Philadelphia.

–. 2023. 'Imagining criminals in the provinces', in Adriaan Lanni, ed., *A Global History of Crime and Punishment in Antiquity*. London, 43–62.

Collins, John J. and Joseph G. Manning, eds. 2016. *Revolt and Resistance in the Ancient Classical World and the Near East: In the Crucible of Empire*. Leiden.

Cornwell, Hannah. 2017. *Pax and the Politics of Peace: Republic to Principate*. Oxford.

de Ste Croix, G.E.M. 1981. *The Class Struggle in the Ancient Greek World*. London.

Courrier, Cyriel and Julio Cesar Magalhães de Oliveira, eds. 2022. *Ancient History from Below. Subaltern Experiences and Actions in Context*. London.

Dyson, Stephen. 1971. 'Native revolts in the Roman Empire'. *Historia* 20(2): 239–74.

–. 1975. 'Native revolt patterns in the Roman Empire'. *Aufstieg und Niedergang der römischen Welt* II.3: 138–75.

Eberle, Lisa P. 2018. '(Ruling through) resistance in the Roman empire', in Antoinette Burton and Carlos F. Noreña, eds., *The Cultural History of Empires in the Western World*. London, 177–99.

Flaig, Egon. 1992. *Den Kaiser herausfordern. Die Usurpation im römischen Reich*. Frankfurt.

Gaca, Kathy L. 2014. 'Martial rape, pulsating fear, and the sexual maltreatment of girls (παῖδες), virgins (παρθένοι), and women (γυναῖκες) in antiquity'. *American Journal of Philology* 135: 33–57.

Gambash, Gil. 2015. *Rome and Provincial Resistance*. New York.

Ginsberg, Lauren Donovan. 2016. *Staging Memory, Staging Strife: Empire and Civil War in the Octavia*. Oxford.

Ginsberg, Lauren Donovan and Darcy A. Krasne. 2018. *After 69 CE – Writing Civil War in Flavian Rome*. Berlin.

Goldhill, Simon. 2023. 'Epilogue: resisting resistance', in Jolowicz and Elsner 2023: 239–56.

Gray, Benjamin. 2018. 'A later Hellenistic debate about the value of Classical Athenian civic ideals? The evidence of epigraphy, historiography and philosophy', in Mirko Canevaro and Benjamin Gray, eds., *The Hellenistic Reception of Classical Athenian Democracy and Political Thought*. Oxford, 139–76.

Grünewald, Thomas. 2004. *Bandits in the Roman Empire: Myth and Reality*, London. Translation of *Räuber, Rebellen, Rivalen, Rächer: Studien zu Latrones im römischen Reich*. Mainz, 1999.

Guha, Ranajit. 1983. 'The prose of counter-insurgency', in id., ed., *Subaltern Studies II: Writings on South Asian History and Society*. Delhi, 45–85.

–. 1999. *Elementary Aspects of Peasant Insurgency in Colonial India*. Durham, NC (originally published Delhi, 1983).

Hermann, Peter. 1990. *Hilferufe aus römischen Provinzen: ein Aspekt der Krise des römischen Reiches im 3. Jahrhundert n. Chr.* Hamburg.

Jolowicz, Daniel and Jaś Elsner. 2023. *Articulating Resistance under the Roman Empire*. Cambridge.

Justice, Steven. 1994. *Writing and Rebellion: England in 1381*. Berkeley.

Kelly, Benjamin. 2007. 'Riot control and imperial ideology in the Roman Empire'. *Phoenix* 61: 150–76.

–. 2011. *Petitions, Litigation, and Social Control in Roman Egypt*. Oxford.

Kosmin, Paul J. and I. S. Moyer. 2022. *Cultures of Resistance in the Hellenistic East*. Oxford.

Lantschner, Patrick. 2014. 'Revolts and the political order of cities in the Late Middle Ages'. *Past & Present* 225(1): 3–46.

Lavan, Myles. 2017. 'Writing revolt in the early Roman empire', in Justine Firnhaber-Baker and Dirk Schoenaers, eds., *The Routledge History Handbook of Medieval Revolt*. London, 19–38.

Lendon, Jon. 1997. *Empire of Honour: The Art of Government in the Roman World*. Oxford.

Lenski, Noel. 1999. 'Assimilation and revolt in the territory of Isauria, from the 1st Century BC to the 6th Century AD'. *Journal of the Economic and Social History of the Orient* 42(4): 413–465.

Lepore, Jill. 2023. 'What the January 6th Report is Missing'. *The New Yorker*, January 9, 2023. https://www.newyorker.com/magazine/2023/01/16/what-the-january-6th-report-is-missing

Ma, John. 1999. *Antiochus III and the Cities of Western Asia Minor*. Oxford.

MacMullen, Ramsay. 1966. *Enemies of the Roman Order: Treason, Unrest, and Alienation in the Empire*. Cambridge, MA.

–. 1985. 'How to revolt in the Roman empire'. *Rivista storica dell'antichità* 15: 67–76. Reprinted in *Changes in the Roman Empire*. Princeton (1990), 198–203.

Magalhães de Oliveira, Julio C. 2012. *Potestas populi: participation populaire et action collective dans les villes de l'Afrique romaine tardive (vers 300–430 apr. J.-C.)*. Turnhout.

–. 2020. 'Late Antiquity. The Age of Crowds?'. *Past & Present* 249(1): 3–52.

–. 2022. 'The crowd in late antiquity: problems and possibilities of an inquiry', in Courrier and Magalhães de Oliveira 2022: 254–277.

Manganaro, Giacomo. 1990. 'Due studi di numismatica greca'. *Annali della Scuola Normale Superiore di Pisa. Classe di Lettere e Filosofia Serie III* 20: 409–27.

McLaren, James and Martin Goodman. 2016. 'The importance of perspective: the Jewish-Roman conflict of 66–70 CE as a revolution', in Collins and Manning 2016: 205–18.

Mildenberg, Leo. 1984. *The coinage of the Bar Kokhba War*. Salzburg.

Morton, Peter. 2012. *Refiguring the Sicilian Slave Wars: From Servile Unrest to Civic Disquiet and Social Disorder*. [Unpublished PhD thesis] University of Edinburgh.

Noreña, Carlos. 2011. *Imperial Ideals in the Roman West: Representation, Circulation, Power.* Cambridge.

Pekáry, Thomas. 1987. '*Seditio*. Unruhen und Revolten im römischen Reich von Augustus bis Commodus'. *Ancient Society* 18: 133–50.

Price, Jonathan J. 2001. *Thucydides and Internal War.* Cambridge.

Rajak, Tessa. 2016. 'Josephus, Jewish resistance and the Masada myth', in Collins and Manning 2016: 219–33.

Richardson, S. 2010. 'Writing rebellion back into the record: a methodologies toolkit', in id., ed., *Rebellions and Peripheries in the Cuneiform World.* New Haven, 1–27.

Riess, Werner. 2001. *Apuleius und die Räuber. Ein Beitrag zur historischen Kriminalitätsforschung.* Stuttgart.

Rutherford, Ian. 2000. 'The genealogy of the *boukoloi*: how Greek literature appropriated an Egyptian narrative-motif.' *The Journal of Hellenic Studies* 120: 106–21.

Schäfer, Peter. 1981. *Der Bar-Kokhba-Aufstand: Studien zum zweiten jüdischen Krieg gegen Rom.* Tübingen.

Schwartz, Seth. 2016. 'The impact of the Jewish rebellions, 66–135 CE: destruction or provincialization?', in Collins and Manning 2016: 234–52.

Scott, James C. 1998. *Seeing like a State.* New York.

Shaw, Brent. 1984. 'Bandits in the Roman empire'. *Past & Present* 105(1): 3–52.

—. 2000. 'Rebels and outsiders', in Alan K. Bowman, Peter Garnsey and Dominic Rathbone, eds., *The Cambridge Ancient History*, Vol. 9. Cambridge, 361–404.

—. 2013. *Bringing in the Sheaves: Economy and Metaphor in the Roman World.* Toronto.

Thonemann, Peter. 2013. 'Phrygia: an anarchist history, 950 BC-AD 100', in id., ed., *Roman Phrygia: Culture and Society.* Cambridge, 1–40.

Woolf, Greg. 1993. 'Roman peace', in John Rich and Graham Shipley, eds., *War and Society in the Roman World.* London, 171–94.

—. 2011. 'Provincial revolts in the early Roman empire', in Mladen Popović, ed., *The Jewish Revolt against Rome: Interdisciplinary Perspectives.* Leiden, 27–44.

Yavetz, Zvi. 1986. 'The urban plebs in the age of the Flavians, Trajan and Nerva', in Adalberto Giovannini und Kurt A. Raaflaub, eds., *Opposition et résistances à l'Empire d'Auguste à Trajan.* Geneva, 135–86.

2. Tell Me How I Conquered You: Theorizing Accommodation and Unrest in the *Book of Daniel*

Dan-el Padilla Peralta

Abstract: *This contribution argues for reading the Book of Daniel as an exercise in theory. Composed in a Mediterranean world of fractious territorial empires, Daniel exemplifies one community's turn to theorizing its own capacity for unrest and accommodation, in a manner analogous to what contemporary Native/Indigenous theorists have termed 'survivance.' The conflicts of the Hellenistic Mediterranean created strong incentives for the adoption of textualization as a strategy for survivance among subjugated and/or minoritized communities; in the case of Judaeo-Palestinian talkbacks to Hellenistic and Roman imperial expansion, this textualization took the form of fictionally emplotted theories about 'proper behaviour' in the teeth of existential menace. In the case of Daniel, such theory simultaneously justified conduct that ensured the ability of the subjugated to remain true to their culturally specific knowledges and looked ahead to the possibility of violent uprising – against empire itself, and against other subjugated communities contending for their share of success and visibility under oppressive conditions. This article works through four propositions that structure Daniel's exercise in theory: (1) the knowledge of subjugated Jews can serve the empire; (2) Jews will die for the Law; (3) Jews can read the mind and the future of the imperial order(s) that subjugate them; (4) the technologies of empire will prove to be their salvation. Shadowing these four propositions, which all act to conceptualize accommodation to and upward mobility within empire, is a threat: that Jewish experts will not work to advance the aims of empire if their pre-eminence is not fully acknowledged.*

I Backgrounds

The slice of cultural time that Hellenistic and Roman historians nowadays designate as the 'second century BCE' saw decisive changes in the theorization of unrest and accommodation, at least to the extent that changes in these concepts can be tracked in literary and para-literary media. These changes responded to, and to varying degrees sought to render intelligible, the disintegration of the Hellenistic kingdoms as the imperial Roman Republic become dominant over broad swathes of the Mediterranean. Faced with hard choices, some communities caught in the vise grip of imperialism did manage to survive the period's ravages of violence: there were options in the face of imperially fuelled calamity, as several ancient historians have documented with reference to the classical and Hellenistic Greek Mediterranean.[1] Indeed numerous communities developed forms of resilience akin to what contemporary Native/Indigenous theorists such as Gerald Vizenor (Minnesota Chippewa) have termed survivance: techniques for the assertion of 'presence over absence, nihility, and victimry.'[2] In general, tactics and strategies of 'resistance' to hegemonic control have lately been the focus of intensive study among ancient historians.[3] This contribution applies pressure to the coherence of 'resistance' as a category by tracking the development of a theory (or set of theories) about accommodation to imperial control, under the sign of anticipated unrest. With Anathea Portier-Young's reading as one inspiration, I will contend that the *Book of Daniel* gives expression to such theory; that excavating this theory's component parts yields insight into the minoritarian politics of the Hellenistic Mediterranean; and that *Daniel*'s formulation of theory should be understood as a form of survivance.

This chapter structures its recovery of theory around two other contemporary historiographical projects, neither directly connected to the ancient world. My title is an homage to José Rabasa's pioneering monograph on processes of 'ethnosuicide' in the colonial Mesoamericas, *Tell Me The Story of How I Conquered You* (2011). A sparkling treatment of the epistemic dislocations of the First Contact, this book attempts to recover the tactics of those communities that saw their knowledges corralled and exploited by the Spaniards. Rabasa explores how Indigenous knowledge-brokers narrativized the subjection of their cultural systems to Spanish imperial domination: even as they responded to the command, 'Tell me the story of how I conquered you', these Indigenous agents created and inhabited 'elsewheres', domains of ex-

---

[1] See Mackil 2004 and the collection of essays in Fachard and Harris 2021.
[2] I quote from Vizenor 2008:1. See Williams 2022 for an application of Vizenor's concept to Native/Indigenous classical reception.
[3] Purely e.g.: Weitzman 2005 and Portier-Young 2011.

perience and trauma and collective identity that remained closed off to their European interlocutors.[4] Even as the Mesoamerican scribes (the *tlacuilo*) represented their world to the missionaries that descended on central America in the wake of the conquest, they also projected, out into the space that was demarcated by a new imperial dispensation, a complex interiority of Indigenous experiences; but this interiority eluded the grasp of subjugators.[5] In a minor key, my title also calls out another powerful intellectual catalyst, the novelist and interpreter Valeria Luiselli's *Tell Me How It Ends: An Essay in 40 Questions* (2017). Patterned after the questions that Luiselli asks Central American child migrants as they prepare to appear before a US judge for deportation proceedings, this essay documents with wrenching precision how undocumented immigrants are compelled into habits of textualization by bureaucratic regimes, such textualization often being their only chance at survival.

I will not graft the findings of Rabasa or of Luiselli on to the Mediterranean world of the second century BCE. The hope here is simply to place their works in conversation with communities around the Hellenistic world that responded to the epistemic ripple-effects of imperial expansion by textualizing theories of resistance. During this era of cultural and political upheavals, strategies for survivance often looked to textualization as a technology for consolation and encouragement. Among the more trenchant examples is the book that was drafted and circulated by the Academic Clitomachus to his peers in captivity after the capture and destruction of Carthage. According to Cicero, the book consisted at least in part of a lecture by his contemporary Carneades and was prepared *consolandi causa* (*Tusc.* 3.22.54). Nicholas Purcell is probably right to observe that '[t]he complicity of men like Clitomachus ... with the Roman rhetorical project constitutes a more interesting and more repellent ethical problem for the historian than

---

4 See the definition of *elsewheres* set out at Rabasa 2011: 1–3; note especially the concept's affinity with and divergence from Doris Sommer's 'rhetoric of particularism': 'the strategies minority writers have developed to produce spaces that bar majority readers from entering'.
5 The affective response prompted by the labour to create and cultivate this interiority is the focus of Rabasa 2011: ch. 6, which works through Freud's 'Mourning and Melancholia' but cautions against 'universalizing our own provincial schemas and modes of understanding affect'. For a repurposing of Freudian melancholy to describe minoritization and racialization in imperial Rome, see Padilla Peralta 2024.

the swagger of Scipio, Censorinus, or Cato'.[6] But the most obvious candidate for a Rabasian reading, and not only because he seems to have been in the grip of Stockholm Syndrome for much of his life, is Polybius, whose *Histories* answer the imperative 'tell me how I conquered you' even as they report and communicate an embodied worldview that would have been remained inaccessible to Polybius' Hellenophile Roman friends – an *elsewhere* of differently configured social relations and in-group dynamics.[7] To skip ahead for a moment to the first century, one of Polybius' historiographical successors may have an even stronger claim to being recast in Rabasian terms: Dionysius of Halicarnassus, characterized recently by Matthew Fox 'as a Greek mediating a newly confident Augustan vision of Rome to a Greek audience across the Mediterranean', can with good sense be included in the roster of Greek writers responsible for the creation of a 'migrant literature' in the early Roman Empire.[8] Reading between the lines of the *Roman Antiquities* brings us closer to the structure of affect that is mapped in Rabasa's work: detectable are the ambition to tell the conquerors who they really were; the production of a cultural *elsewhere* through the re-description of Roman origins within Greek aetiological frameworks; and, more faintly, frustration with Roman rule and its cultural and epistemic exactions.

But for this contribution, I focus instead on *Daniel* as a key to unlocking the types of knowledge that were textualized within the crucible of Judaeo-Palestinian talkbacks to Hellenistic and Roman imperial expansion. Prominent among these types of knowledge is the capacity for generating a theory of 'proper behaviour' in the face of imperial domination. This theory, in addition to outlining the kind of behaviour that would enable the subjugated to remain true to their culturally specific knowledges under arbitrary and capricious rulers, also created a discursive space for the justification of vi-

---

6 Purcell 1995: 146; for more on the content of this text, and the unlikelihood that it mounted a critique of Roman imperialism, see Ferrary 1988: 425–28. For the mediation and ventriloquism of this collective suffering in Roman tragedy, see *Tusc.* 3.53 with Čulík-Baird 2020: 191.

7 On Roman (in)attention to the social dynamics among the Achaean hostages, note Polyb. 35.6 (the request of the hostages to regain their old honours on release, rebuffed dismissively by Cato the Elder) and Pausanias 7.10.11–12 (the varied experiences of the hostages, some of whom ran away successfully).

8 Fox 2018: 180; on Greek migrant literature see de Jonge 2022. In the background to Fox's representation of Dionysius of Halicarnassus is Gabba 1991, which remains useful for situating the Greek historian's project, though I part ways with Gabba on the bright line he draws between the situatedness of Dionysius and that of his predecessor Polybius; cf. Luraghi 2003 and Peirano 2010 for approaches complementary to mine.

olent unrest down the road. At a more abstract level, and with the hope of testing and evaluating this claim beyond the scope of *Daniel* itself, this contribution gestures to two additional premises. First, situations of unrest within imperially subjugated communities give rise simultaneously to non-violent and violent responses; the two are dialectically entangled. In and of itself, this claim is not terribly surprising. What may be more surprising, and for that reason in need of more sustained explanation, is the secondary claim that non-violent responses do more than simply index the shape and directions of their violent complements; it is under the cover of non-violent, because seemingly accommodationist or survivalist, responses that the parameters for violent resistance are developed and concretized. The clarion-call to resist resistance as a default characterization of minoritized dialogues with imperial power, and to think more expansively about 'the imaginary of resistance', should be heeded.[9] I write with this exhortation in mind, engaging a text that has been repeatedly foregrounded in modern formulations of non-violent resistance.[10]

To the extent possible, I seek to read *Daniel* separately from two texts that take shape around and give expression to compatible cultural frictions and ideological dilemmas: the First and Second Books of *Maccabees*. While the nature of Maccabean claims to power and legitimation as refracted through these compositions has been well brought out in recent scholarship,[11] I am more interested in *Daniel*'s commitment to a pragmatics of restless subordination. My attention to *Daniel* has the additional benefit of generating some insight, however indirect or slanting, on the afterlife of this Hellenistic textualization of unrest well into the Roman Empire. *Daniel* has a significant if still relatively understudied literary reception history, beginning with the appearance of the earliest fully extant commentary on a biblical author c. 200 CE.[12]

---

9 See Goldhill 2023, esp. 252–54 on imaginaries.
10 For Mahatma Gandhi's regard for Daniel as 'one of the greatest passive resisters that ever lived' see Cook 2022: 535.
11 Hock et al. 2023 pursue an instructive comparison of Maccabean legitimation strategies with those of the Koglwéogo in contemporary Burkina Faso.
12 For Hippolytus's *Commentary on Daniel* see Bracht 2021.

II Propositions

The *Book of Daniel* was composed in stages. The stories in its early chapters likely came together in the fourth and third centuries, while the major apocalypses – unambiguously pointing in the direction of Hellenistic and Roman power politics – likely originated in the second century. Several versions of *Daniel* were probably floating around during or shortly after the rule of the Seleucid king Antiochus IV Epiphanes (175–164), whose measures against Jewish ritual observance ultimately triggered the revolt at the heart of *1 Maccabees*.[13] Two features of *Daniel*'s structure are noteworthy. First, its linguistic patterning: chapters 1:1 to 2:4a and chapters 8–12 were originally composed in late biblical Hebrew, while chapter 2:4b to the end of chapter 7 first circulated in Aramaic. While Anathea Portier-Young sees this alternation in languages as an attempt 'to underscore the change in situation and call an end to cooperation and accommodation' (2011: 228), Paul Kosmin understands 'the sequence of languages, Hebrew-Aramaic-Hebrew, [as] trac[ing] the shift from covenantal independence to imperial world empire and then to the eschatological reclaiming of that national autonomy …' (2018: 140). This chapter's line on theory and survivance pairs well with either position. Second, the stories of chapters 1–6 seem to have been in motion separately from those of chapters 7–12. Their eventual braiding may have been initiated in a diasporic context but was probably brought to its definitive textual realization in Jerusalem.[14] This locking together of different tales results not only in a text, but in a theorization of unrest and/as resistance across the Book as a whole, one that enjoys a curious afterlife. I will have more to say about this afterlife in the conclusion.

As a textual assemblage, *Daniel* continues to excite and confound in equal measure. *Daniel*'s medley of genres and characters enjoyed a lengthy

---

13 In what follows, I quote from the NRSV HarperCollins English translation. Two Greek versions of *Daniel* have been transmitted in the manuscripts, the 'Old Greek' translation and the 'Theodotion', named after the translator to which it is usually credited. The Masoretic text (MT) aligns considerably more with Theodotion than with OG in chapters 4–6. Generally, see Collins 2001: 2–4 and Segal 2016: 3–6 on the textual tradition of *Daniel*; and Olariub 2022 for the important and well-substantiated claim that Theodotion-Daniel revises the OG version. I will not concern myself extensively with differences between the two Greek texts, though see n. 28 below. For the dating of *Daniel* in relation to the Maccabean revolution see Bickerman 1979: 93–94.

14 For the identity and activity of the scribal class whose interests animate *Daniel* see Portier-Young 2011: 229–32. The 'novelistic' properties of chapters 1–6 receive attention in Wills 1994.

reception history already in antiquity, as the ongoing study and publication of the Huqoq Mosaics has made abundantly clear.[15] The book's obvious familiarity with and direct attention to the jostling for status and power in the Hellenistic Mediterranean have placed it at the centre of contemporary scholarly debates about the extent of Judean Hellenization. These debates in turn orbit around a question given a memorably sharp expression by Seth Schwartz: were Jews a Mediterranean society? To the list of markers of Jewish Mediterraneanness that is supplied by Steven Weitzman in his review of Schwartz's book,[16] one might add the fusion of exemplary pastness and apocalyptic futurity as a discourse for articulating the violence of imperial subjection and for building up collective capacity to resist it. Although this discourse's lengthy pedigree cannot be elaborated here, one of its more salient aspects is the general move in third- and second-century Judaism away from prophetic and towards apocalyptic literature, which is rather more plugged into mainstream Hellenism than some scholars have been willing to concede.[17] In any case, my narrow focus in these pages will be on *Daniel*'s coupling of theory with textualization. At the core of *Daniel*'s storytelling are four interrelated theories about the right forms of accommodation and resistance to imperial domination.

1. *Our knowledge can serve the empire*: the subjugated can preserve their culturally specific knowledge, accumulate new knowledge, and wield the hybridized result in the service of their overlords. This is a theory about the cognitive adaptability and plasticity of the subjugated. In the opening chapter of *Daniel*, Israelites 'of the royal family and of the nobility' are brought to the palace of Nebuchadnezzar of Babylon, 'to be taught the literature and language of the Chaldeans' (1:3–4).[18] Those who are funnelled to the court include Daniel, Hananiah, Mishael, and Aazariah, who are renamed Belteshazzar, Shadrach, Meshach, and Abednego – a renaming that, isomorphic with

---

15 On the new finds at the Huqoq Synagogue see Britt and Boustan 2021. For the critical study of *Daniel*'s contents and themes see the essays in Collins and Flint 2001.
16 See Weitzman 2012 on Schwartz 2010. Note also the assessments of Hellenistic Judaism in Gruen 1998 and Chrubasik 2017, the latter more intent on decoupling local priorities from Mediterranean trends.
17 *Pace* Momigliano 1981: 338–39, for whom the apocalyptic strain is one of the forces that 'remove[s] Judaism from Hellenism'. I sidestep in this paper the archaeological evidence for Judea's Hellenization: see Harrison 1994.
18 For orientation to the historical and intellectual background of the 'Chaldeans' in the context of late Babylonian scholarship see Rochberg 2010: 3–18.

other onomastically mediated processes of social death and rebirth in the slaving worlds of the Hellenistic Mediterranean, carries over the theophoric properties of the former names across cultural and religious gradients. These four choose not to abide by the palace protocol for food and decline the royal rations so as not to defile their bodies (1:8–16). Their reward from their God is to have their knowledge – both the knowledge that they bring with them as observant Jews and the knowledge that they accumulate at the place – even further enhanced, such that, when the king orders them to be presented, '[i]n every matter of wisdom and understanding concerning which the king inquired of them, he found them ten times better than all the magicians and enchanters in his whole kingdom' (1:17–21).

This aptitude will be put to work in interpreting dreams, one of the more famous of which I will scrutinize in a moment. For now, two historical subtexts to this section of *Daniel* merit additional comment. First, hostage-taking as a form of talent requisition is attested in other settings for the second century, one more reason for presuming that the final redaction of *Daniel* took place during this period. To be sure, the thronging of Near Eastern royal courts with specialist interpreters is confirmed for earlier periods too; but *Daniel*'s scene-setting is cut from a Hellenistic cloth, notably in its emphasis on dream interpretation.[19] The machinery of mass enslavement, already in place for several centuries but undergoing a significant escalation in the period of *Daniel*'s redaction,[20] created incentives for captive representatives of subordinated communities not only to show off their cognitive abilities but to make the case that these abilities rested on cultural commitments that were worth safeguarding. Relevant here is the emergence in Hellenistic Jewish circles of a wisdom literature that stressed not only the intrinsic value of its cultivation, but the reputational rewards that would accrue to its holders even as they shuttled (or were trafficked) across the Mediterranean. In the words of the Aramaic Levi Document, composed at some point between the late third and early second century BCE, 'To every la[nd] and country to which he will go / he has a brother and a friend therein / He is [not a]s a stranger in it / and he is not li[ke] a stranger therein … / [Since all of them wi]ll accord

---

19 van der Toorn 2002: 39–41. The prominence attached to oneiromancy in *Daniel* 'seem[s] to depart from the customs at the Assyrian and Babylonian courts'; this departure has much to do with the increasing weight attached to dream interpretation in the ancient Mediterranean from the 5th century on. I return to dream interpretation under the third proposition below.
20 For notices on mass enslavements in the second-century Mediterranean see Volkmann 1990: 21–32 (Balkans), 47–49 (Iberian Peninsula), 51 (Gaul), 58–59 (Africa), and 65 (Asia Minor).

him honour because of it / [s]ince all wish to learn from his wisdom' (*Aramaic Levi Document* 13:8–9).

Second, there is no question that, throughout the Hellenistic period, religious knowledge-brokers derived tangible benefits from opportunistically leveraging their epistemic and world-ordering practices. Michael Segal (2016: 26) correctly notes that *Daniel* 1 'emphasizes the potential for Jews to succeed *as Jews* in the Diaspora … [by] excelling in their training in the foreign king's court, while all the while maintaining the strict restrictions which preserve their unique identity in this context'. The inter-articulation of divinatory skill, racial-ethnic origins, and sociocultural identity was not limited to Jewish dream-interpreters,[21] although the transmission of *Daniel* and other Hellenistic Jewish texts has ensured that we know more about them, or at the very least their literary figuration, than other minoritarian divinatory practitioners. However, other knowledge-brokers, and the communities from which they hailed, did not enjoy this same success; their failure was a necessary part of (imagined) Jewish excellence at accommodating empire. Maia Kotrosits has observed that *Daniel* offers 'an improbable and idealized picture of diasporic negotiation, in which the diasporic subject manages to ascend to the heart of colonial administrations while they themselves stay steadfast and culturally intact, even as kings lose their minds' (2020: 59). Yet in at least one respect the picture is brutally realistic: the prospect of one community's knowledge-brokers trumping another community's expertise incited and fuelled inter-ethnic tensions, as ancient readers of *Daniel* recognized.[22] I revisit this dynamic under the next two propositions.

2. *We will die for the Law*, or at the very least convincingly perform a willingness to die for the Law. By the time that Josephus sat down to compose his *Jewish Antiquities* in the first century CE, this was a well-established trope. In an analysis of the most famous set scenes of 'dying for the law' in Josephus, Steven Weitzman has remarked: 'Although these performances simulated the spectacles of death that so entranced the Romans, they used the histrionics of dying to make possible a different kind of denouement, one in which the performers are spared from actually having to die' (2005: 155). *Mutatis mutandis*, one can see a roughly similar logic at work already in *Daniel*,

---

21 For a Roman effort to grasp and represent this nexus see Cic. *Div.* 1.90–94 with Padilla Peralta 2018.
22 See Jer. *Comm. Dan.* 2:12–13 on Chaldaean envy of the Jews.

which recreates Hellenistic royal courts as spaces for Jews to manifest an unyielding determination to observe the Law, even at the cost of their lives – except that these Jews actually survive. As Tessa Rajak has detailed with reference to *1 Maccabees*, martyrdom is a Hellenizing discourse; so too is the script of facing martyrdom and emerging triumphant (2001: ch. 6). *Daniel* is staked to the fantasy that, when faced by the seemingly black-and-white choice between capitulating to the demands of empire or dying in resistance, the subjugated may have his cake and eat it too. Martyrdom, and with it ethnosuicide – to invoke a term of art in the Rabasian universe – is threatened; but neither martyrdom nor ethnosuicide actually takes place.

The most transparent instance of this occurs in *Daniel* 3, when Shadrach, Meshach, and Abednego are menaced by King Nebuchadnezzar with being 'thrown into a furnace of blazing fire' if they do not worship the sixty-cubit-tall golden statue that the king had erected on the plain of Dura. There will be no deliverance from certain death: 'who is the god that will deliver you out of my hands?' (3:15). The three stick to their refusal to worship the statue, are promptly tossed into the furnace, and, a short time later, are spotted walking around in the flames, apparently untouched. Nebuchadnezzar orders them free, marvels that they 'yielded up their bodies rather than serve and worship any god except their own God', and issues a proclamation that anyone who blasphemes their god 'shall be torn limb from limb, and their houses laid in ruins; for there is no other god who is able to deliver in this way' (3:29). Not only are Shadrach, Meshach, and Abednego vindicated in their decision to die for the Law; they live to be promoted. But the prohibition on any 'blasphemy' that is directed at their god is arguably even more revealing.

The text fantasizes that, as a consequence of successful defiance, the rug will be pulled out from under other individuals and communities whose worship of another divinity on a par with the Jewish god could thenceforth be construed as blasphemous; in other words, that the power of empire will be wielded not just to protect the communal ways of knowing to which Shadrach, Meshach, and Abednego subscribe, but to inflict harm on the agents of other systems of religious knowledge.[23] In this light, the trope of 'dying for the law' veils the desire to see alternative knowledges perish so that one's culturally specific one might live. The wish for the epistemicide

---

23 I do not disagree with readings that take this decree as responding to the blasphemous behavior of Antiochus IV, singled out explicitly at 7:4–25.

of others is coded into its DNA.[24] It is especially significant that the royal decree is figured as a device for epistemicide in *Daniel* 3, since portions of the text were almost certainly being fine-tuned as Antiochus IV handed down some of his more notorious decrees.

3. We can read your mind and your future. This theme, a fixture of *Daniel*'s content and messaging, has been carefully picked over in recent scholarship. 'Tell your servants the dream, and we will reveal the interpretation', the Chaldeans of the court promise Nebuchadnezzar in *Daniel* 2 after he reports being troubled in his sleep. Except Nebuchadnezzar plays murderously coy: he wants the wise men to tell him *his* dream and its interpretation; when the Chaldeans plead with him to divulge the dream first, Nebuchadnezzar accuses them of stalling for time and has them rounded up for execution. At this stage, Daniel rises to the challenge. Having first asked his companions Hananiah, Mishael, and Azariah 'to seek mercy from the God of heaven concerning this mystery, so that Daniel and his companions with the rest of the wise men of Babylon might not perish', the eponymous hero has the mystery of the dream and its interpretation disclosed to him 'in a vision of the night' (2:17–19).

The dream is, famously, of a statue: luminous, colossal, terrifying. Its head is made of gold, upper torso and arms out of silver, lower torso and thighs of bronze, legs of iron, and its feet of iron and clay. As the dream progresses, a stone appears and smashes the feet of clay and iron; then, as the remainder of the statue collapses, its pieces are swept away. But the stone morphs into a mountain, spanning the earth. Daniel's interpretation memorably casts the dream as an evocation of the *translatio imperii*: after Nebuchadnezzar's kingdom (gold), another will rise (silver), and then another (bronze), to be followed by yet another 'strong as iron' that shall 'crush and shatter all these' predecessors; but as a mixed kingdom, it will be fated not to remain together 'just as iron does not mix with clay'. It too will be brought to heel by the one lasting kingdom, installed by the God of heaven and therefore indestructible (2:31–45).[25]

---

24 On Mediterranean epistemicide see Padilla Peralta 2020; I return to this idea in the conclusion.
25 The interpretations of the statue's meanings, and of the cultural and historiographical backdrops to them, are many and varied; Momigliano 1977–1982: 133–39 is an excellent guide. On the long tail of the 'Four Kingdoms' motif, see now the essays in Perrin and Stuckenbruck 2021; note also the remarks at Haubold 2022: 78.

Impressed at Daniel's knowledge of the dream and its significance, Nebuchadnezzar prostrates himself before him, showers him with gifts, and grants him and his close friends promotions: another successful entry in the annals of the advancement of the minoritized under imperial domination. Components of this story find parallels and analogues in other sectors and times of the ancient Near East and the classical and Hellenistic Mediterranean: for testing oracles and dream-interpreters we might compare the trial of dream interpretation in *Daniel* to Croesus' test of the oracle in Herodotus, or Tarquinius Superbus' challenge to the augur Attus Navius in the Roman annalistic tradition. Meanwhile, the four-kingdom paradigm is hardly unique to *Daniel*, as the variations on the theme in the *Fourth Sibylline Oracle*, the Babylonian Dynastic Prophecy, Aemilius Sura,[26] and Pseudo-Daniel all attest. For present purposes, the most important dimension of the episode in *Daniel* is that it marks dream-interpretation as a practice through which the subjugated can reclaim agency over the hegemon: not only by demonstrating their capacity to know the mind of the conqueror, but by laying before him the impermanence of his hegemony. This feat's success is made conditional once again on besting other, rival practitioners of knowledge; and it translates directly into material rewards.

Other dreams are felicitously interpreted in *Daniel*, with prosperity attending the interpreter even when the message of the dream is bleak for the king himself. Without the time to cycle through each one, I want simply to advance one claim on the basis of *Daniel* 3. The inward turn of dream-interpretation fastens on to the response of the subjugated and subaltern to one material imposition of imperial exploitation, namely deracination; it theorizes dream interpretation as one skill that can travel even when its holder is displaced from home and hearth. I already noted with reference to the first proposition that Daniel and his friends were removed from and sent to the king's court. This forced displacement leaves them with nothing except the resources of their embodied knowledge, which they have somehow to wield effectively. In the universe constructed by the text, dream-interpreters from those communities at the end of the imperial spear may not be masters of their time and place, but they are masters of *elsewheres*: precincts of validation and affirmation that are unlocked through dream interpretation. These precincts are shaped by analogy to other commemorative landscapes,

---

26 On this figure (= *FRHist* 103) and his second-century CE date see Swain 1940; for his place in the conceptual evolution of *translatio imperii*, Gotter 2019.

chief among them the honorific spaces of the Hellenistic *polis*. As Kosmin notes, '[t]he statue's destruction', far from belonging exclusively to a 'a distinctly Jewish prophetic discourse and anti-idol polemic', deserves to be located 'within the broad civic culture of the Hellenistic world, [where] destroying the king's statue was a widespread, public, and self-conscious idiom for periodizing a community's history' (2018: 145, 147). Further confirmation of *Daniel*'s taste for Hellenistic idiolects can be found in the dream's visualization of historical time as bodily, an idea tapped in the *Histories* of Polybius.[27]

From mastery over the interpretation of the visions of others, it is only a short step to the generation of mastery through one's own visions, as chapters 10–12 of *Daniel* conjure in stirring terms. The representation of that mastery, which is held to be predicated on the manipulation not only of dream-interpretation but of time itself, brings *Daniel* in line with other efforts under way in the third and second centuries BCE to write back to paradigms of Hellenistic temporality.[28] Daniel is granted a vision that sweeps from the Achaemenid world of Cyrus the Great to the Hellenistic world in the maws of Rome, to the 'time of anguish', and finally to deliverance. The text's exemplification of Daniel as equally adept at navigating the universe of the Neo-Babylonians and the new dispensation of the Achaemenids, apparent already in chapter 2's effort to style Daniel as persisting through changes in imperial regime, is predicated on a capacity to predict the future that allows no space for fallibility.[29] 'But in that time', the archangel Gabriel confidently proclaims, 'your people shall be delivered, everyone who is found written in the book. Many of those who sleep in the dust of the earth shall awake, some to everlasting life, and some to shame and everlasting contempt' (12:1–2). The clause 'everyone who is found written in the book'[30] brings me to the fourth

---

27 See, memorably, Polyb. 1.3.4 on the aggregation of the previously disjointed histories of the *oikoumene* into an 'organic whole' (*somatoeides*), to be read now with Davies 2020: 123–25.

28 The relationship of the visions (or 'beholdings': Remington 2022 for a treatment of their sensorial richness) in *Dan.* 7–12 to the internal chronology of the text and its historical background remains much debated: overview and fresh attempt at reinterpretation in Coşkun 2019. For indigenous rejoinders to Ptolemaic and Seleucid temporalities see Kosmin and Moyer 2021, especially pp. 157–61 on the *Demotic Chronicle*.

29 Notably, the events forecast at 11.40–43 do not come to pass, one reason we can date the final redaction of *Daniel* to the period between 167 and 164 BCE; see Cook 2022: 520–21.

30 Compare כָּל־הַנִּמְצָא כָּתוּב בַּסֵּפֶר(MT); ὃς ἂν εὑρεθῇ ἐγγεγραμμένος ἐν τῶι βιβλίωι (OG); πᾶς ὁ εὑρεθεὶς γεγραμμένος ἐν τῆι βίβλωι (TH). For the importance of minor but revealing differences between OG and TH see Olariub 2022.

and final foundation of *Daniel*'s theorization of accommodation and/as unrest.

4. *The technology of empire will be our salvation.* It is the book that emerges as the technology best suited to deliverance, and most apt for weaponization. The textualization of Jewish communities throughout the Mediterranean has often been assumed to originate in a uniform commitment to the preservation and exegesis of the Torah. According to some accounts, this commitment was scaled up in a dramatic way after the fall of the Second Temple, with the Mishnah and Talmud bearing witness to the multi-generational investment in the production of exegetical texts as a method for safeguarding forms of cultural capital in the wake of collective devastation. Duncan MacRae has dexterously brought this cultural development into conversation with the textualization of Roman theology during the late Republic, a historical conjuncture where one can see the interlacing of writing and systematization to highly transformative effect.[31] But *Daniel* 12's mention of enrolment in the book points in other directions. Why the scroll/book, exactly? Commentators have been quick to point to obvious intertextual parallels (e.g., 'the book of life' in *Psalms*, a concept appropriated with gusto in the New Testament and apocrypha), but the depiction of enrolment in the book brings another set of possibilities to mind. Fiscality and militarism, two basic institutional aspects of the Hellenistic political and cultural universe, are foundations for the futurity envisioned in *Daniel*.

Yet there is another way of taking this reference to enrolment in the book, one more readily harmonized with Duncan MacRae's arguments about the significance of textualization. The theoretical heavy lifting of *Daniel*'s closing vision lies as much in its exaltation of the book as the guardian and vindicator of the subjected as it does in its millenarian tincture. In a Mediterranean where books and bodies were frequently lost on land and at sea,[32] the conviction in the durability of the book is arguably the most utopian feature of *Daniel*. Is it sensible, then, to join Stefan Beyerle in speaking of *Daniel* as a utopian text? In Beyerle's view, which admittedly is not without its detractors, the text's final apocalypse, culminating not only with the resurrection of the dead but with an overhaul of human social organization, clinches its identification as utopian. Addressing a different archive, but with her eye

---

31 MacRae 2016. For more on this systematization see Rüpke 2012.
32 Take Terence, for example: one version of his death had him dying at sea with 108 plays translated from Menander (Suet. *Vita Ter.* 5 with Richlin 2017: 170).

on the second century, and in particular the insurrection of Aristonicus and his 'city of slaves',' Page duBois has encouraged ancient historians to attend more carefully to the fear streaking through the Mediterranean world of mass enslavement: that the boundary-line between free and slave could be destabilized and scrubbed permanently, not just incidentally or temporarily as dramatized on the New Comedy stage.[33] On my reading, the processes of textualization that ultimately give birth to *Daniel* are not only bulwarks against culture loss and epistemicide. They are an education in how to menace the conqueror, through reminders not only that his domination will come to an end but that for its provisional duration he will have to depend on the skills – prophetic as well as literary – of those he has subjugated. It is the subjugated who will tell him how, and when, it all ends.

These, then, are *Daniel's* four pillars for a theory about how productively to conceptualize accommodation to and upward mobility within an imperial order as an unavoidably frictive dynamic. I have, of course, not paid attention to the full spectrum of possibilities for accommodation and/as unrest that *Daniel* exhibits. For a concluding synopsis, I turn again to Anathea Portier-Young:

... the writers of Daniel outlined for their audiences a program of nonviolent resistance to the edict and persecution of Antiochus and the systems of hegemony and domination that supported his rule. New revelation provided an apocalyptic frame for covenant theology and offered hermeneutical keys for interpreting scripture in ways that anchored the writers' self-understanding and understanding of history, current events, and God's future action. Each of these in turn shaped a vision for resistance that included prayer, fasting, and penitence, teaching and preaching, and covenant fidelity even in the face of death. They presented their program for action through prediction and narrative modeling. (Portier-Young 2011: 229)

Portier-Young's 'narrative modelling' approximates my own understanding of theory as a kind of exemplification, as a patterning not merely of a historically contingent response to suffering but of a framework for abstraction. Work on exemplarity in Roman culture has enriched my own grasp of the cognitive affordances of the exemplar, and specifically its ability to organize and direct models for right doing and right *thinking*. But I find equally en-

---

33 See duBois 2007. On Aristonicus' revolt, note also Vavrinek 1975: 129 on its significance as 'one chapter in the history of the struggles of suppressed peoples for freedom and justice – regardless of the fact that in the given historical conditions this fight was necessarily doomed beforehand to failure'.

ergizing the prospect of reading these pillars of resistance theory as *propositional*, in the sense newly put forward by Kaneesha Cherelle Parsard (2022): *Daniel* is best approached as a historical document that bundles together a number of theoretical propositions.

Much like the Josephan discursive strategies analyzed by Katell Berthelot in this volume, the theory incubated in *Daniel* is ultimately inseparable from the identitarian strivings of elites who within their own subordinated communities sought to differentiate themselves from non-elites and rival elites in the process of squaring up to hegemony's demands.[34] Accordingly, it is not a subaltern theory; nor can it offer more than a faint glimpse into the thought corridors of those who, bested by those in their own community when it came to advertising their gifts to empire, had still to make a living under domination somehow.[35] And while I have specified four components to *Daniel*'s theory of resistance, my reading cannot be the final word on the text's generativity. For one, the protagonist's skill at dream interpretation, which I parsed earlier as a signal of the potential displacement of alternative/non-Jewish knowledges, comes laced with a threat: that the subjugated expert might not just withhold their timely wisdom but actively obstruct empire's capacity to sustain itself. Another, similarly menacing prospect that receives airtime in *Daniel* is the conversion of the empire into a kind of carrier vessel for the identities of the subjugated: the use of empire 'as a host body to enter and alter the world that came to colonize them'.[36]

III Futures

It is not out of the question that, at least for some readers, *Daniel* packed a (darkly) comic punch. Comedy was a weapon in the Hellenistic Jewish diasporic arsenal, and certainly in the case of one narrative transmitted with

---

[34] Cook 1995 explores the (elite) social status of those most involved in the production and textualized dissemination of apocalyptic and millenarian literature. Note section I above, on the clear specification of the noble background of Daniel and friends: a semaphore for *Daniel*'s elite-centred imaginary.

[35] The challenges of writing the history of subalterns in antiquity are well brought out in Shaw 2021, introducing a volume on the subject. The need for more ethically calibrated tools for recovering the experiences of those doubly or triply marginalized in antiquity: see now Ahuvia 2023.

[36] I am quoting from Wilner 2022: 114, referring to the anthropologist Franz Boas' translation into a carrier for the embodied knowledges of the Hamatsa.

the Greek text of *Daniel* – the story of Susannah and the Elders – the turn to humor, not as a corrective but as a supplement to the communication of 'serious intent', is hard to miss.[37] Other communicative and affective registers can be traced in *Daniel*. Rabasa discerns in folio 46r of the Codex Telleriano-Remensis 'a sweet melancholy that gives place to mania, to the exhilaration, if not happiness, of crossing languages and forms of life' (2011: 129). Seeing as *Daniel* concludes with the promise of happiness to those who persevere (12:12), it is not a stretch to assert an affective dimension to the construction of its elsewhere through prophecy and apocalypse. This elsewhere did contain a more sinister message for those agents of the hegemon who took the trouble to query and parse it: violence no matter what, at least until the arrival of the prophesied kingdom. On a second read, *Daniel* 10–12 speak to the necessity and indeed unavoidability of such violence as God deemed fit for ushering a new order into being.

The packaging of micro-narratives that extolled idealized aspects of Jewish/Judean exceptionalism gives way in these chapters to visions that put the blame for violence at the door of those who are too lawless to understand (11:36, 12:10). Intriguingly, in the aftermath of the Second Temple's destruction, prescriptions for how to live under empire become markedly less prophetic and apocalyptic in tone, as Natalie Dohrmann's chapter in this volume shows for the tannaitic rabbis. Rule of law, not divinatory excellence, becomes the foundation upon which to base a substantially different paradigm of survivance. Cleaved from the practice of individually vouchsafed revelation, rabbinic law with its bundle of theories and exegeses emerges as a privileged protocol for averting ethnosuicide.

There were risks to *not* redacting theories of resistance and survivance into textual form. Communities that ran out of time to textualize in the teeth of hegemonic brutality do not often leave us with scrutable signs of the abstracting labour to model their own futures. I end by holding up, if only for a moment's contemplation, these Mediterranean communities. Bearing in mind that many were robbed of the time even to lay down basic templates,[38] what urgently calls for additional study is the existence and identification of

---

37 I paraphrase and quote from Gruen 2002: ch. 5; see esp. pp. 170–74. Fontaine 2016 posits the Augustan-era historian Nicolaus of Damascus as the original source for Theodotion's *Susannah*; if correct, the attribution lines up a text that circulated alongside *Daniel* with that generation of Greek-speaking 'migrant intellectuals' that I referenced above (n. 8). On Jewish texts and humour, see now Emanuel 2020's reading of *Revelation*.
38 Discussion of epistemicidal scenarios: Padilla Peralta 2020: 156–57.

minoritized groups who opted against violent resistance, uneasily accommodationist striving, or hyper-textualizing separatism (the last exemplified by the Qumranic community). On the assumption, fragile though it may be, that such groups did in fact exist, where did their elsewheres find expression?

Acknowledgments

My warmest thanks to Lisa Eberle and Myles Lavan, who have been exceptionally patient with me and this project. I wish also to thank the College of the Holy Cross for inviting me to deliver the Thomas More Lecture in 2022, where my faith in this undertaking was restored; Katherine Lu Hsu, Timothy Joseph, Tat-siong Benny Liew, Thomas Martin, Dominic Machado, and Mahri Leonard-Fleckman were delightful hosts and partners-in-thought.

Works Cited

Ahuvia, Mika 2023. 'Critical fabulation and the foundations of classical Judaism'. *Studies in Late Antiquity* 7(1): 29–74.
Bickerman, Elias. 1979. *The God of the Maccabees: Studies on the Meaning and Origin of the Maccabean Revolt*. Leiden.
Bracht, Katharina. 2021. 'The four Kingdoms of Daniel in Hippolytus's *Commentary on Daniel*', in Andrew B. Perrin and Loren T. Stuckenbruck, eds., *Four Kingdom Motifs Before and Beyond the Book of Daniel*. Leiden, 167–90.
Britt, Karen and Ra'anan Boustan. 2021. 'Scenes in stone: newly discovered mosaics from the North Aisle in the Huqoq Synagogue'. *Studies in Late Antiquity* 5(4): 509–79.
Chrubasik, Boris. 2017. 'From pre-Makkabaean Judaea to Hekatomnid Karia and back again.', in id. and Daniel King, eds., *Hellenism and the Local Communities of the Eastern Mediterranean: 400 BCE–250 CE*. Oxford, 83–110.
Collins, John J. and Peter W. Flint, eds., 2001. *The Book of Daniel: Composition and Reception*. 2 vols. Leiden.
Cook, Stephen L. 1995. *Prophecy and Apocalypticism: The Postexilic Social Setting*. Minneapolis.
–. 2022. 'Daniel', in Stephen L. Cook, John T. Strong, and Steven S. Tuell, eds., *The Prophets: Introducing Israel's Prophetic Writings*. Minneapolis, 511–47.

Coşkun, Altay 2019. 'The chronology of the desecration of the Temple and the prophecies of *Daniel* 712 reconsidered'. *Historia* 68(4): 436–62.
Čulík-Baird, Hannah 2020. 'Staging Roman slavery in the second century BCE'. *Ramus* 48(2): 174–97.
Davies, Sarah. 2020. *Rome, Global Dreams, and the International Origins of an Empire*. Leiden.
De Jonge, Casper C. 2022. 'Greek migrant literature in the Early Roman Empire'. *Mnemosyne* 75: 10–36.
duBois, Page. 2007. 'The coarsest demand: utopia and the fear of slaves', in Anastasia Serghidou, ed., Fear of Slaves – Fear of Enslavement in the Ancient Mediterranean = Peur de l'esclave – peur de l'esclavage en Mediterranée ancienne (discours, representations, pratiques). Besançon, 434–44.
Emanuel, Sarah. 2020. *Humor, Resistance, and Jewish Cultural Persistence in the Book of Revelation*. Cambridge.
Fachard, Sylvian and Edward M. Harris, eds., 2021. *The Destruction of Cities in the Ancient Greek World: Integrating the Archaeological and Literary Evidence*. Cambridge.
Ferrary, Jean-Louis. 1988. *Philhellénisme et impérialisme. Aspects idéologiques de la conquête romaine du monde hellénistique, de la seconde guerre de Macédoine à la guerre contre Mithridate*. Rome.
Fontaine, Michael. 2016. 'Is the story of Susanna and the Elders based on a Greek New Comedy? The evidence of Plautus' *Casina* and Burmeister's *Susanna*', in Stavros Frangoulidis, Stephen J. Harrison and Gesine Manuwald, eds., *Roman Drama and its Contexts*. Berlin, 471–87.
Fox, Matthew 2018. 'The prehistory of the Roman *polis* in Dionysius', in Richard Hunter and Caspar C. de Jonge, eds., *Dionysius of Halicarnassus and Augustan Rome: Rhetoric, Criticism and Historiography*. Cambridge, 180–199.
Gabba, Emilio. 1991. *Dionysius and the History of Archaic Rome*. Berkeley.
Goldhill, Simon. 2023. 'Resisting resistance', in Daniel Jolowicz and Jaś Elsner, eds., *Articulating Resistance under the Roman Empire*. Cambridge, 239–56.
Gotter, Ulrich. 2019. 'The succession of empires and the Augustan *res publica*', in Ingo Gildenhard, Ulrich Gotter, Wolfgang Havener, and Louise Hodgson, eds., *Augustus and the Destruction of History: The Politics of the Past in Early Imperial Rome*. Cambridge, 97–109.
Gruen, Erich S. 1998. *Heritage and Hellenism: The Reinvention of Jewish Tradition*. Berkeley.
—. 2002. *Diaspora: Jews Amidst Greeks and Romans*. Cambridge, MA.
Harrison, Robert. 1994. 'Hellenization in Syria-Palestine: the case of Judea in the third century BCE'. *Biblical Archaeologist* 57(2): 98–108.
Haubold, Johannes. 2022. 'Memory and resistance in the Seleucid world: the case of Babylon', in Paul J. Kosmin and Ian S. Moyer, eds., *Cultures of Resistance in the Hellenistic East*. Oxford, 77–94.
Hock, Jana, Valeria Tietze and Nestor Zante. 2023. 'Claiming legitimization: non-state violent local stakeholders and power legitimization of the Maccabees in Judea in the second century BCE and the Koglwéogo in today's Burkina Faso', in Dominique Krüger, Christoph Mohamad-Klotzbach, and Rene Pfeilschifter, eds., *Local Self-Governance in Antiquity and in the Global South*. Berlin, 47–75.

Kosmin, Paul. 2018. *Time and its Adversaries in the Seleucid Empire*. Cambridge, MA.
Kosmin, Paul J. and Ian S. Moyer. 2021. 'Imperial and indigenous temporalities in the Ptolemaic and Seleucid dynasties: a comparison of times', in Christelle Fischer-Bovet and Sitta von Reden, eds., *Comparing the Ptolemaic and Seleucid Empires: Integration, Communication, and Resistance*. Cambridge, 129–63.
Kotrosits, Maia. 2020. *The Lives of Objects: Material Culture, Experience, and the Real in the History of Early Christianity*. Chicago.
Luiselli, Valeria. 2017. *Tell Me How It Ends: An Essay in 40 Questions*. Minneapolis.
Luraghi, Nino. 2003. 'Dionysius von Halikarnassos zwischen Griechen und Römern', in Ulrich Eigler, Ulrich Gotter, Nino Luraghi, and Uwe Walter, eds., *Formen römischer Geschichtsschreibung von den Anfängen bis Livius. Gattungen – Autoren – Kontexte*. Darmstadt, 268–86.
Mackil, Emily 2004. 'Wandering cities: alternatives to catastrophe in the Greek *polis*'. *American Journal of Archaeology* 108(4): 493–516.
MacRae, Duncan. 2016. *Legible Religion: Books, Gods and Rituals in Roman Culture*. Cambridge, MA.
Momigliano, Arnaldo. 1981. 'Greek culture and the Jews', in Moses I. Finley, ed., *The Legacy of Greece*. Oxford, 325–46.
–. [1977–1982] 2016. *Aspects of Hellenistic Judaism: Lectures Delivered in London, Cincinnati, Chicago, Oxford, and Princeton, 1977–1982*. Eds. Lea Niccolai and Antonella Soldani. Pisa.
Olariub, Daniel. 2022. 'Exegetical substitutions in Theodotion Daniel', in Gideon R. Kotzé, Michael N. van der Meer and Martin Rösel, eds., *XVII Congress of the International Organization for Septuagint and Cognate Studies*. Atlanta, 131–63.
Padilla Peralta, Dan-el 2018. 'Ecology, epistemology, and divination in Cicero *De Divinatione* 1.90–94'. *Arethusa* 51(3): 237–67.
–. 2020. 'Epistemicide: the Roman case'. *Classica* 33(2): 151–86.
–. 2024. 'The affects of manumission: racial melancholy and Roman freedpersons', in Rose MacLean, Dorian Borbonus, and Sinclair W. Bell, eds., *Freed Persons in the Roman World: Integration, Diversity, and Representation*. Cambridge, 242–77.
Parsard, Kaneesha Cherelle. 2022. 'Criticism as proposition'. *South Atlantic Quarterly* 121(1): 91–108.
Peirano, Irene. 2010. 'Hellenized Romans and barbarized Greeks. Reading the end of Dionysius of Halicarnassus, *Antiquitates Romanae*'. *Journal of Roman Studies* 100: 32–53.
Perrin, Andrew B. and Loren T. Stuckenbruck. 2021. *Four Kingdom Motifs Before and Beyond the* Book of Daniel. Leiden.
Portier-Young, Anathea. 2011. *Apocalypse against Empire: Theologies of Resistance in Early Judaism*. Grand Rapids.
Purcell, Nicholas. 1995. 'On the sacking of Carthage and Corinth', in Doreen Innes, Harry Hine and Christopher Pelling, eds., *Ethics and Rhetoric: Classical Essays for Donald Russell on his Seventy-Fifth Birthday*. Oxford, 133–48.
Rabasa, José. 2011. *Tell Me The Story of How I Conquered You: Elsewheres and Ethnosuicide in the Colonial Mesoamerican World*. Austin.

Rajak, Tessa. 2001. *The Jewish Dialogue with Greece and Rome: Studies in Cultural and Social Interaction*. Leiden.
Remington, Megan R. 2022. 'Making meaning of touch: revelation and sensorial participation in Daniel 8–10'. *Journal for Interdisciplinary Biblical Studies* 4(1): 157–77.
Richlin, Amy. 2017. 'The traffic in shtick', in Matthew P. Loar, Carolyn MacDonald and Daniel Padilla Peralta, eds., *Rome, Empire of Plunder: The Dynamics of Cultural Appropriation*. Cambridge, 169–93.
Rochberg, Francesca. 2010. *In the Path of the Moon: Babylonian Celestial Divination and its Legacy*. Leiden.
Rüpke, Jörg. 2012. *Religion in Republican Rome: Rationalization and Ritual Change*. Philadelphia.
Schwartz, Seth. 2010. *Were the Jews a Mediterranean Society? Reciprocity and Solidarity in Ancient Judaism*. Princeton.
Segal, Michael. 2016. *Dreams, Riddles, and Visions: Textual, Contextual, and Intertextual Approaches to the Book of Daniel*. Berlin.
Shaw, Brent. 2021. 'Foreword: what is this history to be?', in Cyril Courrier and Julio Cesar Magalhães de Oliveira, eds., *Ancient History from Below: Subaltern Experiences and Actions in Context*. London, x–xxv.
Stone, Michael E. and Esther Eshel, trs., 2013. 'Aramaic Levi Document', in Louis H. Feldman, James L. Kugel and Lawrence H. Schiffmann, eds., *Outside the Bible: Ancient Jewish Writings Related to Scripture*. Lincoln, 1490–1506.
Swain, Joseph W. 1940. 'The theory of the Four Monarchies: opposition history under the Roman Empire'. *Classical Philology* 35(1): 1–21.
van der Toorn, Karel. 2002. 'Scholars at the Oriental court: the figure of Daniel against its Mesopotamian background', in J.J. Collins and P.W. Flint, eds., *The Book of Daniel: Composition and Reception*. Leiden, 37–54.
Vavrinek, Vladimir. 1975. 'Aristonicus of Pergamum: pretender to the throne or leader of a slave revolt?'. *Eirene* 13: 109–29.
Vizenor, Gerald. 2008. 'Aesthetics of survivance', in Gerald Vizenor, ed., *Survivance: Narratives of Native Presence*. Lincoln, 1–23.
Volkmann, Hans. 1990. *Die Massenversklavungen der Einwohner eroberter Städte in der hellenistisch-römischen Zeit*.[2] Stuttgart.
Weitzman, Steven. 2005. *Surviving Sacrilege: Cultural Persistence in Jewish Antiquity*. Cambridge, MA.
–. 2012. 'Mediterranean exchanges: a response to Seth Schwartz's Were the Jews a Mediterranean society?' *Jewish Quarterly Review* 102(4): 491–512.
Williams, Craig. 2022. 'The Latin language and Native survivance in North America'. *American Journal of Philology* 143(2): 219–46.
Wills, L.M. 1994. 'The Jewish novellas', in John R. Morgan and Richard Stoneman, eds., *Greek Fiction: The Greek Novel in Context*. London, 223–238.
Wilner, Isaiah L. 2022. 'Body knowledge, part I: dance, anthropology, and the erasure of history'. *Journal of the History of Ideas* 83(1): 111–42.

3. The Roman Language of Civil War: From Internal War and *Stasis* to *Bellum Civile*

Carsten Hjort Lange

Abstract: *This article attempts to reconstruct Roman conceptual debates about different kinds of unrest and (civil) war in the Republican period. By 'joining the dots' between the revolt of Falerii in the third century as told by Polybius, the destruction of Fregellae in 125 BCE, the subsequent* stasis/seditio *at Rome and, finally, full-blown* bellum civile, *this article will trace the development of the language of internal unrest down to the first civil war between Sulla and Marius. It seems likely that the origins of the concept of* bellum civile, *a relatively late invention, can be traced back to debates that started in the second century BCE, if not earlier.*

This article reassembles what remains of a Roman conceptual debate about different kinds of unrest – internal war and/or rebellion, civil strife, and civil war – down to the first civil war between Sulla and Marius. This debate has left traces, this article will show, in what remains of the contemporary as well as later Roman historiographical tradition. By joining the dots between the revolt of Falerii in the third century BCE as told by Polybius, the destruction of Fregellae in 125 BCE, the subsequent *stasis/seditio* at Rome and, finally, full-blown *bellum civile*, this article will trace the development of conceptualizations of internal unrest down to the first civil war between Sulla and Marius. It offers a reinterpretation of the relationship between concepts such as revolt and/or rebellion – that is, challenges to the Roman order – and the ancient terms of *emphylios polemos, stasis, seditio,* and *bellum civile*. Re-examining the wars of rebellion and wars against the allies may also help us to understand the long second century – from the outbreak of the Second Punic War in 218 BCE to the Social War in 91 BCE and Rome's first civil war in 88 BCE – as an 'antebellum' period to Rome's first civil war.[1]

---

1 A central argument of Lange 2024.

As the Romans of the Middle and Late Republic sought to understand unrest in contemporary history, they looked back on the conquest of Italy and the Punic Wars. The Second Punic War had seen some of Rome's subject-allies rebel or defect from Rome (Fronda 2010). Although allied, these communities were not legally Roman citizens and consequently their rebellion was not a 'civil war', a war between citizens of the same state. There were further revolts during the second century BCE, but mainly outside Italy: rebellions in Spain, the Corsican and Sardinian rebellions of the 180s and 170s, the fourth Macedonian War, the rebellion of the Achaean League, Aristonicus, the Allobroges, the so-called Sicilian Servile Wars, Tolosa's revolt in 109, and Jugurtha. All these were former allies or subject territories that rebelled.[2] But the destruction of Fregellae in 125 BCE was a rupture. Nothing would ever be the same again in *Italia*. The Romans had destroyed an allied city in central Italy. This was recognisably more internecine, domestic, and internal than the revolts of earlier in the century. Fregellae was just as important to the history of Rome's civil wars as the crisis caused by the Gracchan attempts at reform, although scholars tend to overlook it.[3]

Before embarking on this study, it is essential to insist at the outset that the meaning and applicability of loaded terms like 'civil war' must have been as contestable in ancient times as today. Two examples will illustrate the point. In 43 BCE the warmonger Cicero was trying hard to get the proconsul M. Antonius (*cos*. 44) declared a *hostis publicus*. He was strenuously opposed in this endeavour by L. Iulius Caesar (*cos*. 64), who insisted that the situation was a *tumultus* not a *bellum*:[4]

ego semper illum appellavi hostem, cum alii adversarium, semper hoc bellum, cum alii tumultum.

I consistently called Antonius a public enemy [*hostis*], while others [L. Iulius Caesar] called him an adversary [*adversarius*]; I consistently called this a war [*bellum*], while others called it a public emergency [*tumultus*]. (Cic. *Phil.* 12.17)[5]

---

2 Maschek 2018: 83–90 on violence and war during the second century BCE.
3 However, see now Maschek 2018: esp. 22–23; cf. also 64–108. According to Maschek the sack of Fregellae was the symptom of a new period of civil war (23). Whatever we make of this, given the Roman concept of civil war – encompassing both *bellum* and *civile* – the sack of Fregellae was not a civil war; it was an 'internal' war.
4 Chapter 10 of the *Res Gestae* asserts that Lepidus had used the period of *civilis tumultus* to appropriate the title of Pontifex Maximus. Lavan 2017: 22 notes that *tumultus* has 'a technical sense as state of emergency short of war'.
5 Unless otherwise indicated, translations are taken from the Loeb Classical Library edition, with minor changes.

In a different context, the historian Florus, perhaps drawing from Livy, insists that the civil war between Pompeius and Caesar was more than a civil war:

adeo ut non recte tantum civile dicatur, ac ne sociale quidem, sed nec externum, sed potius commune quoddam ex omnibus et plus quam bellum.

It cannot, therefore, justly be called merely a civil war, nor a war between allies, nor yet a foreign war, but was rather a war with all these characteristics and something worse than a war. (Flor. 2.13)

There was never only one narrative. It would be naive to think that the Romans (or Greeks) would have agreed on the definition of such a slippery concept as *war*, or even *civil war*.[6] Can we still believe – in the spirit of positivism – that compiling a list of examples will allow us to arrive at a correct definition of the concepts we are looking at? Hardly! Language has an unfortunate tendency to obscure the extent to which the sources disagree.

Thucydides to Polybius

Before we can understand the Roman debates, we need to begin with a Greek conceptualization of internal unrest: the *stasis* at Corcyra as described by Thucydides. We may prevaricate over whether this *stasis* was also a *polemos*.[7] This raises the fundamental question of when a war is a war and how this changes over time, to be explored later. But, even if one might in principle claim that Corcyra was not a *polemos*, it still remained a key conceptual model for Roman understandings of their own experiences with *stasis* and *bellum civile*. The notion of recurrence is fundamental and becomes a fundamental

---

6 See Lange and Vervaet 2019b; see now also the introduction to Ginsberg and Krasne 2018, König 2018.
7 See Lange 2017 for the argument that it was; *contra* Mynott 2013: 212 n. 1.

element of the tradition.⁸ As we learn from Thucydides' account, *stasis* always reappears:

οὕτως ὠμὴ <ἡ> στάσις προυχώρησε, καὶ ἔδοξε μᾶλλον, διότι ἐν τοῖς πρώτη ἐγένετο, ἐπεὶ ὕστερόν γε καὶ πᾶν ὡς εἰπεῖν τὸ Ἑλληνικὸν ἐκινήθη, διαφορῶν οὐσῶν ἑκασταχοῦ τοῖς τε τῶν δήμων προστάταις τοὺς Ἀθηναίους ἐπάγεσθαι καὶ τοῖς ὀλίγοις τοὺς Λακεδαιμονίους. καὶ ἐν μὲν εἰρήνῃ οὐκ ἂν ἐχόντων πρόφασιν οὐδ' ἑτοίμων παρακαλεῖν αὐτούς, πολεμουμένων δὲ καὶ ξυμμαχίας ἅμα ἑκατέροις τῇ τῶν ἐναντίων κακώσει καὶ σφίσιν αὐτοῖς ἐκ τοῦ αὐτοῦ προσποιήσει ῥᾳδίως αἱ ἐπαγωγαὶ τοῖς νεωτερίζειν τι βουλομένοις ἐπορίζοντο.

Such was the savage progress of the civil strife (*stasis*), and it seemed all the worse because it was the first of its kind, though later practically the whole Greek world was in turmoil as everywhere there were rival efforts by the leaders of the populace to bring in the Athenians and by the oligarchs to bring in the Spartans. In time of peace they would have had neither pretext nor inclination to ask for help; but when these states were at war any faction seeking radical change readily found allies who could be brought in both to help damage their opponents and to bolster their own position. (Thuc. 3.82.1, trans. Mynott 2013)

Thucydides continues: 'Civil strife inflicted many a terrible blow on the cities, as always does and will happen while human nature remains what it is.'⁹ The passage ends with the famous description of *polemos* as a brutal teacher. The concept of *stasis* was thus already closely associated with warfare in Thucydides.¹⁰

Another Greek historian, Polybius, may offer us an invaluable glimpse into the earliest stages of the development of Roman thinking on unrest when he recalls the events of the First Punic War. It is unfortunately impossible to determine whether Polybius' narrative transmits third-century Roman understandings of these events or whether he is imposing a potentially anachronistic second-century perspective, looking back on the great war against Carthage. If the latter, it is not clear if the second-century perspective is one informed by contemporary Roman debates or is a Greek perspective on Roman developments. In attempting a history of Roman

---

8 See Armitage 2017a, Eckstein 1965 on internal war; on the recurrence of civil war, see Collier 2009: 139 ('the most likely legacy of a civil war is further civil war'). Armitage 2017b: 1–18, esp. 2–5 is correct in emphasising the idea of the universal return of civil war but is wrong that this is a Roman invention ('The Romans were the first to try to understand civil war through narrative', 3). The honour surely must go to Thucydides. Armitage also perceives a fundamental difference between *stasis* and *bellum civile*, but see now Lange 2017, Straumann 2017.
9 Thuc. 3.82.2: καὶ ἐπέπεσε πολλὰ καὶ χαλεπὰ κατὰ στάσιν ταῖς πόλεσι, γιγνόμενα μὲν καὶ αἰεὶ ἐσόμενα, ἕως ἂν ἡ αὐτὴ φύσις ἀνθρώπων ᾖ.
10 Thuc. 3.81.4–5; cf. 3.81–85; Lange 2017: 132 on warfare.

The Roman Language of Civil War 59

debates about unrest and internal war, it is vital to remember just how little contemporary evidence we have from the third and second centuries BCE. I focus on Polybius' account of the rebellion of the Falisci, and the Carthaginian Mercenary Revolt with which he connects it (1.65-8). The Falisci revolted in 241 BCE. A consular army was sent against them, and we know from the Fasti Triumphales that both consuls were awarded triumphs in 241 BCE.[11] Livy would later term the conflict a rebellion (*Per.* 20). Polybius describes it as *emphylios polemos*, internal (or civil) war:[12]

μετὰ δὲ τὰς διαλύσεις ταύτας ἴδιόν τι καὶ παραπλήσιον ἀμφοτέροις συνέβη παθεῖν. ἐξεδέξατο γὰρ πόλεμος ἐμφύλιος Ῥωμαίους μὲν ὁ πρὸς τοὺς Φαλίσκους καλουμένους, ὃν ταχέως καὶ συμφερόντως ἐπετέλεσαν, ἐν ὀλίγαις ἡμέραις ἐγκρατεῖς γενόμενοι τῆς πόλεως αὐτῶν.

Shortly after this treaty it so happened that both states found themselves placed in circumstances peculiarly similar. For at Rome there followed intestine war ['civil war' in the Loeb translation of Paton, Walbank and Habicht] (πόλεμος ἐμφύλιος) against the Falisci, but this they brought to a speedy and favourable conclusion, taking Falerii in a few days. (Polyb. 1.65.1-2)

Polybius' discusses the war against the Falisci in a digression on the Mercenary Revolt that Carthage suffered after the First Punic War (Hoyos 2007, Walbank 1970: 130-50). Polybius describes the Mercenary Revolt (1.65-88) as a *stasis* at 1.66.10, 1.67.2, and 1.67.5 – an internal war as well as an internal problem. Yet at 1.65.2 and 1.71.7, he terms it an *emphylios polemos*. Is this merely an example of Polybius' *variatio*, or might it have a deeper significance?

Jonathan Price (2011: 84) has stressed Thucydides' impact on later Greek historians. So powerful was Thucydides' model of *stasis* that almost every subsequent historian writing about *stasis* in Greek, and even some writing in Latin (e.g. Sallust), adopted it and imitated it'; he adds that they were even constrained by it. It is undoubtedly true that Thucydides' famous Corcyra digression was a profound influence on Polybius' narrative here. But we should not overlook the differences either, particularly the use of *emphylios polemos*, which seems to reach for a different tradition or traditions.[13]

---

11 Degrassi 1947: 76-77, 549; see further below for the question of rebellion and triumph.
12 Compare this with Polybius' assessment of Roman warfare at 1.37, where he writes that the Romans use violent force for all purposes.
13 Dreyer 2016 rightly emphasizes that Polybius sees the Mercenary War as a *stasis* ('ohne weiteres in den Kontext einer Stasis', 91). He also talks of an 'erweiterte Anwendung des Stasisbegriffs' (90). Dreyer is also right to emphasize that Polybius took these ideas from Thucydides and Cor-

Indeed, Polybius may be reflecting a Roman tradition as well as a Greek one. While the phrase *bellum civile* appears not yet to have been invented (as we will see), the Romans of the third and second centuries may have known other, analogous terms. Looking forward to Cicero, it is notable that he not only uses the phrase *bellum civile* but also related phrases such as *patriae bellum* ('war against fatherland'), *bellum civile ac domesticum* ('civil and domestic war'), and *bellum domesticum* ('domestic war').[14] Cicero of course uses these phrases deliberately, rhetorically and selectively (see van der Blom 2019). But might they at the same time reflect other, older Roman discussions that predate the first civil war between Marius and Sulla? Potentially even more significant is the phrase *bellum intestinum* ('internal war') – within the polity of Rome – which appears several times in Livy (7.26.15; 41.25.1–6; 42.5.10; 42.13.8; 45.11.5; 42.40.7). It is entirely possible that Polybius, when he described the conflict with the Falisci as *polemos emphylios* was translating a Latin term like *bellum intestinum*. This is not to suggest that Greek phrase *emphylios polemos*, was not an established phrase in Greek, but rather that Polybius used a familiar phrase to translate a Latin concept. Our understanding of its meaning is further complicated by the fact that *emphylios polemos* later became the standard Greek translation for *bellum civile* for Greek writers of the imperial period. The concept unsurprisingly evolved over time.

Whatever we make of his terminology, Polybius' account of the Mercenary War – and indeed that of Rome's war against the Falisci – clearly construed it as an internal war, a war amongst allies or mercenaries, internal to the state and its territory. Moreover, his description of the Mercenary War is marked by numerous episodes of extreme savagery and violence, for example the killing of Gisco and 700 prisoners by the rebels, that anticipate later narratives of the Roman civil wars.[15] Polybius calls it the 'Truceless War (1.65.6: ἄσπονδον πόλεμον). The Roman concept of civil war was not as yet invented, but Polybius's description might still reflect second-century Roman debates

---

cyra, especially regarding violence (92). Gibson 2013 rightly asks why Polybius gives such extensive coverage to the Mercenary War (161). He concludes that the Mercenary War 'is the moment when Carthage was most threatened' (178). While this view is correct, this paper aims to show that this conclusion is not the whole answer.

14 *patriae bellum*: Cic. *Cat*. 1.23; *bellum civile ac domesticum*: Cic. *Cat*. 3.19; *bellum domesticum*: Cic. *Cat*. 2.1, 2.11, *Har. resp*. 49, *Planc*. 49.

15 Polyb. 1.80; cf. 1.88.7. For the difference between foreign – the First Punic War – and civil war: 1.71.5–7; cf. Hoyos 2007: xv, 160–72.

about such internal wars (or even genuine third-century debates). Both conflicts were *internal* wars; though neither would strictly have been *civil* wars.[16] Why, we may ask, did Polybius include this digression? Surely because it revealed a danger: the problem that fickle allies and internal struggles posed for the emerging empire of Rome. The case of Carthage was an outstanding historical example for Polybius' narrative of Roman imperial expansion. The Mercenary War had almost brought about the ruin of Carthage, Rome's great enemy. At the same time both the *stasis* at Carthage and the *emphylios polemos* at Rome were the product of external wars, in both cases the First Punic War. This again reflects Thucydides' description of war as a brutal teacher.

Fregellae

The revolt of Fregellae, an allied city with the Latin right, in 125 BCE was a pivotal moment. The city had remained loyal during the Second Punic War, so the rebellion must have induced great shock in Rome (Osgood 2018: 58). The city was destroyed by the praetor Lucius Opimius (*cos* 121 BCE; *RE* 18/1, 1939: 673–77). The destruction has been confirmed by archaeological excavations by Coarelli and Monti.[17] Rome's response resembles the solutions of 146 BCE, namely the destruction of Corinth and Carthage, followed later by the destruction of Numantia in 133 BCE by Scipio Aemilianus Africanus. But it also foreshadows the last generations of the Roman Republic in its use of political violence (Maschek 2018: 23).

A brief look at a few accounts of the rebellion of Fregellae is revealing. Livy emphasizes that Fregellae had defected (*defecerant*) from Rome (*Per.* 60). *Defectio* implies conscious abandonment of allegiance, clearly indicating an uprising. Valerius Maximus explains that no triumph was awarded because Opimius had merely recuperated what belonged to the Roman people, thus saying much the same (2.8.4, discussed further below). Cicero associates Fregellae with *seditiones* and the war against the rebellious *Socii*:

---

16 Note the description of the defection of the once-loyal allied cities of Hippacritae and Utica to the rebels: 1.82.8–10.
17 Coarelli and Monti 1998: 71–2; cf. *Ad Her.* 4.37; cf. *Ad Her.* 4.9.13, Livy *Per.* 60, Vell. Pat. 2.6.4, Val. Max. 2.8.4, Asc. 17C, Obseq. 30, Amm. Marc. 25.9.10.

multae in hac re publica seditiones domesticae quas praetermitto; bella cum sociis, Fregellanum, Marsicum; quibus omnibus domesticis externisque bellis Capua non modo non obfuit sed opportunissimam se nobis praebuit et ad bellum instruendum et ad exercitus ornandos et tectis ac sedibus suis recipiendos.

[There have been] many domestic seditions within this state, which I will pass over; wars with our allies, the Fregellan war, the Marsic war; in all which domestic and external wars Capua has not only not been in the way but has offered itself to us most suitably for the preparation of war, the equipping of the armies and the reception under their rooves and in their homes. (Cic. *Leg. Agr.* 2.90)

Bella cum sociis, Fregellanum, and *Marsicum* are most fascinating for our purposes; this was neither foreign nor a civil war but an internal war. All three authors see a rebellion against Roman hegemony.

Perhaps surprisingly, L. Opimius did not get at triumph for his victory at Fregellae. The main evidence is Val. Max. 2.8.4: he petitioned but was denied, as the empire had not been expanded. This clearly had not been an issue with the Falisci in 241 BCE (see above). But it is paralleled by the case of Q. Fulvius in 211 BCE after the victory over Capua. Capua, like Fregellae, had rebelled. Valerius Maximus adds the case of Scipio and Spain, but this is a misunderstanding, as that was down to Scipio's lack of a legitimate *imperium*.[18] Valerius Maximus may be wrong on more than one count here. The Fregellae crisis may in fact have resembled a civil war – that is an internal war or, perhaps better, an *emphylios polemos* – in many of its dimensions, although the Latin concept of *bellum civile* had not yet been invented.

One pressing question is why this community rebelled in the first place. Most likely it involved the defeat of a proposal by the consul M. Fulvius Flaccus to enfranchise all Italians in 125 BCE (Dart 2014: 53–61). He tried again in 122 BCE together with Gaius Gracchus; alongside Gracchus, Flaccus was killed by L. Opimius in 121 BCE. Appian is the main evidence.[19] Plutarch draws a clear connection between the rebellion and the policy of Gaius Gracchus (*C. Gracch.* 3). He reports that Gaius Gracchus was accused of encouraging the allies to revolt and being implicated in the rebellion at Fregellae. Whether or not he was involved, there clearly was a fear in Rome of rebellion by the allies. Cicero talks of L. Opimius having freed the state

---

18 Val. Max. 2.8.5, Lange 2016: esp. 32.
19 *B Civ.* 1.21, 1.34; cf. Val. Max. 9.5.1, suggesting that individuals could decide if they wanted Roman citizenship.

from the gravest perils.[20] This is hardly the place for a renewed discussion about the aims of the Italian allies, but the story is interesting in the wider context of internal war.

Chronologically this period of internal war was also one of *stasis/seditio*. L. Opimius himself later became famous after ordering the killing of the supporters of Gaius Gracchus. One of his attendants, Quintus Antyllius, was killed at an assembly on the Capitol at the start of the crisis (Plut. *C. Gracch.* 13, App. *B Civ.* 1.25). L. Opimius used this as a pretext to justify his own killings. Unknowingly anticipating many things to come, he presented the dead body to the Senate as proof of the wrongdoing of the enemies of the state.[21] As in 133 BCE, the corpses of the dead were thrown into the Tiber as an act of purification (Osgood 2018: 60). L. Opimius was tried and exonerated, but later convicted for treason with Jugurtha in 109 BCE. He died in exile in Dyrrachium, Greece; he was hardly welcome in Italy after Fregellae (Kelly 2006: 76–81, 170–71).

In 121 BCE, in commemoration of his deed – and, perhaps at the same time remembering his great internal victory over Fregellae (not least since he had been denied a triumph) – L. Opimius built, on the order of the Senate, what seems to be the first of many conspicuous *stasis*/civil war monuments in Rome: the Temple of Concord, celebrating victory over the Gracchi – fellow Romans, but seditious and potential tyrants.[22] Appian sums up:

καὶ τὴν πόλιν ἐπὶ τοῖς φόνοις ἐκάθαιρεν. ἡ δὲ βουλὴ καὶ νεὼν Ὁμονοίας αὐτὸν ἐν ἀγορᾷ προσέταξεν ἐγεῖραι.

He [Opimius] performed a lustration of the city for the bloodshed, and the Senate ordered him to build a temple to Concord in the forum. (App. *B Civ.* 1.26)

Fregellae (as well as the Gracchi) is in many ways best seen as the pivot between the Middle Republic and the external victories of 146 BCE on one side and continuous problems with the *socii* and internal strife on the other. It was a defining moment in Roman policy towards allies, *stasis* in Italy and relations with the *socii*; but it was also implicated in internal problems at Rome itself that eventually precipitated civil war. All these developments were in-

---

20 *Pis.* 95, *Planc.* 70, echoed later by Young Caesar, 1 August 30 BCE: Arval Fasti (= EJ, p. 49).
21 On the display of severed heads, see Lange 2020.
22 Plut. *C. Gracch.* 17.6 for the famous *dictum* of discord building a temple to Concord; Cic. *Sest.* 140, August. *De civ. D.* 3.25, Pina Polo 2017: 13–14, 19 on this as a monument to the tyrannicide.

tertwined: Between 125 and 121 BCE, L. Opimius played a pivotal role in propagating new methods of violence and war against allies and Romans alike.

From Fregellae to the Social War

I want to pose a question that may at first appear simple: was *seditio* the first step towards civil war?[23] Retrospectively this was undoubtedly the case, as later historians claim with the benefit of hindsight. Tacitus, for example, writes of the Romans being 'ruined one after another by the same poverty and lack of discipline; they were ready to rush into mutiny and dissension (*seditiones et discordias*), and finally into civil war (*bella civilia*)' (*Hist.* 1.46). Isidore of Seville is even more explicit: 'civil war (*civile bellum*) happens when sedition (*seditio*) arises between citizens and tumults are stirred' (*Etym.* 18.1.3).[24] Many of our sources claim after the event that *stasis* and *seditio*, including early internal wars and rebellions, developed into full-blown civil war. But did the contemporaries – during the second century after the fall of Carthage and later – realise that this was in fact what was (slowly) happening? Did the Romans think that their political struggles, including the use of political violence, would develop into *stasis* and/or *emphylios polemos*? Thucydides' model of *stasis* in the Corcyra narrative and Polybius' description of the rebellion of the Falisci would have been enough to show that this could potentially happen.

Modern narratives of *stasis* and *seditio* leading up to civil war can illuminate this question from an unexpected angle. Joanne Freeman (2018) has studied physical violence in the US Congress from 1830 to the outbreak of the Civil War, shedding new light on the systemic breakdown over this period.

---

23 For the use of *seditio* and its interaction with *bellum civile*, see Cic. *Off.* 1.86, Varro, *De Vita* frg. 114 Riposati = Nonius 728 (Lindsey); cf. Tac. *Hist.* 1.2. Here we see interrelated phenomena and civil war as a hybrid.

24 In Roman historiography this goes back to the descriptions of the struggle between Romulus and Remus; cf. famously Livy 1.23.1: *Et bellum utrimque summa ope parabatur, civili simillimum bello, prope inter parentes natosque, Troianam utramque prolem, cum Lavinium ab Troia, ab Lavinio Alba, ab Albanorum stirpe regum oriundi Romani essent* ('And both sides prepared for war with the greatest energy – a civil war, to all intents and purposes, almost as if fathers were arrayed against sons; for both were of Trojan ancestry, since Lavinium had been planted from Troy, Alba from Lavinium, and from the line of the Alban kings had come the Romans.').

She records more than seventy violent incidents in the House and Senate or in nearby streets and duelling grounds. This figure does not include instances of bullying that never went beyond words, though the threat of violence had enormous impact (Freeman 2018: 5–6). One flawed and ineffective attempt at a solution was to 'stop the words': that is, to stop antislavery discussion in Congress in order to avoid 'Union-threatening dissonance' (Freeman 2018: 114). Yet moving violence outside Congress achieved little, if anything. The question we must ask is whether one can have a functioning political system and systemic breakdown at the same time. The build-up to the American Civil War suggests that this is possible. But what about the Roman Late Republic before civil war? I have elsewhere suggested that civil war as such was a development from an incipient phase that began in 133 BCE (or perhaps 146 BCE), emphasising the impact of continuous warfare and of internal and civil wars (Lange 2016: 21). Violence should be at the centre of our attention in looking at this period. But one might also add an ideological dimension: was there, as for Americans from the 1830s onward, a particular *cause* over which the Romans fought (cf. Freeman 2018: 247)? The political process itself is at least part of the answer and, I would suggest, even principally so. Politics is about who gets what, when, and how; but the political process itself is always part of the equation.

Given the growing tendency to critique received concepts such as *optimates* and *populares*,[25] we need a new approach to factional politics.[26] There are numerous alternative ways of conceptualizing alliances and factions within Roman society: *partes*; *factio*; networks of *clientelae*; alliance formations; warring groups; and warlords and alternative states (Rich 2018, Crawford 2008). I myself have added the concept of 'dynasts' to the discussion, as used by Appian and Cassius Dio (Lange 2019). Yet we should always remember that all these concepts were invented to describe the political drama of the Late Republic, often in order to justify and/or understand political violence, *stasis*, and *bellum civile*. These developments bears witness to the collapse of the political system, almost as much as does the carnage upon and beyond the battlefield.

---

25 Robb 2010, Mouritsen 2017: esp. 112–23; *contra* Wiseman 2009: 5–32.
26 Steel 2013: esp. 236: 'The simple binary model of *optimates* (best men) and *populares* is clearly inadequate to explain the position of Pompeius, Crassus and Caesar in 59 and again in 55, or the motives of those men attacking them'; cf. Beard 2015: 342.

The next phase in the struggle between Rome and its allies was the rebellion and/or war of the *socii*, which broke out in 91 BC (Rosenberger 1992: 35–9, Dart 2014). This was variously termed *bellum Marsicum*,[27] *bellum Italicum*, and *bellum sociale*. Florus insists that it was really a *bellum civile* (2.6.1; cf. Strabo 5.4.2), though strictly speaking it was not, since like the Falisci and Fregellae the *socii* were not *cives*, but *peregrini*. This was, however, indubitably an internal war, a rebellion amongst allies. Velleius Paterculus explains:

> *Per omnis annos atque omnia bella duplici numero se militum equitumque fungi neque in eius civitatis ius recipi, quae per eos in id ipsum pervenisset fastigium, per quod homines eiusdem et gentis et sanguinis ut externos alienosque fastidire posset.*

Every year and in every war they were furnishing a double number of men, both of cavalry and of infantry, and yet were not admitted to the rights of citizens in the state which, through their efforts, had reached so high a position that it could look down upon men of the same race and blood as foreigners and aliens. (Vell. Pat. 2.15.2)

This nicely encapsulates the Roman debates, illustrating the problem of how to explain an internal war – that is, something that should not happen.

Sulla

Fighting a civil war invariably necessitated numerous levels and strategies of justification. A pioneer in these strategies was Sulla, who made innovative use of autobiography, a genre that appears to have come to Rome only around the turn of the first century BCE.[28] A passage in Plutarch's *Moralia* which quotes from Sulla's 22-book memoir (*De vita sua*), published shortly after his death, seems to suggest that Sulla played a major role in introducing the novel concept of *bellum civile* into Late Republican politics and literature:

> ὁ δὲ Σύλλας, ὅτε τῶν ἐμφυλίων πολέμων τὴν Ἰταλίαν καθήρας προσέμιξε τῇ Ῥώμῃ πρῶτον, οὐδὲ μικρὸν ἐν τῇ νυκτὶ κατέδαρθεν, ὑπὸ γήθους καὶ χαρᾶς μεγάλης ὥσπερ πνεύματος ἀναφερόμενος τὴν ψυχήν· καὶ ταῦτα περὶ αὐτοῦ γέγραφεν ἐν τοῖς ὑπομνήμασιν.

As he entered Rome for the first time after cleansing Italy of its civil wars, Sulla did not sleep at all that night, borne up in his spirit by great joy and gladness, as by a wind; he has

---

27 The official term: Fasti Cos. (Degrassi 1947): 55; cf. Fasti Venusini (Degrassi 1947): 254.
28 On Sulla's *De vita sua*, see in general Marasco 2011.

written this about himself in his memoirs. (Plut. *Mor.* 786D–E = *FRHist* II.22 F26, trans. Smith)

It is possible that Sulla himself coined the concept, which would be quite characteristic of his unapologetic political methods and conduct. In translating Sulla's concept into Greek, Plutarch would naturally have turned to *emphylios polemos*. The nature and scale of the internal fighting in the years 88–82 BCE and Sulla's record of innovations (including the proscriptions and dictatorship), all suggest that Plutarch's *emphylios polemos* was a direct translation of Sulla's original. Yet Sulla's original *bellum civile* may itself have been a Roman 'translation' of the Greek concept of *emphylios polemos*. The concept itself was of course older than any Roman debates about internal war; but in formulating it as *bellum civile* Sulla gave it a distinctly Roman context, that of citizenship. Importantly, the evidence suggests that when Sulla settled on the concept of *bellum civile*, his emphasis was on *bellum*. The enemy was unusual, but this was yet another victory in war for the great general.[29] Indeed, he may have described 'saving the state' as his crowning victory, even if this had meant fighting fellow (former) Romans; but these, in Sulla's narrative at least, were the Romans that were to blame for the war.

Large Roman legionary armies may have convinced Sulla that a new concept was needed – this was war, but what kind of war? – but it is vital to emphasize that the main difference between, say, Polybius' *emphylios polemos* and Sulla's *bellum civile* is not simply one of scale, despite the emphasis given to this development. Crucially, the key difference is the emphasis on Roman citizenship. On this view, the key question is who did most of the fighting. At least in principle: times of crisis always required the deployment of all the resources of the empire, including manpower.

---

29 With the Senate declining a triumph to L. Opimius, Sulla may after all have thought it less problematic to put on stage a traditional foreign triumph. Nevertheless, Sulla shamelessly incorporated a public celebration of his civil war victory in his curule triumph over Mithridates; see Lange and Vervaet 2019a.

Looking back

Josiah Osgood (2018: 1–3) has recently reminded us just how entrenched the notion of a 'fall' is in our understanding of the Late Republic. He suggests a stimulating alternative conceptualization: the emergence of a world state over the long century from 150 to 20 CE. These two narratives are however interrelated. We can see a development from foreign war to internal war and, later, to *stasis* and civil war. This development tracks Rome's imperial position; it reaches its apex with the onset of full-blown civil war, but it started with conflicts against the allies (that is the revolts of the Falisci and then Fregellae and later the war against the *socii*).

Looking at this development from external war through internal war to civil war, Sallust's description of 146 BCE as the great turning point may be a good start in understanding the transition from Middle to Late Republic.[30] Sallust is also an important point of reference for the adaptation Greek ideas of civil strife to Latin moral vocabulary. He had clearly taken his lead from Thucydides, and this influence is most apparent when he emphasizes the relationship between internecine strife and human nature:[31]

Nobis primae dissensiones vitio humani ingeni evenere, quod inquies atque indomitum semper in certamine libertatis aut gloriae aut dominationis agit.

The earliest conflicts arose among us as a result of a defect of human nature, which restlessly and without restraint always engages in a struggle for freedom or glory or power. (Sall. *Hist.* 1.8)

This echoes the Thucydidean triad of fear, honour, and interest as the universal motives for civil war: 'Fear being our principal motive, though honour and interest afterwards came in'.[32] Similar ideas occur in Sallust's account of the effects of the destruction of Carthage: 'disharmony and greed, as well as ambition and other evils typically arising from success increased very greatly

---

30 Sallust is not however stringent on the matter. The origin of the decline is multifaceted. It lay in the army that Sulla brought from Asia (*Cat.* 11.4–7); in the destruction of Carthage (*Iug.* 41.2); and even in the foundation of the Republic and the confrontation between patricians and plebeians (*Hist.* 1.9–10; see López Barja de Quiroga 2019). Cf. Diod. 34/35.33.5; 33.6, Vell. Pat. 2.1.1.
31 Compare Thuc, 3.82.1–3.
32 Thuc. 1.75.3: μάλιστα μὲν ὑπὸ δέους, ἔπειτα καὶ τιμῆς, ὕστερον καὶ ὠφελίας.

after the destruction of Carthage'.[33] As mentioned earlier, Sallust also clearly associates *seditio* and *bellum civile*:

Postquam remoto metu Punico simultates exercere vacuom fuit, plurumae turbae, seditiones et ad postremum bella civilia orta sunt.

After the fear of Carthage had been removed and the way was clear for pursuing rivalries, there arose a great many riots, insurrections, and in the end, civil wars. (Sall. *Hist.* 1.12R)

Writing early in the imperial period, Velleius Paterculus too saw 146 BCE as pivotal. His Book 2 begins with the destruction of Carthage, or perhaps better, the removal of the fear of Carthage. The result was private *luxuria*. This was not the end of a war, but rather the beginning of *sanguis civilis* (2.3.3), with 133 BCE and the killing of Tiberius Gracchus being one of several further turning points. For Velleius as with Sallust, the destruction of Carthage precipitated civil bloodshed, might prevailing over right, resort to arms rather than the toga to resolve disputes, and fighting for the sake of profit. Velleius continues:

Hunc L. Opimius consul, qui praetor Fregellas exciderat, persecutus armis unaque Fulvium Flaccum, consularem ac triumphalem virum, aeque prava cupientem, quem C. Gracchus in locum Tiberii fratris triumvirum nominaverat, eumque socium regalis adsumpserat potentiae, morte adfecit. Id unum nefarie ab Opimio proditum, quod capitis non dicam Gracchi, sed civis Romani pretium se daturum idque auro repensurum proposuit.

The consul, Lucius Opimius, who, as praetor, had destroyed Fregellae, hunted down Gracchus with armed men and put him to death, slaying with him Fulvius Flaccus, a man who, though now entertaining the same distorted ambitions, had held the consulship and had won a triumph. Gaius had named Flaccus triumvir in the place of his brother Tiberius and had made him his partner in his plans for assuming kingly power. The conduct of Opimius was execrable in this one respect, that he had proposed a reward to be paid for the head, I will not say of a Gracchus, but of a Roman citizen, and had promised to pay it in gold. (Vell. Pat. 2.6.4–5)

L. Opimius here takes centre stage, but even so, it is notable that this description of Roman *stasis* clearly links the internal war against Fregellae and the killing of Gracchus. Flaccus is duly mentioned as a symbol of ambition. L. Opimius is criticized for putting a price on the head of his enemy, thus again beginning a trend that would become highly characteristic of Roman

---

33 Sall. *Hist.* 1.10: *At discordia et avaritia atque ambitio et cetera secundis rebus oriri sueta mala post Carthaginis excidium maxume aucta sunt.*

civil war – the displaying of heads of Roman citizens on the Rostra.[34] When Velleius comes to the war with the allies, he refers to it as *Bellum Italicum* (2.15.1). The choice of phrase is striking, especially because Velleius claims that all of Italy took up *arma adversus Romanos* (2.15.1). This is a description of a rebellion, of an internal war. The Romans, Velleius writes, looked down on people with the same *gens* and *sanguis* as themselves (2.15.2). The conflict that pits Italians against Romans' thus looks similar to that between *optimates* and *populares* (2.3.2). The last part of the story of interest to us is of course the struggle between Sulla and Marius, described as a *factio* (2.18.6). Rome is taken by force and the proscriptions bring the Rostra to the centre of our attention (2.19.1). Marius ends up in Africa amongst the ruins of Carthage (2.19.4). This coda connects the threads of foreign war, internal war, and civil war. *Sanguis civilis* is thus the precursor to civil war; but it in turn was preceded by the defeat of Carthage and all its consequences.[35] At 2.36.2 Sallust himself is (finally) mentioned, the rival of Thucydides and assuredly Velleius' inspiration here. It seems obvious that Velleius' views on the period draw on both historians, Latin and Greek. What we end up with is not *Quellenforschung*, but a Latin tradition focusing on the connection between foreign war, civil strife, and civil war.

Writing in Greek and looking back from the second and third centuries CE, both Appian and Cassius Dio trace a similarly long development, with a notable escalation in 88 BCE.[36] Appian distinguishes three phases of *stasis* at Rome: at *B Civ.* 1.1–2 he distinguishes between the *staseis* of the early Republic on the one hand – which he, unlike Dio, believes to have been bloodless – and the bloody internal disorders from the Gracchi onwards. Then at *B Civ.* 1.55, Appian marks the beginning of a new phase at 88 BCE: civil war as such, with the sack of Rome as a turning point which permanently changed the rules of the game. This turning point opened up the final phase in *stasis* at Rome; from that point onward, the stasiarchs fought one another with great armies in the fashion of war, and with the fatherland as their prize. Cassius Dio appears to have taken much the same view. Neither the term *polemos emphylios* nor the term *oikeios polemos* appears in his extant work until 38.17.4. At 52.16.2, he

---

34 See Lange 2020; the conflict is described as a private feud (2.7.6).
35 Cowan 2019: 246, 'whilst Velleius understood the conflicts in the Sullan period to be civil wars, he nevertheless wished to reserve the expression *bellum civile* in order to demarcate 'The Civil Wars' (the wars of 49–29 BCE) clearly in his narrative.'
36 On Appian and Dio, see Welch 2019, Madsen 2019.

says that the discord arising after Rome's world conquest was at first merely *stasis* 'at home and within the walls,' but was then carried 'into the legions,' implying that 88 BCE was a turning point.[37]

Conclusion

The Greek concepts of *stasis* and *emphylios polemos* are vital to understanding later Roman developments. Yet the relationship is complicated by the fact that Romans writing in Greek (mainly Appian and Cassius Dio) used these terms both with a view to their meaning in the Greek historiographical tradition and to translate the Roman concepts of *seditio* and *bellum civile*. This interaction of different traditions may even go back to Polybius, if his narrative reflects Roman discussions about internal war during the period of expansion and/or the early stages of the Late Republic. Where does this leave us? Whatever we make of it all, it seems likely that the Roman concept of *bellum civile* emerged out of politico-historical debates that began already during the (long) second century BCE, and perhaps even earlier. We should consequently not just talk of foreign *versus* civil war, but rather see a spectrum that also includes *seditio*, *stasis*, and related concepts. How exactly these concepts evolved over time is difficult to discern, chiefly because of the gaps in our evidence, but it seems that interactions between Greek and Latin concepts, and between Greek and Latin historiography, were fundamental to this development.

Abbreviations

EJ = Ehrenberg and Jones, *Documents illustrating the Reigns of Augustus and Tiberius* (2nd edn., Oxford, 1955)

FrHist. = Cornell, T.J. (ed.) (2013) *The Fragments of the Roman Historians*, Vol. 1–3, Oxford.

---

37 Cass. Dio 52.16.2: 'at first it was only at home and within our walls that we broke up into factions and quarrelled, but afterwards we even carried this plague out into the legions' (τὸ μὲν πρῶτον οἴκοι καὶ ἐντὸς τοῦ τείχους κατὰ συστάσεις ἐστασιάσαμεν, ἔπειτα δὲ καὶ ἐς τὰ στρατόπεδα τὸ νόσημα τοῦτο προηγάγομεν).

RE = Realencyclopädie der classischen Altertumswissenschaft

Works cited

Armitage, David. 2017a. *Civil War: A History in Ideas*. New York.
–. 2017b. 'Three narratives of civil war: recurrence, remembrance and reform from Sulla to Syria', in Karine Deslandes, Fabrice Mourlon and Bruno Tribout, eds., *Civil War and Narrative: Testimony, Historiography, Memory*. Cham, 1–18.
Beard, Mary. 2015. SPQR. *A History of Ancient Rome*. London.
Blom, Henriette van der. 2019. 'Bellum civile in Cicero: terminology and self-fashioning', in Carsten H. Lange and Frederik J. Vervaet, eds., *The Historiography of Late Republican Civil War*. Leiden, 111–36.
Coarelli, Filippo and Pier Giorgio Monti. 1998. *Fregellae. Le fonti, la storia, il territorio*. Rome.
Collier, Paul. 2009. *Wars, Guns, and Votes: Democracy in Dangerous Places*. New York.
Cowan, Eleanor. 2019. 'Velleius Paterculus: how to write (civil war) history', in Carsten H. Lange and Frederik J. Vervaet, eds., *The Historiography of Late Republican Civil War*. Leiden, 239–62.
Crawford, Michael H. 2008. 'States waiting in the wings: population distribution and the end of the Roman republic', in Luuk de Ligt and S. Northwood, eds., *People, Land, and Politics: Demographic Developments and the Transformation of Roman Italy 300 BC–AD 14*. Leiden, 631–43.
Dart, Christopher J. 2014. *The Social War, 91 to 88 BCE. A History of the Italian Insurgency against the Roman Republic*. Farnham.
Degrassi, Attilio. 1947. *Inscriptiones Italiae* Vol. 13/1, *Fasti Consulares et Triumphales*. Rome.
Dreyer, Boris. 2016. 'Harmonie und Weltherrschaft. Die *Stasis* bei Polybius', in Henning Börm, Marco Mattheis and Johannes Wienand, eds., *Civil War in Ancient Greece and Rome: Contexts of Disintegration and Reintegration*. Stuttgart, 87–97.
Eckstein, Harry. 1965. 'On the etiology of internal wars'. *History and Theory* 4(2): 133–63.
Freeman, Joanne B. 2018. *The Field of Blood. Violence in Congress and the Road to Civil War*. New York.
Fronda, M. P. 2010. *Between Rome and Carthage. Southern Italy during the Second Punic War*. Cambridge.
Gibson, Bruce. 2013. 'Polybius and Xenophon: the mercenary war', in Bruce Gibson and Thomas Harrison, eds., *Polybius and His World. Essays in Memory of F.W. Walbank*. Oxford, 159–79.
Ginsberg, Lauren D. and Darcy A. Krasne, eds. 2018. *After 69 CE – Writing Civil War in Flavian Rome*. Berlin.
Hoyos, Dexter. 2007. *Truceless War. Carthage's Fight for Survival*. Leiden.
Kelly, Gordon P. 2006. *A History of Exile in the Roman Republic*. Cambridge.

König, Alice. 2018. 'Reading civil war in Frontinus's *Strategemata*: a case-study for Flavian literary studies', in Lauren Donovan Ginsberg and Darcy A. Krasne, eds., *After 69 CE – Writing Civil War in Flavian Rome*. Berlin, 145–77.

Lange, Carsten H. 2016. *Triumphs in the Age of Civil War: The Late Republic and the Adaptability of Triumphal Tradition*. London.

–. 2017. '*Stasis* and *bellum civile*: a difference in scale?', *Critical Analysis of Law* 4(2): 129–40 (http://cal.library.utoronto.ca/index.php/cal/article/view/28855).

–. 2019. 'Cassius Dio on Sextus Pompeius and late republican civil war', in Josiah Osgood and Christopher Baron, eds., *Cassius Dio and the Late Roman Republic*. Leiden, 236–58.

–. 2020. 'Talking heads: the *rostra* as a conspicuous civil war monument', in Carsten H. Lange and Andrew G. Scott, eds., *Cassius Dio: The Impact of Violence, War, and Civil War*. Leiden, 192–216.

–. 2024. *From Hannibal to Sulla: The Birth of Civil War in Republican Rome*. Berlin.

Lange, Carsten H. and Frederik J. Vervaet. 2019a. 'Sulla and the origins of the concept of *bellum civile*', in Carsten H. Lange and Frederik J. Vervaet, eds., *The Historiography of Late Republican Civil War*. Leiden, 17–28.

–. 2019b. *The Historiography of Late Republican Civil War*. Leiden.

Lavan, Myles. 2017. 'Writing revolt in the early Roman empire', in Justine Firnhaber-Baker and Dirk Schoenaers, *The Routledge History Handbook of Medieval Revolt*. London, 19–38.

López Barja de Quiroga, Pedro. 2019. 'Sallust as a historian of civil war', in Carsten H. Lange and Frederik J. Vervaet, eds., *The Historiography of Late Republican Civil War*. Leiden, 160–84.

Madsen, Jesper M. 2019. 'In the shadow of civil war: Cassius Dio and his *Roman History*', in Carsten H. Lange and Frederik J. Vervaet, eds., *The Historiography of Late Republican Civil War*. Leiden, 467–501.

Marasco, Gabriele, ed. 2011. *Political Autobiographies and Memoirs in Antiquity. A Brill Companion*. Leiden.

Maschek, Dominik. 2018. *Die römischen Bürgerkriege. Archäologie und Geschichte einer Krisenzeit*. Darmstadt.

Mouritsen, Henrik. 2017. *Politics and the Roman Republic*. Cambridge.

Mynott, Jeremy. 2013. *Thucydides: The War of the Peloponnesians and the Athenians*. Cambridge.

Osgood, Josiah. 2018. *Rome and the Making of a World State, 150 BCE–20 CE*. Cambridge.

Pina Polo, Francisco. 2017. 'The "tyranny" of the Gracchi and the concordia of the *Optimates*: An ideological construct', in Roberto Cristofoli, Alessandro Galimberti and Francesca Rohr Vio, eds., *Costruire la memoria: uso e abuso della storia fra tarda repubblica e primo principato*. Roma, 5–33.

Price, Jonathan J. 2011. 'Josephus' reading of Thucydides: a test case in the *Bellum Iudaicum*', in Georg Rechenauer and Vassiliki Pothou, eds., *Thucydides – a Violent Teacher?* Göttingen, 79–98.

Rich, John. 2018. 'Warlords and the Roman republic', in Toni Ñaco del Hoyo and Fernando Lopez Sánchez, eds., *War, Warlords and Interstate Relations in the Ancient Mediterranean*. Leiden, 266–94.

Robb, Maggie A. 2010. *Beyond* Populares *and* Optimates. *Political Language in the Late Republic*. Stuttgart.

Rosenberger, Veit. 1992. Bella et expeditiones. *Die antike Terminologie der Kriege Roms.* Stuttgart.

Steel, Catherine. 2013. *The End of the Roman Republic 146 to 44 BC: Conquest and Crisis.* Edinburgh.

Straumann, Benjamin. 2017. 'Roman ideas on the loose'. *Critical Analysis of Law* 4(2): 141–51. (http://cal.library.utoronto.ca/index.php/cal/article/view/28856).

Walbank, Frank W. 1970. *A Historical Commentary on Polybius.* Vol. 1. Oxford.

Welch, Kathryn. 2019. 'Appian and civil war: a history without an ending', in Carsten H. Lange and Frederik J. Vervaet, eds., *The Historiography of Late Republican Civil War.* Leiden, 439–66.

Wiseman, Timothy P. 2009. *Remembering the Roman People. Essays on Late-Republican Politics and Literature.* Oxford.

4. Struggles to Define and Counter-Define Unrest in the Cities of the Early Roman East

Benjamin Gray

Abstract: *This chapter analyses discourses of unrest in the Greek poleis in the early stages of Roman rule (first century BC–first century AD). Like other chapters in the volume, it traces evolutions in the discourse of unrest in response to Roman power and associated social change. Traditional Greek discourse about stasis remained strongly influential. Stasis and division had always been something to be feared for a polis. Nonetheless, many traditional interpretations of it at least grudgingly accepted that participants on each side were engaging (sometimes in wrong, perverted ways) in political activity; this meant that unity could be restored through political processes and political institutions which incorporated all citizens. These tendencies endured in interesting ways into the Roman period, but they also had to contend with alternative ideas and practices, which treated any political unrest (but especially any with democratic aspirations) as a more fundamental challenge to peace, gentleness and civility, requiring new, more ethical styles of resolution. Sometimes even previously routine forms of political self-assertion or confrontation came under this rethought umbrella. This chapter examines the complex interaction of these different conceptualisations, including the ways in which that interaction mirrored ideological developments at Rome and in other provinces. It is argued throughout that evolutions in discourses of political disorder must be studied in tandem with changing discourses of political order and reconciliation.*

The Greek-speaking cities of the early Roman East are famous for their Classicism: their faithful allegiance to the cultural and political traditions of Classical Greece, especially Athens.[1] This was also an important dimension of their approach to issues of internal difference, dissent and unrest. Citizens and intellectuals were adept at manipulating concepts of strife (*stasis*), con-

---

1 See, for example, Swain 1996, Schmitz 1997, Kim 2010, Schmitz and Wiater 2011.

cord (*homonoia*) and political life (*politeia*/τὸ πολιτεύεσθαι) dating back at least to the fifth and fourth centuries BC, a period whose literature and philosophy were central to the educational curriculum in this later period. They also drew on the Hellenistic tradition of preserving and updating these concepts and discourses.[2]

At the same time, as in other areas of their life, the citizens and intellectuals of these cities were well capable of adapting, and even challenging and replacing, Classical assumptions and discourses concerning civic order and disorder.[3] In this chapter, I trace both the preservation and the reworking of earlier Greek paradigms, arguing for important innovations in the discourse of internal unrest in the early Roman poleis. In part these innovations were inspired by the model of the Roman political system and wider empire, but they were also an endogenous response to the evolution of city life and its entanglement with Rome.

My focus is on the transition from the Hellenistic to the Roman period in the cities, roughly the first centuries BC and AD. I consider discourses addressing (or imagining or conjuring into existence) all possible forms of internal unrest: the full or partial breakdown of civic order, and its sustaining relations, institutions and language.[4] To put this in the terms used in the rationale for this volume, my focus is not simply on vocabulary, but on the different conceptual models used to characterise unrest and instability. By their very nature, these conceptual models also characterised the mirroring states of civic harmony and stability; it is necessary to study together the full range of language and ideas about civic order and disorder. Another important link with the rest of this volume is that constructions of order and unrest were usually entwined with the issue of a city's loyalty or disloyalty to Rome, as will emerge from many of the examples I discuss. Conceptualising internal civic order and disorder thus automatically demanded a stance on how to conceptualise the Roman settlement in the East, and the wider Roman Empire.

I first analyse some examples of apparent conservatism in the discourse of unrest: signs of the survival of older conceptual models of civic unrest,

---

2 See Börm 2019, emphasising Hellenistic conservatism in the discourse about *stasis*.
3 Compare Schmitz and Wiater 2011 for the early Roman Greeks' wrestling with their past.
4 For more historical/sociological analysis of different kinds of unrest within cities, see Chaniotis 2008 and Börm 2016 and 2019 (for the late Hellenistic/late Republican period) and Brélaz 2005 and 2008 (for the Imperial period, in Asia Minor); also (crossing the Hellenistic and Imperial periods) Thornton 1999 and 2001.

most famously crystallised in Thucydides' paradigmatic account of *stasis* at Corcyra, as a matter of *stasis* between equal and alike citizens divided by clashing interests and ideologies, democratic and aristocratic.[5] I then argue for contemporary deviation from this pattern, as some citizens and intellectuals reconceptualised destabilising political activity as something more viscerally objectionable than misplaced or perverted political zeal: as a failure to embrace a new civic order of sympathetic, relaxed coexistence under paternalistic elite leadership, mirroring the wider Roman peace. Crucially, these respectively politicising and depoliticising conceptual models of civic order and unrest did not flourish sequentially: they were both vibrant well into the Imperial period, a mutually sustaining pair of discourses, which continued to shape each other.

At the end of this chapter, I analyse the wider implications for the concerns of this volume of the entwining of these different discourses and conceptual models in the cities of the Roman East. This is perhaps principally a story of the flickering of independent or resistant thinking about the Roman settlement in these cities, and the evolution of counter-discourses designed to curtail open and vigorous debate. There were also, however, more paradoxical consequences of these struggles to define and counter-define unrest. Though the two approaches I identify often remained polarised, they could also be fused together, as in some rhetoric of Dio Chrysostom, to recast the Greek democratic and civic tradition on more pluralist lines, with more explicit tolerance (gentle and forgiving) for outspoken dissent, though perhaps not full-scale unrest. I conclude by analysing this unexpected development, and whether it genuinely encouraged – or rather elegantly belittled – independent thinking in the Greek cities.

Traditional *stasis* discourses in the Roman period

In the mid-second century BC, it might still have been plausible to represent Rome as simply the latest entrant into the competition between multiple superpowers (cities and kingdoms) which had long contributed to the polar-

---

5 Thuc. 3.70–85; on this Classical (and Hellenistic) model, see (for example) Lintott 1982, Gehrke 1985, Loraux 2001, Azoulay 2014, Gray 2015, Börm 2019.

isation of Greek poleis into *stasis* between supporters of rival claimants to hegemony. This was changing by the later second and early first century BC, because Rome's increasing monopoly on power in the eastern Mediterranean led to profound changes in political and cultural dynamics, which influenced the discourse of civic *stasis* and unrest in the complex ways explored later in this article. Nonetheless, in a sign of the tenacity of traditional discourses, the philosopher-historian Posidonius represented political conflict at Athens in 88 BC, between supporters and opponents of King Mithridates of Pontus' anti-Roman revolt, almost as an archetypal *stasis* between democrats (led by a demagogue) and wealthy aristocrats.

Posidonius' account is preserved in Athenaeus, who may have adapted Posidonius' text, although the language is not typical of Athenaeus himself (fr. 253 Edelstein-Kidd = Ath. V, 211d-215d).[6] In the preserved fragment, Posidonius recounts how the Peripatetic philosopher and teacher Athenion led a democratic revolt in Athens, against Rome and in favour of Mithridates. He presents Athenion's coup as ostensibly aimed at restoring Athens' democratic institutions, which had apparently been suspended by the Roman Senate after a period of conflict.[7]

As soon as he introduces Athenion, Posidonius draws on some old tropes, very familiar from the Classical Athenian democracy, in order to launch his vilification of Athenion as a demagogue (fr. 253, ll. 12-23).[8] Posidonius claims that Athenion has illegitimately claimed Athenian citizenship: he is the son of an Athenian citizen-father, but of an Egyptian slave-mother. This suggestion of barbarian roots and illegitimate citizenship was a well-established feature of Athenian democratic invective, including against alleged demagogues, well attested in Classical Athenian oratory and comedy.[9] Moreover, Posidonius adds an additional Classical intimation of compromised, opportunistic character, this time drawn from Classical philosophy: despite his

---

6 See Kidd 1988-1999, Vol. 2 ii): 865; compare Kidd 1997: 41 ('this looks to me like straight Posidonius, a quotation: the language is Posidonian and certainly not Athenaean'); compare K. Dowden in his commentary on *BNJ* 87 F36.
7 For historical reconstructions, see Badian 1976: esp. 106-108, 112, Habicht 1997: ch. 13, Haake 2007: 271-3, Grieb 2008: 132-8, Börm 2019: 135-40.
8 Compare now Simonton 2022: 64-7.
9 Compare Kidd 1988-1999, Vol. 2 ii): 866, 1997: 42. For Athenian ethnic rhetoric of vilification and exclusion, including against 'demagogues', compare Connor 1971: 169-71, Lape 2010: esp. chs. 2 and 5.

professions to be a philosopher, Athenion has taken money for his lessons, like the disreputable sophist of Plato's caricature.[10] Posidonius then represents Athenion giving a speech characteristic of the demagogue who exploits civic ideals and symbols to steer the *dēmos* towards his own self-serving ends:

> τί οὖν' εἶπε 'συμβουλεύω; μὴ ἀνέχεσθαι τῆς ἀναρχίας, ἥν ἡ Ῥωμαίων σύγκλητος ἐπισχεθῆναι πεποίηκεν, ἕως <ἂν> αὐτὴ δοκιμάσῃ περὶ τοῦ πῶς ἡμᾶς πολιτεύεσθαι δεῖ. καὶ μὴ περιίδωμεν τὰ ἱερὰ κεκλημένα, αὐχμῶντα δὲ τὰ γυμνάσια, τὸ δὲ θέατρον ἀνεκκλησίαστον, ἄφωνα δὲ τὰ δικαστήρια καὶ τὴν θεῶν χρησμοῖς καθωσιωμένην Πύκνα ἀφῃρημένην τοῦ δήμου. μὴ περιίδωμεν δέ, ἄνδρες Ἀθηναῖοι, τὴν ἱερὰν τοῦ Ἰάκχου φωνὴν κατασεσιγασμένην καὶ τὸ σεμνὸν ἀνάκτορον τοῖν θεοῖν κεκλημένον καὶ τῶν φιλοσόφων τὰς διατριβὰς ἀφώνους.' πολλῶν οὖν καὶ ἄλλων τοιούτων λεχθέντων ὑπὸ τοῦ οἰκότριβος, συλλαλήσαντες αὐτοῖς οἱ ὄχλοι καὶ συνδραμόντες εἰς τὸ θέατρον εἵλοντο τὸν Ἀθηνίωνα στρατηγὸν ἐπὶ τῶν ὅπλων. καὶ παρελθὼν ὁ Περιπατητικὸς εἰς τὴν ὀρχήστραν, 'ἴσα βαίνων Πυθοκλεῖ' εὐχαρίστησέ τε τοῖς Ἀθηναίοις καὶ ἔφη διότι 'νῦν ὑμεῖς ἑαυτῶν στρατηγεῖτε, προέστηκα δ' ἐγώ. καὶ ἂν συνεπισχύσητε, τοσοῦτον δυνήσομαι ὅσον κοινῇ πάντες ὑμεῖς.'

What then,' he said, 'do I advise? Do not tolerate the anarchy which the Roman Senate has caused to be drawn out until it reaches a decision about how we should conduct our civic life. And let us not look on passively at our sanctuaries closed, our gymnasia abandoned, the theatre without assemblies, the law-courts without a voice, and the Pnyx, blessed with oracles to the gods, taken away from the people. And let us not tolerate, men of Athens, the sacred voice of Iacchus silenced, the holy temple of the two gods shut, and the schools of the philosophers without a voice.' After many other such things had been said by this common slave, the masses burst into chatter and came running together into the theatre, where they elected Athenion hoplite general. And the Peripatetic, having come onto the *orchēstra*, 'walking like Pythocles', thanked the Athenians and said: 'Now you are in command of yourselves, and I have taken on the leading position. And if you combine your strength, I will be as powerful as all of you collectively.' (Posidonius fr. 253, ll. 94–110)

Like a first-century reincarnation of the Cleon of hostile Classical polemic, Posidonius' Athenion uses rhetoric skilfully to stir the collective emotions of the *dēmos*, including civic pride, but also shame at 'anarchy' and political emasculation and hostility towards loosely defined enemies of the democratic system. Also like a stereotypical Classical demagogue, he exploits and debases the persuasive and motivational power of Athens' (normally respectable) traditions and institutions. He relies on a distorted sense of Athenian collective strength and freedom, which he presents as rooted in the (supposedly) neglected) collective institutions of sanctuaries, gymnasia,

---

10 See, for example, Plat. *Hp. maior* 282b-283b.

assembly, law-courts and philosophical schools. Athenion is also adept, like the Classical stereotype, at channelling democratic institutions and voting to suit his personal interests: his stirring rhetoric sees him elected hoplite general. Athenion himself then rejoices in the blurring of the boundary between his personal power and the collective power of the *dēmos*: he will be able to take on the strength of the citizens combined. He thus begins to anticipate his own transformation into a tyrant.

Posidonius sets this Classical demagogue of the first-century BC against an opposing group whom he characterises in a way very familiar from Classical representations of anti-democratic *stasis* factions (aristocratic or oligarchic, depending on perspective). According to Posidonius, Athenion attempts rigorously to root out (and expropriate the property of) the 'right-thinking' (τοὺς εὖ φρονοῦντας) among the Athenians. Some try to flee the city, only to be hunted down by Athenion's supporters; they and their purported supporters face extra-judicial killing or corrupt legal proceedings, like victims of a Classical or earlier Hellenistic demagogue or tyrant.[11] Posidonius acknowledges that his language and outlook here are in keeping with Classical traditions of aristocratic political theory: he says that Athenion's opposition to these right-thinking citizens went against the precepts of his own supposed philosophical inspirations as a Peripatetic, Aristotle and Theophrastus (fr. 253, ll. 99–123). Aristotle himself had indeed used the same expression ('right-thinking') in his *Rhetoric* to describe the perceptive few (as opposed to the many) who have a superior ability to decide on appropriate laws, of general application, and to make legal judgements.[12]

As well as attaching himself to the aristocratic tradition in political theory, Posidonius here also perpetuates a historiographical tradition of presenting the elite victims of *stasis* violence in a polis as distinguished by good sense and virtue. Xenophon, for example, twice presents the pro-Spartan Corinthians who fell victim in 392 BC to a massacre by their fellow citizens, seeking to avoid a return to the Spartan alliance, as 'the best

---

11 Compare the political persecutions of Molpagoras of Cius, a 'greedy demagogue' (δημαγωγικὸς καὶ πλεονέκτης), at Polyb. 15.21.1. Polybius goes on to use moral language to describe the opposition between 'the worst' and their opponents (προάγοντες ἀεὶ τοὺς χειρίστους καὶ κολάζοντες τοὺς ἐναντιουμένους τούτοις, 15.21.4).
12 Arist. *Rh*. 1354a34–1354b1: πρῶτον μὲν ὅτι ἕνα λαβεῖν καὶ ὀλίγους ῥᾷον ἢ πολλοὺς εὖ φρονοῦντας καὶ δυναμένους νομοθετεῖν καὶ δικάζειν.

men' (οἱ βέλτιστοι, Hell. 4.4.1, 4.4.3).[13] Thucydides, for his part, was more dispassionate than either Xenophon or Posidonius in his account of *stasis* at Corcyra in the *Peloponnesian War*, finding fault and hypocrisy on both sides. He recognised the same way of talking about the anti-democratic faction, but was more alert to its ideological workings. For Thucydides, the language of 'self-controlled aristocracy' or 'sound-minded aristocracy' (ἀριστοκρατία σώφρων) was the Corcyrean oligarchs' cloak for their less noble motives, mirroring the way democrats hid behind slogans of political equality.[14]

Standing within this tradition, Posidonius resolves this confrontation between anti- and pro-Romans at Athens into quite a conventional *stasis*, in which his own sympathies are clear, between an unruly *dēmos* striving for absolute equality and democratic sovereignty under a demagogue and, on the other side, their aristocratic opponents, distinguished by superior wisdom and prudence. This same traditional pattern for understanding unrest clearly endured well into the Roman period. This is evident in the record of (supposedly now resolved) unrest in the famous Lycian *stadiasmos* of c. AD 46, the still imperfectly understood monument celebrating the establishment of Roman control and peace in Lycia under the Emperor Claudius.[15] The relevant part of the inscription on the monument is the following:

Τιβερίωι Κλαυδίωι Δρούσου [υἱ]ῶι Καίσαρι Σεβαστῶι Γερμανικῶι, ἀρχιερεῖ με[γ]ίστωι, δ[η]μαρχικῆς ἐξου[σί]ας τὸ πέμπτον, [αὐ]το[κρατο]κράτορι τὸ ἐνδέκατον, πατρὶ πατρίδος, ὑπάτω[ι] τὸ τέταρτον ἀποδεδειγμέν[ω], σωτῆρι τοῦ ἑαυτῶν ἔθνους Λύκιοι φιλορώμαιοι καὶ φιλοκ[αί]σαρες πιστοὶ σύμμαχοι ἀπαλλαγ[έ]ν[τε]ς στάσεως καὶ ἀνομίας καὶ λῃσ[τ]ειῶν [δι]ὰ τὴν θείαν αὐτο[ῦ] πρόνοιαν, ἀπειλη[φ]ότες δὲ ὁμό[νοι]αν καὶ τὴν ἴσην δ[ικαιοδ]οσίαν καὶ τοὺς [π]α[τρίο]υς νόμους τῆς πολειτείας τοῖς ἐξ ἀρίστων ἐπιλελεγμένοις βουλευταῖς ἀπὸ τοῦ ἀκρίτου πλήθους πιστευθείσης [- - -]

To Tiberius Claudius, son of Drusus, Caesar Augustus Germanicus, *pontifex maximus*, in his fifth year of tribunician power, in his eleventh year as emperor, father of his country, who has been appointed consul for the fourth time, the saviour of our community: the Lycians, lovers of the Romans and the Caesars, faithful allies, after being released from civil strife and lawlessness and plundering through his divine foresight, and having recovered concord and equal legal justice and the ancestral laws, and with our constitution now

---

13 For Xenophon's representation of oligarchs and their opponents, compare *Hell.* 7.3.4 (on Sikyon), discussed further below.
14 Thuc. 3.82.8: οἱ γὰρ ἐν ταῖς πόλεσι προστάντες μετὰ ὀνόματος ἑκάτεροι εὐπρεποῦς, πλήθους τε ἰσονομίας πολιτικῆς καὶ ἀριστοκρατίας σώφρονος προτιμήσει, τὰ μὲν κοινὰ λόγῳ θεραπεύοντες ἆθλα ἐποιοῦντο.
15 For historical interpretation, see especially Jones 2001, Thornton 2001, Şahin and Adak 2007.

entrusted to councillors selected from the best citizens rather than the common people lacking in judgement.... (SEG 51.1832, A, ll. 1–30, updated in accordance with Şahin and Adak 2007)

There are some clear signs here of a changed world, with a Roman monopoly on power determining local loyalty and identity ('lovers of the Romans and the Caesars'). There are also hints of the changed approaches to unrest explored further in the next section, especially in the reference to the democratic insurrection as 'plundering', which seems to relegate it below true political confrontation into more meaningless violence,[16] though it is also true that similar language had been used even in the Classical period to describe exiled dissidents harrying their home city.[17]

The unquestioned acknowledgement of the absolute power of the emperor, grounded in a 'foresight' which is 'divine' and exists outside normal politics, also heralds a new political world. Crucially, however, the local Lycian elite are not presented here as exercising in miniature this new type of power, unlike some of the local elite figures considered in my next section. On the contrary, despite some minor innovations, the local political conflict is represented very much as a traditional *stasis* between a virtuous elite, true defenders of law, tradition and the common good, and unruly democrats. The new post-*stasis*, Roman-backed councillors are presented as drawn from 'the best men' (ἄριστοι), a classic description of oligarchs (compare Xenophon's βέλτιστοι, above). The democratic faction, by contrast, are denied all legitimacy, in rhetoric very much in line with the Classical anti-democratic tradition:[18] not only are the democrats described as a *plēthos*, little more than a mob, but the adjective ἄκριτον is added, perhaps to mean 'countless', 'undistinguished', but more probably to suggest they lack the capacity for good judgement, including formal judgement in the law-courts central to the text's presentation of the conflict.[19] The victorious aristocrats

---

16 Compare Thornton 2008 for analysis of this ambiguous invective; it could be a pejorative description of judicial or extra-judicial redistribution of property, now corrected through the re-establishment of 'fair' legal process, emphasised here.
17 Compare Thuc. 3.85.2 (exiles from Corcyra settled on the mainland and plundered their rivals on the island, ἐλῄζοντο τοὺς ἐν τῇ νήσῳ) and 4.75 (on Samian exiles in the Samian peraea at Anaia, described with different language of disruption, esp. τοὺς ἐν τῇ πόλει Σαμίους ἐς ταραχὴν καθίστασαν).
18 Thornton 2001: 437–45 analyses the anti-democratic resonances of this part of the text.
19 Şahin and Adak 2007: 35 translate 'die gesetzlose Volksmenge' (compare Adak in that volume, pp. 53–6, suggesting that civic, rather than federal, assemblies are implied, because the League

thus represent themselves as restoring lawful government and justice to Lycia, superseding the democrats' 'lawlessness'. Though there is no explicit suggestion that the democrats were anti-Roman (Şahin and Adak 2007: 56), an association between Roman power and respectable aristocracy is implied.

In both Posidonius' text and the Lycian inscription, there is a paradoxical symmetry between the two factions, despite all the fundamental differences in the ways they are presented. In the development of traditional Greek conceptual models of *stasis*, it had usually been outside observers, without a clear commitment to one faction, who had most clearly represented the two factions in a *stasis* engaging in symmetrical forms of political agitation: most famously, the democrats and oligarchs at Thucydides' Corcyra contribute to social breakdown in mirroring ways.[20] Nevertheless, even more partisan analysts of *stasis* had also sometimes implied a certain symmetry between two factions, their favoured one and its opponents: Xenophon, for example, uses a genitive absolute which makes both his favoured aristocrats and their democratic opponents in early fourth-century Sikyon subjects of the same verb, στασιάζειν ('to engage in *stasis*').[21] This implies that, despite the moral differences between 'the best men' and the *dēmos*, the two factions are still somehow engaged in the same political game, with one following rules of legitimacy and the other perverting or misunderstanding (but not ignoring) them.[22]

I would like to suggest that both Posidonius and the Lycians, unlike the early Roman Greeks of my next section, reproduced this pattern. They did everything they could to vilify and delegitimise the respective democratic factions, helping to cast anti-Roman dissent in general as dubious. At the same time, their rhetoric does imply, however grudgingly, an unexpected symme-

---

would not have criticised its own assemblies so bitterly); compare Petzl 2011: 52 (translating 'die urteilslose Masse'). For this meaning of *akritos* in a post-Classical text, compare Polyb. 3.19.9 (on Demetrios of Pharos: ἀνὴρ θράσος μὲν καὶ τόλμαν κεκτημένος, ἀλόγιστον δὲ ταύτην καὶ τελέως ἄκριτον); for an older example, see Thornton 2001: 439 on Hom. *Il*.2, l. 246. See Walser 2011 on the continued vitality of civic courts in the Hellenistic period, clearly sustained in Lycia at the time of this inscription.

20 See the parallel descriptions of the two factions' transgressions in Thuc. 3.82; compare the analysis of the shared basic motivations of different *stasis* factions (for gain and honour) in Arist. *Pol*. V.

21 Xen. *Hell*. 7.3.4: στασιασάντων γὰρ ἐν τῷ Σικυῶνι τῶν τε βελτίστων καὶ τοῦ δήμου.

22 On the paradoxes of symmetry and asymmetry between *stasis* factions, still somehow imagined as part of one single organism, in Classical Greek representations, see Loraux 2005: chs. 1–3, 6, 8, analysed further and criticised in Azoulay 2014.

try between the two parties in these conflicts. Both sides engage in parallel in the political game in its less idealistic sense, each seeking to win the power struggle for its own interests (for example, through control of law and the courts in Lycia). Posidonius betrays grudging respect for Athenion's effectiveness as a demagogue and power broker, like the grudging admiration of the fifth-century Old Oligarch for Athenian democrats, who have stitched up Athenian politics in their own interests.

Yet the two factions in each of these two texts also engage in mirroring ways with the more respectable, even elevated dimensions of politics. In both texts, the two factions are clearly composed of fellow citizens: the elite faction are simply 'the best' among a notionally equal group. The descriptions of the elite citizens as the 'right-thinking' and 'the best' might seem to gesture at moral excellence which transcends politics, as in the examples in my next section, but they also evoke the vocabulary and sentiments of a long tradition of aristocratic engagement with political institutions and process. This connection is made explicit in the Lycian text: the role of 'the best' was precisely to supply councillors to run political and legal institutions (the council, the courts), in such a way as to defend clearly political values of concord, equal justice and ancestral law.

The strange symmetry here is that the respective democratic factions are also represented as engaging in these types of distinctively political activity, characterised by particular institutions and values: however mistaken they are, the different democrats promote through speech and action a particular interpretation of shared values of autonomy, justice and the common good, which they tie closely to political institutions. Posidonius represents Athenion carrying out in an illegitimate and deeply misguided way precisely the types of activities which his 'right-thinking' citizens would know how to carry out correctly and sincerely. He makes Athenion appeal in his rhetoric to shared civic values of freedom, self-government and law, of interest to all, which are rooted in the institutions of Pnyx, courts, education and civic religion. For their part, the Lycians go much further in denying any true political activity to the democrats, but their rhetoric still implies that the democrats had succeeded in running their own (degenerate) versions of both deliberative and judicial institutions, now safely superseded: they claim that 'equal' administration of justice and 'ancestral' laws have been restored and the constitution entrusted to the best men, implying that inferior political arrangements prevailed in the interim. That their cherished solution is the restoration of good, ancestral civic law and institutions, equally binding on all citizens, is further testament to the fact that they conceive this episode as very much a traditional *stasis*, in which all participants have continuously oriented themselves around shared basic political structures and ideals and can be seamlessly integrated into the reconstituted *politeia*. Once again, this looks particularly significant when contrasted with the quite different emphasis in some of the projects of reconciliation and restoration in my next section.

The tenacity of traditional civic conceptual models in Lycia might be ascribed to its unusual history, as an independent *koinon* until this belated provincialisation under Claudius. It is, however, in fact in keeping with wider trends in Imperial Anatolia and beyond, even if the pattern was even stronger in Lycia. Recent research has demonstrated the endurance of traditional civic politics, including relatively wide political participation and vibrant assemblies.[23] Our most detailed witnesses to local civic life around AD 100, Plutarch and Dio Chrysostom, both innovate considerably in their political thinking (see next sections). Yet their preserved writings are so rich and varied that they engage with many varied conceptual models of order and disorder. They certainly engage closely with these continuity-phenomena and continuity-discourses, creating a picture of continued political interaction (and sometimes confrontation) between politicised aristocrats and self-conscious organised *dēmos* at city-level, even with Roman power always looming over the scene. This is perhaps especially true of Dio's representation of his own relationship with the people of Prusa, in which he emerges as a post-Classical philosophical mentor and effective operator with the Romans, but also as a latter-day Pericles promoting civic projects (including public building projects) and managing through political oratory (with varying success) the changing mood of the *dēmos*, which at one point sent him into exile.[24]

The dominance of elite voices in our evidence may, if anything, conceal the extent of the survival of traditional civic spirit. If even some figures who leaned towards aristocratic ideas, like the Lycians responsible for the inscription, could perpetuate traditional conceptual models of participatory political life and conflict, that makes it all the more probable that convinced Imperial-era democrats, whose words are much less well preserved, would also

---

23 Zuiderhoek 2008, 2009, Heller 2009, 2020, Fernoux 2011, Salmeri 2011, Brélaz 2013.
24 E.g. Dio Chrys. *Or.* 40.42–51, with Jones 1978: chs. 6 and 11, Swain 1996: 225–41, Ma 2000. Compare Plut. *Prae. ger. reip.* with Roskam and van der Stockt 2011.

have done so. They would have had even more incentive to resist pressures towards depoliticised civility (compare my next section) and present their activities, as Posidonius' Athenion does, in a long civic tradition, in their case of democratic pride and agitation.[25] This endurance of traditional conceptual models and practices throws into relief the simultaneous evolution of quite different ideas of civic order and disorder, to which I now turn.

Alternative conceptualisations of civic (dis)order in the Roman period

Other Greek citizens and intellectuals began in the Roman Empire to conceptualise civic order more as a pre-political or apolitical state of civility and calm coexistence, which they often regarded as underpinned by Roman power and peace (and their local representatives). Viewed through this lens, concerted dissent within a polis was less traditional political agitation than disturbance of peace and civility. There are already hints of this changed perspective in Polybius' analysis of unrest in third-century BC Arcadian Cynaetha. According to Polybius, the bitterness of the factional unrest was a symptom of the Cynaethans' neglect of traditional Arcadian music and dance, which had normally served to soften harsh Arcadian character, toughened by climate and topography. Indeed, these practices had helped to make the Arcadians famous for 'humanity' (*philanthrōpia*) and 'love of foreigners' (*philoxenia*) (4.17–21).

Polybius was elsewhere, perhaps especially in his Book VI, an advocate of traditional categories and methods of political analysis, focussed on constitutions, institutions and hard-headed political values of justice and the common good. Yet in this particular discussion of Arcadian unrest, he implies that civic cohesion and stability rely on deeper forms of sociability, humanity and sympathy, which exist beyond the narrowly political or institutional plane. These are put at risk during periods of violent unrest. This outlook has something in common with Thucydides' account of *stasis* (at Corcyra and elsewhere) as the breakdown of human interaction in general, though Polybius' specific stress on gentle, sympathetic virtues, sustained by music, is a

---

25 Compare Thornton 1999, 2001 (e.g. 445), 2008, Ma 2000.

distinctive touch which foreshadows developments of the first centuries BC and AD.

The most programmatic statement of these emerging new approaches comes in Diodorus Siculus' analysis of order and disorder in households and cities in his account of the Second Sicilian Slave War:

Ὅτι οὐ μόνον κατὰ τὰς πολιτικὰς δυναστείας τοὺς ἐν ὑπεροχῇ ὄντας ἐπιεικῶς χρὴ προσφέρεσθαι τοῖς ταπεινοτέροις, ἀλλὰ καὶ κατὰ τοὺς ἰδιωτικοὺς βίους πρᾴως προσενεκτέον τοῖς οἰκέταις τοὺς εὖ φρονοῦντας. ἡ γὰρ ὑπερηφανία καὶ βαρύτης ἐν μὲν ταῖς πόλεσιν ἀπεργάζεται στάσεις ἐμφυλίους τῶν ἐλευθέρων, ἐν δὲ τοῖς κατὰ μέρος τῶν ἰδιωτῶν οἴκοις δούλων ἐπιβουλὰς τοῖς δεσπόταις καὶ ἀποστάσεις φοβερὰς κοινῇ ταῖς πόλεσι κατασκευάζει. ὅσῳ δ' ἂν τὰ τῆς ἐξουσίας εἰς ὠμότητα καὶ παρανομίαν ἐκτρέπηται, τοσούτῳ μᾶλλον καὶ τὰ τῶν ὑποτεταγμένων ἤθη πρὸς ἀπόνοιαν ἀποθηριοῦται· πᾶς γὰρ ὁ τῇ τύχῃ ταπεινὸς τοῦ μὲν καλοῦ καὶ τῆς δόξης ἑκουσίως ἐκχωρεῖ τοῖς ὑπερέχουσι, τῆς δὲ καθηκούσης φιλανθρωπίας στερισκόμενος πολέμιος γίνεται τῶν ἀνημέρως δεσποζόντων.

For not only in political regimes should those in power behave decently towards the more humble, but also in private life the right-thinking should behave gently towards their slaves. For arrogance and heavy-handedness produces in cities internecine *staseis* among the free, and in private households plots of slaves against masters and terrible co-ordinated rebellions against cities. The more power inclines towards severity and lawlessness, the more the characters of subjects are made savage and driven to desperation. For anyone whose fortune is to be humble willingly submits to superiors in recognition of excellence and reputation, but, when deprived of fitting humane treatment (*philanthrōpia*), becomes hostile to those ruling in an ungentle manner. (Diod. Sic. 34/35.2.33)

The analogy of household and polis had often sustained thoroughly politicising conceptualisations of human society in Greek thought (Brock 2013: ch. 2). In this case, by contrast, Diodorus uses the parallel to paint a picture of civic order far removed from the traditional political conception. The elite in a polis rule well through kindness and humanity, rather than through attention to conventional political institutions and values. When they fail in this duty, the poor respond with savage hostility. This is not the politicised rage of the democratic citizen, but a beast-like savagery resembling that of revolting slaves in a household, who should more properly be, as Diodorus spells out (ἐλευθέρων ... δούλων), the antithesis of free citizens.
Even though Diodorus was here partly relying on Posidonius' account of the Second Sicilian Slave War, he adds his own moral tone and structure.[26] The conceptual model of *stasis* is a world away from the traditional one evident

---

26 Morton 2018, Wozniczka 2018; compare Sacks 1990, Rathmann 2016.

in Posidonius' Athenion episode and my other examples in the previous section. Mass and elite are no longer clearly fellow citizens engaged in a common game of politics, as symmetrical factions. There is now a fundamental asymmetry between a benevolent, paternalistic elite and needy, poorer citizens, who require sympathy and guidance to prevent them from turning to mindless violence. This alternative conceptualisation of conflict carried with it a fundamentally different understanding of the relationships which hold the polis together: what are now important are no longer so much *political* relations based on debate, exchange and struggle mediated through shared institutions, but rather *ethical* or *social* relations of peaceful coexistence, personal sympathy and mutual understanding, well summed up with the term *philanthrōpia* ('humanity') which is central to Diodorus' (like Polybius') approach to *stasis*.[27]

In this particular case, Diodorus is tolerant towards popular unrest provoked by elite severity. It is less clear, however, how tolerant he is of democratic demands and agitation in less extreme conditions: on his picture, what might earlier have been accepted as legitimate political dissent or jockeying might easily be condemned as disregard for the norms of civility and humane society. This different perspective was put into practice by the geographer Strabo, in his account of unrest at Tarsus during the transition from Antony's to Octavian's dominance in Asia Minor (14.5.14; Börm 2019:157). Strabo again uses familiar anti-democratic tropes, already encountered in my previous section, to discredit Mark Antony's faction, led by a certain Boethos, who had come to power in Tarsus: he explicitly portrays Boethos' power as based on demagoguery.[28]

In the representation of the democratic faction alone, there are already subtle hints of shifts in civic life, because the democrats' shortcomings are viscerally linked to (failings in) culture and *paideia*, which were evolving into ever more central dimensions of citizenship.[29] This ever closer entanglement of citizenship and culture is vividly symbolised in the condemnation of Boethos as 'bad poet and bad citizen' (κακοῦ μὲν ποιητοῦ κακοῦ δὲ πολίτου). Scarcely less threatening to cultured civility is Boethos' siphoning off of oil from the gymnasium, which he is supposed to be running as the heart

---

27 See Gray 2013 for the crucial role of this concept in the evolution of new understandings of civic order at this point.
28 See now Simonton 2022: 68–70.
29 For these wider trends in the Imperial Greek world: Swain 1996, Schmitz 1997.

of politico-cultural life in Tarsus. After incurring a sentence of exile, the members of Boethos' faction exemplify their attachment to bad poetry by inscribing scatological verse graffiti, and one even soils the house of the philosopher Athenodoros (for whom, see below). The political dimensions of this democratic dissent are thus played down by Strabo, in favour of an emphasis on the intrusion of ignorance, boorishness and greed into an evolving world of cultured civility, as those driven by the body and appetites corrupt the practices and spaces of the life of mind and soul.

The most significant departure from earlier patterns is the way that Strabo represents the opposition to the democrats. Strabo does not describe opposition from a symmetrical aristocratic faction struggling for control of the *politeia* from within the city, though such a faction may well have existed. Rather, Strabo puts all his emphasis on the intervention to restore order by the expatriate Tarsian Stoic philosopher Athenodoros Cananites, who returns from Rome, where he had been a respected teacher of Octavian. This Athenodoros 'uses the power given to him by Caesar', rather than the punitive power of regular civic law and courts, to exile Boethos' faction (ἐχρήσατο τῇ δοθείσῃ ὑπὸ τοῦ Καίσαρος ἐξουσίᾳ καὶ ἐξέβαλεν αὐτοὺς καταγνοὺς φυγήν). He then presses ahead single-handedly with local reforms, despite continued opposition. He succeeds in doing so through condescending humour and calm poise – personal attributes rather than institutional methods: he revises and sanitises the inscribed graffiti, and makes light of the soiling of his house. This is not to say that Athenodoros is ignorant of the Greek civic tradition: Strabo makes him evoke, after the incident at his house, the traditional civic metaphor of *stasis* as sickness.[30] Yet the dominant impression is of an outsider who has absorbed but moved beyond Greek civic *mores*, and returns out of consideration for his (former) compatriots.

Athenodoros thus partly fits the pattern identified by Gauthier and others of a new role for many elite civic figures in the later Hellenistic and early Imperial poleis, increasingly king-like and unconstrained by traditional civic checks and balances.[31] Yet he is even more distant from his notional fellow citizens, as a long-term expatriate and Roman courtier. Indeed, Athenodoros emerges from Strabo's text as a figure standing well above the civic political fray, an enlightened (philosophical) superior and representative of the new

---

30 Simonton 2022: 70, with Brock 2013: ch. 5.
31 See Gauthier 1985, with Fröhlich and Müller 2005, Mann and Scholz 2012 (including especially Hamon 2012); Quaß 1993 offers a different but related picture.

cosmopolitan (Stoic and Roman) world order, of which Strabo himself was a zealous advocate.[32] Indeed, as a doctrinal (Stoic) cosmopolitan with personal links to the Roman elite, Strabo's Athenodoros is an ideal mediator to bring to his home polis the blessings of the new Roman peace and order. With regard to questions of dissent and unrest, Strabo's implication is not so much that the democratic supporters of Antony are playing the established game of civic politics wrong, or perverting it through their corrupt decisions, but rather that they have missed the point that the traditional political cut-and-thrust is no longer appropriate within the new Roman cosmopolis. Strident assertion of factional interests, or even of traditional civic values, is now merely disruptive and destabilising; Tarsian and other Greek citizens need to learn some of the post-political or supra-political poise of the expatriate Athenodoros. This requires them to turn away from energetic, boisterous political competition and embrace instead the gentle, almost bourgeois virtues of contemplation and elegant self-control, exemplified by Athenodoros. To express dissent through traditional political channels is now, on this view, a category mistake which fails to recognise a new social and moral order, which goes beyond politics.

It is instructive to compare Strabo's representation of this process of civic conflict-resolution with preserved epigraphic examples of the same phenomenon, which suggest similar tendencies. For the pre-Roman Hellenistic world, inscriptions richly attest processes of civic conflict resolution through the summoning of a group of (supposedly impartial) foreign judges or arbitrators.[33] In that earlier period, these judges and arbitrators almost always worked in groups, to prevent any individual wielding decisive power. For the later Hellenistic period, however, preserved inscriptions of this kind are much rarer, which may in itself indicate a change in civic values and practices of publicity and accountability.[34] Those that survive attest lone individuals effecting settlements after conflict, in the manner of Athenodoros of Tarsus, which confirms that a new style of conflict resolution was a key part of the transitions noted by Gauthier and others (see above). The individual entrusted with this unusually wide-ranging power could be, like Athenodoros, an august home citizen. In later Hellenistic Mylasa, the

---

32 Compare Strabo 1.1.16–18, Engels 1999, Dueck, Lindsay and Pothecary 2005. On cosmopolitan theory and the Roman Empire: Richter 2011: esp. ch. 4.
33 See recently Scafuro 2013, Magnetto 2016.
34 Compare Börm 2019: 271–2.

elite citizen Ouliades acted as sole arbitrator and judge after acute disputes relating to legal cases, probably concerning financial contracts and debts. Some leading individuals had played similar roles in poleis in earlier Greek history, though this kind of behaviour would earlier have been quick to attract suspicions of tyranny or tyrannical ambitions.[35] Ouliades' unusual role is recorded in a section of the civic honorific decree for him, which makes explicit the shift in values which is the focus of this section (*I.Mylasa* 101, ll. 38–9). A well-established formula in epigraphic texts concerning reconciliation was that the settlement was geared to enable citizens to 'conduct their political life' (πολιτεύεσθαι) in concord (ὁμονοία).[36] The decree for Ouliades literally depoliticises this formula, by adapting it to state that Ouliades aimed to enable his fellow citizens to 'conduct their shared life together' (τὴν μετ' ἀλλήλων συναναστροφὴν ποιεῖσθαι) in concord (*I.Mylasa* 101, ll. 37–46). This removal of the expected reference to political life implies that the recent discord was not, as in the standard pattern, an example of political conflict which burst the bounds of the political game, for which the required solution was the restoration of political institutions and normal political activity. Rather, the unrest was perceived in this case to breach a more diffuse form of social (and economic) coexistence and interaction (συναναστροφή),[37] which Ouliades was able to revive.

Similar shifts in emphasis and values are revealed in a partly comparable honorific decree from later Hellenistic Sagalassos, which also details the resolution of acute civic conflict by a lone individual, in this case a foreigner: Manesas, from nearby Termessos.[38]

τὴν ἐκεί[νων] εἰς τὰ ἡμέτερα πράγματα σπουδὴν καὶ φιλοτειμίαν ὑπερέθετο καὶ κατ' ἰδίαν
ἑκάστωι τῶν συντετευχότων αὐτῶι ἡμετέρων χρησιμώτατον ἑαυτὸν παρεσχημένος, ἐξ ὧν
αὐτῶι συνφώνως ἐμαρτυρήθη ὑπὸ πάντων ἐπὶ τῆς βουλῆς, καὶ κοινῆι τοῖς δημοσίοις πράγ-
μασιν εὐνούστατον παρεσχημένος, καὶ τὰ νῦν φιλοτειμίας πολειτικῆς καὶ πολέμου χαλεπω-
τάτου περιέχοντος τὴν πόλιν ἡμῶν ἐπιγνοὺς τὴν καθ' ἡμᾶς περίστασιν ἴδιον ἐλάσωμα διαλα-

---

35 Compare Diodorus' representation (drawing on earlier analyses) of Agathokles' brokering role as general and 'protector of the peace' between incumbent citizens and returned exiles at Syracuse (19.5.5, δημαγωγήσας ποικίλως τὰ πλήθη στρατηγὸς κατεστάθη καὶ φύλαξ τῆς εἰρήνης, μέχρι ἂν γνησίως ὁμονοήσωσιν οἱ συνεληλυθότες εἰς τὴν πόλιν) as a stepping-stone on his route to tyrannical power.
36 See *IG* XII 4 1 132 (Telos, later fourth century BC), ll. 4–5, 38–9, *IG* XII 6 1 95 (Samos, third century BC), ll. 16–17, *Tit. Cal.* Test. XVI (Kalymna, third century BC), ll. 37–8.
37 This was a newly prominent concept in the later Hellenistic world, which I explore in Gray 2022.
38 Compare Waelkens 2002: 316, Börm 2019: 272 n. 637.

βὼν εἶναι τὸν πάντα χρόνον προσεκαρτέρησεν καὶ συνὼν ἡμεῖν καὶ πρὸς τὰ ἄριστα προτρεπόμενος καὶ συμβουλεύων σωτηρίως καὶ κακοῦ ἔχθραν οὐδεμίαν ἐκκλείνων αἰτιώτατος τῆς καθ' ἡμᾶς εἰρήνης καὶ ὁμονοίας ἐγένετο.

... he exceeded their enthusiasm and love of honour concerning our affairs, and in private having made himself most useful to each of our citizens who has come across him, as a result of which there was univocal testimony about him from all before the council, and in public having conducted himself with the greatest good will towards our public affairs; and when he recognised the recent situation, with civic strife and most harsh war enveloping our polis, treating our situation as a personal setback, he showed endurance throughout the whole time, and spending time with us, urging us towards the best, offering advice like a saviour and not deviating from any hatred of evil, he was most responsible for the peace and concord among us. (*TAM* III 1 7, ll. 1–15)

Manesas is again, like Athenodoros and Ouliades, an almost king-like figure above politics. He does not pursue reconciliation through the traditional Greek civic route of a combination of law, institutional mechanisms and appeal to shared political values, especially justice and the common good (Dössel 2003, Gray 2015: chs. 1–2). Rather, he relies on personal charisma, sympathy and advice. According to the decree, he spent time among the Sagalassians (συνὼν) and urged them towards the best things (πρὸς τὰ ἄριστα προτρεπόμενος), driven by hatred of evil. These are activities and vocabulary more readily associated with ethical and philosophical mentoring than with the expectations and formulae of official civic decrees.[39] Personal emotion is also given unusual prominence, in a context where institutions and standard civic values would normally be dominant: Manesas mourned the discord as a personal setback for himself. There is also much language here which is strongly in keeping with older norms, perhaps especially the reference to Manesas giving advice using a verb (συμβουλεύειν) very familiar from traditional political contexts.[40] However, the addition of the adverb σωτηρίως ('like a saviour') is very striking: he was not so much a civic adviser as a charismatic 'saviour' standing outside political struggle.[41]

This changed conceptualisation of political interaction is also evident in the handling of the concept of *philotimia*. At the start of the decree, Manesas himself is praised for *philotimia* in the sense of 'love of honour', a traditional civic

---

39 Compare Robert 1960: 213, 1967: 12 n. 1, on the migration of προτρέπεσθαι from fourth-century ethical literature to later Hellenistic official decree language.
40 See already, for example, Herodotus 7.237 or *IG* II² 223, C, ll. 11–12.
41 Compare similar language in the second-century BC decree of Abdera for Teian envoys to Rome: *SIG*³ 656, ll. 17–19 (ἀρίστην ἅμα καὶ σωτήριον [πραγμάτω]ν ἀπορουμένων ἀεὶ προτιθέντες γνώμην).

virtue, but interestingly this word is itself used later in the decree with the different meaning of 'political strife' (with connotations of honour-driven competition), to describe the conflict in Sagalassos itself. This suggests an ambivalence about this central attribute of the traditional engaged, rivalrous citizen: this kind of highly politicised behaviour can lead to unrest as much as stability. The preferable end state, achieved with Manesas' help, is both *homonoia*, the traditional Greek concept of internal civic harmony, and *eirēnē*, peace. As I have argued in another article, this apparent use of *eirēnē* to refer to internal civic order is striking and significant: since the Peloponnesian War, the Greeks had almost always made a sharp distinction between the internal *homonoia* which holds together a polis, a high level of integration achieved through political debate and institutions, and, on the other hand, the looser *eirēnē* or peace which binds together multiple different states when they are not at war. By blurring the distinction between these concepts, the Sagalassians succeeded in reinforcing the impression that traditional civic politics, based on the institutionalised political interaction of a highly engaged and ambitious citizenry, was giving way to a different type of civic order, based on looser and less politicised coexistence and mutual tolerance (Gray 2017).

This new valuing of internal *eirēnē* also soon took on an institutionalised form in Asia Minor, in a new magistracy adopted by many cities in the Imperial period: the office of *eirēnarch* ('magistrate in charge of peace'), charged with maintaining internal 'peace' in the city against any kind of disruption, including internal insubordination by (for example) Christians (Brélaz 2005: 90–122; 2008: 197–204). The developments in ideas and institutions in the Greek world were probably partly inspired by the rise to prominence of *pax* ('peace') as a way of conceptualising internal order in Rome during the Civil Wars, sometimes in combination with *concordia* ('harmony') and sometimes as an alternative to it (Cornwell 2017: esp. chs. 1–2). A sharp distinction between internal 'harmony' and external 'peace' certainly continued to appeal to later city-states: the Stadttor of the Hanseatic city-state of Lübeck proclaims *domi concordia, foris pax*. In this period, however, both Greeks and Romans were experimenting with blurring the two, with important consequences for conceptual models of unrest: to this way of thinking, any political assertiveness, even previously routine democratic activity, might potentially breach the peace.

It speaks in favour of the interconnection of the Greek and Roman discourses around this time that there is evidence for the Roman introduction to the eastern Mediterranean of their own variants of these new ways of thinking about unrest, and solutions to it. In a letter to the Knidians, Augustus represents his intervention as geared at resolving what he presents as a feud between leading local families, though it was perhaps in reality not so different from many Hellenistic *staseis* (Börm 2019: 222–6). Nocturnal domestic attacks had threatened the 'security' of all (τὴν κοινὴν ἁπάντων ὑμῶν ἀσφάλειαν [ἀναι]ροὐντων; *I. Knidos* I 34 (6 BC), ll. 34–5). Augustus thus depoliticises civic order: even in the 'free' city of Knidos, order is now a matter of preserving civic safety and security (*asphaleia*, not political *homonoia* or *dēmokratia*) from random disturbances (presented as lacking any broader political basis).

I have concentrated in this section on the later Hellenistic and Augustan periods, but these developments set the pattern for many conceptualisations of unrest in the early Imperial Greek East, as already evident from the development of the office of *eirēnarch*. For example, Dio Chrysostom often gives the impression, as noted above, that the world of Pericles and Demosthenes endures at civic level. However, at other times he suggests that civic order is now principally a matter of genteel civility, more aesthetic or philosophical than political. For example, in his speech to the Alexandrians (*Or.* 32), he presents the unruliness and ribaldry of the Alexandrian *dēmos* as a departure from the sober, cultivated habits which true education and music can instil. The truly desirable democracy is the one which is 'reasonable and gentle and truly mild' (εὐγνώμων καὶ πρᾷος καὶ γαληνὸς ὄντως) and willing to accept good, frank advice from mentors like Dio, rather than arrogant, tyrannical and beast-like (*Or.* 32.27; compare 32.7 on the quality of Dio's advice). In this ideal scenario, both leaders and *dēmos* are mild and considerate, which helps to enable debate between them (compare my conclusion).[42]

Plutarch, for his part, explicitly disparages traditional styles of civic and democratic rhetoric, especially those suited to arousing strong emotions and decisive political action, in favour of the pursuit of calm, gentle civic order. In a well-known passage of his *Praecepta reipublicae gerendae*, Plutarch argues that magistrates rising in the assembly to incite the *dēmos* with heroic examples of Classical Athenian deeds and ideals are now out of step with the times and conditions (814ac; see Kokkinia 2004 for the wider context). He later makes clear he has in mind references to Greek military victories in the name of collective liberty, naming Eurymedon, Plataea and Marathon. This makes clear that his target is any contemporary Greek who uses Clas-

---

42 For much deeper analysis of this speech from this angle, see Dubreuil, forthcoming.

sical Greek history in an aggressive manner to incite freedom from Roman hegemony. It is probably also not coincidental that these were all democratic military victories: any kind of assertive political intervention or dissent on behalf of the *dēmos* is also now, for Plutarch, anachronistic.

Plutarch does think Classical Athens offers other positive models to emulate, but, revealingly, these all involve, for him, a turning away from the cut-and-thrust of political struggle and striving in favour of social peace and civility: he mentions the Athenian amnesty of 403 BC, and also some other famous Classical Athenian examples of decency, sensitivity to others' feelings, or sympathy for the unfortunate.[43] Plutarch's desire is that contemporary polis citizens should focus on getting along with one another as smoothly as possible, through the kind of gentle reflection and sympathy familiar from other examples in this section, from Sagalassos to Dio's Alexandria. As at Strabo's Tarsus, for Plutarch, almost any energetic political self-assertion was now tantamount to boorish disturbing of the peace. Indeed, Plutarch's (and Dio's) example brings out something implicit in my examples from earlier in the Roman period, especially Strabo's account of Tarsus: it was not simply that outright unrest was being reconceptualised, but this reconceptualisation dragged into the category of unrest previously routine forms of political oratory, competition, and confrontation.

Coexistence, rivalry, and fusion of old and new discourses of unrest

Plutarch's example makes clear the vibrant and contested interaction between different conceptual models of order and disorder in the Greek poleis of the early Roman Empire. There was no straightforward, progressive hollowing out of Greek political and democratic traditions (de Ste. Croix 1981's 'death of Greek democracy'), including traditional ideas of *stasis* and 'taking a stand'. Rather, many continued to advocate, and enact, traditional civic modes of political interaction and confrontation. To put this another way,

---

43 Plutarch mentions how the Classical Athenians fined Phrynichos for his tragedy on the fall of Miletus, wore garlands when Cassander refounded Thebes, held an expiatory sacrifice after the Argive *skytalismos*, and abstained from searching the house of a newly married man while investigating the Harpalos affair.

two pictures of the Roman-era polis dominant in modern historiography were true simultaneously. The old picture of the Roman-era polis as a depoliticised *town* where politics had been diluted into festivals, associations and gentility has considerable force; but so too does the more recent picture, advanced by Heller, Fernoux and others, according to which the traditional polis of vibrant assembly debate endured.[44]

In fact, I would like to suggest, these two cities were indissolubly linked with each other. It must have been partly precisely the threat of those to whom Plutarch alludes – those who continued to engage in traditional civic politics and rhetoric to argue for autonomy, or even democracy and equality – which provoked their opponents in civic elites, including Plutarch himself, to seek new or adapted ways to delegitimise political agitation and assertion as obsolete and damaging to the hard-won Roman *pax*, including peace (and resulting cultured civility) at civic level. Whereas Posidonius, for example, used traditional conceptual models of *stasis* to attack radical appeals to the Classical democratic past to justify anti-Roman and anti-elite dissent in the new world, for Plutarch, as for Diodorus, Strabo and others before him, it was not that these dissenters were doing politics wrong, but that they should not be doing politics at all. According to this (contested) way of thinking, it was now genteel social and cultural interaction, in a spirit of peace, which was demanded of good citizens.

The new conceptual models of unrest and stability which emerged must have drawn much inspiration from Roman discourses of peace and security (see previous section) and from developments in other provinces (studied elsewhere in this volume). In particular, there are close links with the evolution of Roman discourses, central to this volume, of unrest within the empire as a matter of internal disturbance within an unequal political system, perpetrated by insider miscreants who would not accept benevolence from above. These new Greek approaches had in common with this wider evolution the aspiration to conceptualise unrest as something clearly internal to a single political organism, but significantly different from established models of conflict between equal fellow citizens of a single citizen-state. Yet it also made a significant difference that here the main older reference points were distinctively Greek conceptual models of *stasis* and *homonoia*, which gave the new Greek approaches their distinctive cast, especially their preoccupation with transformation of citizenship in a cultured, gentle di-

---

44 See again, among recent work, Heller 2009, Fernoux 2011, Brélaz 2013.

rection. As explored for the wider Roman world in this volume, the complex Greek discourses of the period itself should make historians hesitate to adopt too readily the language of 'dissent' or 'revolt' against an unequivocal established 'peace' or orthodoxy; the conflicts and wider political field were more dynamic and multipolar than that language implies, with concepts of peace and order themselves deeply contested even long after Greece and Asia Minor were free from war.

Mutual counter-definition was the dominant relationship between the two conceptual models of civic order and disorder I have discussed, but they could also be fused into a new hybrid. As already noted in this chapter, Dio Chrysostom straddled older and newer approaches, moving between politics, ethics, philosophy and aesthetics, or between Periclean and Socratic citizenship. At times he fused these different approaches. In his speech to the council of Apameia on concord with Prusa (*Or.* 41), Dio reflects on opposition to him back in Prusa:

τὸ δὲ εἶναί τινας, ὡς ἂν ἐν δήμῳ, τῶν ἐνθάδε ἐμοὶ σχεδὸν μὴ σφόδρα ἡδομένους οὐκ ἂν θαυμάσαιμι διὰ τὴν τῶν πόλεων φιλοτιμίαν. καίτοι ἐπίσταμαι σαφῶς οὐδὲ τοὺς ἐκεῖ πολίτας ἅπαντας ἀρέσαι δυνάμενος, ἀλλ' ἐνίους δι' αὐτὸ τοῦτο ἀχθομένους ὅτι λίαν δοκῶ φιλόπολις καὶ πρόθυμος. δεῖ δὲ τὸν ἐπιεικῆ καὶ μέτριον ἄνδρα καὶ ταύτην παρέχειν τὴν ἐξουσίαν τοῖς ἑαυτοῦ πολίταις. τὸ γὰρ μηδένα ἐν πόλει μήτε ἀντιλέγειν ἑνὶ μήτε μέμφεσθαι κἂν ἅπαντα φαίνηται ποιῶν καλῶς, οὐ δήμων ἐστὶν οὐδὲ ἐπιεικές, ἀλλὰ μᾶλλον φιλεῖ τὸ τοιοῦτον συμβαίνειν τοῖς τυράννοις ἢ τοῖς εὐεργέταις. εἰ οὖν εἰσί τινες πρὸς ἐμὲ δυσκόλως διακείμενοι, τούτοις μάλιστα πιστεύω.

I would not be surprised that there should be some of those here, as should be the case in a democracy, who are not particularly pleased with me, on account of the rivalry between the cities [Apameia and Prusa]. Indeed, I well know that I cannot even please all of the citizens there [in Prusa], but rather some of them are troubled by the very fact that I seem to be too polis-loving and enthusiastic. It is necessary for the decent and moderate man to extend this power to his fellow citizens. For no-one in a polis to contradict or to blame someone, even someone who is evidently acting virtuously in all respects, is not characteristic of democracy or decent; such things tend to happen to tyrants rather than benefactors. If, therefore, there are some who are hostile towards me, it is in them that I have the most trust. (Dio Chrys. *Or.* 41.2–3)

According to Dio here, it is, in fact, a mark of decency (*epieikeia*) and moderation to tolerate, or even encourage, dissent and criticism (if not full-scale unrest), in the democratic tradition. This adds a new dimension to the new ideas of civility in citizenship: a grace, magnanimity and trust towards political enemies which unexpectedly reintroduces the intense political debate associated with rival models of civic order and disorder. Especially since Dio is here addressing the civic elite on the council of Apameia, there is more than a hint of elite condescension and tolerance: perhaps the most effective way to defuse serious dissent was, in fact, not to vilify it, but graciously to tolerate it.

On the other hand, there is also more to this passage. In older Greek civic discourse, it had often been very difficult to acknowledge disagreement and division within one's own citizen-body, supposedly united in *homonoia*, especially after a vote had been taken. For all their language of *parrhēsia*, Classical Athenians rarely made explicit the existence of divisions within their *dēmos*, let alone celebrating it.[45] Dio, by contrast, here has no difficulty in accepting, and even embracing, the fissures in his own home polis; he even 'trusts most of all' those at odds with him (τούτοις μάλιστα πιστεύω).[46] He also openly states before the council of Apameia that there is inevitably continued vigorous opposition to him in that city, even *after* a vote has been taken to honour him. Dio's rhetoric here raises the tantalising possibility that the rise to prominence of 'bourgeois' civility and decency also opened the door to revised ideas of democracy in the Roman East, themselves more 'bourgeois' in their new pluralism and intimations of proto-liberal tolerance and mutual trust between political enemies. A fusion of the contrasting models I have discussed in this chapter was, at least, conceivable: a fusion which calls into question any simplistic argument, which this chapter might seem to invite, for the incompatibility of civility and agonistic debate as bases of democracy. In any case, complex evidence such as this for discourses about unrest, dissent and stability in the Romano-Greek world make sense only as the product of dynamic interaction between different conceptual models: still vibrant older ones and transformative new ones, inspired by the new Roman world.

Acknowledgments

I am very grateful to Lisa Eberle and Myles Lavan for organising the stimulating Tübingen conference and for help with this chapter.

---

45 Compare Saxonhouse 1992, Loraux 2001, 2005, Gray 2015: chs. 4–5.
46 But compare and contrast Dio's disparaging engagement with his domestic opponents at *Or.* 40.8.

Works cited

Azoulay, Vincent. 2014. 'Repolitiser la cité grecque, trente ans après'. *Annales. Histoire, Sciences Sociales* 69(3): 689–719.
Badian, Ernst. 1976. 'Rome, Athens and Mithridates'. *American Journal of Ancient History* 1: 105–28.
Börm, Henning. 2016. 'Hellenistische Poleis und römischer Bürgerkrieg – *Stasis* im griechischen Osten nach den Iden des März (44 bis 39 v. Chr.)', in Börm, Mattheis and Wienand 2016: 99–125.
–. 2019. *Mordende Mitbürger. Stasis und Bürgerkrieg in griechischen Poleis des Hellenismus*. Stuttgart.
Börm, Henning, Marco Mattheis and Johannes Wienand. 2016. *Civil War in Ancient Greece and Rome: Contexts of Disintegration and Reintegration*. Stuttgart.
Brélaz, Cédric. 2005. *La sécurité publique en Asie Mineure sous le principat*. Basel.
–. 2008. 'L'adieu aux armes: la défense de la cité grecque dans l'empire romain pacifié', in Brélaz and Ducrey 2008: 155–96.
–. 2013. 'La vie démocratique dans les cités grecques à l'époque impériale romaine. Notes de lectures et orientations de la recherche'. *Topoi* 18(2): 367–99.
Brélaz, Cédric and Pierre Ducrey, eds. 2008. *Securité collective et ordre public dans les sociétés anciennes*. Geneva.
Brock, Roger. 2013. *Greek Political Imagery from Homer to Aristotle*. London.
Chaniotis, Angelos. 2008. 'Policing the Hellenistic countryside. Realities and ideologies', in Brélaz and Ducrey 2008: 103–153.
Connor, W.R. 1971. *The New Politicians of Fifth-Century Athens*. Princeton.
Cornwell, Hannah. 2017. *Pax and the Politics of Peace: Republic to Principate*. Oxford.
Dössel, Astrid. 2003. *Die Beilegung innerstaatlicher Konflikte in den griechischen Poleis vom 5.-3. Jahrhundert v. Chr.* Frankfurt.
Dubreuil, Raphaëla. Forthcoming. 'The leader as doctor: healing the city in Dio's *Oration* 32', in Gavrielatos and Nicholson, forthcoming.
Dueck, Daniela, Hugh Lindsay and Sarah Pothecary, eds. 2005. *Strabo's Cultural Geography. The Making of a* Colossourgia. Cambridge.
Engels, Johannes. 1999. *Augusteische Oikumenegeographie und Universalhistorie im Werk Strabons von Amaseia*. Stuttgart.
Fernoux, Henri-Louis. 2011. *Le Démos et la Cité: communautés et assemblées populaires en Asie Mineure à l'époque impériale*. Rennes.
Forsen, Björn and Giovanni Salmeri, eds. 2008. *The Province Strikes Back: Imperial Dynamics in the Eastern Mediterranean*. Helsinki.
Fröhlich, Pierre and Christel Müller, eds. 2005. *Citoyenneté et participation à la basse époque hellénistique*. Geneva.
Gauthier, Philippe. 1985. *Les cités grecques et leurs bienfaiteurs*. Athens.
Gavrielatos, Andreas and Emma Nicholson, eds. Forthcoming. *Literary Genre and Leadership Values in Antiquity*. London.

Gehrke, Hans-Joachim. 1985. *Stasis: Untersuchungen zu den inneren Kriegen in den griechischen Staaten des 5. und 4. Jahrhunderts v. Chr.* Munich.
Gray, Benjamin. 2013. 'The polis becomes humane? *Philanthrōpia* as a cardinal civic virtue in later Hellenistic honorific epigraphy and historiography', in Mari and Thornton 2013: 137–62.
–. 2015. *Stasis and Stability. Exile, the Polis, and Political Thought, c. 404–146 BC*. Oxford.
–. 2017. 'Civic reconciliation in later classical and post-classical Greek cities: a question of peace and peacefulness?', in Moloney and Williams 2017: 66–85.
–. 2022. 'L'invention du social? Délimiter la politique dans la cité grecque (de la fin de la période classique au début de la période impériale).' *Annales. Histoire, Sciences Sociales* 77(4): 633–71.
Grieb, Volker. 2008. *Hellenistische Demokratie. Politische Organisation und Struktur in freien griechischen Poleis nach Alexander dem Großen*. Stuttgart.
Griffin, Miriam and Jonathan Barnes, eds. 1997. *Philosophia Togata I: Essays on Philosophy and Roman Society*, revised paperback edition. Oxford.
Haake, Matthias. 2007. *Der Philosoph in der Stadt: Untersuchungen zur öffentlichen Rede über Philosophen und Philosophie in den hellenistischen Poleis*. Munich.
Habicht, Christian. 1997. *Athens from Alexander to Antony*. Cambridge, MA.
Hamon, Patrice. 2012. 'Gleichheit, Ungleichheit und Euergetismus: die *isotes* in den kleinasiatischen Poleis der hellenistischen Zeit', in Mann and Scholz 2012: 56–73.
Hau, Lisa, Alexander Meeus, and Brian Sheridan, eds. 2018. *Diodoros of Sicily: Historiographical Theory and Practice in the* Bibliotheke. Leuven.
Heller, Anna. 2009. 'La cité grecque d'époque impériale: vers une société d'ordres ?' *Annales. Histoire, Sciences Sociales* 64(2): 341–73.
–. 2020. *L'âge d'or des bienfaiteurs. Titres honorifiques et sociétés civiques dans l'Asie Mineure d'époque romaine (Ier s. av. J.-C. – IIIe s. apr. J.-C.)*. Geneva.
Jones, Christopher P. 1978. *The Roman World of Dio Chrysostom*. Cambridge, MA.
–. 2001. 'The Claudian monument at Patara'. *Zeitschrift für Papyrologie und Epigraphik* 137: 161–8.
Kidd, Ian G. 1988–1999. *Posidonius*. Vol. 2 (i) *and* (ii): *The Commentary and* Vol. 3: *The Translation of the Fragments*. Cambridge.
–. 1997. 'Posidonius as philosopher-historian', in Griffin and Barnes 1997: 38–50.
Kim, Lawrence. 2010. *Homer between History and Fiction in Imperial Greek Literature*. Cambridge.
Kokkinia, Christina. 2004. 'Ruling, inducing, arguing: how to govern (and survive) a Greek province', in de Ligt, Hemelrijk and Singor 2004: 39–58.
Lape, Susan. 2010. *Race and Citizen Identity in the Classical Athenian Democracy*. Cambridge.
de Ligt, Luuk, Emily Hemelrijk and Henk W. Singor, eds. 2004. *Roman Rule and Civic Life: Local and Regional Perspectives*. Amsterdam.
Lintott, Andrew. 1982. *Violence, Civil Strife and Revolution in the Classical City*. London.
Loraux, Nicole. 2001. *The Divided City: On Memory and Forgetting in Ancient Athens*. New York.
–. 2005. *La tragédie d'Athènes: la politique entre l'ombre et l'utopie*. Paris.
Ma, John. 2000. 'Public speech and community in the *Euboicus*', in Swain 2000: 108–124.

Magnetto, Anna. 2016. 'Interstate arbitration and foreign judges', in Mirko Canevaro and Edward Harris, eds., *The Oxford Handbook of Ancient Greek Law*. https://doi.org/10.1093/oxfordhb/9780199599257.013.20.

Mann, Christian and Peter Scholz, eds. 2012. *"Demokratie" im Hellenismus: Von der Herrschaft des Volkes zur Herrschaft der Honoratioren?* (Die hellenistische Polis als Lebensform 2). Berlin.

Mari, Manuela and John Thornton, eds. 2013. *Parole in movimento. Linguaggio politico e lessico storiografico in età ellenistica. Studi ellenistici XXVII*. Pisa.

Moloney, Eoghan and Michael Williams, eds. 2017. *Peace and Reconciliation in the Classical World*. Abingdon.

Morton, Peter. 2018. 'Diodorus Siculus' "slave war" narratives: writing social commentary in the *Bibliotheke*'. *Classical Quarterly* 68(2): 534–51.

Petzl, Georg. 2011. Review of Şahin and Adak 2007. *Gnomon* 83(1): 50–55.

Quaß, Friedemann. 1993. *Die Honoratiorenschicht in den Städten des griechischen Ostens*. Stuttgart.

Rathmann, Michael. 2016. *Diodor und seine "Bibliotheke". Weltgeschichte aus der Provinz*. Berlin.

Richter, Daniel. 2011. *Cosmopolis: Imagining Community in Late Classical Athens and the Early Roman Empire*. Oxford.

Robert, Louis 1960. *Hellenica 11/12*. Paris.

—. 1967. 'Sur les inscriptions d'Ephèse'. *Revue de philologie, de littérature et d'histoire anciennes* ser. 3, no. 4: 7–84.

Roskam, Geert and Luc van der Stockt, eds. 2011. *Virtues for the People: Aspects of Plutarchan Ethics*. Leuven.

Sacks, Kenneth. 1990. *Diodorus Siculus and the First Century*. Princeton.

Şahin, Sencer and Mustafa Adak. 2007. *Stadiasmus Patarensis. Itinera Romana Provinciae Lyciae*. Istanbul.

Salmeri, Giovanni. 2008. 'Empire and collective mentality: The transformation of *eutaxia* from the fifth century BC to the second century AD', in Forsen and Salmeri 2008: 137–55.

—. 2011. 'Reconstructing the political life and culture of the Greek cities of the Roman empire', in van Nijf and Alston 2011: 307–36.

de Ste Croix, G.E.M. 1981. *The Class Struggle in the Ancient Greek World*. London.

Saxonhouse, Arlene. 1992. *Fear of Diversity: The Birth of Political Science in Ancient Greek Thought*. Chicago.

Scafuro, Adele. 2013. 'Decrees for foreign judges: judging conventions or epigraphic habits?' *Symposion* 2013: 365–95.

Schmitz, Thomas. 1997. *Bildung und Macht. Zur sozialen und politischen Funktion der zweiten Sophistik in der griechischen Welt der Kaiserzeit*. Munich.

Schmitz, Thomas and Nicolas Wiater, eds. 2011. *The Struggle for Identity: Greeks and their Past in the First Century BCE*. Stuttgart.

Simonton, Matthew. 2022. 'Demagogues and demagoguery in Hellenistic Greece'. *Polis* 39(1): 35–76.

Swain, Simon. 1996. *Hellenism and Empire: Language, Classicism, and Power in the Greek World, c. AD 50–250*. Oxford.

–, ed., 2000. *Dio Chrysostom: Politics, Letters and Philosophy*. Oxford.

Thornton, John. 1999. 'Una città e due regine. Eleutheria e lotta politica a Cizico fra gli Attalidi e i Giulio Claudi'. *Mediterraneo antico* 2: 497–538.

–. 2001. 'Gli *aristoi*, l'*akriton plēthos* e la provincializzazione della Licia nel monumento di Patara'. *Mediterraneo antico* 4: 427–46.

–. 2008. '*Lesteiai* nella dedica a Claudio del monumento di Patara: una sommessa proposta d'interpretazione'. *Mediterraneo antico* 11: 175–98.

van Nijf, Onno, and Alston, Richard, eds. 2011. *Political Culture in the Greek City after the Classical Age*. Leuven.

Waelkens, Marc. 2002. 'Romanization in the East. A Case Study: Sagalassos and Pisidia (SW Turkey)'. *Istanbuler Mitteilungen* 52: 311–368.

Walser, Andreas Victor. 2011. 'ΔΙΚΑΣΤΗΡΙΑ – Rechtsprechung und Demokratie in den hellenistischen Poleis', in Mann and Scholz 2011: 74–108.

Wozniczka, Piotr. 2018. 'Diodoros' narrative of the first Sicilian slave revolt (ca. 140/35–132 BC). A reflection of Poseidonios' ideas and style?' in Hau, Meeus, and Sheridan 2018: 221–46.

Zuiderhoek, Arjan. 2008. 'On the political sociology of the imperial Greek city'. *Greek, Roman and Byzantine Studies* 48: 417–45.

–. 2009. *The Politics of Munificence in the Roman Empire: Citizens, Elites and Benefactors in Asia Minor*. Cambridge.

5. Josephus's Multilayered Discourse on the Judean Revolt against Rome

Katell Berthelot

Abstract: *This article argues that Josephus's account of the Judean revolt in BJ reflects his situation in Rome and his exposure to Roman norms, values and discourses on unrest. It analyses Josephus's discourse from three perspectives, as the Judean historian describes the war as (1) a conflict with or revolt against Rome (polemos, neōterismos, apostasis), (2) a civil war (stasis), and (3) a rebellion against the God of Israel. These interwoven narratives reflect Josephus's historiographical and theological perspectives but also some apologetic concerns – to defend not the Romans or the Flavian dynasty, as scholars have sometimes argued, but rather the people of Judea (at least the majority), a great part of its nobility and Josephus and his historical work. In addition, the interpretation of the revolt as a war against God, closely connected to Josephus's dismissal of the rebels' religious motives and theological vision, probably aimed to defend the Jewish religio against Roman discourses that mocked Jewish superstitio and celebrated the failure of the Jewish God, and to reassert the soundness of the Jewish faith in the God of Israel. Yet while some aspects of Josephus's discourse on the war may reflect a subaltern perspective (that of the Jews under Roman domination), others are connected to his original social milieu and express the view not of a subaltern but rather of an aristocratic leader who was once in a dominant position and understood unrest as a threat to his station.*

The topic of Josephus's discourse on unrest in Judea shortly before and during the 66–74 CE war against Rome, as expressed in his first work, the *Jewish* (or *Judean*) *War* (henceforth *BJ*), is hardly new. Countless studies have been devoted to Josephus's account of the Great Jewish Revolt, among which the recent synthesis by Steve Mason (2016), deserves special mention. Several publications have attempted to reconstruct the causes of the revolt, the course of events and the rebels' motivations,[1] or to analyse *BJ*'s literary construction, Josephus's terminology, his rhetorical strategies and his own understanding of the war.[2] In connection with Josephus's rhetorical strategies, considerable attention has also been paid to the apologetic dimension of his works, including *BJ*.[3]

The present contribution owes a lot to these previous studies. It analyses Josephus's discourse on unrest in *BJ* from three perspectives, arguing that the Judean historian describes the events as (1) a conflict with or revolt against Rome (*polemos*, *neōterismos*[4], *apostasis*[5]), (2) a civil war (*stasis*) (in a way that does not exactly reflect the Thucydidean use of the term, as we shall see),[6] and (3) a rebellion or a war against God. These categories aligned with the cultural norms of Josephus's Roman, Greek and Jewish audiences in various ways, even though Josephus's theological interpretation of the revolt remains thoroughly Jewish (and may even be characterized as Deuteronomistic: the disasters that befell the Jews were due to the people's sins).[7] This article argues that viewing the Judeo-Roman war through the lenses of these three

---

[1] See, e.g., Farmer 1956: 11–23, Goodman 1987, Goodman 1990, Berlin and Overman 2002, Tomasino 2008, Popović 2011, Mason 2016, Giambrone 2021.

[2] Lindner 1972, Bilde 1979, Rajak 1991, Krieger 1999, Lanfranchi 2000, Mader 2000, Sterling 2000, Kelley 2004, Price 2007, Brighton 2009, Wiater 2010, Price 2011, Vandenberghe 2016, Sievers 2021. On Josephus's mastery of classical rhetoric, see Runnals 1997.

[3] See, e.g. Nikiprowetzky 1971, Berthelot 2008. On Josephus's apology for himself, see in particular *BJ* 6.107.

[4] On *neōterismos* / *to neōterizon* / *hoi neōterizontoi* / *neōterizein* in connection with rebellion against Rome, see, e.g., *BJ* 1.4, 2.318, 2.332, 2.407, 2.410, 2.417, 2.494, 2.513, 2.593, 2.652, 3.108, 3.289, 3.445 (with *aphestanai* as a parallel), 3.447, 3.463, 4.114, 4.120, 4.133, 6.239, 6.343, 7.4, 7.447 (as a risk); Sterling 2000, 147.

[5] Or *epanastasis* (in *BJ* 3.3). On *apostasis* as revolt against Rome, see, e.g., *BJ* 2.39 and 2.73 (unrest in 4 BCE, at the time of Varus), 2.238 (unrest caused by Judas the Galilean, who exhorted people not to pay taxes to Rome, in 6 CE), 2.264, 2.333–34, 2.342, 2.347, 2.371, 2.385, 2.404, 2.412, 3.465, 4.4, 4.83, 5.183, 6.290 (with *polemos* as a parallel), 7.76–77 and 82–89 (revolts by Germans and Scythians), 7.113, 7.164, 7.257 (where *apostasis* seems to refer to the first phase of the war, designated as *polemos*), 7.370; Krieger 1999: 209–10; Mason 2008: 28 n. 236. Another word used by Josephus in connection with the revolt is *kinēma* (*BJ* 1.4), but it is rare and tends to designate the instability before the revolt rather than the war itself (*BJ* 6.290).

[6] On war against the Romans as *polemos* and civil war in Jerusalem as *stasis*, see *BJ* 1.27, also 1.10.

[7] Nicole Kelley (2004: 259) argues that 'Josephus's orations [*his own speech at Jotapata and Eleazar's oration at Masada*] ought to be understood as a cosmopolitan expression of ideas that were equally at home – and intentionally so – in Jewish and Greco-Roman philosophical thought'. On Josephus's primarily Roman audience in *BJ*, see Mason 2005. On Josephus's theological interpretation of the war, see, e.g., Nikiprowetzky 1971, Lindner 1972, Bilde 1979, Rajak 1991, Spilsbury 2003, Price 2005, Sievers 2021.

categories allowed Josephus to develop a multilayered apologetic discourse. From a sociological perspective, some aspects of this discourse may reflect a subaltern perspective (that of the Jews under Roman domination), but others are connected to Josephus's original social milieu and express the view not of a subaltern but rather of an aristocratic leader who was once in a dominant position and understood unrest as a threat to his station.

A revolt against Rome

Describing the 66–74 war as a revolt against Rome is not as uncontroversial among modern scholars as one may think at first glance. Mason, in particular, has put great emphasis on the conflict's regional dimension and the role played by tensions between the Judeans and other ethnic groups (Greeks, Syrians, Samarians, etc.).[8] Mason also insists that some of the decisions taken by the Judeans were not necessarily anti-Roman. In his opinion, even though the conflict ended up in an open war between the Judeans and the Roman legions, it did not start this way, nor was it originally fuelled by anti-Roman ideology.[9]

Leaving aside this debate about the real causes of the conflict, I wish to focus on Josephus's discourse and its rhetorical strategies. Josephus explicitly states that some people in Jerusalem could no longer stand Florus's administration of Judea (2.293–94), and that this led to the rejection of Roman rule more generally. He tells how Eleazar, the son of the (former) high priest Ananias, and thus a member of Jerusalem's priestly elite, incited the inhabitants to put an end to the sacrifices offered in the Temple for the well-being of the emperor and the Roman people (2.409–10). Josephus duly acknowledges that such a decision was tantamount to rebellion against Rome. He also admits that those whom he describes as 'moderate' voluntarily joined the rebellion after the Judeans' victory at Bethoron against the Twelfth Ro-

---

8 The events in Caesarea under Felix (*BJ* 2.266–70), followed at the time of Florus by the massacre of the Jewish population (2.457) and subsequent massacres (by Greeks and Judeans) in other cities (2.458–80), provide illuminating examples of such a dynamic.
9 See, e.g., Mason 2016: 109, 200, 412, 449 (concerning the Zealots: 'there is nothing in their name, presumed tradition, or behaviour to suggest that these people were motivated by anti-imperial grievances. They came into conflict with Rome as a result of regional strife, which persuaded them to arm themselves and look to God for protection'), 451–53 (on John of Gischala, with caution).

man Legion, commanded by Cestius Gallus (2.541–55).[10] In short, Josephus writes quite openly about the desire of many Judeans to reject Roman rule.

Insofar as Josephus was writing *BJ* in the city of Rome, where he faced hostility against Jews that was at least partly connected to the war, we might reasonably expect him to downplay the Jews' rebelliousness. Such attempts are in fact perceptible in his later works – namely, in *Jewish Antiquities* (e.g., *AJ* 1.6) and *Life* (*Vit*. 24–27), where he claims that the Jews had no choice but to wage war and were thus drawn into the war against their will. (In *Vit*. 17–23 he also presents himself as reluctant to get involved in the revolt, whereas in *BJ* he does not mention reservations on his part at the outbreak of the war.) In *BJ*, however, he clearly attributes to at least part of the people the desire to get rid of Rome's yoke and regain their freedom, even though he assesses their project and their hopes as mad and deceptive.[11] The theme of the desire for freedom and liberation from the Romans runs throughout the whole work, from book 2 (§§ 259, 264, 443 and repeatedly in Agrippa II's speech to the Jerusalemites[12]) to Eleazar's speech at Masada in book 7 (§§ 325–27, 334). Moreover, Josephus connects Eleazar to Judas the Galilean and his 'Fourth Philosophy' (7.253–55), which he already describes at the beginning of book 2 as focused on the issue of liberation from the Roman 'masters' and submission to God alone (2.118, 433).[13]

Myles Lavan has shown that the characterization of submission to Rome as 'enslavement' and a longing for liberty are recurring themes in Tacitus's accounts of rebellions in various parts of the empire (2017: 27). Josephus's insistence on the motif of freedom and scorn for enslavement to Rome among

---

10 On the support given by numerous members of the Judean elite to the revolt, see Goodman 1987; 1990.
11 See, e.g., *BJ* 2.264: 'And even when these [parts] had been put in order, just as in a body that is diseased a different part again was becoming inflamed. For the enchanters (*goētes*) and bandit-types (*lēstrikoi*) got together and were inciting many to rebellion (*apostasis*) and cajoling them toward "freedom", threatening death to those who submitted to the Roman imperium and saying that they would remove by force those "who willingly chose slavery"' (trans. Mason 2008: 214–15).
12 Lanfranchi 2000: 131 notes that there are eleven references to *eleutheria* in Agrippa II's speech to the rebels (*BJ* 2.345–401): see 2.346, 348–49, 355, 358, 361, 365, 368, 370, 373–74. This speech, which aims to discourage the Judeans from revolting against Rome, contains many echoes of Roman and pro-Roman discourses on Rome's power and management of empire. See Rajak 1991, Mason 2008 ad loc., Kaden 2011.
13 Judas and his partisans triggered the insurrection of 6 CE against Quirinius's census and Roman rule more widely. See also *BJ* 7.253–55, *AJ* 18.4–9, 23.

the rebels may thus reflect both the insurgents' aspirations and the Roman perception of what caused people to revolt more generally.

Other aspects of Josephus's discourse on the Judean revolt against Rome have parallels from the pens of Roman authors, most notably in Tacitus's descriptions of other uprisings within the empire. As Lavan argued, the rebels' speeches in Tacitus regularly refer to the vices of Roman rulers, especially greed, cruelty and lust (2017: 27). Similarly, Josephus's presentation of the events leading to the revolt leaves no doubt as to the personal responsibility of the Roman procurator Florus Gessius, as well as other Roman administrators before him, for the outburst in Jerusalem. In his famous speech in book 2, Agrippa II exhorts the Judeans to differentiate between Roman rule in general and the misbehaviour of bad governors, who may be replaced and do not embody the quintessential nature of Rome's government (§§ 352–54). Such passages in *BJ* are congruent with a Roman senatorial perspective on the causes of unrest within the empire. Thus, even though Josephus is supposed to embody the voice of a subaltern – a member of the conquered and defeated people – he endorses a discourse on revolt that was fully at home in a Roman elite context.

A striking feature of *BJ* is Josephus's designation of the rebels, be they Sicarii, Zealots or people associated with other groups:[14] he encompasses all of them under the appellation *lēstai* (brigands, robbers), even though some passages of his work show that among the insurgents there were members of the nobility, who were probably wealthy.[15] *Lēstai* thus appears as a derogatory appellation meant to present the rebels as despicable 'gangsters' motivated by greed and to minimize the political (or political-religious) dimension of their actions.[16]

---

14 See *BJ* 2.254 (Sicarii), 2.264, 2.441, 2.587 (John of Gischala), 2.653 (Sicarii), 3.450 (Jesus son of Saphat), 4.97, 4.504 (Sicarii), 4.510 (Simon bar Giora's men), etc.; Grünewald 2004: 94. Josephus seems to use the lexical field of *lēsteia* to a greater extent than other authors; see Nickel 2018: 45–47. Note that the term *lēstēs* (*listim*) is also present in rabbinic literature; see Isaac 1984. On banditry see also Shaw 1984, Isaac 1992, 66–67, Grünewald 2004.
15 In *BJ* 3.450, Josephus calls Jesus son of Saphat the head of a robbers' band, but according to *BJ* 2.599 he was in fact the chief magistrate of Tiberias. The best example of Josephus's strategy of delegitimization is John of Gischala, his archenemy, whose nobility he tries to conceal; see Grünewald 2004: 100–104. The fact that many leaders of the revolt (including himself, originally) stemmed from the Judean elites was embarrassing to Josephus.
16 Rhoads 1976: 160–61, Grünewald 2004: 109, Vandenberghe 2016: 506–7. Against this scholarly trend, Richard Horsley (1979, 39) argues that 'much of Josephus' use of the nomenclature of banditry evidently refers to actual bandits', whom Horsley deems to be social bandits.

According to Lavan, this strategy is absent from Tacitus's writings: he does not use the 'language of *latrocinium*' to speak about the provincials who rebelled against Rome (2017: 30, 34). Yet in his study of bandits in the Roman empire, Thomas Grünewald found examples of such a rhetoric of *latrocinium* in connection with revolts against Rome (2004: ch. 2). The first case is that of Viriatus in second-century BCE Spain, who successfully led Lusitanian resistance against the Republic. Numerous Roman authors call him a *latro* (because of his mountain origins and his practice of guerrilla warfare, often associated with *latrocinium*), yet he enjoys a positive reputation in their writings, since they put the blame for the revolt on the original breach of trust by the Roman *praetor* of the province of Hispania Ulterior, Galba. The second example is Tacfarinas in Africa Proconsularis in 17–24 CE, whose image is wholly negative, as he combined the crime of rebellion with that of desertion. Even though these examples differ from the Judean revolt in significant ways, they show that labelling insurgents as *lēstai* would not have been alien to the Roman or Greek pro-Roman rhetoric Josephus is likely to have encountered in Rome.

Josephus's adoption of a Roman perspective on unrest to speak of the Judean revolt certainly enhanced the credibility of his historical work for his Greco-Roman audience in Rome. It thus primarily served his purposes of self-promotion and apology for himself and his work.

A civil war

Josephus's use of *lēstai* to describe rebel leaders may have mimicked Roman trends in yet another way, which draws our attention to the second dimension of the Judean conflict, that of civil war. Grünewald has shown that labelling political enemies as *lēstai* was not uncommon at the end of the Republic and the beginning of the Principate (2004: ch. 4). This practice seems to have vanished under Augustus but later Roman authors echoed the use of *latro* and *latrocinium* in the period running from Cicero to Augustus. Josephus's characterization of John of Gischala, his personal enemy, as *lēstēs* fits in this Roman tradition. In a chapter dedicated to *lēstai* in Josephus's *BJ*, Grünewald concludes that 'Josephus deployed the term "bandit" entirely pejoratively and described the rival politicians to whom he applied it using the same conventional clichés as used by Roman writers' (2004: 109).

Josephus's derogatory discourse on the rebels and their leaders again reflects a perspective that was consonant with an upper-class Roman milieu in the case of the Sicarii. Marijn Vandenberghe has shown that the characterization of some groups as *sikarioi* (a Greek spelling of the Latin word *sicarii*, which he translates as 'skilled users of the *sica*-type dagger') reflects Josephus's familiarity with Roman legal and rhetorical uses of the term.[17] The *Lex Cornelia de sicariis et veneficiis* was directed against killing, arson, illegal carrying of weapons, bribery of magistrates and false testimony.[18] An example of references to the *lex de sicariis* in vituperative speeches is found in Cicero's *Stoic Paradoxes*, where Cicero addresses an imaginary character (to be identified with his enemy Clodius) with 'You caused a massacre in the forum, you held the temples with armed brigands, you burnt private persons' houses and consecrated buildings' (*Parad*. 30, trans. Rackham), and then cites three clauses of the *lex de sicariis*. This list of crimes parallels Josephus's statements about the Sicarii in *BJ*.[19] Vanderberghe further adds that the legal category of 'bandit' could be 'used as a weapon of accusation against political rivals if the rhetorician could prove that the opponent used illegal means in political conflicts. ... Clodius accused Milo, for example, of being a 'bandit and assassin' (*latronem ac sicarium*) who acted on Cicero's orders (Cicero, *Mil*. 18)' (2016: 484–85). Josephus's use of *sikarioi* and his association of Sicarii with *lēstai* (as in *BJ* 2.254, 2.653, 4.504, etc.) is thus congruent with Roman rhetorical practice. Moreover, his tendency to libel political enemies as *sicarii* and brigands in order to cast the rebel leaders in a negative light contributed to establishing his position in Rome as one who, despite his initial participation in the revolt, had opposed these leaders (at least in the case of John).[20]

As mentioned in the introduction, Josephus's narrative is also the story of a war within the war, a succession of inner conflicts in the Judean camp that

---

17 Vandenberghe 2016: quotation at 480. For the view that the term refers not to a more or less unified movement but to various groups that were not connected to one another, see also Mason 2008: 207–8 n. 1604, Brighton 2009: xiii, 141–50, which concludes that 'the label *sicarii* was used not primarily to describe a group of people but to marginalize and condemn certain types of behavior' (150).
18 According to Vandenberghe (2016: 481–83), this law is known from Cicero's speeches, Ulpian (quoted in *Collatio Legum Mosaicarum et Romanarum* 1.3.1) and the *Digest* (48.8.1).
19 See, e.g., *BJ* 2.254–57, 2.425–29 (in association with another group called *lēstai*), 4.398–409. See also *AJ* 20.163–65.
20 See Grünewald 2004: 109.

he describes as civil strife. He makes this point clear right from the outset, in a crucial passage of the preface:

I shall faithfully recount the actions of both combatants; but in my reflections on the events I cannot conceal my private sentiments, nor refuse to give my personal sympathies scope to bewail my country's misfortunes. For, that it owed its ruin to civil strife (*stasis oikeia*; cf. *BJ* 5.257), and that it was the Jewish tyrants (*tyrannoi*) who drew down upon the holy temple the unwilling hands of the Romans and the conflagration, is attested by Titus Caesar himself, who sacked the city; throughout the war he commiserated the populace who were at the mercy of the revolutionaries (*stasiastoi*), and often of his own accord deferred the capture of the city and by protracting the siege gave the culprits time for repentance. Should, however, any critic censure me for my strictures upon the tyrants (*tyrannoi*) or their bands of marauders (*to lēstrikon*) or for my lamentations over my country's misfortunes, I ask his indulgence for a compassion which falls outside an historian's province. (*BJ* 1.10, trans. Thackeray)

The theme of civil war also appears at the very beginning of Josephus's historical narrative, when he first recalls the events that occurred during the Hasmonean period (*BJ* 1.31, trans. Thackeray): 'At the time when Antiochus, surnamed Epiphanes, was disputing with Ptolemy VI the suzerainty of Syria, dissension (*stasis*) arose among the Jewish nobles (*hoi dynatoi*)'. According to Josephus, both the crisis under Antiochus IV and the destruction of the Temple in 70 CE were thus linked to the same phenomenon, *stasis* among the Judeans (Price 2011: 85).

From book 2 onward, *BJ* narrates how the leadership of Judea, composed mainly of priestly families or clans and wealthy families associated with the Herodian dynasty,[21] was gradually overpowered by the *neōterizontoi* (some of whom were also from a priestly background) and their followers. Already under Albinus, a 'revolutionary party' (τῶν νεωτερίζειν βουλομένων, 2.274) was active in Jerusalem, whose leaders Josephus describes as 'chief-robbers' (*archilēstai*) and tyrants (*tyrannoi*). Later on, new leaders, characterized by Josephus as reckless, cruel and tyrannical, successively gained power and control over the city or some of its parts: Menahem son (or rather descendant) of Judas the Galilean, whose followers apparently formed the core group of the Sicarii later found in Masada; Eleazar son of Simon (head of the Zealots); John of Gischala (originally from Galilee); and Simon bar Giora, to name only the main actors. Books 4 to 6 of the *Jewish War* are replete with

---

21 In *BJ* 2.411, Josephus also includes among these elites 'the notables among the Pharisees'.

accounts of the atrocities committed by these men and their supporters, as well as by other groups, such as the Adiabenians and the Idumeans.[22]

Josephus repeatedly refers to this state of affairs with the lexicon of *stasis*, a term that already had a strong Thucydidean connotation in his time.[23] It brought to the minds of educated readers passages of the *Peloponnesian War*, such as the description of the *stasis* in Corcyra (3.82–84).[24] As Gottfried Mader suggests, Josephus's description of the atmosphere of systematic deceit, betrayal and transgression of the law within the city echoes Thucydides's account at 3.82.6–7 (2000: 90). He also notes that the typology of *stasis* includes 'trust and oaths perverted (3.82.6–7), religion disregarded (3.82.8), sacred space violated (3.70.4, 3.81.3–5)', all elements that are present in Josephus's account of the rebels' behaviour (2000: 132). Thucydides's comparison of *stasis* to a plague that spreads through the social body has parallels in Josephus as well (Price 2011: 86). Josephus's use of Thucydidean references and *stasis* terminology, which his educated Greco-Roman audience in Rome would have readily identified, was certainly meant to strengthen his legitimacy as an historian.[25]

Josephus was no servile imitator of his Greek predecessor, however. Jonathan Price has shown that his use of the word *stasis* differs from that of Thucydides. While in *BJ*'s book 2 *stasis* refers to internal divisions and unrest within Judean society, later on the lexical field of *stasis* (especially *stasiastai* – 'agents of civil strife' or 'insurgents' – which seems to be Josephus's favourite form[26]) is associated only with the factions that opposed the traditional rulers of Judea, just as in *AJ* 4.11–56, the episode of Korah's rebellion against Moses, *stasis* characterizes Korah and his group, not Moses, Aaron and the Israelites who remained faithful to them.[27] In other words, *stasis* is used to refer to the actions of the revolutionaries rather than to the conflict between them and their rivals (Jerusalem's nobility). In Josephus's account of the

---

22 The process of *stasis* associated with the 66–74 war may be considered to start with Eleazar's decision to put an end to the sacrifices on behalf of the emperor and the Roman people in *BJ* 2.409, but it takes on a new dimension with the arrival in Jerusalem of exterior groups. On *BJ* 4.121–282, see Mader 2000: ch. 3.
23 The influence of Thucydides's work on *BJ*, in terms of both structure and writing style, is massive and has received extensive attention. See, e.g., Hadas-Lebel 1989: 245, Mader 2000, Sementchenko 2010, Price 2011.
24 Feldman 1994: 50, Mader 2000: esp. 56, Sementchenko 2010, Price 2011.
25 Mader 2000, Price 2011: 84 ('These imitations lend power and authority to Josephus' account').
26 Mason 2008: 11.
27 See *AJ* 4.12–13, 30, 32, 36, Sementchenko 2010, Price 2011.

Judean civil war, it is thus not the *dēmos* that rejects the authority of the traditional, aristocratic elite,[28] but specific groups that inflict great harm on a powerless people.[29] The responsibility for *stasis* lies with the groups that Josephus characterizes as 'revolutionaries' (*neōterizontoi*) or 'robbers' (*lēstai*).

Stasis thus comes to designate an insurrection against the established power (leading to the destruction of the archives, the abolition of debt, the liberation of slaves and measures against the wealthy). In most passages of *BJ*, this power is that of the Judean elites who ruled the country before the war, not Roman power.[30] The civil war within the war against Rome therefore appears as a revolt against the Judean aristocracy, of which Josephus was a prominent member.

It is thus unsurprising that we should find under Josephus's pen 'what [Ranajit] Guha calls the "prose of counter-insurgency"', which includes 'not just the obvious rhetorics of barbarism, criminality, and immorality, which deny legitimacy to the rebels, but also more subtle tropes, such as spontaneity or hysteria, which deny them agency and rationality' (Lavan 2017: 20, quoting Guha 1999: 333). The leaders of the insurgents are *tyrannoi*, which means that they establish a type of power that is marked by lawlessness. Both the insurgents and their leaders are described as inhuman, ferocious and impious. Moreover, Josephus depicts them as deprived of rationality.[31] Josephus's description of the rebels thus conforms to what modern authors have identified as the norms of colonial discourse about subalterns' efforts to shake off imperial or colonial oppression.

Lavan emphasizes that 'one of the most remarkable features of the Latin discourse on revolt is the lack of strategies of delegitimisation' (2017: 34). Josephus's *BJ* represents the opposite case: a consistent and systematic

---

28 See Gray's chapter in this volume, which notes that 'Posidonius thus here presents the unrest at Athens in 88 BC very much like a Classical *stasis*, of the kind known from Thucydides, Xenophon and Aristotle, fought between an unruly *demos* striving for absolute equality under a demagogue and, on the other side, their aristocratic opponents, who insist on their superior virtue and self-control'.

29 See, e.g., *BJ* 2.304, 2.449–50, 3.448, 3.454, 5.53, 5.566.

30 Rhoads 1976: 162; Sementchenko 2010. In some cases, *stasis* and other words from the same lexical field may refer to the insurrection against the Judean elites and the empire taken together, as in *BJ* 2.418–19. See also 2.421 (with *aphistēmi*).

31 See, e.g., *BJ* 2.265 (*aponoia*), 2.346 (*elpis alogistos*), 2.412 (*alogos*), 3.454 (*aponoia*), 3.479 (*tolma, thrasos* and *aponoia*, in Titus's exhortation to his troops), 4.147 (*aponoia*), 4.211 (*alogos*, in connection with John), 4.261 (*aponoia*), 4.362 (*aponoia*), 4.571 (*aponoia*), 5.121 and 316 (*aponoia*, again attributed to Titus), 5.424 (*aponoia*), 5.566 (*aponoia*), 6.39 (*aponoia*, again in one of Titus's speeches).

effort to delegitimize the rebels by labelling them as murderers (*sicarii*), brigands (*lēstai*), seditious people (*stasiastai*) and rebels/revolutionaries (*neōterizontoi*),[32] and by ascribing to them all kinds of crimes, impious acts and irrational behaviour.

Moreover, Josephus's description of Judean society as deeply unsettled by *stasis* sharply differentiates his account of the Great Revolt from Tacitus's passages on provincial rebellions against Rome. Lavan has drawn attention to the fact that 'in each case [in Tacitus], a subject people rises in its entirety against their Roman oppressors' (2017: 29). Such a vision could not be further from Josephus's understanding of the Judean revolt. On the contrary, he repeatedly laments that kinship ties and ethnic solidarity have become meaningless, the rebels showing more cruelty than the Romans themselves toward other Jews.[33] The divisions and hatred among the Jewish people, which Josephus views as a major sin (see section 3 below), represent a thread that runs through the whole book.

Yet Josephus's argument that the people (including part of the nobility, of which he was himself a member) were forced to endure the rebels' decision not to compromise, to continue the war until the ultimate catastrophe, arouses suspicion. He may have exaggerated the divisions within the people to downplay the responsibility of the majority in the eyes of his audience in Rome. Martin Goodman notes that it still would have been possible to escape Jerusalem in the summer of 68, and even 69.[34] Josephus's rhetoric of cruelty and madness on the rebels' part thus plays an apologetic function again: in this case, an apology for the 'people', and implicitly the nobles who remained in Jerusalem and suffered at the hands of the 'tyrants' but were probably more involved in the war than Josephus is willing to admit.[35]

Moreover, looking at the Great Revolt through the prism of civil war could serve Josephus's apologetic goals in yet another way, helping him to reduce the gap between Jews and Romans by suggesting that Jews were no

---

32 Already in *B.J.* 1.4, Josephus uses the phrase *to neōterizon*, the 'revolutionary' faction or party; and at the very end of *BJ* (7.421) he still speaks of *neōteropoiia* to describe the seditious activities of Jews in Alexandria.
33 See, e.g., *BJ* 2.466, 2.469–76, 2.581, 4.16, 4.134, 4.181–83, 6.4.
34 Goodman 1990: 42, referring to *BJ* 4.353, 5.421, 5.450.
35 Goodman 1990: 41–42. Mason 2016: 465, focusing on the refugees who had lost everything and for whom surrender was an empty option, writes that perhaps 'Jerusalem itself would have capitulated, had it not been for the large numbers of desperate men who fled to Jerusalem from elsewhere and who could not surrender'.

barbarian, irrational people. In 68–69, the Romans had experienced civil war throughout the empire and within the city of Rome itself. In the latter case too, the inhabitants had witnessed horrific scenes and acts of impiety, culminating in the burning of the most holy temple of Jupiter Capitolinus. Josephus's detailed retelling of these events in book 4 (§§ 545–655, esp. 647–53), after his account of the crucial turning point reached by the *stasis* in Jerusalem, is certainly not coincidental but rather meant to suggest a parallel. Mason aptly notes that

> structure and language reveal that Josephus is doing much more than merely supplying information. He is bringing the Judaean and Roman civil wars into direct conversation. Just when Simon bar Giora reaches the height of his power, menacing Jerusalem from outside, Josephus makes the comparison: "Not only in Judaea were there civil strife and internecine war (στάσις ἦν καὶ πόλεμος ἐμφύλιος), but also in Italy" (4.545). After briefly covering the murder of Galba in the forum, Otho's war with Vitellius, who "craved kingship" just as John and Simon did (4.208, 390, 510), and Otho's suicide in defeat (4.545–49), Josephus returns to Simon's entry into Jerusalem (4.556–84) and remarks, "around this time terrible sufferings also enveloped Rome" (4.585). Just as John and Simon turn Jerusalem into a scene of bloody conflict and pollute the temple, so Vitellius and his rough German soldiers "made the whole of Rome into a military camp" (4.586). The switching back and forth, applying similarly charged language to Jerusalem and Rome, encourages his Roman audience to view both conflicts as species of the same genus. The Judaeans are not strange barbarians; their leaders face the same problems as those of every polis, of Rome itself. Josephus implicitly portrays himself as a man of the same cast as his cultured audiences. … In addition, he points to what every intelligent person knows to be the real basis of the Flavian triumph, the victory over Roman rivals. (Mason 2016: 417)[36]

In short, the designation of the war as a *stasis* in the sense of a civil war between the Judean authorities and 'revolutionary' groups serves Josephus's apologetic efforts to defend the Jewish people, the Judean nobility who had remained in Jerusalem until the end of the war and his own historical work in the eyes of his Roman audience: the people, because he argues that the responsibility for the revolt lay with the seditious groups that triggered the *stasis*; the nobility, because he implicitly aligns its members both with the Roman authorities against whom the *stasiastai* fought (for the latter opposed Rome and Jerusalem's nobility) and with the Roman elites who had experienced the civil war in 68–69 CE; and himself, since by using *stasis*

---

36 See already Mason 2005: 97–99.

language and Thucydidean language and images more widely he could hope to increase his legitimacy as an historian.

A rebellion against God

As Klawans observes, 'Although *Jewish War* is, primarily, a work of history … Josephus's account is liberally peppered with theological observations' (2012: 187). Joseph Sievers similarly notes that 'Josephus uses what we would call religious categories, values, and experiences to explain what happened and why it happened' (2021: 196). And Price has demonstrated that we should take Josephus's theological thought about the war seriously (2005).

We must first make a distinction between Josephus's personal theological reflection on the revolt and the way he describes the rebels' religious motivations, which, as Mader argues, he tends to belittle and not explain adequately to his audience.[37] Mader states that 'one significant function of Josephus' polemic against the Jewish insurgents is to counteract and downplay the religious substratum which gave the revolt its broad ideological cohesion'. Taking issue with the theological assumptions of the revolutionaries, Josephus provides a rationalizing, psychological and moralistic account of their motivations (2000: 10–11, quotation at 10). Moreover, consistently describing the rebels as impious – emphasizing that they transgressed the divine laws, committed various sacrileges and polluted the sacred precinct – is also a way for Josephus to invalidate their beliefs.[38] Ultimately, he dismisses the rebels' religious discourses and reasonings not only as expressions of wrong religiosity (manifested in the inability to decipher signs and oracles properly as at BJ 6.288–315) or wrong theology (such as John's confidence in Jerusalem's invincibility in 6.98 or the 'end of history' interpretation of the Judean defeat by Eleazar son of Jairus in book 7) but also to preserve the respectability and

---

37 These motivations have been interpreted by scholars in various ways, and even put in doubt; but the coins minted during the revolt focus on 'Holy Jerusalem' and 'the redemption/freedom of Zion', and display temple vessels and religious symbols such as the four species of Sukkot (Meshorer 2001: 115–31). See, e.g., Hengel 1976: esp. 235–318, Rajak 2002a, Tomasino 2008, McLaren 2011.
38 On the rebels' transgressions and impiety, see, e.g., BJ 2.258, 2.413–14, 4.148, 4.242, 4.314–18, 5.401–2, 7.254–74.

credibility of the Jewish *religio* (which, we must keep in mind, was mocked and loathed by part of the Roman elite).[39]

Josephus's account of the revolt dismisses the rebels' theological claims but conveys an alternative theological reading of the events. Civil strife is a major sin, not merely a human, political and military disaster.[40] Moreover, Josephus claims that the tragedy that befell Jerusalem was foretold by prophecies. He recalls an oracle 'that the city would be taken and the sanctuary burnt to the ground by the right of war, whensoever it should be visited by sedition (*stasis*) and native hands should be the first to defile God's sacred precincts' (*BJ* 4.388, trans. Thackeray). Again, in a speech addressed to John of Gischala and the besieged, he recalls how ancient prophets foretold that Jerusalem 'would be taken whensoever one should begin to slaughter his own countrymen (*homophylou phonou*)' and adds: 'God it is then, God Himself, who with the Romans is bringing the fire to purge His Temple and exterminating a city so laden with pollutions' (*BJ* 6.109–10, trans. Thackeray). In a similar vein, some rabbinic sources, which are admittedly later than Josephus's writings, refer to wanton hatred between Jews as a major sin and the main cause of the defeat by Rome.[41]

Josephus's theological interpretation of the war and his understanding of divine wrath are, however, more complex than the above quotations suggest, because in *BJ* civil war is both a *sin* and a *punishment* for previous offenses committed by Israel. That the Judean people (or at least the Jerusalemites) had sinned before *stasis* fully spread in Jerusalem comes to the fore in several places in book 2.

First, Josephus presents Eleazar son of Ananias's decision to interrupt the daily sacrifices at the Jerusalem Temple for the well-being of the emperor and the Roman people not only as a clear political message of rebellion against Rome but also as a major impiety (*BJ* 2.409–17, esp. 413–14). Eleazar's aim

---

39 Tacitus refers to oracles and omens that occurred during the war and claims that Jews were unable to interpret them correctly, in a way that recalls Josephus's statements in *BJ* 6.288–315 but is much less sympathetic: Jews were both prone to superstition and unwilling to practice the propitiatory rites that would have been needed in such circumstances. See Tacitus, *Hist.* 5.13; Suetonius, *Vesp.* 4.5; Tomasino 2008.
40 According to Tessa Rajak (2002b: 95), this is even 'the ultimate sin'. It runs against the Mosaic law's logic, which is to create *homonoia* among Jews (*Ap.* 2.179, 283).
41 Tosefta, Menahot 13:22; Jerusalem Talmud, Yoma 1:1, 38c; Babylonian Talmud, Yoma 9b; Goldenberg 1982:523. On the similarities between Josephus's understanding of the causes of the Temple's destruction and those found in rabbinic literature, see Price 2005: 109; Klawans 2010; Klawans 2012: 187; Sievers 2021: 196.

was to reject offerings and sacrifices brought or funded by foreigners (2.409), but 'the chief priests and the notables' replied that

their ancestors had furnished the shrine mostly from the foreigners, always welcoming the gifts from outside nations. And not only had they not prohibited the sacrifices of certain people, for this is most impious, but they also [did not prohibit] them from dedicating the votive offerings around the temple, which can be seen and remain in place for such a long time. ... Along with the danger, they [*i.e., Eleazar and his partisans*] had voted to condemn the city for impiety – if among the Judeans alone an outsider could neither sacrifice nor make obeisance. (*BJ* 2.412–14, trans. Mason 2008: 416–17)

Josephus was aware that accusations of misanthropy and atheism (or impiety) were formulated against the Jews in his time (Schäfer 1997, Berthelot 2003). Therefore, he wanted to clearly condemn Eleazar's decision, which, beyond its political significance, could appear to Josephus's audience as both a mark of impiety and an indication of 'hatred of foreigners'. Josephus even characterizes Eleazar's 'reform' as 'a foreign cult' (*thrēskeia xenē*, 2.414), meaning that it ran against Judean customs and laws.

Eleazar's initiative opened the way to a series of crimes that also qualified as impious acts from Josephus's perspective. Especially appalling was the slaughter of the Roman garrison in Jerusalem on a Sabbath, despite oaths sworn to the soldiers that they would be allowed to leave the city in peace if they surrendered their weapons (*BJ* 2.450–56). The crime of Eleazar and his followers was triple: they betrayed the word given to the Romans, they murdered unarmed men, and they desecrated the Sabbath. As a consequence, the people in Jerusalem understood 'that the causes of the war were already irremediable, and that the city had been defiled with such a great pollution (*miasma*), as a result of which it was reasonable to expect some other-worldly wrath, even if not the vengeance from the Romans' (2.455, trans. Mason 2008: 335–36). This divine wrath manifested itself in the subsequent disasters that afflicted the city, ultimately including the destruction of the sanctuary (see also *BJ* 4.323). Josephus later adds that as a consequence of the temple's pollution, God prevented the war from reaching an early conclusion (2.539). This remark means that the *stasis* that developed in Jerusalem with the arrival of John of Gischala, Simon bar Giora and others was already a consequence of God's punishment of his people. The idea that the *stasis* in Jerusalem was a consequence of God's rejection of the city and its inhabitants is also found in a speech attributed to Vespasian's generals, who argue that 'divine providence has come to our aid by turning our adversaries against each other' (*BJ* 4.366, trans. Thackeray). Even the insurgents themselves come close to formulating such an idea. At a later stage of the war, the rebels try to unite their forces to resist the Romans but admit that God may very well deny them 'lasting concord' and thus be the driving force behind their divisions (5.278). These passages reflect Josephus's perception of the situation.

That Josephus repeatedly asserts that God sided with the Romans is well known. Ultimately, he goes so far as to accuse the rebels of waging war not only against the Romans but against God himself. In book 5, he addresses the besieged in the following terms:

> Will you not turn your eyes and mark what place is that whence you issue to battle and reflect how mighty an Ally you have outraged? Will you not recall your fathers' superhuman exploits and what mighty wars this holy place has quelled for us in days of old? For myself, I shudder at recounting the works of God to unworthy ears; yet listen, that you may learn that you are warring not against the Romans only, but also against God (ἀκούετε δ' ὅμως, ἵνα γνῶτε μὴ μόνον Ῥωμαίοις πολεμοῦντες ἀλλὰ καὶ τῷ θεῷ; see also BJ 6.4). (BJ 5.378, trans. Thackeray)

This passage provides the third and final key to decipher Josephus's vision of the war: not only a revolt against Rome and an episode of civil strife, but a war against the God of Israel. As in the case of *stasis*, this war is waged by only a portion of the Judeans, not the people as a whole (whereas the revolt was, originally at least, supported by at least a vast majority of the Judeans, including Josephus himself in BJ's version). Yet all Jews suffer the consequences of the rebellion against God (see also AJ 20.166).

Price has argued that 'Josephus was not immune from the traumatic question which afflicted all Jews after 70 CE: why did God let it happen?' (2005: 110). This statement raises an additional question: namely, is it appropriate to see Josephus's theological discourse as an apology for the God of Israel? Per Bilde has answered this question negatively, emphasizing the difference between Josephus's BJ and 4 Ezra, a work that focuses entirely on the issue of theodicy (Bilde 1979). As a matter of fact, nowhere does Josephus raise doubts about God's justice. Nevertheless, his theological explanation of the war has an apologetic dimension. Yet what he aimed to defend by so strongly putting the responsibility for the war on the 'revolutionaries' was not God or divine justice but the very possibility of keeping faith in the God of Israel – in other words, the legitimacy of the Jews' *religio*.

Conclusion

Josephus's account of the Judean revolt in *BJ* reflects his situation in Rome and his exposure to Greco-Roman norms, values and discourses on unrest. To a large extent he embraced a Roman elite perspective on the events, which did not necessarily conflict with that of the Judean rebels themselves, as the theme of liberation and freedom, for example, shows.

Yet Josephus's work cannot be reduced to the story of the uprising of a provincial people against the empire, because it is interwoven with two other narrative strands, with their own respective terminologies and discursive strategies, which describe the events as the result of civil strife (*stasis*) on the one hand and a revolt against the God of Israel on the other. The discourse about *stasis* would have resonated deeply with educated readers or listeners familiar with Thucydides, as well as with a Roman aristocratic audience who had vivid memories of the 68–69 CE civil war in Rome. It must also have resonated with Jewish concerns about Israel's unity and the deleterious consequences of division. Envisioning the war as a revolt against God was, on the other hand, meaningful mainly for a Jewish audience.

These interwoven narratives about the Judean revolt – operating on different levels and with different categories of discourse – reflect Josephus's historiographical and theological perspectives but also some apologetic concerns. His work is not an apology for the Romans or the Flavian dynasty, as scholars have sometimes argued, but rather a defence of the people of Judea (at least the majority), of a great part of the nobility and of Josephus himself (his person and his historical work). Moreover, I have argued that the interpretation of the revolt as a war against God, which goes hand in hand with Josephus's dismissal of the rebels' religious motives and theological vision, also aimed to defend the Jewish *religio* against Roman discourses that mocked Jewish *superstitio* and celebrated the failure of the Jewish God, and to reassert the soundness of the Jewish faith in the God of Israel.

Ultimately, analysis of Josephus's multi-layered discourse on the Judean war shows that even though he was a representative of a people that had been defeated and crushed by Rome, his perspective was not so much that of a subaltern as that of a member of an aristocratic elite which had faced a revolt that aimed to destabilize and appropriate its power. His labelling of the insurgents as bandits, assassins and revolutionaries characterized by madness, cruelty and impiety betrays his privileged position in Judean society on the eve of the revolt. A final remark may illustrate this point: In Tacitus's works, the rebel leaders often speak of their peoples' desire for freedom and liberation from the Roman governors' brutality, whereas in Josephus's *BJ* such arguments are expressed first and foremost in the speech attributed to Agrippa II, who was Rome's ally (*BJ* 2.345–401). In Agrippa's discourse, the validity of these arguments is both acknowledged and undermined. Josephus thus simultaneously echoes and silences the subaltern's voice, a position that is best explained by his social status both before the war, as a member of an aristocratic elite that had much to lose in the conflict with Rome, and after the Judean defeat, as a privileged protégé of the imperial house.[42]

Works cited

Berlin, Andrea and J. Andrew Overman, eds. 2002. *The First Jewish Revolt: Archaeology, History, and Ideology*. New York.

Berthelot, Katell. 2003. *Philanthrôpia judaica: Le débat autour de la "misanthropie" des lois juives dans l'Antiquité*. Leiden.

–. 2008. 'Les liens étroits entre historiographie et récit de soi dans l'œuvre de Flavius Josèphe', in Maryline Crivello and Jean-Noël Pelen, eds., *Individu, récit, histoire*. Aix-en-Provence, 38–51.

Bilde, Per. 1979. 'The causes of the Jewish War according to Josephus'. *Journal for the Study of Judaism* 10: 179–202.

Brighton, Mark Andrew. 2009. *The Sicarii in Josephus's Judean War: Rhetorical Analysis and Historical Observations*. Atlanta.

Farmer, William R. 1956. *Maccabees, Zealots, and Josephus: An Inquiry into Jewish Nationalism in the Greco-Roman Period*. New York.

Feldman, Louis H. 1994. 'Josephus' portrayal of the Hasmoneans compared with 1 Maccabees', in Fausto Parente and Joseph Sievers, eds., *Josephus and the History of the Greco-Roman Period*. Leiden, 41–68.

Giambrone, Anthony, ed. 2021. *Rethinking the Jewish War: Archaeology, Society, Traditions*. Leuven.

Goldenberg, Robert. 1982. 'Early rabbinic explanations of the destruction of Jerusalem'. *Journal of Jewish Studies* 33: 517–25.

Goodman, Martin. 1987. *The Ruling Class of Judaea: The Origins of the Jewish Revolt against Rome A.D. 66–70*. New York.

---

42. This conclusion complements David Kaden's (2011: 481) analysis of 'Josephus' hybrid posture as conquered Judean and Roman citizen'.

–. 1990. 'The origins of the Great Revolt: a conflict of status criteria', in Arieh Kasher, Uriel Rappaport and Gideon Fuks, eds., *Greece and Rome in Eretz-Israel: Collected Essays*. Jerusalem, 39–53.

Grünewald, Thomas. 2004. *Bandits in the Roman Empire: Myth and Reality*. London.

Guha, Ranajit. 1999. *Elementary Aspects of Peasant Insurgency in Colonial India*. Durham, NC.

Hadas-Lebel, Mireille. 1989. *Flavius Josèphe*. Paris.

Hengel, Martin. 1976. *Die Zeloten: Untersuchungen zur jüdischen Freiheitsbewegung in der Zeit von Herodes I. bis 70 n. Chr.* Leiden. First published 1961.

Horsley, Richard. 1979. 'Josephus and the bandits'. *Journal for the Study of Judaism* 10(1): 37–63.

Isaac, Benjamin. 1984. 'Bandits in Judaea and Arabia'. *Harvard Studies in Classical Philology* 88: 171–203.

–. 1992. *The Limits of Empire: The Roman Army in the East*. Oxford.

Kaden, David A. 2011. 'Flavius Josephus and the *gentes devictae* in Roman imperial discourse: hybridity, mimicry, and irony in the Agrippa II speech (*Judean War* 2.345–402)'. *Journal for the Study of Judaism* 42(4–5): 481–507.

Kelley, Nicole. 2004. 'The cosmopolitan expression of Josephus's prophetic perspective in the Jewish War'. *Harvard Theological Review* 97: 257–74.

Klawans, Jonathan. 2010. "Josephus, the rabbis, and responses to catastrophes ancient and modern." *Jewish Quarterly Review* 100(2): 278–309.

–. 2012. *Josephus and the Theologies of Ancient Judaism*. Oxford.

Krieger, Klaus-Stefan. 1999. 'Beobachtungen zu Flavius Josephus' Terminologie für die jüdischen Aufständischen gegen Rom in der Vita und im Bellum Judaicum', in Jürgen U. Kalms, ed., *Internationales Josephus-Kolloquium Brüssel 1998*. Münster, 209–21.

Lanfranchi, Pierluigi. 2000. 'Flavio Giuseppe personaggio della "Guerra Giudaica"'. *Acme* 53(2): 125–62.

Lavan, Myles. 2017. 'Writing revolt in the early Roman empire', in Justine Firnhaber-Baker and Dirk Schoenaers, eds., *The Routledge History Handbook of Medieval Revolt*. London, 19–38.

Lindner, Helgo. 1972. *Geschichtsauffassung des Flavius Josephus im Bellum Judaicum*. Leiden.

Mader, Gottfried. 2000. *Josephus and the Politics of Historiography: Apologetic and Impression Management in the Bellum Judaicum*. Leiden.

Mason, Steve. 2005. 'Of audience and meaning: reading Josephus' *Bellum Judaicum* in the context of a Flavian audience', in Joseph Sievers and Gaia Lembi, eds., *Josephus and Jewish History in Flavian Rome and Beyond*. Leiden, 71–100.

–. 2008. *Josephus, Judean War 2*. Leiden.

–. 2016. *A History of the Jewish War: A.D. 66–74*. New York.

McLaren, James S. 2011. 'Going to war against Rome: the motivation of the Jewish rebels', in Mladen Popović, ed., *The Jewish Revolt against Rome: Interdisciplinary Perspectives*. Leiden, 129–53.

Meshorer, Ya'akov. 2001. *A Treasury of Jewish Coins: From the Persian Period to Bar Kokhba*. Jerusalem.

Nickel, Jesse. 2018. 'Jesus and the *lēstai*: competing kingdom visions'. *Ex Auditu* 34: 42–61.

Nikiprowetzky, Valentin. 1971. 'La mort d'Éleazar fils de Jaïre et les courant apologétiques dans le De Bello Judaico de Flavius Josèphe', in André Caquot and Marc Philonenko, eds., *Hommages à André Dupont-Sommer*. Paris, 461–90.
Popović, Mladen. 2011. *The Jewish Revolt against Rome: Interdisciplinary Perspectives*. Leiden.
Price, Jonathan J. 2005. 'Some aspects of Josephus' theological interpretation of the Jewish War', in Mauro Perani, ed., *"The Words of a Wise Man's Mouth Are Gracious" (Qoh 10,12): Festschrift for Günter Stemberger on the Occasion of his 65th Birthday*. Berlin, 109–19.
–. 2007. 'The failure of rhetoric in Josephus' Bellum Judaicum'. *Ramus* 36.1: 6–24.
–. 2011. 'Josephus' reading of Thucydides: a test case in the *Bellum Iudaicum*', in Georg Rechenauer and Vassiliki Pothou, eds., *Thucydides – a Violent Teacher? History and its Representations*. Göttingen, 79–98.
Rajak, Tessa. 1991. 'Friends, Romans, subjects: Agrippa II's speech in Josephus' Jewish War', in Loveday Alexander, ed., *Images of Empire*. Sheffield, 122–34.
–. 2002a. 'Jewish millenarian expectations', in Andrea Berlin and J. Andrew Overman, eds., *The First Jewish Revolt: Archaeology, History, and Ideology*. London, 164–88.
–. 2002b. *Josephus: The Historian and His Society*. London.
Rhoads, David M. 1976. *Israel in Revolution, 6–74 C.E.: A Political History Based on the Writings of Josephus*. Philadelphia.
Runnalls, Donna. 1997. 'The rhetoric of Josephus', in Stanley E. Porter, ed., *Handbook of Classical Rhetoric in the Hellenistic Period, 330 B.C.-A.D. 400*. Leiden, 737–54.
Schäfer, Peter. 1997. *Judeophobia: Attitudes toward the Jews in the Ancient World*. Cambridge.
Sementchenko, Lada. 2010. 'La notion de stasis chez Thucydide et Flavius Josèphe', in Valérie Fromentin, Sophie Gotteland and Pascal Payen, eds., *Ombres de Thucydide: La réception de l'historien depuis l'Antiquité jusqu'au début du XXe siècle*. Bordeaux, 63–70. Open access at https://books.openedition.org/ausonius/2357.
Shaw, Brent D. 1984. 'Bandits in the Roman empire'. *Past & Present* 105(1): 3–52.
Sievers, Joseph. 2021. 'Religious language in Josephus's *Judean War*', in Anthony Giambrone, ed., *Rethinking the Jewish War: Archaeology, Society, Traditions*. Leuven, 182–96.
Spilsbury, Paul. 2003. 'Flavius Josephus on the rise and fall of the Roman empire'. *Journal of Theological Studies* 54: 1–24.
Sterling, Gregory S. 2000. 'Explaining defeat: Polybius and Josephus on the wars with Rome', in Jürgen Kalms, ed., *Internationales Josephus-Kolloquium, Aarhus 1999*. Münster, 135–51.
Tomasino, Anthony J. 2008. 'Oracles of insurrection: the prophetic catalyst of the Great Revolt'. *Journal of Jewish Studies* 59(1): 86–111.
Vandenberghe, Marijn J. 2016. 'Villains called *sicarii*: a commonplace for rhetorical vituperation in the texts of Flavius Josephus'. *Journal for the Study of Judaism* 47(4–5): 475–507.
Wiater, Nicolas. 2010. 'Reading the Jewish War: narrative technique and historical interpretation in Josephus's Bellum Judaicum'. *Materiali e discussioni per l'analisi dei testi classici* 64: 145–85.

6. Narrating Mutiny: Towards a Discursive History of Military Unrest

Hans Kopp

Abstract: *Although the idea of the legions as a perfectly functioning fighting force has had a long-lasting influence on modern images of the Roman army, scholarship on the Roman military has long recognized the frequency and significance of mutinies and other forms of military unrest. However, as with other forms of revolt, the sources for mutinies in the Roman world rarely allow for the straightforward reconstruction of these events beyond their basic outlines. The motives and intentions of those involved, as well as the details of their organization, were always open to imaginative reconstruction or outright invention on the part of the ancient historiographers. This paper argues that by focusing on the textual record of Roman accounts of mutinies, we can move towards a more comprehensive understanding of both the literary traditions in which narratives of military revolt were embedded and the peculiar cultural presence of mutiny in the Roman world, building on recent moves to study the Roman discourse on revolt in its own right.*

Despite popular and persistent images of the Roman army as a machine-like fighting force, mutiny was a recurring feature within the Roman legions, particularly during the Republican period.[1] As Jon E. Lendon reminds us,

---

1 There is no scholarly consensus on the applicability of the concept of mutiny to the ancient world. Carney 2015 rightly emphasizes the difference between conditions in Greek (classical and Macedonian) and Roman armies. Only for the latter, she argues, can mutiny be reasonably applied because the 'idea of mutiny assumes two things' that were lacking in Greek and Macedonian armies, namely, 'very considerable and consistent emphasis on unquestioning obedience to orders, even in non-combat situations, and a clear distinction between the rights and behavior' of the citizen as political subject and soldier (37). Part of the confusion certainly stems from the term's contested nature. As Dwyer 2017: 15 (see also Rose 1982: 561–65) points out, '[a]lthough it is a punishable offence in any military, there is no consensus over what precisely constitutes a mutiny. It is often an emotive term, which can be used or substituted strategically, both by soldiers and authorities.' The single most distinguishing feature of mutiny as opposed to other forms of disobedience in

'a close look at the record of the Roman army, a litany of mutinies, rebellions, and individual and mass disobedience, can easily raise doubts as to whether the army of the Romans was, by the standards of modern armies, very well disciplined at all'.[2] Given the historical record's general tendency to downplay or even altogether ignore mutiny,[3] we appear to know a surprising amount about Roman mutinies. Yet it is still unclear what kind of history of Roman mutinies we can confidently write given the complicated and frequently limited nature of the available sources. This is a characteristic that mutiny shares with other, possibly all, forms of riotous revolts in the ancient world.[4] Mutinies, like any revolt in history, 'are both narratives and events', and as narrated events, they only live on if someone writes them down and preserves their memory.[5] Accounts of mutinies, as narrative constructs, not only served specific political and historiographical agendas, but were also open to imaginative reconstruction and outright manipulation.[6]

In this paper, I build on the reflections of Myles Lavan and others, arguing that despite the severely limited possibilities for writing reliable social histories of revolt in the Roman world,[7] there is something to be gained by studying accounts of Roman mutinies through the lens of discursive history. Rather than focusing on a single aspect, author, or event, I will outline two

---

the military sphere is its *collective* nature: a single individual may be disobedient or guilty of misconduct, but only the coordinated action of a group of individuals can be mutiny (Dwyer 2017: 16–17). Physical violence was not necessarily part of mutiny in the Roman understanding because every act of insubordination on the part of a crowd against a Roman magistrate's commands was *seditio*, the term most commonly used to label military revolts (see below, pp. 128–29), regardless of whether it involved physical violence (Mommsen 1899: 562–63).

2 Lendon 2005: 170. See also MacMullen 1984: 454, Lee 2020: 100. There were most likely many more mutinies than we are aware of; see Hinard 1990: 151, Wolff 2012: 109.

3 Rose 1982: 562–64, Frykman, Anderson, and van Voss 2013: 3, Dwyer 2017: 16. For Rome, see Hinard 1990: 151, Pagán 2005: 415.

4 Kelly 2007: 151–56, Lavan 2017. On the specific character of the sources for military unrest, see Kaegi 1981: 4–5.

5 Quotation from Brummett 1998: 94. What Turner and Clark 2017: 5 argue for accounts of military defeats also applies to mutinies: we know about them 'not (or not only) because of some Roman desire to keep track of the past, but because someone, for some reason, wanted them remembered'.

6 See Goodyear 1972: 196–97, Fulkerson 2006: 172, 2013: 165–66 (both on Tacitus). Schauer (2016: 170–71) emphasizes that, while ancient authors were unable to change the basic facts of military events, such as mutinies, due to their public nature, they were able to use their literary techniques to work out and strengthen certain aspects while weakening or completely ignoring others (such as moods, circumstances, motives of those involved, inner logic of events, etc.).

7 Kelly 2007, Woolf 2011, Lavan 2017; see also the introduction to this volume.

distinct ways in which accounts of mutinies can be productively analysed using a textual record of military unrest: first, by analysing the terminology used in Livy's account of a mutiny among the Roman legions encamped in southern Italy in 342 BCE, I will discuss how close lexical analysis can shed a light on the conceptual diversity (and fluidity) of the Roman notion of mutiny; second, I will focus on specific tropes and broader narrative patterns as parts of Roman narratives of military unrest, paying particular attention to, on the one hand, the idea of an independently acting soldiery and, on the other, to the trope of 'murmuring' and the 'soundscapes of mutiny' depicted in Roman accounts of military unrest.

Terminology: Livy's account of the mutiny of 342 BCE

Analysing the lexemes used to describe and explain such revolts is one obvious starting point for studying Roman mutiny narratives and their discursive contexts.[8] Although *seditio* is the term most commonly used to describe what we would call a mutiny, Roman authors had a plethora of terms that could be used to describe military unrest, each with its own set of connotations.[9] Livy's account (7.38–42) of the mutiny of the Roman forces at Capua in 342 BCE is a particularly good illustration, for it is distinguished by a considerable lexical variety of terms denoting 'revolt'. Livy – whose sources, while disagreeing on most details of the story, only agreed that some kind of 'revolt' (*seditio*) had occurred (7.42.7) – appears to have gone to great lengths, not only in his narrative, but also in his terminology, to determine exactly what kind of unrest had occurred in 342 BCE. According to Livy's 'mainstream' version of the story,[10] following the victory over the Samnites, the Roman soldiers stationed at Capua mutinied, enticed by the amenities of the fertile Campanian countryside. Instead of returning to Rome, where they were forced to cultivate infertile soil and suffered economic hardships such as usury, they desired to own their own good land, just as the Campanians did. After their plans were revealed, the soldiers marched on Rome, and it was only through

---

8 On the significance of the labels attached to revolts, see Firnhaber-Baker 2017: 8.
9 On the Latin vocabulary for military disobedience, see Brice 2015b: 105 n. 6.
10 For other accounts of the 342 BCE mutiny, see Dion. Hal. *Ant. Rom.* 15.3.1–15 (on the first half of the mutiny), App. *Sam.* 1.1–2, Frontin. *Str.* 1.9.1, Zonar. 7.25.9; see also [Aur. Vict.] *De vir. Ill.* 29.3.

the intervention of the dictator M. Valerius Corvus, who confronted the mutineers outside the city gates, that outright civil war was avoided and legal reforms enacted, which temporarily settled the dispute. Scholars have questioned the historicity of the entire event,[11] but for the purposes of this chapter, I will set aside this question, as well as the related problem of the historiographical traditions on which Livy's report was ultimately based.[12] Instead, I will focus on Livy's terminology in describing the mutiny because his account can serve as an example of how Roman authors used various terms from the lexical field of 'unrest' to describe and conceptualize mutiny in various ways.

Mutiny as seditio

Given the prevalence of *seditio* as the Latin term for what we would call a mutiny, it is not surprising that Livy refers to the events of 342 BCE as a *seditio* (7.38.10, 7.39.4, 7.42.7). If Livy's remark that the only thing earlier authors agreed on was that there had been some form of *seditio* (7.42.7) can be understood in this way, this was possibly also how his sources referred to the event. It may be significant that Livy never qualifies this particular *seditio* as specifically military (*seditio militum* or *militaris*), as he and later authors do in case of other mutinies.[13] This corresponds to how Roman authors understood the relationship between military and civil *seditio* at the time. Cicero (*Rep.* 6.1) defines *seditio* as the state of affairs when citizens in discord quite literally drift away from each other (*eaque dissensio civium, quod seorsum eunt alii ad alios, seditio dicitur*). *Seditio* was also a broad term that encompassed both civilian and military forms of unrest. Valerius Maximus, writing during Tiberius' reign and thus shortly after Livy, recognizes two types of *seditio*, one of civilian, one of military character (*seditionis tam togatae quam etiam armatae*, 9.7.1). Some *seditiones* occur *in foro*, others *in castris* (9.7 *mil. Rom.* 1), but both can be categorized as unrest from within the *populus Romanus*. Referring to the mutiny of 342 BCE as a *seditio* thus fits well with the overall logic and purpose of Livy's story, as the main narrative purpose of the extended account of this mutiny

---

11 See Oakley 1998: 363–64.
12 On the historiographical tradition of the mutiny, see Poma 1990 (with the comments by W. Kierdorf, pp. 205–6); Scardigli 1996.
13 E.g. Livy 22.33.7, 28.38.14, Tac. *Hist.* 4.46 (*seditio militaris*), Livy 29.19.4, 32.3.2, Curt. 10.4.3 (*seditio militum*).

is to explain the origins of the important legislative reforms that were carried out in Rome as an immediate result of the soldiers' revolt. Livy also refers to the first and second plebeian secessions as *seditiones* (2.32.1, 3.50.1), and by referring to the mutiny of 342 as *seditio*, he connects this instance of military unrest to the tradition of plebeian struggle for economic relief and political participation. This particular civilian-political framing of the soldiers' revolt recurs even more pronouncedly in connection with another term, *secessio*.

Mutiny as *secessio*

Livy refers to the events of 342 BCE as a *secessio* four times, three times explicitly (7.40.2, 7.41.2, 7.41.3), and once in a historical comparison (7.40.11). Referring to a revolt by Roman soldiers as *secessio* inevitably connects the event to other instances of plebeian *secessiones* in the early days of the Republic, and thus to the broader theme of the so-called Struggle of the Orders. This is not only implied by Livy's terminology, but also stated explicitly in the narrative. Whereas Livy, in an authorial comment, looks forward to his own present and compares the 342 BCE mutiny to the civil wars he had witnessed (7.40.1), Valerius Corvus, in his speech to the mutineers, directs the reader back in time. Corvus compares the mutiny to two previous plebeian revolts, the *secessio* to the Sacred Mountain in 494 and to the Aventine in 449 BCE (7.40.11). Usury, cancellation of debts, and the Struggle of the Orders are among the dominant themes of Livy's Book 7, and they also serve as the backdrop to the mutiny of 342 BCE.[14] Calling this mutiny a *seditio* and a *secessio* relates the soldiers' revolt to earlier outbursts of plebeian discontent and thus into larger patterns of early Roman societal development. Thus, the mutiny at Capua, framed as a *secessio* of the *plebs*, appears in Livy's account as the culmination of the fundamental political conflict that shapes his historical narrative in the early books.[15] This may also explain why Livy views this mutiny with a degree of sympathy: it was unrest and may have involved serious threats to the authority of Roman magistrates, but it was not wholly condemnable and,

---

14 Oakley 1993: 20, 1998: 365, Humm 2015: 355–56.
15 Cf. Raaflaub 2005:190, Hölkeskamp 2011:108. Based on Livy's note that after the end of the revolt, the *populus* enacted a law *ne cui militum fraudi secessio esset* (7.41.3; cf. 3.54.5, 3.54.14, App. *Sam.* 1), Daube (1972: 147) argues that *secessio* reflects the original terminology of the law passed in 342 BCE. On the authenticity of Livy's note, see Oakley 1998: ad loc., Hölkeskamp 2011: 102.

to some extent, it was justifiable, as it could be understood as being part of the long tradition of *iustae seditiones*, 'justified' or 'righteous revolts', in Roman history.[16]

Mutiny as *defectio*

The labels *seditio* and *secessio* are hardly surprising for the 342 BCE mutiny. However, near the end of his account, Livy refers to the mutiny as a *defectio* (7.42.2). This is a striking and hardly self-explanatory choice, as the term was only very rarely used to describe unrest among Roman citizens (Hoben 1978: 23). At least in Republican Latin, '*defectio* and *seditio* were mutually exclusive: *seditio* was the act of citizens; *defectio* that of allies and subjects' (Lavan 2017: 23). Only during the imperial period could the term be used to describe the actions of Roman soldiers who defected or otherwise assisted Rome's foreign enemies.[17] Livy himself is keen to maintain the 'Republican' distinction between the two types of revolt elsewhere in his narrative. In the context of his report about the mutiny in Scipio's army at Sucro in 206 BCE, he explicitly distinguishes between *seditio* in the Roman camp and *defectio* of Roman allies, even explicitly contrasting both concepts (*seditionem civilem ... defectionem sociorum*, 28.31.4; cf. 28.24.4 for the mutiny as *civilis furor*). Up to that point, there does not appear to be any confusion regarding how to classify the events in the camp at Sucro. However, Livy had already referred to the mutiny as a *seditio* and a *defectio* at the beginning of his account (*seditionis defectionisque*, 28.24.10), without providing any explanation for this choice of terms. Later, when he relates the Roman deliberations on how to punish the mutineers, it is argued that the mutiny, which is otherwise referred to as *seditio* throughout, was a *defectio* rather than a simple soldiers' revolt (*defectio magis quam seditio*, 28.26.2). Only in Scipio's subsequent speech does the reader learn why this mutiny could have been a *defectio*. In what appears to be an addition by our sources, inspired primarily by Polybius' account,[18] Scipio accuses the mutineers of conspiring with Rome's former Spanish al-

---

16 On the notion of *iustae seditiones* in late Republican Rome, see Cic. *De or.* 2.199, Osthoff 1952: 105–9.
17 Lavan 2017: 23. On *defectio*, see generally Hoben 1978: 21–25.
18 In Polybius' account, Scipio accuses the mutineers of *apostasis* (11.28.11) and of having 'defected' from their fatherland (ἀποστάτας γενομένους τῆς πατρίδος, 11.28.6), *apostasis* being the Greek equivalent to Latin *defectio* (Hoben 1978: 23–24).

lies who had defected in order to exacerbate the soldiers' guilt (28.27.13; cf. 28.19.2, 28.25.11–12).[19] Overall, then, the traditional distinction between the two types of revolt is apparent in Livy's account, even though we can also detect traces of a usage that tends to conflate the two, if desired, for narrative purposes.

It is thus all the more striking that Livy refers to the military *seditio* of 342 BCE as a *defectio* at 7.42.2, employing a term that undermines his otherwise cautiously sympathetic treatment of the mutiny. Whereas *seditio* and especially *secessio* conceptually linked the mutiny to memories of (at least partially) justified resistance of the Roman *plebs*, *defectio* had no such connotations and was a purely condemnatory term. Apart from the not entirely implausible possibility of different historiographical traditions,[20] one reason for Livy's surprising choice could be that any military *seditio* was much 'closer' (also in a literal sense) to *defectiones* than were civilian *seditiones*. Mutinies were, by definition, both internal and external. Even if a mutiny occurred far from Rome, it was still internal because Roman citizens were involved; in Livy's words, a mutiny is a *seditio civilis in castris* (28.31.4), and historiography frequently explains the outbreak of revolt in the army by referring to civilian influences (e.g. Tac. *Ann.* 1.31.4, Cass. Dio fr. 100 and 57.5.4). At the same time, mutinies occurred on the outskirts of the expanding Roman empire, in close contact with (and sometimes under the influence of) foreign people and Rome's external enemies. As Scipio's accusations against the mutinous soldiers in his army in 206 BCE demonstrate, rebel soldiers were easily accused of conspiring with Rome's enemies, whether this was true or not, and thus of transforming *seditio* into something even worse: *defectio*. The mutineers of 342 BCE not only revolted but, according to Livy, initially even lost their *memoria patriae* while attempting to settle the fertile lands around Capua themselves (7.38.5–7). The proximity of foreign luxuries had enticed them into revolt, transforming their internal dissatisfaction with Rome's political and economic conditions into a desire to defect from Rome and establish themselves as a separate community.[21] Given the conciliatory ending of Livy's ac-

---

19 Chrissanthos 1997: 181. It must be noted that both Roman citizens and *socii* were involved in the mutiny (28.24.13, 28.32.6), which may have contributed to Livy's terminological ambiguity.
20 Daube 1972: 147 argues that *secessio* reflects a contemporary 'conciliatory' perspective on the political revolt (shared to some extent by Livy), whereas *defectio* stems from a later, more hostile attitude towards the mutiny.
21 This theme is even more prominent in Dionysius' account, as the mutineers there consider ravaging Roman territory and supporting Rome's enemies from the start (*Ant. Rom.* 15.3.9). Dionysius

count, it remains difficult to explain why *defectio*, rather than the more placatory *seditio* or *secessio*, appears at the very end of it, in conjunction with an enumeration of the important political and legal reforms that were the long-term result of the mutiny.

Mutiny as *coniuratio*

Livy refers to the mutiny of 342 BCE as a 'conspiracy' (*coniuratio*) or to the participants as 'conspirators' (*coniurati*) at several points (7.38.8, 7.39.6, 7.41.5, 7.41.8, 7.42.3, 7.42.4). When compared to the other terms used in his narrative, *coniuratio* is by far the most evocative and emotive, suggesting, to a late-first century BCE audience in particular, images of secret gatherings at night, shady characters involved in dubious and morally outrageous activities, and the ultimate threat directed against the *res publica*. The Bacchanalian affair of 186 BCE and the Catilinarian conspiracy of 63 BCE leap to mind for the modern, and presumably also for the contemporary, reader of Livy's narrative. However, it is critical not to over-emphasise this negative image of *coniuratio*. The term's etymology simply referred to the act of taking a collective (rather than individual) oath in order to pursue a common goal.[22] In a military context, it was particularly used to denote the oath of allegiance sworn by soldiers during times of crisis, as Livy writes of the previously voluntary, now mandatory oath sworn by all recruits (he uses *coniurare*) before the battle of Cannae in 216 BCE (22.38.4). When we read about soldiers who 'conspire' to mutiny and separate themselves from the main body of the troops in ancient texts, the double nature of *coniuratio* becomes especially evident, as both semantic layers of the term are simultaneously present. On the one hand, the mutinying soldiers followed a well-established model of achieving battlefield cohesion and ensuring loyalty among themselves (Rawlings 2007: 51). On the other hand, they also 'conspired' against the *res publica* and its authorities, transforming their capacity for cohesion into a threat to public order. Although, as Habinek emphasizes, the term *coniuratio* is in essence 'ethically neutral, with the potential of being applied to

---

accordingly terms the revolt not only a 'conspiracy' (15.3.10, 15.3.12, 15.3.13), but also an *apostasis* (15.3.14).

22 On the range of meanings of *coniuratio*, see Hoben 1978: 6–17, Habinek 1998: 76–78, Pagán 2005: 10–14.

good or bad swearings together' (1998: 77), in Livy, with very few exceptions, *coniuratio* tends to denote 'plots hatched to subvert the legitimate or established authority' (Nousek 2010: 161 n. 17). This interpretation of the term is undoubtedly present in his account of the 342 BCE mutiny. By referring to it as a *coniuratio*, Livy emphasizes the gravity of the situation and the threats posed by the soldiers against the *res publica*. In Roman reports on political and military betrayals, the next step after a *coniuratio* is often *defectio* (Hoben 1978: 21). Livy's repeated emphasis on the soldiers' 'conspiracy' thus terminologically prepares him to refer to the mutiny as a *defectio* towards the end of his account.

To sum up this section, Livy's account, far from confronting us with a clear-cut definition of what a mutiny exactly is, thus highlights the inherent conceptual fluidity and ambiguity of soldierly revolt and the Roman notion of *seditio*. This should perhaps be attributed less to a striking 'perplexity' of the historian and his 'lexical uncertainty' in handling the events ('la perplessità di Livio ... incertezza lessicale', Poma 1990: 156) than to a deliberate attempt on his side to highlight the various possible ways of understanding and presenting a mutiny within a Roman cultural and historical context. A mutiny was in a way everything at once: a dangerous conspiracy, civil unrest, social upheaval, a condemnable insurrection threatening the very foundations of Roman order, and at the same time a form of 'justified revolt' rooted in a genuinely Roman tradition of seeing rebellion as the trigger of societal and legal evolution. As such, it was a serious challenge for an elite perspective wishing to come to terms with the phenomenon of soldierly revolt, be it far-back in time or of more recent character. This perplexing complexity of the Roman idea and cultural presence of mutiny is mirrored in lexical usage, as Livy's account of the 342 BCE mutiny amply demonstrates.

Narrative models

The example of Livy's account of the 342 BCE mutiny demonstrates how Roman authors could conceptualize mutiny in various ways and link the events described with broader discourses through lexical variation and specification. Yet lexemes 'are only the smallest building blocks of the Latin discourse on revolt. There is a higher order of patterning at the level of whole narratives' (Lavan 2017: 24). Historiographical accounts of mutiny contain a variety of patterns of explanation and conceptualization as well as narrative tropes that help to bring out specific features within their presentation of military unrest. These different narrative devices cut across the straightforward presentation of events in our (primarily historiographical) sources, which is reinforced by the fact that much of ancient writing about revolts was a highly intertextual affair, with different models of explanation handed down from one generation of historians to the next.[23] In what follows, I will sketch the outline of two particular models that are prominent in historiographical discourse: the model of mutiny as the action of an independent soldiery and the narrative trope of mutiny as a sonic phenomenon.

The independent soldiery

Simon Hornblower has developed the concept of an independent soldiery with regard to Greek armies, noting 'their tendency to slide back into political habits at short notice', by acting as voting bodies and by exerting 'democratic' pressure from below on their commanders (2007: 32 and 37, 2011). Hornblower considers such behaviour to be markedly 'un-Roman' (2007: 32). It is thus all the more striking that such collective behaviour is a common feature of Roman mutiny narratives. Mutinying soldiers were capable of 'united and purposeful action to achieve their ends', they 'elected their own officers', and they had a council and commissars, thereby establishing 'rudimentary political organization'; this, admittedly, is not an ancient historian's characterization of military unrest, but Geoffrey Parker's description of the regular course of mutinies in the Spanish army of Flanders in the 16th century (1973: 40).[24] However, Roman authors also depict mutinying soldiers deliberating, voting, and imitating regular procedure and rituals, in short: establishing themselves as an independent, self-organizing community, if only for a short time. This not only reflects certain historical features of the Roman army, as scholarship has long pointed out,[25] but is also part of a broader discourse on what has recently been termed 'plebeian agency' (Logghe 2017).

---

23 See Lavan 2017: 32 on intertextuality in revolt narratives.
24 On this topic, see also Sherer 2017: 121–24 ('the soldiers demonstrated a surprising ability to organize themselves', 121).
25 MacMullen 1984: 455, Rowe 2002: 155–57, Taylor 2018: 150–51; on the imperial period, see also Faure 2007.

Despite the *plebs*' limited ability to exert political influence on a formal level, the Roman elites were concerned about their informal potential to do so (Knopf 2019). These concerns were expressed, *inter alia*, in historiographical narratives of soldiers in mutinies acting independently and, according to the participants' assumed logic, rationally. Mutinies occurred, according to this model's (mostly implicit) explanatory reasoning, not only because of significant immediate grievances, but also because Roman soldiers were accustomed to being part of a 'political culture that was participatory rather than passive' (Rowe 2002: 155–56), and thus could easily switch into self-organizing modes.

Assemblies and other forms of participatory behaviour are common in Livy, both during mutinies and in other, related circumstances.[26] The rebel soldiers of 342 BCE, having gathered in great number on the outskirts of Rome almost like a regular army, exchange *sententiae* on how to proceed (7.39.9); Livy also describes their reasoning as *deliberatio* (7.39.11; cf. 7.38.5: *consilia*), implying a certain logic and structure to their debate. Even the mutineers of 206 BCE, who are initially depicted as an undisciplined gang acting solely from *libido* and *licentia* (28.24.9), are shown to have some regard for order. Livy emphasizes how they attempted to maintain the appearance of regular command structures (Taylor 2018: 151). They chose two common soldiers as their commanding officers, for which Livy uses the striking *delatum omnium consensu imperium est* (28.24.13), a phrase hardly expected in the context of mutinies but rather evocative of earlier periods of Roman political harmony (3.34.5) or concerns (for Livy, contemporary ones) about unity and *concordia* (Instinsky 1940, Lobur 2008: ch. 1). This phrase connects the mutineers' actions to other instances of soldiers taking matters into their hands, particularly elections of officers.[27]

In each case, extreme circumstances – whether the loss of regular leadership following a defeat or the overturning of regular command structures during mutinies – necessitate the same response: independent action on the part of the soldiery that imitated regular procedures. This is even more

---

26 This theme was not invented by Livy; it was already present in Caesar. Commenting upon the mutiny (*secessio*) of the soldiers at besieged Corfinium in 49 BCE (*BCiv*. 1.20), see Grillo 2020: 130: 'the mutinous soldiers maintain a well-organized and well-defined structure to communicate with various parties within the town. The first effect of their *secessio* is that they find intermediaries and confer successfully and in an orderly manner. They function like separate states within the walls ...'.
27 Livy 22.14.15 (with 14.1), 22.53.3, 25.37.5–6.

prominent in Appian's version of the 206 BCE mutiny (*Hisp.* 7.34). The mutineers, he reports, 'defected' (ἀφίσταντο) from Marcius (Scipio's otherwise unknown temporary replacement) and 'set up camp by themselves' (ἐφ' ἑαυτῶν ἐστρατοπέδευον);[28] they then 'appointed generals and company commanders from their own number' (ἀπὸ σφῶν ἑλόμενοι), 'put everything else in order on their own authority, before arraying themselves on parade and exchanging oaths with each other' (ἐφ' ἑαυτῶν ἐτάσσοντο καὶ συνώμνυον ἀλλήλοις, trans. McGing). Despite Appian's apparent hostility towards the mutineers (Leidl 1996: 268), it has been argued that his version of the mutiny reflects the 'unbroken and rich tradition of self-government peculiar to the Roman army' (MacMullen 1984: 455). This is undoubtedly true, but Appian's account also comes at the end of a long historiographical tradition.[29] The independent soldiery model was most likely not part of the 'original' Polybian version of the mutiny and was imposed later, probably by Livy, who was heavily influenced by his own experiences as an eyewitness to the dangerously independent soldiery of the civil war period and projected this experience into earlier material.[30]

Appian's use of the model suggests that it remained relevant even in the imperial period. Following the reorganization of Roman politics after the civil wars of the late Republic and the establishment of a monarchical system, elite fears of an independently acting populace evidently lost some of their force. One might think that imperial historiography, written when the professional volunteer army had replaced the Republican militia and mutinies

---

28 The mutineers' separation from the main camp is reported only by Appian. Leidl 1996: 273 suspects that the mutineers' takeover of the camp, reported in detail by Livy (28.24.10–14) and implied in Polybius (11.29.6), was further elaborated by Appian in a story of actual physical secession; cf. also Richardson 2000: ad loc. Appian may have been inspired by actual events closer to his own times. In a letter to Cato from Cilicia (late 51/early 50 BCE), Cicero reports that five cohorts were in 'a kind of mutiny' and had encamped 'without a legate, a military tribune, in fact even without a single centurion' apart from the main body of the army (*seditione quadam exercitus esset dissipatus, quinque cohortes sine legato, sine tribuno militum, denique edam sine centurione ullo apud Philomelium consedissent, Fam.* 15.4.2).

29 On the differences between the three main accounts of the mutiny (Polybius, Livy, and Appian), especially regarding the presentation of the soldiers and their motives, see Fulkerson 2013: 170–74.

30 Chrissanthos 1997: 174. Polybius' general disinterest in the soldiers and their complaints in his account (Chrissanthos 1997: 173) makes it seem unlikely that he would have spent much time depicting their actions and modes of behaviour. Cf., however, Taylor 2015: 151 n. 17, who suspects that 'the basic vision of mutineers self-organizing' had already been part of the now lost parts of Polybius' account.

were far less frequent than during the Republic (Lee 2020: 101–2), would have had no place for an independent soldiery. It is thus all the more remarkable that, as several scholars have noted, traces of this pattern of narrating and explaining military unrest can be found even in imperial historiography, most notably in Tacitus' accounts of the Pannonian (1.16–30) and German (1.31–49) mutinies of 14 CE in the *Annals* (Rowe 2002: 162–63, 172, Bhatt 2016: 167). What I am interested in here is not the historical reality of these mutinies, nor the (disputed) question of whether it can be reconstructed at all on the basis of Tacitus' vivid and highly imaginative account (Goodyear 1972: 196–97, Fulkerson 2006: 172), but rather whether Tacitus' narrative of these mutinies contains traces of the narrative pattern of explanation as outlined above.

The concept of the independent soldiery, it should be noted, is far from being the dominant theme of Tacitus' accounts of the 14 CE mutinies. As one commentator observed, Tacitus 'emphasizes disorder, rebellion, and violence and contrasts this with discipline, rational effort, and calmness' (Williams 1997: 57). However, there are times when, beneath this superstructure, a secondary narrative pattern emerges, one that resembles the model outlined above. Just as in the other narratives analysed thus far, the mutinous soldiers are depicted as inverting regular modes of participation and communication in the legions. The institution of the military assembly, the *contio*, is especially important in this context, as Tacitus emphasizes from the start. Percennius, the instigator of the Pannonian mutiny, spoke to the other *ministri seditionis* in an assembly of the soldiers that resembled a *contio* (*velut contionabundus*, 1.17.1) after inciting the soldiers' rage and 'assembled' (*congregare*, 1.16.3) the 'worst' of them.[31] Although under normal circumstances, the military *contio*, like its civilian counterpart, could only be summoned by the commander-in-chief, the event was not entirely one-sided. Rather, while it was primarily a listening assembly, it also provided a forum for the communication of grievances and negotiation within the forces.[32]

The mutineers appropriate this institution and create a 'topsy-turvy world' (Breebaart 1987: 64) under the leadership of the 'pseudo-politician' Percennius (Fulkerson 2013: 170), calling an assembly to air their grievances

---

31 On *contionabundus*, see Goodyear 1972: ad loc., Rosenblitt 2019: 137.
32 On the military *contio* as an instrument of communication between soldiers and commanders, see Chrissanthos 2004: 359–62.

and to draft their demands. In another imitation of regular procedures, the soldiers construct a common assembly space and erect a raised platform, a *tribunal*, from which the commanders would normally speak in a regular *contio* (1.18.2 with Pina Polo 1995: 213). Tacitus' use of the term *velut* emphasizes that the mutineers' assembly was a mirage, a travesty of order. However, as in Livy's or Appian's accounts of mutinies, the collective action and spirit of self-organization that were also part of the mutiny are revealed.[33] This becomes even clearer when we compare Tacitus' account to a source almost contemporary to the events. In Velleius Paterculus' account of the mutiny (2.125.1–3), the soldiers are depicted as having no organizational or rational capacity and are driven solely by frenzy and their desire for anarchy. In contrast, Tacitus not only gives ample space to articulating the soldiers' grievances, which is noteworthy in and of itself (Breebaart 1987: 64–65, Fulkerson 2013: 165), but also sketches their actions as a kind of ordered chaos. Given that the majority of the colourful details in Tacitus' account are most likely his own invention and not based on an earlier source (Goodyear 1972: 196–97), this distinction is striking and emphasizes the importance of this theme for how he wanted the mutiny to be understood.[34]

These themes are elaborated upon in the subsequent narrative of the German mutiny. Tacitus writes that the soldiers attacked their centurions in a 'sudden frenzy' (*repente lymphati*), killing some and throwing their corpses into the river (1.32.1). He then confronts the reader with the paradoxical fact that the mutiny's violence leads directly to 'the creation of its own society' (Bloomer 1997: 179) in what is undoubtedly 'one of the most salient passages from Tacitus' work with reference to military psychology' (Breebaart 1987: 67). Tacitus suggests that amidst all the frenzy and bloodshed, there was still some kind of order – or at least the outward semblance of order and rationality:

No tribune, no camp prefect wielded authority any further: watches, pickets, and anything else which their immediate need indicated, were assigned by the men themselves (*ipsi partiebantur*). To anyone making a deeper diagnosis of the soldiers' spirits (*militares animos altius coniectantibus*), a principal symptom of the extent and irremediability of their distur-

---

33 Cf. O'Gorman 2000: 39: 'The construction of a tribunal mirrors the collection of the three standards, but also, as an organised project, manifests the unity of the mutineers, countering descriptions of them as a disorderly mass.'
34 As Rowe (2002: 162) notes, comparing both accounts from 'a disinterested perspective, the same mutinies appear remarkable for their orderliness. Soldiers deliberated in assemblies, made moderate demands, and demonstrated a keen grasp of the political system to which they belonged.'

bance (*praecipuum indicium magni atque inplacabilis motus*) was the fact that they were neither scattered in disarray nor under the influence of a minority but flared up together and fell silent together – with such uniformity and consistency that you would have believed them to be directed (*tanta aequalitate et constantia, ut regi crederes*). (Tac. *Ann.* 1.32.3, trans. Woodman)

The passage is similar to other accounts of the collective action of mutinous soldiers, such as Livy's (or later Appian's) version of the 206 BCE mutiny.[35] As O'Gorman notes, the issue of unity and resolve is especially prominent at the beginning of Tacitus' account of the German mutiny (2000: 34–35). Tacitus emphasizes that the soldiers in Lower Germany did not require someone like Percennius to rouse them and make them aware of their grievances; rather, they voiced their demands *collectively* from the start (*multa seditionis ora vocesque*, 1.31.5). The result of their organized behaviour is that the mutiny, rather than looking like disorderly chaos, has the outward appearance of control and rationality. Tacitus contrasts an ordinary reader's (superficial) assumption about the mutiny's characteristics with an expert's deeper understanding (*altius coniectantibus*), drawing his readers' attention to the event's inherent paradox: the outwards signs that might lead one to believe that the mutiny was an act of order and structure, he argues, were in fact the *indicia* for the utterly disturbed state of the troops (*motus*). Moving away from well-worn tropes about the soldiers' depravity or inability to act in unison,[36] Tacitus summarizes and condenses the ambiguity that had already been present in earlier mutiny narratives but had not been made explicit: chaotic frenzy and coordinated action were not mutually exclusive ways of understanding mutiny, but only two ways of looking at it. The account reveals the unique character of mutiny as a collective insurgency against authority that, in order to succeed, must rely on the same modes of collective organization that regular authority relies on.

Tacitus' direct address to his readers, who were most likely members of the Roman elite of senatorial and, to a lesser extent, equestrian rank,[37]

---

35 Cf. also Livy's description of the mutiny of 342 BCE, where the soldiers, rather than being instructed by a *dux*, decide to march into Rome (*suo magis inde impetu quam consilio duci*, 7.39.16); or his account of the first plebeian secession, where the soldiers *sine ullo duce* decide to encamp on the Sacred Mountain (2.32.4). On lack of leadership as a characteristic of plebeian revolt in Livy's first pentad, see Vasaly 2015: 102–3.
36 Breebaart 1987: 67. For an overview of literary *topoi* about mutinies, see Fulkerson 2013: 162–65. On Tacitus' views on crowd behaviour, soldierly and civilian, see Kajanto 1970, Breebaart 1987.
37 On the (presumed) audience of Tacitean historiography, see Marincola 2009: 12–13.

is perhaps the most remarkable aspect of this passage. He at least hints at the predispositions and expectations of a contemporary audience on the causes and course of military revolts by alluding to their attitude towards the mutiny. When Roman authors wrote about the minute details of mutinies, events that had often occurred far away or long ago, they had to fill the (mostly inevitable) gaps in their knowledge in order to produce vivid, coherent, and professionally acceptable literary narratives.[38] They drew on shared ideas about collective behaviour to fill these gaps; but because they were literary men, their presuppositions about unrest and its motives were also shaped to a large extent by literary models and traditions (Woolf 2011: 34–35). Tacitus is apparently alluding to widespread beliefs that, due to crowds' innate inability to act in coordination, any uprising from below is necessarily chaotic and uncoordinated, unless some leader lends them his voice, a credo that can also be found in Tacitus' own works (Kajanto 1970: 707). If 'elements of structure, of order, appear in such a movement, without being brought about by identifiable individuals, this is at least a θαυμάσιον' (Breebaart 1987: 67), or so Tacitus' audience would have been inclined to speculate.

One may wonder whom Tacitus was addressing with *crederes* and which particular audience he may have had in mind with this astute analysis of the military psyche. As Greg Woolf has remarked, 'Tacitus' own reconstructions of revolts and their causes can be taken to reflect the *kind* of explanation formed by members of the imperial ruling classes when they considered individual revolts.'[39] Tacitus' striking remark about the paradoxical outward appearance of mutiny could be interpreted as addressing a readership comprised of those in administrative control of the empire who had only a cursory interest in *animi militares*, as opposed to the scholarly-minded (like Tacitus), who, in Thucydidean fashion (1.22.4), try to 'look through the surface of things' for a better understanding. If, as Woolf further argues, 'discussions of revolts by historians like Sallust, Tacitus, Arrian and Dio must have re-

---

38 On the temporal and geographical distances between writing about revolts and the events themselves, see Lavan 2017: 35. On Roman and modern historians' sometimes contradictory task of providing plausible, convincing accounts of events about which they can know very little, see Pagán 2004: 3–4.
39 Woolf 2011: 35. See also Kelly 2007: 155–56. As Fulkerson 2013: 166 notes, given the way our sources operate with literary manipulation and allusions, 'we should not necessarily expect to discover how individual mutinies occurred or were quelled in the Roman army, only how historians (and their audiences) expected these events to occur'.

flected and shaped their own service in the provinces, and the experience of their peers and readers',[40] one could reasonably conclude that Tacitus' remark about different interpretations of the mutinies of 14 CE was likewise a cautionary tale about soldiers' psychology aimed at those who were likely to face soldierly disobedience in one form or another during their own tenure in the provinces.[41]

'Soundscapes of mutiny'

A second noteworthy narrative feature of Roman accounts of mutiny is what I would like to call the sonic quality of soldierly revolt, or – to borrow an expression coined primarily for the naval mutinies of the early modern period – the 'soundscapes of mutiny'.[42] The various components of these 'soundscapes', from hardly audible murmurs to articulate complaints, accompany the early stages of military revolt in particular, a specific phase within the development of rebellion that has been termed 'expression of grievances' in order to distinguish it from outright, often violent revolt, the last stage within such a chains of events.[43] Scholarship on mutinies in the modern era has stressed that the sonic backdrop of 'murmuring' was an ever-present 'technique of dissent and warning of mutiny' that, if mentioned in official accounts, 'always evoked the spectre of dissent and mutiny'.[44] 'Murmuring' in particular helped to communicate grievances and hostilities to officers and was thus a potential way to signal, and perhaps

---

40 Woolf 2011: 43. Cassius Dio's notable interest in mutinies and military unrest was likely considerably influenced by the events of his own times as well, perhaps even by personal experience; see de Blois 1997: 2663, 2666. Mutinies and military discipline in general are also an important theme in Appian; see Leidl 1996: 264–65.
41 On Tacitus' interest in the psychology of mutiny, see Kajanto 1970: 705, Breebaart 1987: 63. On Roman authors' interest in the relationship between mutiny, military leadership, and crowd psychology, see Hardie 2010. Fulkerson 2013: 185 understands the evolution of Roman mutiny narratives as part of 'a broader shift in the empire towards interest in the soldiery in its own right, and as a locus of power'.
42 The phrase 'soundscapes of mutiny' is borrowed from Buchan 2017.
43 On 'expression of grievances' as a regular phenomenon of military unrest in antiquity, see Brice 2015a: 72–73.
44 Maddison 2014: 131. See also Frykman, Anderson, and van Ross 2013: 11 on 'a broad definition of mutiny that includes all forms of collective resistance ..., from muttering and murmuring all the way to bloody massacre'.

ultimately avoid, mutiny.[45] These 'soundscapes', however, were as much a feature of the written discourse about revolt in its own right as they were an element of the actual genesis of rebellion. References to 'murmurs' and related forms of inarticulate complaints served a specific purpose in the eyes of those writing about dissent and revolt: 'the murmuring trope allowed elite writers to acknowledge the fact of dissent without actually engaging with its content by representing underclass speech as excessively embodied and thus apolitical' (Mazzaferro 2018: 7). Informing readers about mutinous soldiers' discontented 'grumbling' and 'shouting' occupies a middle ground between simply ignoring their grievances and concerns and fully engaging with the content (and thus potentially the justification) of the causes of *seditio*. The extent to which authors gave mutineers a voice was one of the literary tools they used to significantly influence the evaluation and perception of incidents and thus shape their meaning for contemporary and future audiences.[46]

The presence of this narrative trope is marked in Latin literature by a corresponding vocabulary, in particular the terms *fremitus/fremere* – 'murmuring', but also 'clamour' – and *vociferatio/vociferare* – 'hue and cry' or simply loud shouting of various kinds. The latter term in particular highlights the sonic quality of mutiny in Roman accounts. What makes it particularly important and noteworthy from our present perspective is that it was a term of historiography and legal writing alike. As such, it was particularly associated with traditional Roman forms of 'popular justice' (Lintott 1999: 6–10). According to Ulpian's *On the Edict*, which was likely based on Labeo's commentary from the Augustan period, *vociferatio* is an integral feature of 'public defamation' (*convicium*): a group of people gathered in front of a person's house and raised an abusive clamour. Ulpian claims that in order to be a *convicium* in a legal sense, this verbal abuse must be performed in public gatherings (*in coetu*) and with loud shouting (*vociferatio*) (*Dig.* 47.10.15.11). However, it has been argued that the *convicium* should not only be understood as a form of 'defamatory popular justice' bordering on mob violence, but also as a regulated extrajudicial practice for resolving disputes that was intended as a means of resolving existing quarrels between individuals, by forcing the opposing side to change its behaviour or by strengthening one's own position (Seelentag

---

45 Mazzaferro 2018: 17 ('a kind of early warning sign for underclass political innovation'). On 'murmuring' as a distinct preliminary stage and feature of mutiny, see also Buchan 2017.
46 On 'vocalization' in Roman mutiny narratives, see Worley 2018.

2017). *Vociferatio* was thus inextricably linked with Roman traditions for conflict resolution that relied on the social pressure exerted by the public vocalisation of complaints and accusations and was mostly independent of formal legal procedures.

Aside from the term's legal use, there was also a historiographical tradition of *vociferatio*. Particularly in Livy, *vociferatio* frequently refers to the loud shouting and the desperate outcries of those who have been wronged and, in the absence of other means of obtaining justice, appeal to the support of assembled crowds and bystanders. *Vociferatio* thus becomes the sonic mark of popular resistance, mostly inarticulate, but nonetheless powerful. Livy presents *vociferatio* as the next step after discontented 'murmuring' (*fremitus/fremere*), delineating the sonic panorama of mutiny as an escalation of public vocal utterances.[47] One episode from the first pentad is particularly illuminating: according to Livy, during the campaign against the Aequi in 414 BCE, a mutiny (*seditio*, 4.50.2; cf. 4.51.5) broke out in the Roman camp due to the conduct of the soldiers' commander. The soldiers were already irritated (*in castris maiorem indignationem*, 4.50.1) because they felt cheated out of their spoils. They first 'murmured openly' (*fremitus aperte esset*, 4.50.2) after learning that the consular tribune M. Postumius Regillensis had publicly threatened them in Rome with harsh treatment 'if they don't keep quiet' (*nisi quieverint*, 4.49.11), and then broke out in 'loud cries' (*clamor*, 4.50.2) and 'strife' (*iurgium*) after a quaestor tried to arrest a 'bawling soldier' (*vociferantem ... militem*, 4.50.2).[48] In response, Postumius himself appeared in the camp and imposed harsh penalties, sentencing several soldiers to death. Those he had sentenced cried out, and a crowd of enraged bystanders gathered after hearing their cries (*ad vociferationem eorum ... concursu facto*, 4.50.4). Postumius was eventually stoned by his soldiers, and the matter was delegated to Rome (4.50.6–8). The prominence of *vociferatio* and other terms for vocal utterances in this scene is noteworthy, beginning with Postumius' demand that the soldiers should be 'quiet', and ending with the loud *vociferatio* of the

---

47 Livy 7.12.14, 22.43.3, 24.21.2; cf. 3.45.4–5, 8.32.9–33.2, 29.9.4, Curt. 9.7.9, Cass. Dio fr. 36.7. On 'murmuring' and the 'voice of the people' in Livy's first pentad, see Vasaly 2015: 101–4. On the various 'soundscapes' of Roman warfare, see now Diemke 2022: 585–98.
48 Within the narrative sequence of Livy's account, the soldiers' unrest in the camp is referred to as *seditio* (focalized through the quaestor, 4.50.2) even before it becomes violent, which corresponds to the Roman concept of *seditio*, which did not always include physical violence (see n. 1 above). According to Livy, both the words and deeds of soldiers could be regarded as *seditiosus*, 'mutinous' (45.37.2, though the text is not secure at this point).

condemned which led to the tribune's death. Livy's attention to the sonic quality of military unrest not only adds to the story's vividness, but also demonstrates an understanding of the dual nature of 'murmuring' as, on the one hand, a warning sign of mutiny in its early stages and, on the other, a dialogic instrument for communication within the hierarchical order of the troops.

Historiography was not, however, the only site of discourse about military unrest, as the use of the term *vociferatio* in connection with mutiny in quite a different literary genre suggests. Given the near complete absence of references to mutinies in imperial documents,[49] another obvious place to look for traces of the discourse on mutiny is the writings of Roman jurists,[50] in whose domain mutiny fell as one of the most serious (military) crimes.[51] However, there is not much on this subject in the surviving corpus of Roman jurisprudence. The 49th book of the *Digest* of Justinian contains two provisions for military offences labelled *seditio*, both originally drafted in the first half of the third century CE by the jurist Herennius Modestinus in the fourth book of his *De poenis*, a monograph on criminal law.[52] Even if Modestinus' interest in *seditio* was limited, it was part of a broader trend in jurisprudence. As Sara Phang notes, the emphasis of jurists like Arrius Menander and Modestinus 'on obedience is, like other such prescriptions, an aristocratic response to the coups and civil wars that had broken out afresh in these jurists' lifetimes' (2008: 139). The first statement notes that those who 'stir up' a 'wild' or 'severe' mutiny shall be sentenced to death (*qui seditionem atrocem militum concitavit, capite punitur*, Dig. 49.16.3.19).[53] The second states that if a *seditio* occurred in

---

49 A fascinating exception is suggested by the editors of the *SC de Cn. Pisone Patre* (20 CE), who argue (Eck, Caballos and, Fernández 1996: 168) that in the senatorial praise of Tiberius, the claim that the emperor had 'buried' the 'evils of civil war' (*virtutibusq(ue) Ti(beri) Caesaris Aug(usti)* | *omnibus civilis belli sepultis malis*, ll. 46–47) refers to the quelling of the mutinies of 14 CE: 'Gerade diese dramatischen Ereignisse, die erst wenige Jahre zurücklagen, mußten jedem im Senat noch gegenwärtig sein.' They are followed by Griffin 1997: 256, Fishwick 2007: 298, and (cautiously) Cooley 2023: 179, ad loc. This would have been an intriguing case of official discourse glossing mutiny as civil war, a thematic link that is also crucial in Tacitus' account of the mutinies (Ash 2019). However, Malloch 2004: 201 n. 15 argues that the 'meaning may simply be that Tiberius maintained by his *virtutes* the stability established by Augustus at the end of the civil wars'.
50 On the relationship between historiographical and juridical models and discourses on unrest, see Myles Lavan's paper in this volume.
51 On Roman military law, see generally Mommsen 1899: 27–34, Jung 1982, Campbell 1984: 300–14.
52 On Modestinus, see Liebs 1997: 195–201 (§ 427), on *De poenis* p. 197.
53 Cf. 49.16.16.1 (Paulus 5 *sent.*): *Miles turbator pacis capite punitur*, Campbell 1984: 310.

an environment where there had already been 'loud shouting' or 'minor accusations', those responsible would be punished by a reduction in rank (*si intra vociferationem aut levem querellam seditio mota est, tunc gradu militiae deicitur*, *Dig.* 49.16.3.20). The precise meaning of both statements and their relationship is not wholly clear, however. It is left vague, for instance, what is meant by *seditio atrox*, 'wild' or 'severe' mutiny. Is it only defined by the fact that it is not of the type mentioned next, a *seditio* that arose in the midst of tumultuous circumstances? Or did it include the use of physical violence, which, as previously stated,[54] was not necessarily part of the Roman concept of *seditio* but was one of the features that could define an offence as *atrox*, 'aggravated' (*Dig.* 47.10.7.8, 47.10.9pr), in a legal context? Finally, if the second statement can be understood in the way proposed here, it is remarkable that it was apparently understood as a mitigating circumstance if soldiers were carried away to mutiny in an already heated atmosphere.[55]

Be that as it may, the presence of the term *vociferatio* in a juridical context which highlights either the different grades of severity of a mutiny or, as has been argued here, mitigating circumstances, is in any case noteworthy. It is also possible, perhaps even likely, that the occurrence of *vociferatio* as a mitigating factor in Modestinus' statement was no mere coincidence. The 414 BCE mutiny, like other instances of plebeian revolt in Livy's first pentad, demonstrates that 'many of the people's most passionate reactions are presented as justified responses to extreme provocation' (Vasaly 2015: 99). The story of the mutiny against Postumius was apparently remembered as a *popularis* tale about one of many *iustae seditiones* in Roman history (Ogilvie 1965:

---

54 See n. 1 above. Livy (32.3.2) describes the mutiny among the Roman soldiers in northern Greece in 199 BCE as an *atrox seditio* yet says nothing about any violence; its 'dangerous' character likely resulted from the great number of those involved.

55 There is some (implicit) disagreement about how to interpret the phrase, *si intra vociferationem aut levem querellam seditio mota est*. Some understand both *vociferatio* and *levis querella* as defining the type of *seditio* the regulation concerns, and thus a less severe form of it than the *seditio atrox* mentioned in the preceding statement. In this sense the regulation is translated in Watson 1998: 'If the disorder stirred up was confined to a noisy argument or a trivial complaint'; cf. Campbell 1984: 310 ('but if the uproar ... stopped short at "abuse" and "minor complaints"'), Phang 2008: 139 ('a lesser degree of insubordination [a *vociferatio* or *levis querella*]'). However, this seems to contradict the sense of the Latin phrase: *mota est* surely denotes not the extent but the origin of the *seditio*, and *vociferatio* and *levis querella* define the circumstances 'in which' (as *intra* clearly marks) this less punishable military revolt could have originated (see for this sense also Jung 1982: 996). On the phrase *seditio mota* denoting the outbreak of unrest, see, e.g. Livy 4.16.3, 4.50.2, SHA *Alex. Sev.* 53.3; cf. Curt. 10.4.3.

609); by the time of the early principate, Postumius' 'thoughtless' disregard for his soldiers and subsequent death had already achieved exemplary status (Val. Max. 9.8.3). The story was also remembered in the high empire as a warning about what could happen in a *seditio* if the soldiers were treated unjustly and disrespectfully (Flor. 1.17.2). Thus, by the time of Modestinus, it was widely available as an *exemplum* of justified soldierly discontent that demonstrated the potential consequences when commanders were unresponsive to the sonic early warning signs of mutiny.

The Severan jurists by and large took some interest in the concerns of the common soldiers, as well as the circumstances and motives of their offences. They attempted to add structure and predictability to the arbitrariness of military jurisdiction by defining and structuring offences (Jung 1982: 1011–12). Modestinus' distinction between *seditiones* arising from different circumstances could have been part of a larger trend towards systematisation. He appears to have drawn inspiration not only from civilian legal practices such as *vociferatio* in the *convicium*, but also from exemplary historiographical discourses on justified soldiery discontent and its various manifestations. Despite their interest in matters of obedience and military discipline, the early third-century jurists were not military experts; rather, they were intellectuals, comparable to rhetorically skilled philosophers (de Blois 2001: 142). It is not surprising, then, that when they wrote about military discipline, they frequently drew on the seemingly limitless reservoir of exemplary tales from early Roman history (Phang 2008: 134–36). Although the jurists' references to earlier *exempla* mostly served to illustrate the harsh discipline of the 'good old days' (Phang 2008: 136), the choice of *vociferatio* as a mitigating factor for *seditiones* also evoked an exemplary tradition that treated mutinies as unavoidable and even necessary expressions of soldiers' grievances in certain circumstances. In some ways, this corresponds to recent scholarship's tendency to understand mutinies not only as outrageous and abnormal outbursts of organized violence, but also as an intensified form of otherwise accepted practices of communication and negotiation within armed forces.[56]

---

56 See generally Dwyer 2017: esp. ch. 1; for Roman antiquity, see Lee 2019: 278–79, 2020: 100.

Conclusion: Roman mutinies between event, narrative, and discourse

This analysis of Roman discourses on mutiny was not meant to suggest that military unrest was primarily a textual phenomenon. Nevertheless, mutinies were much more to the Romans than mere events. They were something that was *talked about*, the object of remembrance, debate, and rhetorical appropriation, and thus a fitting object for the type of discursive analysis attempted in this paper. Mutinies were, as one modern historian succinctly describes, 'un sujet de préoccupation' (Hinard 1990: 152) for not only modern historians but also the Romans themselves. This preoccupation, it should be noted, manifested itself in literary production as well as in specific cultural and political practices. Mutinies, it can be argued, thus had a far greater presence in Roman politics and culture than their location on the empire's outskirts might suggest. However, we know almost exclusively about this peculiar presence from literary, primarily historiographical, sources, texts that were governed by their own literary and ideological agendas. As the final section of the chapter has demonstrated, even the seemingly technical discourse of jurisprudence was influenced to some extent by explanatory models for military unrest borrowed from historiographical traditions. To return to a quote with which I began, mutinies are always and inevitably 'both narratives and events' (Brummett 1998: 94) in any society that keeps a record of its own past. In the case of the Romans, even more than in other periods of history, we know much about the narratives but very little about the minute details of events. If we want to fully understand why the Romans were so surprisingly 'preoccupied' with mutiny, we must study the Roman discourse(s) on mutiny in as comprehensive a way as possible, paying close attention to the various discourses in which accounts of mutinies and their afterlives were embedded. To be sure, a much larger project is required to accomplish this,[57] but the preceding analysis of several approaches to Roman accounts of mutiny as discursive history should have already indicated the potential of focusing on the textual record of mutinies. Far from being a mere supplement to a social history of military unrest, such an approach is a field of study in its own right.

---

57 The author of this paper is working on a comprehensive study of mutiny discourses in the Roman world, for which this chapter is a preliminary foundation.

Works cited

Ash, Rhiannon. 2019. 'Civilis rabies usque in exitium (Histories 3.80.2): Tacitus and the evolving trope of republican civil war during the principate', in Carsten Hjort Lange and Frederik Juliaan Vervaet, eds., *The Historiography of Late Republican Civil War*. Leiden, 351–75.
Bhatt, Shreyaa. 2016. 'Rhetoric and truth: Tacitus' Percennius and democratic historiography'. *Helios* 43(2): 163–89.
Bloomer, W. Martin. 1997. *Latinity and Literary Society at Rome*. Philadelphia.
Breebaart, A. B. 1987. 'Plebs and soldiers: social history and mass psychology in Tacitus', in *Clio and Antiquity: History and Historiography of the Greek and Roman World*. Hilversum, 51–70.
Brice, Lee L. 2015a. 'Military unrest in the age of Philip and Alexander of Macedon: defining the terms of debate', in Timothy Howe, E. Edward Garvin, and Graham Wrightson, eds., *Greece, Macedon and Persia: Studies in Social, Political and Military History in Honour of Waldemar Heckel*. Oxford, 69–76.
–. 2015b. 'Second chance for valor: Restoration of order after mutinies and indiscipline', in id. and Daniëlle Slootjes, eds., *Aspects of Ancient Institutions and Geography: Studies in Honor of Richard J.A. Talbert*. Leiden, 103–21.
Brummett, Palmira. 1998. 'Classifying Ottoman mutiny: the act and vision of rebellion'. *Turkish Studies Association Bulletin* 22(1): 91–107.
Buchan, Bruce. 2017. 'Civility at sea: from murmuring to mutiny'. *Republic of Letters* 5(2): 1–14.
Campbell, J. Brian. 1984. *The Emperor and the Roman Army, 31 BC AD 235*. Oxford.
Carney, Elizabeth Donnelly. 2015. 'Macedonians and mutiny: Discipline and indiscipline in the army of Philip and Alexander', in *King and Court in ancient Macedonia: Rivalry, Treason and Conspiracy*. Swansea, 27–59.
Chrissanthos, Stefan G. 1997. 'Scipio and the mutiny at Sucro, 206 B.C.'. *Historia* 46(2): 172–84.
–. 2004. 'Freedom of speech and the Roman republican army', in Ineke Sluiter and Ralph M. Rosen, eds., *Free Speech in Classical Antiquity*. Leiden, 341–67.
Cooley, Alison E. 2023: *The senatus consultum de Cn. Pisone patre: Text, Translation, and Commentary*. Cambridge.
Diemke, Justine. 2022. 'Was sahen, hörten und rochen die römischen Soldaten? Versuch einer multisensorischen Rekonstruktion römischer Kriegserfahrung'. *Historische Zeitschrift* 315(3): 571–605.
Daube, David. 1972. *Civil Disobedience in Antiquity*. Edinburgh.
de Blois, Lukas. 1997. 'Volk und Soldaten bei Cassius Dio'. *Aufstieg und Niedergang der römischen Welt* II 34(3): 2650–76.
–. 2001. 'Roman jurists and the crisis of the third century A.D. in the Roman empire', in id., ed., *Administration, Prosopography and Appointment Policies in the Roman Empire*. Amsterdam, 136–53.

Dwyer, Maggie. 2017. *Soldiers in Revolt: Army Mutinies in Africa*. Oxford.

Eck, Werner, Antonio Caballos and Fernando Fernández. 1996. *Das senatus consultum de cn. Pisone patre*. Munich.

Faure, Patrice. 2007. 'Le *suffragium legionis*: une forme d'expression des soldats dans l'armée romaine', in Julie Dalaison, ed., *Espaces et pouvoirs dans l'Antiquité de l'Anatolie à la Gaule: Hommages à Bernard Rémy*. Grenoble, 319–31.

Firnhaber-Baker, Justine. 2017. 'Introduction: medieval revolt in context', in Justine Firnhaber-Baker and Dirk Schoenaers, eds., *The Routledge History Handbook of Medieval Revolt*. London, 1–15.

Fishwick, Duncan. 2007. 'Cn. Piso pater and the numen Divi Augusti'. *Zeitschrift für Papyrologie und Epigraphik* 159: 297–300.

Frykman, Niklas, Clare Anderson and Lex Heerma van Voss. 2013. 'Mutiny and maritime radicalism in the age of revolution: an introduction'. *International Review of Social History* 58: 1–14.

Fulkerson, Laurel. 2006. 'Staging a mutiny: competitive roleplaying on the Rhine (*Annals* 1.31–51)'. *Ramus* 35: 169–92.

–. 2013. *No Regrets: Remorse in Classical Antiquity*. Oxford.

Goodyear, F. R. D. 1972. *The Annals of Tacitus: Books 1–6*. Vol. 1. Cambridge.

Griffin, Miriam. 1997. 'The senate's story'. *Journal of Roman Studies* 87: 249–63.

Grillo, Luca. 2020. 'Caesar and the crisis of Corfinium', in Jacqueline Klooster and Inger N. I. Kuin, eds., *After the Crisis: Remembering, Re-anchoring and Recovery in Ancient Greece and Rome*. London, 121–34.

Habinek, Thomas N. 1998. *The Politics of Latin Literature: Writing, Identity, and Empire in Ancient Rome*. Princeton.

Hardie, Philip. 2010. 'Crowds and leaders in imperial historiography and in epic', in John F. Miller and Anthony J. Woodman, eds., *Latin Historiography and Poetry in the Early Empire: Generic Interactions*. Leiden, 9–27.

Hinard, François. 1990. 'Les révoltes militaires dans l'armée républicaine'. *Bulletin de l'Association Guillaume Budé* 2: 149–54.

Hoben, Wolfgang. 1978. *Terminologische Studien zu den Sklavenerhebungen der römischen Republik*. Wiesbaden.

Hölkeskamp, Karl-Joachim. 2011. *Die Entstehung der Nobilität: Studien zur sozialen und politischen Geschichte der römischen Republik im 4. Jhdt. v. Chr.* 2nd edn. Stuttgart.

Hornblower, Simon. 2007. 'Warfare in ancient literature: the paradox of war', in Philip Sabin, Hans van Wees, and Michael Whitby, eds., *The Cambridge History of Greek and Roman Warfare*. Vol. 1, *Greece, the Hellenistic World and the Rise of Rome*. Cambridge, 22–53.

–. 2011. '"This was decided" (ἔδοξε ταῦτα): The army as *polis* in Xenophon's *Anabasis* – and elsewhere', in *Thucydidean Themes*. Oxford, 226–49.

Humm, Michel. 2015. 'From 390 BC to Sentinum: Political and ideological aspects', in Bernard Mineo, ed., *A Companion to Livy*. Malden., 342–66.

Instinsky, Hans Ulrich. 1940. 'Consensus universorum'. *Hermes* 75(3): 265–78.

Jung, Jost Heinrich. 1982. 'Die Rechtsstellung der römischen Soldaten. Ihre Entwicklung von den Anfängen Roms bis auf Diokletian'. *Aufstieg und Niedergang der römischen Welt* II 14: 882–1013.

Kaegi, Walter Emil, Jr. 1981. *Byzantine Military Unrest, 471–843: An Interpretation*. Amsterdam.

Kajanto, Iiro. 1970. 'Tacitus' attitude to war and the soldier'. *Latomus* 29(3): 699–718.

Kelly, Benjamin. 2007. 'Riot control and imperial ideology in the Roman empire'. *Phoenix* 61(1/2): 150–76.

Knopf, Fabian. 2019. 'Circuli – Statuen – Funera. "Unverfasste" Partizipationsformen der spätrepublikanischen Plebs'. *Klio* 101(1): 107–41.

Lavan, Myles. 2017. 'Writing revolt in the early Roman empire', in Justine Firnhaber-Baker and Dirk Schoenaers, eds., *The Routledge History Handbook of Medieval Revolt*. London, 19–38.

Lee, Alan Douglas. 2019. 'Food supply and military mutiny in the late Roman empire'. *Journal of Late Antiquity* 12(2): 277–97.

–. 2020. *Warfare in the Roman World*. Cambridge.

Leidl, Christoph. 1996. *Appians Darstellung des 2. Punischen Krieges in Spanien (Iberike c. 1–38 § 1–158a): Text und Kommentar*. Munich.

Lendon, Jon E. 2005. *Soldiers and Ghosts: A History of Battle in Classical Antiquity*. New Haven.

Liebs, Detlef. 1997. 'Jurisprudenz', in Klaus Sallmann, ed., *Handbuch der lateinischen Literatur der Antike*. Vol. 4, *Die Literatur des Umbruchs: Von der römischen zur christlichen Literatur, 117 bis 284 n. Chr.* Munich, 83–217.

Lintott, Andrew. 1999. *Violence in Republican Rome*. 2nd edn. Oxford.

Lobur, John Alexander. 2008. *Consensus, Concordia, and the Formation of Roman Imperial Ideology*. London.

Logghe, Loonis. 2017. 'Plebeian agency in the later Roman republic', in Richard Evans, ed., *Mass and Elite in the Greek and Roman Worlds: From Sparta to Late Antiquity*. London, 63–81.

MacMullen, Ramsay. 1984. 'The legion as a society'. *Historia* 33(4): 440–56.

Maddison, Ben. 2014. *Class and Colonialism in Antarctic Exploration, 1750–1920*. London.

Malloch, Simon J. V. 2004. 'The end of the Rhine mutiny in Tacitus, Suetonius, and Dio'. *Classical Quarterly* 54(1): 198–210.

Marincola, John. 2009. 'Ancient audiences and expectations', in Andrew Feldherr, ed., *The Cambridge Companion to the Roman Historians*. Cambridge, 11–23.

Mazzaferro, Alexander. 2018. '"Such a murmur": innovation, rebellion, and sovereignty in William Strachey's "True Reportory"'. *Early American Literature* 53(1): 3–32.

Mommsen, Theodor. 1899. *Römisches Strafrecht*. Leipzig.

Nousek, Debra L. 2010. 'Echoes of Cicero in Livy's Bacchanalian narrative (39.8–19)'. *Classical Quarterly* 60(1): 156–66.

Oakley, Stephen P. 1993. 'The Roman conquest of Italy', in John Rich and Graham Shipley, eds., *War and Society in the Roman World*. London, 9–37.

–. 1998. *A Commentary on Livy Books VI–X*. Vol. 2, *Books VII–VIII*. Oxford.

Ogilvie, Robert M. 1965. *A Commentary on Livy: Books 1–5*. Oxford.

O'Gorman, Ellen. 2000. *Irony and Misreading in the* Annals *of Tacitus*. Cambridge.

Osthoff, Gerhard. 1952. 'Tumultus – seditio: Untersuchungen zum römischen Staatsrecht und zur politischen Terminologie der Römer'. Diss. phil. University of Cologne.

Pagán, Victoria Emma. 2004. *Conspiracy Narratives in Roman History*. Austin.

–. 2005. 'The Pannonian revolt in the *Annals* of Tacitus', in Carl Deroux, ed., *Studies in Latin Literature and Roman History XII*. Brussels, 414–22.

Parker, Geoffrey. 1973. 'Mutiny and discontent in the Spanish army of Flanders 1572–1607'. *Past & Present* 58(1): 38–52.

Phang, Sara Elise. 2008. *Roman Military Service: Ideologies of Discipline in the Late Republic and Early Principate*. Cambridge.

Pina Polo, Francisco. 1995. 'Procedures and functions of civil and military *contiones* in Rome'. *Klio* 77: 203–16.

Poma, Gabriella. 1990. 'Considerazioni sul processo di formazione della tradizione annalistica: il caso della sedizione militare del 342 a.C.', in Walter Eder, ed., *Staat und Staatlichkeit in der frühen römischen Republik: Akten eines Symposiums, 12.–15. Juli 1988, Freie Universität Berlin*. Stuttgart, 139–57.

Raaflaub, Kurt A. 2005. 'From protection and defense to offense and participation: stages in the conflict of the orders', in id., ed., *Social Struggles in Archaic Rome: New Perspectives on the Conflict of the Orders*. 2nd ed. Malden, 185–222.

Rawlings, Louis. 2007. 'Army and battle during the conquest of Italy (350–264 BC)', in Paul Erdkamp, ed., *A Companion to the Roman Army*. Malden, 45–62.

Richardson, John S. 2000. *Appian: Wars of the Romans in Iberia, with an Introduction, Translation and Commentary*. Warminster.

Rose, Elihu. 1982. 'The anatomy of mutiny'. *Armed Forces and Society* 8: 561–74.

Rosenblitt, J. Alison. 2019. 'Sulla's long shadow: Sallust in Tacitus and Tacitus in Sallust', in Alexandra Eckert and Alexander Thein, eds., *Sulla: Politics and Reception*. Berlin, 125–42.

Rowe, Greg. 2002. *Princes and Political Cultures: The New Tiberian Senatorial Decrees*. Ann Arbor.

Scardigli, Barbara. 1996. 'Una marcia su Roma nel 342 a.C.? A proposito di Appiano, *Samn.* fr. 1', in Luisa Breglia Pulci Doria, ed., *L'incidenza dell'antico: studi in memoria di Ettore Lepore*. Vol. 2. Naples, 403–10.

Schauer, Markus. 2016. *Der Gallische Krieg: Geschichte und Täuschung in Caesars Meisterwerk*. Munich.

Seelentag, Anna Margarete. 2017. 'Das *convicium* als Beispiel außergerichtlicher Konfliktlösung in Rom', in Guido Pfeifer and Nadine Grotkamp, eds., *Außergerichtliche Konfliktlösung in der Antike: Beispiele aus drei Jahrtausenden*. Frankfurt am Main, 105–39.

Sherer, Idan. 2017. *Warriors for a Living: The Experience of the Spanish Infantry in the Italian Wars, 1494–1559*. Leiden.

Taylor, Michael J. 2018. 'The election of centurions during the Republican period'. *Ancient Society* 48: 147–67.

Turner, Brian and Jessica H. Clark. 2017. 'Thinking about military defeat in ancient Mediterranean society', in Jessica H. Clark and Brian Turner, eds., *Brill's Companion to Military Defeat in Ancient Mediterranean Society*. Leiden, 1–22.

Vasaly, Ann. 2015. *Livy's Political Philosophy: Power and Personality in Early Rome*. Cambridge.

Watson, Alan, ed., 1998. *The Digest of Justinian*. Rev. edn. Vol. 4. Philadelphia.
Williams, Mary Frances. 1997. 'Four mutinies: Tacitus *Annals* 1.16–30; 1.31–49 and Ammianus Marcellinus *Res gestae* 20.4.9–20.5.7; 24.3.1–8'. *Phoenix* 51(1): 44–74.
Wolff, Catherine. 2012. *L'armée romaine: Une armée modèle?* Paris.
Woolf, Greg. 2011. 'Provincial revolts in the early Roman empire', in Mladen Popović, ed., *The Jewish Revolt against Rome: Interdisciplinary Perspectives*. Leiden, 27–44.
Worley, Andrew. 2018. 'A percennial problem: The development of vocalization within the mutiny narrative in Roman historiography', in Olivier Devillers and Breno Battistin Sebastiani, eds., *Sources et modèles des historiens anciens*. Bordeaux, 111–23.

7. Aporetic Unrest: Reimagining Materialism and Empire in Appian

Lisa Pilar Eberle

Abstract: *This paper re-envisions the place of materialism in Appian's historiographical project in the Romaika. The often fragmentarily preserved books in which Appian recounted Rome's military confrontations with the various people that made up the empire in his own day contain a model of unrest – 'aporetic unrest' – that has a distinctly material dimension: on several occasions Appian suggests that people became bandits and pirates (lēistai and peiratai) and engaged in rebellion and civil strife (apostasis and stasis) because they were at a loss (aporia), a predicament that more often than not seems to have been connected with a lack of land (aporia gēs). While clearly related to various intellectual traditions, this figure of thought in its unadulterated consistency seems to be unique to Appian's writing. It constituted a vital aspect of his historiographical project and was also deeply imbricated in his personal identity and imperial politics. The suggestion that people had only opposed Rome because a lack of land had somehow forced them to do so opened the door for re-thinking how imperial subjects should be treated and for re-conceptualizing imperial rule more generally, not least to move beyond the conqueror-conquered divide. Related developments can also be traced in various actions and artefacts associated with the emperor Hadrian, many of which Antoninus Pius, his successor, during whose reign Appian most likely composed the* Romaika, *quickly moved to undo. Ultimately, then, the lens of 'aporetic unrest' provides a precious window into the multiplicity of empires (and the histories that they required) that might have existed at any one point throughout the Roman empire's long life.*

...he gets to the bottom of the material basis of things in these civil wars. (Marx to Engels, 27 February 1861; *Marx-Engels-Werke* 30.160)

Few men (or women) have been as enthusiastic in their praise of Appian and his work as Karl Marx, who spent several wintry London evenings reading parts of Appian's *Romaika* in the original Greek.[1] In fact, for a long time ancient historians did not even think about Appian as an author in his own right. The materialism that Marx identified, near-unique within the Graeco-Roman tradition, is largely considered a problem of Quellenforschung: not Appian, an Alexandrian-born member of Rome's second-century CE imperial elite, but some earlier, possibly republican, and most likely Roman author is assumed to have been its author.[2] In the 1980s, as ancient historians finally began giving Appian credit as a historical thinker, any notion of materialism quickly disappeared from view.[3] As Gregory Bucher put it, Appian did not 'concern himself with politics, social problems, or other mechanisms of the decay'; instead, the author of the *Romaika* has emerged as a monarchist with tendencies to credit the divine (*ho theos*) for the events he was recounting.[4]

This paper reclaims materialism for Appian – in relation to how he explained different forms of unrest throughout the *Romaika*. To do so, I explore the parts of his work that are not concerned with late republican history: the often fragmentarily preserved books in which Appian recounted Rome's military confrontations with the various people that made up the empire in his own day.[5] There, I contend, Appian articulated a model of unrest – 'aporetic unrest' – that has a distinctly material dimension: on several occasions Appian suggests that people became bandits and pirates (*lēistai* and *peiratai*) and engaged in rebellion and civil strife (*apostasis* and *stasis*) because they were at a loss (*aporia*), a predicament that more often than not seems to have been connected with a lack of land (*aporia gēs*).

'Aporetic unrest' is not simply a recurring figure of thought in the *Romaika*. While clearly related to various intellectual traditions, this idea in its unadulterated consistency seems to be unique to Appian's writing. As it turns out, it is deeply imbricated in both his imperial politics and personal iden-

---

1 Bonnell 2015 discusses the intellectual context of this reading, Famerie 1990 its impact on Appian's reception.
2 Schwartz, *RE* s.v. 'Appianus 2' remains central. Iconic, if now generally rejected, are Gabba 1956, 1958. Goukowsky 2008: cciv-ccxxxi outlines the (un)certainties of the debate.
3 On Appian's life: Gowing 1992: 9–18, Brodersen 1993: 352–54, Goukowsky 1998, Brodersen 2015, Goukowsky 2021. On Appian as a historian: Goldman 1988, Gowing 1992, Hose 1994, Bucher 2000, 2005, 2007, Goukowsky 2001a, Pitcher 2016, Welch 2019. See also the contributions in ANRW II 34(1), published in 1993, and in Welch 2015 as well as the various commentaries on individual books by Goukowsky. His fading materialism: Gowing 1992: 9–10, McGing 1993: 512–14.
4 Bucher 2000: 436, 442–48; compare also Goldman 1988: 24–29, Gowing 1992: 297, Brodersen 1993: 355–56, Hose 1994: 258–66, 348–50, Welch 2019.
5 For other takes on Appian's materialism beyond the *Civil Wars* see Kühne 1969, Cuff 1983.

tity. Appian's materialism as embodied in 'aporetic unrest' thus is very much his own – on more than one level. It should be considered a vital aspect of his historiographical project and a deeply original contribution within the discursive history of unrest in the ancient world. From the perspective of this volume, then, not just materialism but also enthusiasm may be restored to Appian and his work.

Aporetic Unrest in Appian

'Aporetic unrest' – the idea that people engaged in different forms of unrest because they were at a loss (*aporia*) for some reason connected to a lack of land (*aporia gēs*) – is neither straightforward nor obvious, its presentation by Appian both elliptical and allusive. As such 'aporetic unrest' deserves some explication. The account of the efflorescence of piracy after the First Mithridatic war in 88 BCE constitutes the most elaborate and rich articulation of the notion in the preserved parts of the *Romaika*. The passage in question provides a helpful starting point for outlining its various dimensions:[6]

When Mithridates first went to war with the Romans and subdued the province of Asia, he thought that he should not hold the province long, and accordingly plundered it in all sorts of ways, as I have mentioned above, and sent out pirates on the sea. ... Having enjoyed large gains, the pirates did not desist when Mithridates was defeated, made peace, and retired. For having lost both livelihood (*bios*) and fatherland (*patris*) by reason of the war and having fallen into extreme *aporia*, they harvested the sea instead of the land, at first with pinnaces and hemiolii, then with two-bank and three-bank ships, sailing in squadrons under pirate chiefs, who were like generals of an army. ... Perhaps this evil had its beginning among the men of the Crags of Cilicia, but thither also men of Syrian, Cyprian, Pamphylian, and Pontic origin and those of almost all the Eastern nations had congregated, who, on account

---

6 *Mithr.* 92.416–22: Μιθριδάτης ὅτε πρῶτον Ῥωμαίοις ἐπολέμει καὶ τῆς Ἀσίας ἐκράτει, ἡγούμενος οὐκ ἐς πολὺ καθέξειν τῆς Ἀσίας, τά τε ἄλλα, ὥς μοι προείρηται, πάντα ἐλυμαίνετο, καὶ ἐς τὴν θάλασσαν πειρατὰς καθῆκεν ... γευσάμενοι δὲ κερδῶν μεγάλων, οὐδ' ἡττωμένου καὶ σπενδομένου τοῦ Μιθριδάτου καὶ ἀναχωροῦντος ἔτι ἐπαύοντο· οἱ γὰρ βίου καὶ πατρίδων διὰ τὸν πόλεμον ἀφῃρημένοι, καὶ ἐς ἀπορίαν ἐμπεσόντες ἀθρόαν, ἀντὶ τῆς γῆς ἐκαρποῦντο τὴν θάλασσαν, μυοπάρωσι πρῶτον καὶ ἡμιολίαις, εἶτα δικρότοις καὶ τριήρεσι κατὰ μέρη περιπλέοντες, ἡγουμένων λῃστάρχων οἷα πολέμου στρατηγῶν. ... ἀρξαμένου μὲν ἴσως τοῦ κακοῦ παρὰ τῶν Τραχεωτῶν Κιλίκων, συνεπιλαβόντων δὲ Σύρων τε καὶ Κυπρίων καὶ Παμφύλων καὶ τῶν Ποντικῶν καὶ σχεδὸν ἁπάντων τῶν ἑῴων ἐθνῶν οἳ πολλοῦ καὶ χρονίου σφίσιν ὄντος τοῦ Μιθριδατείου πολέμου δρᾶν τι μᾶλλον ἢ πάσχειν αἱρούμενοι τὴν θάλασσαν ἀντὶ τῆς γῆς ἐπελέγοντο.

of the long continuance of the Mithridatic war, preferred to do wrong rather than to suffer it, and for this purpose chose the sea instead of the land. (*Mithr.* 92.416–22)

Appian's account is multi-layered and complex. He attributes the rise of piracy to Mithridates' strategic calculations – the Pontic king did not think that he was going to hold Asia for long, so he decided to plunder it using piracy – while also suggesting that people turned to piracy because of human psychology in the context of war: due to the length of the war with Mithridates people preferred to partake in the war and reap its benefits to potentially becoming its victims, and so they joined the pirates. However, when it comes to explaining the persistence of piracy after the war, Appian ties all the different strands of his account together in one sentence: by becoming pirates people lost their fatherland (*patris*) and livelihood (*bios*); this meant 'extreme *aporia*', which in turn led the pirates to continue 'harvesting the sea'.

Elusive though Appian's account may be, the passage allows us to begin outlining 'aporetic unrest' as explanatory model. I have left *aporia* untranslated, and purposefully so. It seems to me that here the word does not mean poverty or destitution, as it is often translated.[7] After all, in the sentence before talking about the pirates' *aporia*, Appian had just described their *kerda*, their gains and profits. Instead, in this passage *aporia* seems to refer to the lack or loss of a specific resource: landed possessions. Appian's memorable image that the pirates were now harvesting the sea and not the land supports this idea. So, when Appian stated that these men had lost their *bios*, he was thinking of one way of making a living: by cultivating land in a place that was their *patris*. A set of complex circumstances, including the strategic calculations of kings and various aspects of human psychology, had made them lose this land; these circumstances gave rise to *aporia* – they were at a loss – and this *aporia* in turn forced them to continue engaging in piracy: it put them in a position where they could not help but 'harvest the sea'. Arguably, then, Appian's use of *aporia* here also resonates with its use in the Greek philosophical tradition, where it refers to a seemingly insoluble impasse, an intellectual place from which there was no way out.[8]

Appian's narrative presentation, both in this passage and elsewhere, supports this suggestion. In the preserved parts of his work, we only have one

---

7 Veh 1987: 394 ('Not'), Goukowsky 2001b: 93 ('dénuement'), McGing 2019: 329 ('poverty').
8 On *aporia* in the Greek philosophical tradition see now Karamanolis and Politis 2018.

passage in which Appian speaks of *aporia gēs*: *Hisp.* 42.171. In all other instances of 'aporetic unrest' we can infer from context that a lack of land was the issue, but Appian did not explicitly qualify the *aporia* as being related to land. Arguably, this presentation encouraged his audience to understand *aporia* both materially and philosophically. *Aporia* could and had to be both: a lack of land and a situation from which there was no way out. More specifically, it was both at the same time. Lack of land was a situation from which there was no way out. Somehow lack of land forced people to be unrestful; they could not help it, there was no (other) way out.

The *Iberikē*, Appian's account of the Roman conquest of the Iberian Peninsula, contains several instances of this intertwining of *aporia*, land, and unrest. Appian saw revolts on the Iberian peninsula in the 170s BCE as the result of *aporia gēs*, the sole instance of the actual phrase preserved in his entire work.[9] He also had Servius Sulpicius Galba feign sympathy with some Lusitanian rebels in the early 150s BCE: these men had only become bandits, they had only taken up arms, they had only broken their oaths because of their *aporia*; so really, Galba stated, it was the wretchedness of their land, which had forced them to take up arms against Rome.[10] At the end of the Lusitanian war Appian showed Quintus Servilius Caepio dealing with defeated rebels: Caepio settled them on enough land 'so that they would not take to banditry because of *aporia*'.[11] In the fourth and final passage Appian attributed an instance of Iberian banditry to *aporia* and showed the Roman general Titus Didius remedy the situation by giving the (former) bandits new plots of land.[12]

In all these four cases Appian and/or his Roman protagonists posit a causal connection between various forms of unrest – banditry, rebellion, and warfare – and *aporia* (*gēs*). The passage concerning Sulpicius Galba is particularly revealing because there, in direct speech, we find the explicit mention of necessity – *anankazein* is the verb that he uses – to describe the exigency of lack of land: it forced people to engage in banditry and warfare.

---

9 *Hisp.* 42.171: πολλοὶ τῶν Ἰβήρων γῆς ἀποροῦντες ἀπέστησαν ἀπὸ Ῥωμαίων.
10 *Hisp.* 75.321: καὶ ὑπεκρίνετο αὐτοῖς καὶ συνάχθεσθαι ὡς δι' ἀπορίαν λῃστεύουσί τε καὶ πολεμοῦσι καὶ παρεσπονδηκόσιν· Τὸ γὰρ λυπρόγεων, ἔφη, καὶ πενιχρὸν ὑμᾶς ἐς λῃστείαν ἄγει· δώσω δ' ἐγὼ πενομένοις φίλοις γῆν ἀγαθὴν καὶ ἐν ἀφθόνοις συνοικιῶ, διελὼν ἐς τρία.
11 *Hisp.* 75.321: ὁ δὲ ὅπλα τε αὐτοὺς ἀφείλετο ἅπαντα, καὶ γῆν ἔδωκεν ἱκανήν, ἵνα μὴ λῃστεύοιεν ἐξ ἀπορίας.
12 *Hisp.* 100.433–34: ἐλῄστευον δ' ἐξ ἀπορίας οὗτοι ... ἔφη τοῖς ἐπιφανέσιν αὐτῶν ἐθέλειν τὴν Κολενδέων χώραν αὐτοῖς προσορίσαι πενομένοις.

This idea constitutes a more concrete formulation of the dynamic I sketched in my analysis of 'aporetic unrest' in the case of first-century BCE piracy. As such, this passage might be taken to confirm my suggestion that the *aporia* in 'aporetic unrest' combined both material and philosophical dimensions. In the *Libykē*, Appian's account of Roman warfare in North Africa, we find further instances of *aporia* operating as a causal force in relation to unrest. At the end of the First Punic War the Carthaginians took to plundering merchant ships that were sailing past their coast. According to Appian, this form of banditry arose because they were running out of supplies; it arose, he claimed, because of their *aporia*.[13] While this passage does not concern a lack of land, a second passage quite likely does. Appian suggested that Gaius Gracchus' attempt to resettle Carthage resulted from civil strife (*stasis*) in Rome, which in turn had been the result of *aporia*.[14] The phrasing is short and elusive. The context of land-distributions in North Africa, however, makes it likely that here too Appian was thinking of *aporia* in relation to land.

I have not been able to find further instances of 'aporetic unrest' in the remaining parts of the *Romaika*. While three books might seem a meagre sample in a work that might have contained twenty-four books in total, it seems worth remembering the fragmentary state of the *Romaika*'s preservation.[15] Apart from the five extant books on civil strife in late republican Rome, only six books on separate regions of the empire are preserved in more than mere fragments. The absence of 'aporetic unrest' from Appian's account of the demise of the republic is indeed significant, and I will discuss (and try to explain) this absence in the final section of the paper. For now, I would highlight three justifications for concluding that Appian was invested in the idea.

One, Appian presented *aporia* as a powerful causal force throughout the *Romaika*.[16] Examples range from the mundane and purely material to the dramatic and psychologically complex. They include ethnographic obser-

---

13 *Pun.* 5.21: ἐμπόρους δ', ὅσοι παρέπλεον, ἐλῄστευον ἐξ ἀπορίας.
14 *Pun.* 136.644: Γαΐου Γράχχου δημαρχοῦντος ἐν Ῥώμῃ καὶ στάσεων οὐσῶν ἐξ ἀπορίας.
15 Goukowsky 2020: 12 provides an overview.
16 *ex aporias*: *Hisp.* 75.321, 82.355, 100.434, *Pun.* 5.21, 94.442, *Mithr.* 99.456, *BCiv.* 2.13.93, 4.9.65, 4.14.107, 4.16.123, 5.12.113, 5.14.142; *hyp' aporias*: *Samn.* 4.18, *Hisp.* 16.60, *Pun.* 28.116, *Syr.* 35.183, *Mithr.* 88.398, 99.495, *Fragm.* 19.3, *B Civ.* 1.6.49, 3.14.97, 5.14.140; *di' aporian*: *Hisp.* 59.249, *Hann.* 18.78, *Pun.* 39.161, *BCiv.* 5.8.67; other constructions attributing causal force to *aporia*: App. *Hisp.* 79.339, *Hann.* 17.77, *Pun.* 37.155, 108.509, *Ill.* 17.50, *Mithr.* 54.217, 92.417, 96.444, 97.451, *BCiv.* 3.12.58, 4.13.103.

vations about Celtic peoples and their habit of eating herbs when no other food was available as well as the legendary moment when the Samnites made the Romans pass under the yoke; the Romans agreed to these terms, Appian writes, *hup' aporias* – because they saw no other way out (*Celt.* 1.9, *Sam.* 4.18). He also used *aporia* to explain the surrender of infamous enemies of Rome, including Hannibal and Mithridates.[17] Crucially, Appian had recourse to *aporia* when explaining his own decision to entrust his fate to the mantic skills of his Arab guide when fleeing the Jewish Diaspora Revolt in 115–117 BCE: there was simply nothing else that he could do (*Fragm.* 19.3.5). Arguably, then, throughout the *Romaika* Appian familiarized his audience with the idea that *aporia* was a powerful explanation for human behaviour, thus making the instances in which it he claimed that it caused unrest less surprising and more comprehensible.

Two, Appian acknowledged that alternative explanations of unrest were possible and explicitly argued against them. On his telling, Pompey settled the defeated pirates in various parts of Cilicia because he was convinced that they had not resorted to piracy because of some innate wickedness (*mochthēria*); it was lack of livelihood, *aporia biou*, that had led them to do so.[18] Beyond the twofold verbal echo of Appian's own explanation for post-Mithridatic piracy – *aporia* and *bios* – this passage is also striking because it mentions a readily available and widespread explanation for piracy: moral depravity on the part of the pirates. Here Appian invokes Pompey's authority and actions to counter the idea. He also seems to have tailored his narrative to counter a second well-known explanation for piratical behaviour. In conceding that the origins of this piracy might have lain in Cilicia while also insisting that in the context of the Mithridatic war many people from all over the eastern Mediterranean had joined these Cilician pirates, he seems to have sought to counter explanations of piracy that were ethnically and geographically based.[19]

---

17 Hannibal: *Pun.* 37.155, 37.157, 39.161; Mithridates: *Mithr.* 97.451, 99.455, 99.456; Sextus Pompeius: *B Civ.* 5.14.140, 5.14.142; Caesar: *B Civ.* 2.13.93; Romans: *Pun.* 94.442.
18 *Hisp.* 96.444: τοὺς δὲ πειρατὰς οἳ μάλιστα ἐδόκουν οὐχ ὑπὸ μοχθηρίας ἀλλ' ἀπορίᾳ βίου διὰ τὸν πόλεμον ἐπὶ ταῦτα ἐλθεῖν, ἐς Μαλλὸν καὶ Ἄδανα καὶ Ἐπιφάνειαν, ἢ εἴ τι ἄλλο πόλισμα ἔρημον ἢ ὀλιγάνθρωπον ἦν τῆσδε τῆς τραχείας Κιλικίας, συνῴκιζε·
19 *Mithr.* 92.422. For accounts that put the responsibility for piracy in the eastern Mediterranean squarely onto Rome—a take that Appian seems to largely ignore—see Goukowsky 2001b: 226 n. 872.

Three, as Appian presents it, he was not the only person to explain unrest with reference to *aporia* in both its material and philosophical sense; Roman generals did so too, both in their words and in their actions. Just consider Pompey in the aftermath of his defeat of the pirates. Not only did he (re)articulate Appian's own account of the origins of piracy after the Mithridatic Wars; his decision to settle the pirates also constituted the only effective means of preventing the recurrence of such actions in the future that this account prescribed. In the *Iberikē* Servius Sulpicius Galba, Quintus Servilius Caepio and Titus Didius also referred to *aporia* (*gēs*) – both in their words and in their actions.

The case of Galba, who only feigned agreement with this mode of explanation, is particularly illuminating. Infamous for his slaughter of Lusitanians to whom he had promised land, Galba is portrayed in a thoroughly negative light. Upon Galba's first appearance in the book his military successes are attributed to luck, and his military inexperience is highlighted (*Hisp*. 58.244–45). As he exits the narrative Appian dwells on his greed, the wealth it led him to amass, and how this wealth allowed him to escape the charges brought against him for his brutal treatment of the Lusitanians (*Hisp*. 60.254–55). While Appian concedes that Galba's treatment of the Lusitanians amounted to repaying treachery with treachery, he also states that in so doing Galba behaved like a barbarian and that such behaviour was 'unworthy of Rome'.[20] Along more pragmatic lines, Appian suggested that Galba's slaughter of the Lusitanians lay at the origins of Rome's drawn-out and traumatic conflict with Viriatus (*Hisp*. 61–62). In short, Roman commanders not only endorsed and acted in line with 'aporetic unrest'; in Appian's narrative it was also unbecoming and unwise for them to not do so.

As persuasive as Appian might have tried to make 'aporetic unrest' appear within the confines of his work, it is worth remembering that this way of explaining unrest was rather unusual in the context of what we know about Roman imperial elites and their thoughts on why people took to plundering, piracy and rebellion. In his recent analysis of Tacitean thinking on the origins of unrest Myles Lavan has identified two patterns.[21] On one level, Tacitus invoked prejudice based on class, geography, and race to portray people

---

20 *Hisp*. 60.253: οὐκ ἀξίως δὲ Ῥωμαίων μιμούμενος βαρβάρους; compare *Hisp*. 61.256, where Appian speaks of Galba's behavior as 'lawlessness' (*paranomēsis*).
21 Lavan 2017: 24–32, discussing also one passage from Suetonius. Woolf 2011: 36–41 focuses on the second model.

as essentially and unavoidably unrestful. At the same time, he also cast their actions as the predictable response to morally corrupt Roman officials. As should be clear, 'aporetic unrest' refrains from essentializing people. As the case of post-Mithridatic piracy illustrates, 'aporetic unrest' is not about people without land in general; instead, it concerns people who have happened to lose attachment to land. More generally, 'aporetic unrest' implies a belief that people can be made restful: by settling them on land. As for corrupt Roman officials, one of the distinguishing features of 'aporetic unrest' is its refusal to even raise the question of blame at all. Arguably, the elliptical shorthand of *aporia gēs* seems designed to sidestep the matter altogether.

Tacitus's thinking on unrest has been taken as representative of a wider senatorial and/or imperial elite in the late first and early second centuries CE (Woolf 2011: 34, Lavan 2017: 35–36). Most likely, Appian, an equestrian by the end of his life, only started work on the *Romaika* in the 150s CE.[22] Where, then, does 'aporetic unrest' stand in the intellectual and political landscape of the empire? Representative of a tradition of explaining unrest that Tacitus had ignored? A complete innovation at the hands of Appian? A sign of changing times and/or different elites in the middle of the second century CE? As I hope to show, all these options have something to recommend themselves, though none of them fully captures the complex intervention in the discursive structures of imperial society that 'aporetic unrest' constituted. In the following section I situate 'aporetic unrest' in the context of Graeco-Roman thought more broadly to argue that the idea shows affinity but also persistent non-identity with at least three well-established ways of thinking about unrest (and other things) in this world. Doing so also allows me to further parse the intellectual operations that 'aporetic unrest' entailed.

Aporetic Unrest beyond Appian?

The historiographical and encomiastic writings of Posidonios of Apamea, a leading Stoic philosopher in the first half of the first century BCE, have been

---

22 Bucher 2000: 415–29. Goukowsky 2021: 209–17 sees the possibility for a more drawn-out composition process.

posited as a possible source for several books and passages in which 'aporetic unrest' appears.[23] There is no suggestion that Appian mindlessly copied Posidonios's writings. Such a view would go against current understandings of how Appian dealt with his sources (Goukowsky 2001b: xcvii-ciii). In addition, at least two instances of 'aporetic unrest' in Appian lie beyond the chronological remit of Posidonios's works (*Pun.* 5.21, third century BCE; *Hisp.* 42.171, 179 BCE). The real question, then, is if Appian found 'aporetic unrest' as a figure of thought in the first-century BCE author and then deployed it for his own purposes throughout the *Romaika*. Due to the state of preservation of Posidonios's writings – only fragments, and few of them direct quotations – there is no way to arrive at a definitive answer to this question. However, the one fragment that we have in which Posidonios does seem to mobilize *aporia* to explain unrest would suggest that if 'aporetic unrest' was in any way inspired by Posidonios's works, it might have been inspired by elements of it that were not exclusively Posidonian.

Why did so many slaves on Sicily take to banditry just before they revolted in 135 BCE? Their masters were not giving them enough food or clothing, so they had to provide for their livelihood (*zēn porizein*) through banditry (*lēisteia*). While scholars have long attributed this account of the run-up to the First Sicilian Slave War to Posidonios, it should be noted that we only have it preserved in the Byzantine excerpts of the works of Diodoros, another, later first-century BCE author (*BNJ* 87 F 108a2 = Diod. Sic. 34/35.2.2).[24] In this case there are indeed good reasons to think that Diodoros and his Byzantine excerptors followed Posidonios quite closely.[25] That being said, regardless of who the author of that passage was, the idea as such is not original. The suggestion that people took to plunder by land or sea because they lacked food and supplies is well attested elsewhere in the Greek historiographical tradition.[26] Arguably, 'aporetic unrest' is closely related to this idea, but also

---

23 Posidonios as (a source for Appian) in general: Schwartz, *RE* s.v. 'Appianus 2', Capelle 1932, Hahn 1982: 267. Posidonios as a source for the *Mithridatikē*: Strasburger 1982: 42–44, 50–52, Goukowsky 2001b: cxvii-cxxv. And for the *Iberikē*: García Quintela 1991: 95–96, Gómez Espelosín 1993: 420, Richardson 2000: 5, Baray 2015: 253–56.
24 Pfuntner 2014 discusses the Byzantine context of Diodoros's excerptors.
25 Cf. Ken Dowden's commentary on *BNJ* 87 F 108 f. For Diodoran reworkings of the revolt narrative as a whole see Morton 2018, Wozniczka 2018; Sacks 1994 discusses Diodoros's treatment of his sources in general.
26 Thuc. 1.11 (land), Dion. Hal. *Ant. Rom.* 36.37.4–5 (sea). Appian's account of Carthaginian plundering after the First Punic War (*Pun.* 5.21) also invokes this idea.

differs from it in meaningful ways. It limits the kind of resource at issue, just land, and extends the events that may be explained: not just economic crime, but also (*apo*)*stasis*, rebellion, and civic unrest. In fact, in the *Iberikē* Appian has Sulpicius Galba enact this extension at a narrative and syntactic level: *aporia* led the Lusitanians 'to become brigands, make war, and break treaties'.[27]

A similar tension between affinity and divergence may be observed as regards the relationship between 'aporetic unrest' and another well-established idea in the Graeco-Roman world: the suggestion that people had been forced to become unrestful. This idea is best attested in direct speech in historiographical narrative. The Athenians' appeal to 'necessary nature' (*physis anankaia*) to justify their highhanded treatment of the Melians in the fifth book of Thucydides' *Peloponnesian War* might be the best known and most unconventional illustration of this idea.[28] For a more typical example we may turn to the *Roman Antiquities* of Dionysios of Halikarnassos and Coriolanus's invective against the plebeians contained therein. When imagining what people might say in defence of the plebeians and their secession, Coriolanus invokes notions of necessity and force; in so doing, he uses not only the widespread *anankē* (necessity) but also *aporia* (impasse).[29] Given the close affinity between historiography and rhetoric, not least in relation to *inventio* and the fictive speeches of historical actors (Woodman 1988, Marincola 2007), it seems likely that talk of *aporia*, also in a more abstract, less material sense, was an established move in conciliatory political rhetoric.

Appian's invocation of this apologetic strategy not just in speeches but in his own narrative reminds us that the *Romaika*, just like any historiographical work in the Graeco-Roman tradition, was a rhetorical enterprise connected to a distinct political goal (on the nature of which I will have more to say in the following section).[30] At the same time, we may note that Appian was not alone in considering this way of thinking not just an argument fitting for conciliatory oratory but also an instance of compelling social analysis. Aeneas Tacticus, the third-century BCE expert on military matters, rec-

---

27 *Hisp.* 59.249–50: καὶ ὑπεκρίνετο αὐτοῖς καὶ συνάχθεσθαι ὡς δι' ἀπορίαν λῃστεύουσί τε καὶ πολεμοῦσι καὶ παρεσπονδηκόσιν.
28 Thuc. 5.105. On *anankē* in Thucydides, especially as it relates to the famous passage at 1.23.6, see Ostwald 1988.
29 Dion. Hal. *Ant. Rom.* 7.22.1. Other, more conventional, examples include Dion. Hal. *Ant. Rom.* 36.37.4–5 and App. *Pun.* 50.215–52.228.
30 For Appian as rhetor and sophist see Goukowsky 2001b: lix.

ommended that during the siege of a city the civic leaders should take care that no man currently experiencing poverty, the pressure of some agreement or any other kind of difficulty (*allēn tina aporian*, Aen. Tact. 5.1-2) should be appointed gatekeeper; such men might readily join or themselves incite a revolt, he claimed. I have not been able to find an analogous appeal to *aporia* in the context of provincial unrest beyond Appian, and so again 'aporetic unrest' may have widened the explananda of an established figure of thought – now from the civic to the imperial. At the same time, 'aporetic unrest', in its striking focus on land, also reshaped the nature of the explanation.

What about land, then? Land occupied a powerful role in the social imaginary of Graeco-Roman writers. At the broadest level we may regard this as a form of class bias. The authors of Graeco-Roman literature were all members of a socioeconomic elite whose status depended on landed property. Unsurprisingly, then, for this elite lack of land was a cause for concern (both for themselves and as it pertained to others) and thus could be imagined as a powerful social force. Graeco-Roman migration narratives and their regular invocation of the insufficiency of land as prime motivator are a good illustration of this dynamic.[31] As for unrest, the best example I have been able to find comes from Strabo.

This late first-century BCE author suggests that the sterility of land, the fact that people lack all resources except for strongholds (*aporia tōn allōn, erymatōn d'euporia*), made people keen to revolt, which explains why the emperor and the ample military resources at his disposal had to control such regions.[32] As should be clear, this is not 'aporetic unrest' as we find it in Appian. Strabo's ultimate interest lies in geographic and environmental matters. At the same time, the passage in question also shows a distinct parallel with 'aporetic unrest' in that it posits a material background for a form of unrest that it describes as political (*aphēniazein, apeithein*). The means by which the two authors accomplish that transition from economics to politics are different, though. If Strabo leverages the environment – the ready supply of strongholds and lack of all other resources – Appian arguably draws on the philosophical sense of *aporia* and the conventions of conciliatory political rhetoric. *Aporia gēs* was an *aporia* after all, and as such, it could also motivate unrest.

---

31 E.g. Pl. *Leg.* 4.707e, 5.740, Livy 39.54.1-10.
32 Strabo 17.3.25: αὕτη δ' ἐστὶν ἡ βάρβαρος καὶ πλησιόχωρος τοῖς μήπω κεχειρωμένοις ἔθνεσιν ἢ λυπρὰ καὶ δυσγεώργητος, ὥσθ' ὑπὸ ἀπορίας τῶν ἄλλων ἐρυμάτων δ' εὐπορίας ἀφηνιάζειν καὶ ἀπειθεῖν.

The picture of repeated affinity and divergence between 'aporetic unrest' and other, often wide-spread patterns of thought and argument in the Graeco-Roman world helps to further nuance our understanding of 'aporetic unrest' in Appian. On one level, it increases the likelihood that 'aporetic unrest' was indeed Appian's creation – a problem, of course, in which certainty is out of the question. At the same time, it also helps us understand how Appian (and possibly others) could have hoped that what might have been a novel idea in certain respects would also persuade: because it evoked and combined several figures of thought that were widely shared among the empire's socioeconomic elite. What remains to be understood, then, is why Appian wanted 'aporetic unrest' to be persuasive. Why did he articulate this highly unusual account of unrest? Why was he so invested in the idea that unrest might result from *aporia* (*gēs*)? To explore these questions, I now situate his person and his work in the changing imperial politics of the second century CE.

Aporetic Unrest, Appian, and Hadrian

Upon his accession in 117 BCE Hadrian scaled back the empire's extent. Trajan's initial success beyond the Danube and the Euphrates turned out to be precarious at best, and since 115 BCE the Jewish Diaspora Revolt had spread insecurity and unrest throughout the Eastern Mediterranean. In this context the new emperor chose to focus on the people and places that were already subject to Roman rule rather than on those that might become subject to that rule. In so doing, Hadrian seems to have recovered Augustus as a model – Augustus the administrator, the man of the *breviarium totius imperii*, in which he summarized the conditions of the empire at the end of his life and recommended that the empire be kept within its current bounds; his successors should steward the resources that were there rather than seek to add new ones.[33]

As Josiah Osgood (2015) has argued, Appian's *Romaika* displays the same conservative imperial mindset.[34] Appian's original plan for the *Romaika* included a final book that would set out the size of the army, the revenues

---

33 Suet. *Aug.* 101.4, Tac. *Ann.* 1.9.5, Osgood 2015: 28–33.
34 Goukowsky 2001a: 176–79 also locates Appian's project in a Hadrianic context.

from each people over whom the Romans ruled, expenses on the navy and similar matters.[35] The affinity with Augustus's *breviarium* are obvious. At a more profound level, the rather unusual structure of the *Romaika* – its unique arrangement of books *kat'ethnos*, according to peoples that Rome had conquered – might also have had its origins in Hadrian's imperial politics. Arguably, this structure constituted the historiographic realization of 'empire-as-collection' that Augustus's *breviarium* embodied and Hadrian demonstrably revived.[36]

A second layer of affinities between Hadrian's empire and Appian's *Romaika* can be added. While inspired by Augustus's mandate to survey and look after the empire's existing resources, Hadrian also articulated an innovative vision of the empire that broke with centuries-long tradition. Augustus had claimed to be the *restitutor rei publicae*, Trajan the restorer of *Italia*; Hadrian, by contrast, extended his imperial care-work to the entire world: he was the *restitutor orbis terrarum* (Seelentag 2011: 306–11). In a series of coins he showed himself extending a hand to raise up personifications of various parts of the empire, including provinces, cities, and Italy (Zahrnt 2007). The inclusion of *Italia* en par with the provinces is striking and seems to have gone against a long tradition of thought and action that assimilated the Italian peninsula to Rome and the imperial center (Cooley 2016, Carlà-Uhink 2017, 164–74). Arguably, Hadrian had also taken steps towards governing Italy like a province when he appointed four *legati Augusti pro praetore* to oversee its different regions (Eck [1991] 1995). The fact that Antoninus Pius no longer featured *Italia* in the same coin series as the provinces and also abolished the *legati Augusti pro praetore* adds further weight to the idea that these were iconographic and institutional expressions of an innovative and rather controversial idea.[37]

In his *Romaika* Appian also presented the peoples of Italy on a par with those living in the provinces. Just as the Greeks and the Thracians were subject (*hupekoos*) to Rome, so were the Italians (*Praef.* 3.10). Just like there was an

---

35 *Praef.* 15.61: ἡ δὲ τελευταία καὶ τὴν στρατιὰν αὐτῶν, ὅσην ἔχουσιν, ἢ πρόσοδον, ἣν καρποῦνται καθ' ἕκαστον ἔθνος, ἢ εἴ τι προσαναλίσκουσιν εἰς τὰς ἐπινείους φρουρὰς ὅσα τε τοιουτότροπα ἄλλα ἐπιδείξει.

36 On the structure more generally see Brodersen 1990; Bucher 2000: 454 discusses the oddity of the structure within the Graeco-Roman historiographical tradition.

37 Eck [1991] 1995: 325 n. 45 and Seelentag 2011: 312–13 discuss the changes introduced by Antoninus Pius.

Iberikē and a *Libykē*, there was an *Italikē*.[38] The Samnites, just like other great foes of Rome, received a separate book. Arguably, 'aporetic unrest' itself can also be seen as intimately connected with the visions of the empire that we see on Hadrian's coins. On several levels this figure of thought provided the empire with the kind of history that fit and justified the emperor's claims to restore not just the *res publica* or *Italia* but the entire *orbis terrarum*, including those people who had fought against Roman rule – at times repeatedly, in conflicts recurring across decades and centuries.

'Aporetic unrest' as explanatory model suggests that unrest, not least when it took the form of military opposition to Roman rule, was nothing to worry about. Such unrest was bound to happen because, well, *aporia* was a powerful motivator of human action. At the same time, *aporia* also led people to do the unexpected: powerful generals surrendering, mighty cities caving, Appian trusting Arab mantic skills. When unrest did happen, then, it was an aberration from the norm and not the expression of an underlying pathology. Above all else, it did not constitute an expression of opposition to Roman rule – something that might chronically weaken or threaten the empire, something that had to be met with exceeding force. 'Aporetic unrest' negated politics, not to delegitimize, but to de-escalate.

Within the context of the *Romaika* 'aporetic unrest' also soothed anxiety at another level. For Appian the hallmark of the Roman empire was its *euporia* (*Praef.* 10.41, *Hann.* 132.628, *B Civ.* 1.1.11). Any behaviour that had its origins in *aporia* could only lose out against Rome's richness in resources. For Appian the only thing that could topple empires was civil war – because it destroyed their resources (*Praef.* 10.42). Here we can begin to understand why 'aporetic unrest' made no appearance in how Appian narrated late republican history in the five books of his Civil Wars. This was the one instance of unrest that could potentially threaten the empire; consequently, the quietist model of 'aporetic unrest' had no place in explaining it.

'Aporetic unrest' also constituted an apologetic account of unrest. At first glance the model elided the question of blame and responsibility altogether. By means of the short-cut 'through *aporia*', it papered over the thorny problem of how this *aporia* had come about. The model's focus seems to have lain on enjoining on Roman commanders a distinct course of action: rather than punishing unrestful people, they should give them land. Not only was this the logically correct thing to do to prevent future recurrences of unrest. From a

---

38 For the title *Italikē* see *Ital.* frgm. 5.

moral perspective it was also the only course open to such commanders; for how could they justify punitive action against people that had been forced into rebellion? In the *Romaika* Appian also makes explicit arguments against the harsh punishment of defeated enemies. In the aftermath of the battle of Zama in 202 BCE Appian has Hasdrubal spell out the lessons that he himself sought to convey in his account of Sulpicius Galba and the massacre of the Lusitanians that I discussed above. In his effort to convince Scipio Africanus to refrain from destroying Carthage Hasdrubal suggested that Carthage had in fact been forced to enter the war, and that the *aporia* that could result from harsh punishment may push Carthaginians to commit new transgressions, to be unrestful again (*Pun.* 50.215–52.228; for *aporia* see 52.226). *Aporia* here might well imply the lack of land that would result from a destruction of the city.

Hasdrubal's speech – especially the passage concerning *aporia* – is replete with well-known keywords in Appian's historiographical thought: *euboulia*, *eutychia*, and *atychia*.[39] Quite likely, an inextricable connection between *aporia* and unrest should also be counted among the key aspects of his thought. As I have tried to show, this aspect was also intertwined with the imperial politics of the first half of the second century CE. By enjoining the lenient treatment of unrestful peoples, by making land-distributions to them the only strategically and ethically correct response to their behaviour, by recommending what Hadrian might have called *restitutio* as the only possible course of action, 'aporetic unrest' as explanatory model made Hadrian's view of the empire inescapable – a necessary consequence of any correct assessment of Rome's past conquests.

Of course, Appian knew that Roman commanders had not always followed the course of action that 'aporetic unrest' enjoined. As István Hahn noted long ago, Appian thought that the self-restraint that had once been part of Roman nature (*physis*) had become a matter of personal choice and excellence by the second century BCE (Hahn and Nemeth 1993: 383–95). Appian's account of the destruction of Carthage is telling. The narrative is filled with pathos and horror; the account of the whole war a tragic narrative, very different from the dry accounts of Polybios and Diodoros: even his Roman commanders consider the plan to destroy the city monstrous.[40] Appian's

---

39 Cf. App. *Praef.* 7, 11–12, Goldman 1988: 6–17, 24–49.
40 *Pun.* 81.381, 128.610–130.620 with Goukowsky 2001c: xix–xxiii.

description of how Scipio Aemilianus, the destroyer of Carthage, wreaked havoc on Numantia and its inhabitants is similarly revealing – not least because at the end of the passage Appian explicitly connected the destruction of the two cities (*Hisp.* 97.422–23, 98.424–27). After describing in great detail the dehumanizing effects of Scipio's siege on the Numantians, including the abandonment of personal hygiene, cannibalism, and suicide, he also lists various possible explanations for Scipio's behaviour: Was the destroyer of Carthage and Numantia vengeful? A pragmatist, considering such actions useful to Rome? Or committed to gaining great glory by great atrocity? Appian knew that people in history and in his own day could rationalize the horrifying actions that the destruction of Carthage and Numantia entailed. In his presentation, however, he distanced himself from them – also at a narrative level, when he refrained from committing to a particular version of Scipio's motivations.

It is tempting to imagine what Appian made of the Jewish Diaspora Revolt that temporarily uprooted his own life in Alexandria – of its origins, Hadrian's response, and its connection to the Bar Kochba uprising that occurred less than fifteen years later. In a fragment of the *Syriakē* we learn that Appian could see Jerusalem's history as a series of repeated destructions at the hands of Roman commanders: first Pompey, then Vespasian and now, in his own time, Hadrian – these Roman commanders had all destroyed what for the Jews was 'the holiest city' (*Syr.* 50.252–53). Appian could also describe Trajan as trying to 'exterminate' (*exollusthai*) the Jewish *genos* (*B Civ.* 2.90.380). There is, then, at least the possibility that he saw Jewish unrest in his own day as confirmation of the inextricable link between unrest and *aporia*, but not without an added twist that spelt out the implications of 'aporetic unrest' for questions of responsibility and blame. By not following the injunctions of 'aporetic unrest', by themselves causing *aporia*, Roman commanders themselves risked becoming the cause of further unrest – yet another illustration of the dynamic that Appian highlighted with Sulpicius Galba and the Lusitanians in the *Iberikē*.

While committed to a vision of the empire that we can best trace through some of Hadrian's actions, Appian most likely composed the *Romaika* under Antoninus Pius, Hadrian's successor.[41] As mentioned above, Antoninus seems to have undone some of the Hadrianic efforts to level the difference between *Italia* and the provinces. On his coins Antoninus showed people be-

---

41 See n. 22 above.

yond Italy paying taxes, an act that contemporaries could interpret as a sign of subjection and enslavement (Eberle 2021: 77–87). And while his famous *nationes* relief in Rome did not depict Rome's subject as defeated enemies, hints of the triumphs celebrated over them pervade the monument.[42] It remains impossible to know if Appian himself thought that he was living through changing times, if he saw himself as advocating for a view of the empire that was under siege. If my speculation about his take on the various Jewish revolts is anything to go by, it seems at least likely that he did not subscribe to an idealized view of the Hadrianic empire that was now coming undone. He probably understood that symbolic claims and lived reality were two rather different things.

Furthermore, we may note that Appian's commitment to 'aporetic unrest' and the vision of the empire and imperial rule with which it was connected might not have been a matter of intellectual choice alone; for the Alexandrian-born author, who described himself as *Aigyptios* in the preface to his work, this commitment might also have been bound up with the personal, with his own presentation of himself and his identity.[43] Some of his contemporaries might have considered 'the Egyptians' a defeated people, one of the many *ethnē* over which Roman commanders had triumphed. Appian, however, may well have seen them as one of the many equipollent parts of a world empire, all equally worthy of imperial care-work and attention. As a result, a member of the imperial elite, possibly a priest of Venus and Rome and *advocatus fisci*, insisted not on his *Romanitas* but proudly advertised his Egyptian identity instead. This interplay of the personal, the political, and the historiographical is striking indeed. Maybe this interplay also explains why I have not been able to find echoes of 'aporetic unrest' in works postdating the *Romaika*.

Just like the account of the agrarian background to the Gracchan crisis in the first book of the Civil Wars, 'aporetic unrest' can claim a certain measure of uniqueness within the preserved parts of the ancient intellectual landscape. However, the materialisms that these two aspects of Appian's work embody would appear to be quite different. If the former dwelt on the economic and demographic background to a specific instance of unrest, the latter uses two words – *aporia* (*gēs*) – to both insist on the material

---

42 Osgood 2015: 35–39, who places the emphasis on continuity, not rupture with Hadrianic thought and practice.
43 Brodersen 1993: 354 discusses Appian's investment in Egypt in relation to the structure of his work.

background to potentially any form of unrest while also obfuscating its details. Quite likely, this was not the kind of materialism that Marx would have appreciated. That being said, 'aporetic unrest' does share a certain universalizing quality with the social sciences as we know them today: *aporia* (*gēs*) was an undiscriminating force that might cause anyone to be unrestful; before *aporia* (*gēs*) all people were created equal. It should not come as a surprise, then, that for Appian this figure of thought provided the basis for imagining an empire in which people beyond the emperor did not have to become equal (i.e. Roman) but were simply considered to be equal (and not Roman). Somewhere between utopia and a path not taken, 'aporetic unrest' should thus also inspire some enthusiasm as a precious window into the multiplicity of empires (and the histories that they required) that may have existed at any one point in Roman history.

Acknowledgments

I thank the participants at the conference in which this paper originated for their encouraging feedback. Felix Maier provided helpful comments on the very first draft of these arguments in 2019. In the summer of 2023 the participants in the Ancient History Oberseminar at Tübingen helped me see what was important about them in the last phase of revisions. All remaining mistakes remain my own.

Works cited

Baray, Luc. 2015. 'Le 'brigand lusitanien' reconsidéré. Analyse du problème de la terre chez Appien'. *Gerion* 33: 229–60.
Bonnell, Andrew G. 2015. 'A "very valuable book": Karl Marx and Appian', in Kathryn Welch, ed., *Appian's Roman History. Empire and Civil War*. Swansea, 15–22.
Brodersen, Kai. 1990. 'Die Buchtitelverzeichnisse, das Lexikon Περὶ Συντάξεως und der Aufbau von Appians Werk'. *Wiener Studien* 103: 49–55.
–. 1993. 'Appian und sein Werk'. *Aufstieg und Niedergang der römischen Welt* II 34(1): 339–63.
–. 2015. '*Epitaphios*: Appianos and his treasured Eutychia', in Kathryn Welch, ed., *Appian's Roman History. Empire and Civil War*. Swansea, 341–50.

Bucher, Gregory S. 2000. 'The origins, program, and composition of Appian's Roman History'. *Transactions of the American Philological Association* 130: 411–58.

–. 2005. 'Fictive elements in Appian's Pharsalus narrative'. *Phoenix* 59: 50–76.

–. 2007. 'Toward a literary evaluation of Appian's Civil Wars, Book 1', in John Marincola, ed., *The Blackwell Companion to Greek and Roman Historiography*. Oxford, 454–60.

Capelle, Wilhelm. 1932. 'Griechische Ethik und römischer Imperialismus'. *Klio* 8: 86–113.

Carlà-Uhink, Filippo. 2017. *The 'Birth' of Italy: The Institutionalisation of Italy as a Region, 3rd-1st Century BCE*. Berlin.

Cooley, Alison. 2016. 'Coming to terms with dynastic power, 30 BC–AD 69', in Alison Cooley, ed., *A Companion to Roman Italy*. Chichester, 103–12.

Cuff, P. J. 1983. 'Appian's Romaika: a note'. *Athenaeum* 61: 148–64.

Eck, Werner. [1991] 1995. 'Die italienischen *legati Augusti pro praetore* unter Hadrian und Antoninus Pius', in Werner Eck, ed., *Die Verwaltung des römischen Reiches in der hohen Kaiserzeit*. Vol. 1. Basel, 315–26.

Eberle, Lisa Pilar. 2021. 'Fiscal semantics in the long second century: citizenship, taxation and the *constitutio Antoniniana*', in Clifford Ando and Myles Lavan, eds., *Roman Citizenship in the Long Second Century*. Oxford, 69–99.

Famerie, Etienne. 1990. 'Appien, ses traducteurs francais et Marx'. *Acta Classica Universitatis Scientiarum Debreceniensis* 26: 91–99.

Gabba, Emilio. 1956. *Appiano e la storia delle Guerre Civili*. Florence.

–. 1958. *Appiani Bellorum civilium liber primus*. Florence.

García Quintela, Marco V. 1991. 'Sources pour l'étude de la protohistoire d'Hispanie. Pour une nouvelle lecture'. *Dialogues d'histoire ancienne* 17(1): 61–99.

Goldmann, Bernhard. 1988. *Einheitlichkeit und Eigenständigkeit der Historia Romana des Appian*. Hildesheim.

Gómez Espelosín, Francisco Javier. 1993. 'Appian's Iberiké'. *Aufstieg und Niedergang der römischen Welt* II 34(1): 403–27.

Goukowsky, Paul. 1998. 'Appien d'Alexandrie, prêtre de Rome sous Hadrien?'. *Comptes rendus de l'Académie des Inscriptions et Belles-Lettres* 142(3): 835–56.

–. 2001a. 'Un "compilateur" témoin de son temps: Appien d'Alexandrie et la révolte juive de 117 ap. J.-C.'. *Publications de l'Académie des Inscriptions et Belles-Lettres* 11(1): 167–203.

–. 2001b. *Histoire Romaine / Appien*. Vol. 7, *La guerre de Mithridate*. Paris.

–. 2001c. *Histoire Romaine / Appien*. Vol. 8, *Le livre africain*. Paris.

–. 2008. *Histoire Romaine / Appien*. Vol 13, *Guerres civiles. Livre I*. Paris.

–. 2020. *Histoire Romaine / Appien*. Vol. 1, *Préface et fragments des livres I-V*. Paris.

–. 2021. *D'Alexandrie à Rome. L'itinéraire de l'historien Appien*. Paris.

Gowing, Alain M. 1992. *The Triumviral Narratives of Appian and Cassius Dio*. Ann Arbor.

Hahn, István. 1982. 'Appian und seine Quellen', in Gerhard Wirth, ed., *Romanitas – Christianitas*. Berlin, 251–76.

Hahn, István and György Németh. 1993. 'Appian und Rom'. *Aufstieg und Niedergang der römischen Welt* II 34(1): 364–402.

Hose, Martin. 1994. *Erneuerung der Vergangenheit. Die Historiker im Imperium Romanum von Florus bis Cassius Dio*. Stuttgart.

Karamanolis, Giorgos and Basileios Politis. 2018. *The Aporetic Tradition in Ancient Philosophy*. Cambridge.

Kühne, Heinz-Jürgen. 1969. 'Appians historiographische Leistung'. *Wissenschaftliche Zeitschrift der Universität Rostock* 18: 345–77.

Lavan, Myles. 2017. 'Writing revolt in the early Roman empire', in Justine Firnhaber-Baker and Dirk Schoenaers, eds., *The Routledge History Handbook of Medieval Revolt*. London, 19–38.

Marincola, John. 2007. 'Speeches in Classical Historiography', in John Marincola, ed., *A Companion to Greek and Roman Historiography*. Malden, MA, 101–15.

McGing, Brian. 1993. 'Appian's Mithridateios'. *Aufstieg und Niedergang der römischen Welt* II 34(1): 496–522.

–. 2019. *Appian. Roman History*. Vol. 3. Cambridge, MA.

Morton, Peter. 2018. 'Diodorus Siculus' "slave war narratives: writing social commentary in the Bibliothēkē'. *The Classical Quarterly* 68(2): 534–51.

Osgood, Josiah. 2015. 'Breviarium totius imperii: the background of Appian's *Roman History*', in Kathryn Welch, ed., *Appian's Roman History. Empire and Civil War*. Swansea, 23–44.

Ostwald, Martin. 1988. *Anankē in Thucydides*. Atlanta.

Pfuntner, Laura. 2014. 'Reading Diodorus through Photius: The case of the Sicilian slave revolts'. *Greek, Roman, and Byzantine Studies* 55(1): 256–72.

Pitcher, Luke. 2016. 'Future's bright? Looking forward in Appian', in Alexandra Lianeri, ed., *Knowing Future Time in and through Greek Historiography*. Boston, 281–92.

Sacks, Kenneth. 1994. 'Diodorus and his sources: conformity and creativity', in Simon Hornblower, ed., *Greek Historiography*. Oxford, 213–32.

Seelentag, Gunnar. 2011. 'Die Herrschaftszeit der Kaiser Trajan, Hadrian und Antoninus Pius. Deutungsmuster und Perspektiven', in Aloys Winterling, ed., *Zwischen Strukturgeschichte und Biographie. Probleme und Perspektiven einer Römischen Kaisergeschichte der Zeit von Augustus bis Commodus*. Munich, 295–315.

Strasburger, Hermann. 1982. 'Poseidonios über die Römerherrschaft', in Walter Schmitthenner und Renate Zoepffel, eds., *Hermann Strasburger: Studien zur Alten Geschichte*. Hildesheim, 920–45.

Richardson, John. 2000. *Appian. Wars of the Romans in Iberia*. Warminster.

Veh, Otto. 1987–89. *Römische Geschichte. Appian von Alexandria*. Stuttgart.

Welch, Kathryn. ed. 2015. *Appian's Roman History. Empire and Civil War*. Swansea.

–. 2019. 'Appian and civil war: a history without an ending', in Carsten Hjort Lange and Frederik Juliaan Vervaet, eds., *The Historiography of Late Republican Civil War*. Leiden, 439–66.

Woodman, Anthony J. 1988. *Rhetoric in Classical Historiography*. London.

Woolf, Greg. 2011. 'Provincial revolts in the early Roman empire', in Mladen Popović, ed., *The Jewish Revolt against Rome: Interdisciplinary perspectives*. Leiden, 27–44.

Wozniczka, Piotr. 2018. 'Diodoros' narrative of the first Sicilian slave revolt (ca. 140/35–132 BC). A reflection of Poseidonios' ideas and style?', in Lisa Irene Hau, Alexander Meeus and Brian Sheridan, eds., *Diodoros of Sicily: Historiographical Theory and Practice in the Bibliotheke*. Leuven, 221–46.

Zahrnt, Michael. 2007. 'Hadrians "Provinzmünzen', in Rudolf Haensch and Johannes Heinrichs, eds., *Herrschen und Verwalten. Der Alltag der römischen Administration in der hohen Kaiserzeit.* Wien, 195–212.

8. From War to Criminality: The Roman Discourse of Provincial Revolt

Myles Lavan

Abstract: *This chapter sketches a history of how the Roman elite conceptualised provincial revolt from the later republic to the early third century CE. It illustrates the persistence of an 'externalising' perspective that conceives of unrest as occurring outside the political community. This perspective was associated with a republican conception of empire that drew a sharp distinction between the Roman people and foreign peoples they ruled. The chapter begins with what might seem evidence to the contrary: two famous juristic definitions that limit the term 'enemy' to foreign peoples with whom the Roman state is at war, labelling all other armed groups 'bandits'. These definitions have led many scholars to conclude that the Roman elite delegitimised provincial revolt by classifying it as criminality not war. I argue that this is to misunderstand the original function of these definitions, the concerns of the jurists who formulated them and the cultural authority of their theorisations. The rest of the chapter highlights the persistence of an externalising perspective that equates unrest with war through the works of Cicero, Tacitus and Cassius Dio, among others. Only in the later second century do we begin to see the more systematic construction of unrest as criminality. I argue that this change was associated with developments in the field of jurisprudence: both the extension of its scope to criminal and administrative law and the growing influence of jurists in imperial administration.*

'Enemies' (*hostes*) are those who have publicly declared war on us or on whom we have publicly declared war; others are 'bandits' (*latrones*) or 'brigands' (*praedones*). (Sextus Pomponius 2 *ad Muc.* apud *Dig.* 50.16.118)

'Enemies' (*hostes*) are those on whom the Roman people has publicly declared war, or who themselves have declared war on the Roman people; others are termed 'bandits'(*latrunculi*) or 'brigands' (*praedones*). (Ulpian 1 *Inst.* apud *Dig.* 49.15.24)

The first text above, attributed to the Antonine jurist Sextus Pomponius, appears in a section of Justinian's *Digest* devoted to 'the meaning of terms', where it provides the authoritative definition for the term 'enemy'. Pomponius' definition was repeated almost verbatim by the great Severan jurist Ulpian in a passage quoted elsewhere in the *Digest*. These juristic pronouncements might seem to be doing ideological work familiar to modern readers. The restrictive definitions of 'enemy' appear to anticipate the practices of modern states that seek to delegitimise violent collective action by subordinated populations by representing it as forms of criminality, often 'terrorism'. The definitions of Pomponius and Ulpian have often been taken to prove that the Roman state elite used the category of banditry to similar effect, delegitimising armed resistance by subject populations as a form of criminality (e.g. Riess 2001: 14, 50–1, Grünewald 2004: 16–17, 40).

The first goal of this paper is to argue that this conventional view risks misrepresenting metropolitan Roman discourse about unrest in the provinces in the late republic and early empire. It rests on a misunderstanding of the context in which the quoted definitions were originally formulated and of the position of jurisprudence in elite culture. It also has the effect of obscuring the fact that most elite texts of the late republic and early empire in fact assimilate provincial revolts to the domain of warfare, not that of criminality.

The second goal is to suggest that this tendency to assimilate provincial revolts to warfare rather than banditry or criminality gives expression to a particular conception of empire that we might term 'republican empire'. This conception imposes a fundamental, binary divide on the population of the empire; the divide is usually articulated in terms of Roman citizenship, distinguishing 'citizens' (*cives*) from 'allies' (*socii*). This binary is reproduced in the sphere of unrest. The citizen population is the domain of criminous *seditio* or civil war, while large-scale unrest in the subject population is something different: revolt (*defectio*), rebellion (*rebellio*), or simply war (*bellum*).[1] Indeed, one of the most striking features of this conception of empire is that it sees a sharper boundary between citizens and subjects than between subjects and non-subjects – to the extent that the latter two groups are often conflated into an undifferentiated category of foreign peoples (*nationes exterae* etc) and the domain of war.

Finally, I will argue that it is this tendency to 'externalise' provincial revolt, rather than any delegitimisation of provincial revolts as banditry, that is the most salient ideological operation in the Roman discourse of unrest of this

---

1 On *seditio* by citizens and soldiers, see Kopp in this volume. All translations are my own, unless stated otherwise.

period. The homogeneity of the Roman citizen population was of course a construct. So too was the alterity of Rome's non-citizen subjects. We should understand the many Roman narratives of whole peoples rising organically in resistance to Rome as the expression of a particular conception of empire, rather than reading them straight as a description of events. In the few cases where we have more granular evidence for the unfolding of provincial revolts, we find more selective participation and more complex lines of alliance, often reaching across the putatively decisive citizen-alien divide.[2]

Like other papers in this volume, this paper seeks to illustrate what can be gained by focusing on revolt narratives as narratives, rather than on the events they purport to describe. Whatever these narratives may or may not tell us about unrest in the provinces of the Roman empire, they reveal a lot about how the imperial elite conceived of the empire as a state and political community.

Pomponius and Ulpian on non-state violence

Three misconceptions have elevated the definitions of *hostes* quoted above to a status they do not deserve. The first concerns their original context and function. The doctrine represented by Pomponius and Ulpian, which may well be considerably older than Pomponius, was not developed in the context of criminal or public law, as one might at first suppose. It emerged rather in the context of private law and served to address problematic uncertainties in the sphere of status and property.

Pomponius' definition was stripped of its context when it was excerpted in the Digest, but it is attributed to Book 2 of his 39-book commentary on Q. Mucius Scaevola. We know that the subject of Book 2 was wills (Lenel 1889: ii 60). The less than obvious connection between a definition of 'enemies' and the law of inheritance lies in the effect of captivity on personal status and

---

2 Provincial revolts often involved Roman citizens of local descent: Arminius in the German revolt of 9 CE (Vell. Pat. 2.118.2), Iulius Florus and Iulius Sacrovir in the Gallic revolt of 21 CE (Tac. *Ann.* 4.40.1), Iulius Civilis, Iulius Classicus, Iulius Tutor and Iulius Sabinus in the Batavian revolt of 69–70 CE (Tac. *Hist.* 4.13–14, 4.55). Narrative accounts occasionally hint at the complicity of Roman administrators or other colonial elements, including the suggestion that Roman governors were complicit in the Gallic revolt of 21 CE (Tac. *Ann.* 4.18.1, 4.28.2). See further Lavan 2017: 29.

hence family relations and property. By the Roman construction of the *ius gentium*, a person who was captured in war became a slave. This applied to Roman citizens as much as to foreign peoples. But the legal effects of the capture and enslavement of a Roman citizen were complex, because the status of the captive was considered to be in suspense until it was eventually determined by the event of death in captivity (in which case most matters were regulated as if the captive had died at the moment of capture) or return to the Roman state (in which case the captive could recover his former status and most of his former rights by the right of *postliminium*). This gave rise to a complex body of law and jurisprudence on the effects of *captivitas* and *postliminium* on family relations, property and inheritance.[3] This must have been the larger context for Pomponius' definition. The question it addressed was what kinds of capture would be recognised as effecting enslavement and hence triggering the ramifying effects of *captivitas*.

The connection with enslavement is even clearer in the case of Ulpian's definition. Unlike that of Pomponius, Ulpian's is quoted as part of a longer passage. The much-excerpted definition continues: 'Therefore, a person who is captured by bandits (*latrones*) is not the bandits' slave; ... after capture by the enemy, however as, say, by the Germans and the Parthians, he is the slave of the enemy.'[4] The context appears to have been a discussion of enslavement by capture as an institution of the *ius gentium* (Lenel 1889: ii 927).

By restricting the definition of *hostes* to polities with which a formal state of war existed, the jurists ensured that capture by any other armed group, whether internal or external, would not affect the captive's legal status in Roman law and hence their rights over persons or property. Anna Tarwacka has shown that that this doctrine can be traced back to the time of Plautus, at least for the case of capture by pirates (2022: 43–46). It bears noting that the first legal theorisation of war was motivated by Roman society's need to circumscribe the consequences of its commitment to the legitimacy of the use of violence to make free persons chattel. In any case, it should be clear that the juristic distinction between *hostes* and *latrones* was originally developed

---

[3] On *captivitas* and *postliminium* ('perhaps the subtlest part of Roman legal science', Watson 1993: 1361), see Buckland 1908: 291–317.

[4] *Dig.* 49.15.24. Ulpianus 1 *inst.*: *et ideo qui a latronibus captus est, servus latronum non est, nec postliminium illi necessarium est: ab hostibus autem captus, ut puta a Germanis et Parthis, et servus est hostium et postliminio statum pristinum recuperat.*

to manage complications affecting the transmission of property and status, not to regulate how the Roman state dealt with collective violence.

The second misconception concerns the scope of jurisprudence as a discipline. The relatively narrow, private-law concern that motivated these two definitions is entirely in keeping with the trajectory of jurisprudence. For most of the classical period – from Scaevola through to the reign of Hadrian – the work of the jurists focused almost exclusively on private law. Discussion of what Ulpian calls 'public law', including what we would term criminal and administrative law, was an innovation of the Antonine period. This can be seen in the sudden proliferation of treatises on the public (i.e. criminal) courts, on penalties and on the duties of magistrates (Sirks 2015: 349–50). When a series of jurists began writing about the duties of a governor (*De officio proconsulis*) – Venuleius Saturninus in the 160s, Paul, Ulpian and Aemilius Macer in the 210s – and others wrote treatises *De iudiciis publicis* (Marcianus, Macer, Paul), *De poenis* (Venuleius Saturninus, Modestinus and Paul) and *De cognitionibus* (Callistratus), they were colonising new territory for the science of the law.[5] Pomponius was writing at the beginning of this period of expanding horizons, but he was not one of the pioneers. His attested works focus exclusively on the traditional domain of private law (Mommsen and Kruger 1963: 943–5).

The third misconception concerns the cultural status and influence of the jurists, particularly in the early imperial period. It is fairly obvious that genres such as poetry or historiography represent relatively autonomous cultural practices that stood at some distance from the everyday practice of government – even when they were composed by men who commanded armies and governed provinces. The writings of the jurists may seem much more closely enmeshed in government. Yet they too should be seen as the product of a cultural practice with a degree of autonomy. Jurisprudence of the early and high classical period was – not unlike historiography – a project pursued alongside the rigours of a political career by a few leading senators and equestrians. The writing of treatises on the law was somewhat removed from the everyday practice of law in the courts, where litigants were usually represented by advocates who were trained in rhetoric, not legal science (men like Cicero, Pliny and Tacitus); magistrates and judges might come from either group – or neither (Crook 1995: 40–1, 68). It was only in the late second century, when imperial patronage began to favour trained jurists for the

---

5 See dell'Oro 1960 on the genre *De officio proconsulis*.

equestrian cursus, that we might expect the jurists' theorisations to permeate public discourse more broadly. In short, to take the definitions of *hostes* as a statement of how the Roman state elite categorised collective violence in the late republic and early empire would be to misunderstand the original function of these definitions, the concerns of the jurists who formulated them and the cultural authority of their theorisations. As I will show, numerous other texts show that members of the imperial elite routinely framed provincial revolts in terms of warfare rather than criminality, long into the imperial period.

Cicero

Cicero inherited a republican conception of empire that divided the world into Roman citizens (*cives*), allies (*socii*) and enemies (*hostes*), where 'allies' was a vague and capacious term for all Rome's non-citizen dependents, encompassing both conquered populations and loyal allies, both the provinces and nominally autonomous states.[6] This structuring of the world can be observed, for example, in the text transmitted to us as Cicero's first letter to his brother Quintus (*Qfr.* 1.1). Purporting to be a private letter advising Quintus on his governorship of the province of Asia, it was clearly intended for circulation and amounts to a treatise on the duties of a provincial governor. The letter describes Quintus as governing two fundamentally different kinds of subject, Roman citizens (*cives, provinciales viri* or *homines*, 'men in the provinces') and non-citizens (*socii* or *Graeci*), while the enemy (*hostes*) lurk vaguely in the background.[7]

This ternary scheme entailed a corresponding taxonomy of unrest. The Roman citizen body was the domain of *seditio* (sedition), encompassing both mutinies by citizens at war and disturbance or disobedience by citizens in the city, and civil war (*bellum civile*).[8] Revolts by subject populations constituted *defectio* ('defection' or 'desertion') or *rebellio* (literally, a renewal of war).[9] Conflict with foreign powers was *bellum* ('war'). Again, Cicero's letter to Quin-

---

6 See e.g. *Leg. Man.* 48, *Prov. cons.* 12 with Lavan 2013: 37–49.
7 Lavan 2013: 43–4, 55.
8 See, in this volume, Kopp on *seditio* and Lange on *bellum civile*.
9 See e.g. *Pis.* 84, *Qfr.* 1.5.

tus provides an illustration, when he remarks reassuringly on the absence of threats at the present: 'We do not, I think, have to fear any attack by the enemy (*insidias hostium*), ... any revolt by the allies (*defectionem sociorum*) ... or any sedition by the army (*seditionem exercitus*)'.[10]

A further characteristic of this republican view of the Roman order is that the most salient distinction is that between Roman citizens and everyone else. This can be seen from the fact that the citizen-ally-enemy triad coexists with a simpler dyad that divides the world into Roman citizens (or *nos* or *nostri*) and foreign peoples (*exterae nationes*), a binary schema that assimilates the non-citizen inhabitants of Rome's provinces to hostile powers beyond the frontiers.[11]

The three domains of unrest too are often collapsed to a simple dyad, contrasting conflict within the citizen body (*bellum civile* or *seditio*) with *bellum* with foreign peoples – regardless of whether or not they had been subject to Rome.[12] A good example is Cicero's description of unrest among the Allobroges, the largest Gallic people in the province of Transalpine Gaul. Catiline and his allies were accused of trying to incite the Allobroges to revolt in 63 BCE and there seems to have been an actual revolt two years later. Cicero refers to the prospective revolt of 63 BCE variously as *tumultus* (a vague term for an emergency) and *bellum* (*Cat.* 3.4, 3.22). The actual revolt of 61 he refers to as the 'war of the Allobroges' (*bellum Allobrogum, Prov. Cons.* 32).

The early empire

One might have expected some change in the conceptualisation of revolt over Augustus' long reign, given the regime's emphasis on *pax*.[13] Yet it is striking that there is not a single appearance of *latrocinium* or its cognates in Augus-

---

10 *Qfr.* 1.1.5; Cicero does, it bears noting, mention banditry later in the letter when he praises Quintus for his work in suppressing *latrocinia* (*Qfr.* 1.1.25) but this seems to denote a form of small-scale criminality distinct from the large-scale revolt envisaged earlier (*defectio sociorum*, ibid. 5).
11 See e.g. *Div Caec.* 18, *1Verr.* 2, *2Verr.* 5.127.
12 See e.g. *Leg. Agr.* 2.90
13 Gruen 1985 surveys the rhetoric of peace, while also stressing continuities with republican discourse.

tus' own *Res Gestae*, which instead foregrounds the language of war.[14] Particularly striking is the text's second sentence:

> *Bella terra et mari civilia externaque toto in orbe terrarum saepe gessi, victorque omnibus veniam petentibus civibus peperci. Externas gentes, quibus tuto ignosci potuit, conservare quam excidere malui.*
>
> I waged many wars, on land and sea, civil and foreign, across the whole world. Victorious, I granted pardon to all citizens who begged it. As for foreign peoples, those who could safely be forgiven I preferred to preserve rather than destroy. (*Res Gestae* 1.3)

The latter two sentences give expression to the familiar republican vision of a world divided into Roman citizen (*cives*) and foreign peoples (*externae gentes*), with the latter category conflating populations both within and outside Rome's provinces. The first sentence similarly recognises just two types of conflict, civil and foreign. The latter category implicitly encompasses the many revolts that were suppressed under his reign, such as those in Iberia and Pannonia.

It is certainly the case that justifications for wars of conquest written in the Augustan period sometimes resort to the trope of denigrating their victims as peoples irredeemably prone to 'banditry', implicitly justifying wars of aggression as necessary to safeguard peace and prosperity. Perhaps the best example is Strabo's account of the Alpine Salassi, a powerful and prosperous people who had rivalled Rome for control of traffic over the Alps and were conquered and enslaved in 25 BCE.[15] But this habit of labelling some rivals to Roman power as bandits is not the same as systematically delegitimising revolt as banditry.

The concept of *latrocinium* seems to have been particularly prominent in imperial ideology during the reign of Tiberius. It is striking that both Velleius Paterculus and Suetonius associate him with claims to have protected the world from banditry: 'The Augustan Peace preserves every corner of the world secure from the fear of banditry (*latrocinia*)' wrote Velleius, during his reign (2.126.3). Suetonius records that 'he gave special attention to protecting the peace from robbery and banditry (*latrocinia*) and the lawlessness of sedition (*seditionumque licentia*)' (Suet. *Tib.* 37.1). There is also Tacitus' famous anecdote that Tiberius was furious when the Numidian rebel Tacfarinas sought to make peace with Rome, denouncing him as a bandit (*desertor et praedo, latro*), not a *hostis*. (Tac. *Ann.* 3.73.2).

---

14 The closest to an exception is the reference to piracy: *mare pacaui a praedonibus* (1.25).
15 Strabo 4.6.7 with Clavel-Lévêque 1978 and Riess 2001: 14, 51.

These passages suggest that Tiberius placed particular emphasis on the threat posed by banditry and his measures to suppress it, as part of a wider rhetoric of *securitas*.[16] But there is no evidence that this was bound up with new strategies to delegitimise unrest in the provinces. Thomas Grunewald has argued convincingly that the dismissal of Tacfarinas as *latro* is sufficiently determined by his low status – as a commoner, barbarian and crucially deserter – and should not be seen as part of a systematic effort to delegitimate revolt in general (Grünewald 2004: 48–53). Moreover, it is surely significant that the Tiberian historian Velleius Paterculus explicitly describes the two major provincial revolts of his reign – both that of Tacfarinas and the Gallic revolt of 21 CE – as *wars*:

Quantae molis bellum principe Galliarum ciente Sacroviro Floroque Iulio mira celeritate ac virtute compressit ... ! Magni etiam terroris bellum Africum et cotidiano auctu maius auspiciis consiliisque eius brevi sepultum est.

How huge was the *war* instigated by the leaders of the Gauls, Iulius Sacrovir and Iulius Florus, which [Tiberius] suppressed with astonishing speed and courage. Even the African *War*, a source of terror and growing day by day, was quickly put to rest through his auspices and plans. (Vell. Pat. 2.129.3–4)

Tacitus' later account of the Florus-Sacrovir revolt represents it as (exceptionally) blurring the divide between external and internal conflict (Tac. *Ann.* 4.40–47 with Lavan 2017: 30–2). But the perspective in Velleius' contemporary account is unambiguously externalising.

The most substantial provincial revolt of the first century CE, the unrest in Judea from 66 to 70 CE, conforms to the pattern. The Flavians famously celebrated the eventual suppression of Jewish resistance as victory in a great war against a foreign people, as can be observed in the spectacular triumph of 71 CE and the numerous coins assimilating the defeated Jews to conquered barbarians of the late Republic.[17] Even for Tacitus, writing in the early second century, this was the 'Jewish War' (*bellum Iudaicum*: Tac. *Hist.* 1.10.3, 2.4.3, 4.51.2). His excursus on the origins of the revolt notes the moment 'war broke out' (*bellum ortum*, Tac. *Hist.* 5.10.1). Suetonius refers to it variously as rebellion (*rebellio*) and a disturbance (*motus*) (Suet. *Vesp.* 4.5). It is to the Jewish Josephus, not Roman accounts, that we must look to find the rebels, or at least a faction within them, delegitimised as 'bandits' (*lēstai*) and criminals, as Katell

---

16 Michéle Lowrie is working on a history of *securitas* in the early principate.
17 Triumph: Jos. *BJ* 7.119–157. Coins: Cody 2003.

Berthelot shows in her contribution to this volume. She links these strategies of delegitimisation to the particular threat the revolt had posed to the Jewish aristocratic elite to which he belonged.

Tacitus

Tacitus' historical works, which look back at the events of the first century CE from the early decades of the second, continue to set provincial revolt in a recognisably republican frame. The proem to his *Histories* does famously thematise a blurring of the boundary between civil and foreign conflict as it surveys its subject matter, promising 'wars, three civil, more foreign and often combined' (*trina bella civilia, plura externa ac plerumque permixta*, *Hist*. 1.2.1). This appears to be an allusion to the Batavian Revolt of 69–70 which is narrated in Books 4 and 5 (Damon 2003: 84). The idea recurs in a further foreshadowing of the revolt in Book 2, when Tacitus records that Vitellius sent Batavian auxiliaries back to the Rhine, where they would later mutiny: 'for the Fates were preparing the beginning of a war at once internal and foreign' (*interno simul externoque bello*, *Hist*. 2.69.1). The vision is realised in the early stages of Tacitus' narrative of the revolt, when an army of rebel Batavians and Germans swelled by the mutinous Batavian auxiliaries besieges two Roman legions in the camp at Vetera: 'on one side the standards of veteran cohorts; on the other, images of wild beasts brought out from forests and groves, however each people was accustomed to enter battle – these astounded the besieged by combining the appearance of civil and foreign war (*mixta belli civilis externique facie*) (*Hist*. 4.22.2).

But this interest in how provincial revolt might blur the boundary between civil and foreign conflict seems to be specific to the Batavian revolt in particular. Ellen O'Gorman has shown that the narrative of the Batavian revolt has a special place in the *Histories*, a work that is a profound meditation on civil war (O'Gorman 1995). The Batavian revolt of Books 4 and 5 can be read as revisiting the civil wars narrated in the preceding books, raising troubling questions about the possibility of closure (O'Gorman 1995: 117, 124–9). Several features of the revolt may have made it particularly apposite for this purpose, not least the identity of its leader – not just a Roman citizen and a Iulius, but even having the cognomen Civilis – and the involvement of mutinous cohorts. (In the passage just quoted, it is the juxtaposition of Roman and barbaric standards that gives the attacking force its extraordinary, boundary-destabilising aspect.) These distinctive features give the Batavian revolt a thematic importance in the *Histories*.

Yet it is striking that there are no parallels to the notion of blurred boundaries in Tacitus' account of the Jewish revolt, when he turns to its final stages in Book 5 (5.1–13). By contrast, the Jews are marked as indisputably foreign, indeed barbarous. Nor is there any real development of the theme of blurred boundaries in the numerous accounts of provincial revolts in the later *Annals*. Those instead manifest themselves as variations on a small number of narrative types that are clearly externalising in their perspective. One presents revolt as a natural feature of unruly landscapes and their populations and hence needing no further explanation (Lavan 2017: 26). Another narrates revolts as the work of a foreign people rising organically against Rome out of outrage at Roman injustice and/or a desire for freedom (Lavan 2017: 27–30).

The account of the Florus-Sacrovir revolt in Gaul in 21 CE (noted earlier in the context of the reign of Tiberius) is the single notable exception in the *Annals*. It seems to conflate the model of rebellion by a subject people with themes of debt, destitution, immorality and criminality that are familiar from narratives of domestic conflict in Rome but notably absent from Tacitus' other accounts of revolt in the provinces. The rebels include 'all the fiercest men and those who had the greatest need to do wrong (*peccandi necessitudo*) due to destitution (*egestas*) and fear born of past crimes (*flagitia*)' (Tac. *Ann*. 3.40.2). This is language and ideas normally confined to accounts of revolution and sedition within the citizen body. I have argued that the idiosyncrasies of this narrative probably reflect Tacitus' particular interest in a later Gallic revolt, that led by Gaius Iulius Vindex in 68, which must have featured in the lost final books of the *Annals* (Lavan 2017: 30–2). If I am right, Tacitus' account of that revolt may have problematised distinctions between domestic and foreign conflicts in ways that paralleled his account of the Batavian Revolt in the *Histories*. But that is speculation. What is clear is the consistently externalising perspective of the vast majority of Tacitus' revolt narratives across his works.

In that respect, it is worth returning to the figure of Iulius Civilis, the instigator of the Batavian Revolt in Tacitus' account. Tacitus prefaces his account of Civilis's role in fomenting revolt by tracing his hostility to Rome back to his trial for alleged complicity in the revolt of Vindex in 68:

Iulius Paulus et Iulius Civilis regia stirpe multo ceteros anteibant. Paulum Fonteius Capito falso rebellionis crimine interfecit; iniectae Civili catenae, missusque ad Neronem et a Galba absolutus sub Vitellio rursus discrimen adiit, flagitante supplicium eius exercitu: inde causae irarum spesque ex malis nostris.

Iulius Paulus and Iulius Civilis were by far the most eminent [among the Batavians], being of royal blood. Paulus was executed by Fonteius Capito on a false charge of rebellion. Civilis was thrown in chains, sent to Nero and acquitted by Galba. Yet he found himself in jeopardy again under Vitellius, when the army demanded he be punished. This was the cause of his anger and why he saw opportunity in our misfortune. (Tac. *Hist.* 4.13.1)

Though Vindex is not mentioned by name, the context – a *rebellio* that happened under Nero and towards which Galba showed leniency – strongly suggests that his was the revolt in question (Chilver 1979 *ad loc.*). Tacitus suggests that Civilis' compatriot Iulius Paulus was falsely accused of complicity, but nonetheless convicted and executed. The implication is that Civilis himself was also falsely accused, but – unlike Paulus – sent to Rome for the emperor's judgement. It is not clear why Paulus was executed on the spot, but the governor perhaps claimed that the urgency of the situation demanded immediate action.[18]

In his excellent survey of the legal underpinnings of Roman responses to threats to internal order, Benjamin Kelly cites this passage as a rare description of a judicial response to a provincial revolt: 'Presumably, those guilty of rebelling against Roman rule in a province could have been brought before the relevant provincial governor and (at least from the late Republic) charged with *maiestas* or *vis*. Reports of such judicial responses to provincial revolts are, however, exceedingly rare. ... The few examples of such reports include ... Tac. *Hist.* 4.13' (Kelly 2016: 381–2 and n. 44). One would indeed expect Paulus and Civilis, both Roman citizens, to have been tried under Roman law. Indeed, the fact that Civilis was sent to Rome is precisely what one would expect in such a trial, since provincial governors did not have the authority to execute Roman citizens.

What draws my attention is a single incongruous detail: the charge was *rebellio*. This does not seem to have been a term with meaning under the laws under which Paulus and Civilis must have been charged. One would rather expect the *crimen* to have been *seditio*, *maiestas* or some other crime of a Roman citizen against the state. By contrast, Tacitus's reference to *rebellio*

---

18 See e.g. Ulpian at *Dig.* 28.3.6.9 on extra-judicial killing in emergencies.

has an estranging effect, representing the two Iulii as Batavian rebels rather than seditious citizens. The choice perfectly illustrates Tacitus' tendency, even with the Batavian revolt, to set provincial revolt in an externalising frame.

Cassius Dio

Cassius Dio's *Roman History* provides another, somewhat later, senatorial perspective on the history of unrest in the provinces, this time mediated through the Greek historiographical tradition. Dio's accounts of provincial revolts tend to be quite short, but they display a consistency of structure and vocabulary that is entirely consistent with what recent scholarship has revealed about the importance of authorial design in shaping his sprawling narrative.[19]

Dio often forgoes explanation, presenting provincial revolts as a quasi-natural occurrence that requires no investigation of cause and effect. One particularly characteristic pattern is to record that a particular people or peoples 'made war again', *vel sim*. For example, in 54 BCE, during Caesar's campaigns in Gaul, the Treveri 'began war against [the Romans] once more' (ἐξεπολεμώθησαν αὖθις αὐτοῖς, 40(40).11.2). In 22 BCE, 'the Cantabri and the Astures made war again' (ἐπολέμησαν αὖθις, 54(54).5.1). In Africa in 42 CE, the Mauri 'made war again' (αὖθις ... πολεμήσαντες, 60(60).9.1). In 79 CE, 'war had again broken out in Britain' (πολέμου αὖθις ... γενομένου, 66(66).20.1 [Xiph]).[20]

The phrasing is distinctive to Dio. The collocation of *polemein* (wage war) or cognate verb with the adverb *authis* (again) recurs numerous times across his work, almost always in the context of revolt.[21] By contrast, it appears only once each in Herodotus, Polybius, Dionysius Halicarnassus and Appian – and never in the context of revolt.[22] This seems to be Dio's gloss on the Latin

---

19 See especially Hose 1994: ch. 6, Kemezis 2014: ch. 3, Fromentin et al. 2016 and Lange and Madsen 2016 (and subsequent volumes in the same series).
20 This passage survives only in Xiphilinus' paraphrase, but the parallels suggest the distinctive phrase is Dio's.
21 See also 40.26.1, 42.10.3, 42.47.4, 46.24.2, 48.1.2, 48.24.7.
22 Hdt. 5.120, Polyb. 1.6.7, Dion. Hal. *Ant. Rom.* 3.9.3, App. *Hisp.* 297.

verb *rebellare* (literally, 'wage war again'), so common in Latin revolt narratives, where it often plays a similar role in substituting for explanation, representing conquest as always provisional and rebellion as a natural feature of an imperial state. As such, Dio's language seems to perpetuate republican conceptions of provincial revolt, presenting subject peoples as rising organically and spontaneously against Roman rule.

A second pattern is different, and more idiosyncratic. A notable cluster of Dio's notices of provincial revolt focus on the fiscal burden of Roman rule. Unrest in Egypt in 48 BCE occurs because 'the Egyptians were oppressed by the exaction of money' (ταῖς τῶν χρημάτων ἐσπράξεσι βαρυνόμενοι, 43(43).34.44) In 6 CE, the Pannonians revolted after having been 'oppressed by levies of money' (ἐσφοραῖς τῶν χρημάτων … βαρυνόμενοι, 55(55).29.9). Britons and Gauls revolt in 68 CE because they were 'oppressed by levies' (βαρυνόμενοι ταῖς εἰσφοραῖς, 63(63).22.1a [Zon]).[23] Vindex's revolt relies on Gauls 'who had suffered much by the numerous forced levies of money' (πολλὰ πεπονθότας τε ἐν ταῖς συχναῖς ἐσπράξεσι τῶν χρημάτων, 63(63).22.11 [Xiph.]). Across 86 and 87 CE 'many of the peoples tributary to the Romans revolted when contributions of money were forcibly extorted from them' (χρήματα βιαίως πρασσόμενοι, 67(67).4.6–7 [Zon].) Across a span of three decades of his work, we find a systematic attention to the weight of taxation, as opposed to for example sexual violence, the levying of troops, or the census – all of which feature prominently in comparable narratives in Tacitus. And the explanations are couched in a distinctive shorthand, characterised above all by the verb *barunesthai*.[24]

This apparently innovative pattern of explanation, which stresses the burden of taxation and its capacity to spark unrest, is in many ways more interesting than the first, which its familiar republican tropes. Its materialism bears comparison with the similarly distinctive analyses of Appian and the anonymous fourth-century *De rebus bellicis*, discussed respectively by Lisa Eberle and Bruno Pottier in their chapters. It is also just one facet of Dio's broader and equally unusual interest in taxation and its effects.[25] The

---

23 Again it seems possible to detect Dio's distinctive ideas and language in the paraphrases of Zonaras and Xiphilinus in this and the next two examples.
24 The works of Herodotus, Thucydides, Polybius, Dionysius and Appian together offer only a single parallel for the collocation of *barunesthai* with *chrēmata* or *eisphora*: Polyb. 5.94.9, and that not related to revolt.
25 See for example the fiscal proposals in the speech of Maecenas (52.27–30, with Burden-Strevens 2023: 374–6).

focus on taxation might seem to construct revolt as arising within a state, and in that regard to be 'internalising' in the sense of this paper. Yet it is striking that Dio, like Cicero and Tacitus before him, continues to present even these revolts as the work of foreign peoples acting as a whole, rather than criminous individuals. Notably absent from these narratives is the language of immorality and criminality, not to mention the particular concept of banditry.

The rise of the jurists

The texts I have discussed so far illustrate the longevity of republican perspectives on unrest in the provinces, and their externalising frames. But there were other ways of framing the phenomenon which may have become increasingly prominent during the mid-second century CE. It is plausible that men who were trained in the juristic tradition saw things differently than other members of the office-holding elite, such as Tacitus or Dio. It is also plausible that their perspective became more influential as their numbers increased and they became more prominent in the imperial administration, thanks to imperial patronage.

Ulpian's handbook *De officio proconsulis* is a notable example of the colonisation of the domain of public administration by jurisprudence in the Antonine and Severan periods that I discussed earlier. Ulpian's guidance to governors includes an exhortation to rid their provinces of 'evil men' (*mali homines*):

Congruit bono et gravi praesidi curare, ut pacata atque quieta provincia sit quam regit. quod non difficile optinebit, si sollicite agat, ut malis hominibus provincia careat eosque conquirat: nam et sacrilegos latrones plagiarios fures conquirere debet et prout quisque deliquerit, in eum animadvertere, receptoresque eorum coercere, sine quibus latro diutius latere non potest.

It befits a good and responsible governor to see that the province he rules is peaceful and orderly. This he will achieve without difficulty, if he works conscientiously at ridding the province of wicked men and at seeking them out to that end. For he is duty-bound to search out blasphemers, robbers, hijackers, and thieves and to punish them each according to the evil he has done and to jail those who harbor them, without whose help a robber cannot lie hidden for too long. (Ulpianus 7 *De off. procons.* apud *Dig.* 1.18.13.pr, trans. D. N. MacCormick)

We also know from Ulpian that imperial *mandata*, the instructions given to governors when they left for their province, had by this period begun to include a directive to purge one's province of 'evil men' (*mali homines*):[26]

> nam et in mandatis principum est, ut curet is, qui provinciae praeest, malis hominibus provinciam purgare.
>
> For it is to be found in the imperial warrants of appointment that he who has charge of the province shall attend to cleansing the province of evil men. (Paulus 13 *Ad Sab.* apud *Dig.* 1.18.3, trans. D. N. MacCormick)

We cannot date the introduction of this language into imperial *mandata*, since Ulpian is the only evidence for it. Yet it seems plausible that it was a relatively recent development and reflected the growing influence of jurists like Ulpian himself. Both these texts construct provincial territory as a space uniformly subject to law, where unrest is the work of wicked criminals. There seems no opening here for rebellion by a foreign people.

It is probably not a coincidence that the language of *latrocinium* begins to feature more prominently in official discourse in the latter half of the second century. An honorific inscription for M. Valerius Maximianus, an equestrian who had pursued a career in the emperor's service and was raised to the Senate by Marcus Aurelius, includes a reference to a special appointment 'to expel the band of Brisean bandits (*latrones*) on the borders of Macedonia and Thrace' (*AE* 1956, 124, from Diana Veteranorum, Numidia). Under Commodus, the governor of Pannonia Inferior oversaw the construction of forts along the Danube and commissioned inscriptions advertising the emperor's efforts to repel crossings by bandits (*latrunculorum transitus*).[27] Here we do see unrest in the provinces constructed as the actions of criminal *latrones*, not foreign peoples. Both these texts represent provincial governors as delivering on an imperial commitment to the suppression of *latrocinium* that would seem to parallel or at least anticipate the later instructions to hunt down *mali homines*.

The rise of internalising perspectives on provincial unrest continued into Late Antiquity, as Bruno Pottier illustrates in the next chapter in this volume. Pottier observes new tendencies to narrate provincial revolts as the work of opportunists of low status who take advantage of moments of crisis to set themselves up as rivals to the Roman state, or alternatively as a legitimate

---

26 On *mandata*, see Corcoran 2014: 176. On the 'evil men', see Bryen 2023, especially 67–8.
27 See *RIU* 5 1127–36.

defence of republican principles against the depredations of a tyrant. Both patterns of explanation tend to integrate provincial revolt into the 'internal' politics of the empire. But Pottier also illustrates the parallel persistence, well into late Antiquity, of the old, republican association of provincial revolt with ethnic difference.

Conclusion

This paper has sought to illustrate the longevity of externalising perspectives in Roman discourse on unrest in the provinces. Not just Cicero, but Tacitus and even Cassius Dio seem to conceive of much of the population of the empire as somehow 'foreign' – more like populations beyond the limits of the provinces than like the Roman citizen body. It followed that the decisive boundary between 'internal' and 'external' conflict lay well within the territorial limits of Roman control – and not at them, as some might expect.

It may well be that perspectives on unrest began to change in the later second century, following the expansion of the scope of jurisprudence from private to public law and the concomitant increase in the presence of jurists in the imperial bureaucracy. New, internalising accounts that constructed all agents of unrest as individualised, criminal subjects may have come to rival the old republican tendency to distinguish between *seditio* by citizens and *defectio/rebellio* by subject peoples. But change was slow and never complete.

Finally, it is worth noting that juristic discourse, despite its general tendency to set unrest in an internalising frame, could still externalise some forms of unrest. The jurists' use of *latrocinium* is particularly revealing. Although in principle crimes were the same everywhere, in practice the jurists tend to use *seditio* of unrest in urban contexts and *latrocinium* of unrest in rural contexts. Insofar as *seditio* remained the master term for unrest in the citizen body, this use of *latrocinium* implicitly excluded non-urban populations from the civic sphere. Here too the discourse on unrest can be seen to reveal underlying conceptions of political community.

Works cited

Ando, Clifford. 2011. *Law, Language, and Empire in the Roman Tradition*. Philadelphia.
Buckland, William Warwick. 1908. *The Roman Law of Slavery: The Condition of the Slave in Private Law from Augustus to Justinian*. Cambridge.
Bryen, Ari. 2023. 'Imagining criminals in the provinces', in Adriaan Lanni, ed., *A Global History of Crime and Punishment in Antiquity*. London, 43–62.
Burden-Strevens, Christopher. 2023. 'The Agrippa-Maecenas debate', in Jesper Majbom Madsen and Andrew G. Scott, eds., *Brill's Companion to Cassius Dio*. Leiden, 371–405.
Chilver, G. E. F. 1979. *A Historical Commentary on Tacitus' Histories I and II*. Oxford.
Clavel-Lévêque, Monique. 1978. 'Brigandage et piraterie: représentations idéologiques et pratiques impérialistes au dernier siècle de la République'. *Dialogues d'histoire ancienne* 4: 17–31.
Cody, Jane M. 2003. 'Conquerors and conquered on Flavian coins', in Anthony Boyle and William J. Dominik, eds., *Flavian Rome: Culture, Image, Text*. Leiden, 103–24.
Corcoran, Simon. 2014. 'State correspondence in the Roman empire: imperial communication from Augustus to Julian', in Karen Radner, ed., *State Correspondence in the Ancient World: From New Kingdom Egypt to the Roman Empire*. Oxford, 172–209.
Crook, John. 1995. *Legal Advocacy in the Roman World*. London.
Damon, Cynthia. 2003. *Tacitus: Histories Book 1*. Cambridge.
dell'Oro, A. 1960. *I libri de officio nella giurisprudenza romana*. Milan.
Fromentin, Valérie, Estelle Bertrand, Michèle Coltelloni-Trannoy, Michel Molin and Gianpaolo Urso, eds., 2016. *Cassius Dion: Nouvelles lectures*. Bordeaux.
Gruen, Erich S. 1985. 'Augustus and the ideology of war and peace', in Rolf Winkes, ed., *The age of Augustus*. Louvain-la-Neuve and Providence, RI, 51–72.
Grünewald, Thomas. 2004. *Bandits in the Roman Empire: Myth and Reality*. London. Trans. of *Räuber, Rebellen, Rivalen, Räucher*. Mainz, 1999.
Hose, Martin. 1994. *Erneuerung der Vergangenheit: die Historiker im Imperium Romanum von Florus bis Cassius Dio*. Stuttgart and Leipzig.
Kelly, Benjamin. 2016. 'Repression, resistance and rebellion', in Paul J. Du Plessis, Clifford Ando and Kaius Tuori, eds., *The Oxford Handbook of Roman Law and Society*. Oxford, 374–85.
Kemezis, Adam M. 2014. *Greek Narratives of the Roman Empire under the Severans: Cassius Dio, Philostratus and Herodian*. Cambridge.
Lange, Carsten Hjort and Jesper Majbom Madsen, eds., 2016. *Cassius Dio: Greek intellectual and Roman politician*. Leiden.
Lavan, Myles. 2013. *Slaves to Rome: Paradigms of Empire in Roman Culture*. Cambridge.
Lavan, Myles. 2017. 'Writing revolt in the early Roman empire', in Justine Firnhaber-Baker and Dirk Schoenaers, eds., *The Routledge History Handbook of Medieval Revolt*. London, 19–38.
Lenel, Otto. 1889. *Palingenesia iuris civilis*. Leipzig.

Mommsen, Theodor and Paul Kruger. 1963. *Corpus Iuris Civilis. I. Institutiones, Digesta.* 13th edn, Berlin.

O'Gorman, Ellen. 1995. 'Shifting ground: Lucan, Tacitus and the landscape of civil war'. *Hermathena*, 158: 117–31.

Riess, Werner. 2001. *Apuleius und die Räuber. Ein Beitrag zur historischen Kriminalitätsforschung.* Stuttgart.

Sirks, Adriaan J. B. 2015. 'Public law', in David Johnston, ed., *The Cambridge Companion to Roman Law.* Cambridge, 332–52.

Tarwacka, Anna. 2022. 'Pirates' captives in light of Roman law', in Peter Candy and Emilia Mataix Ferrandiz, eds., *Roman law and maritime commerce.* Edinburgh, 41–55.

Watson, Alan. 1993. 'Thinking Property at Rome'. *Chicago-Kent Law Review* 68: 1355–71.

9. Usurpers, Bandits and Barbarians: Narratives of Provincial Unrest in the Fourth Century

Bruno Pottier

Abstract: *Understandings of provincial unrest evolved in the fourth century AD owing to changing political conditions after the Antonine Constitution of 212 and the third century crisis. Ancient historians distinguished two types of revolts. Some were supposed to have an ethnic character, involving peoples who were not fully integrated, often dwelling in mountains. They were paradoxically viewed as barbarians inside the Empire, maintaining a way of life characterized by predation against their neighbours. At the same time, contemporary authors had growing concern about the danger of separatist tendencies in some parts of the Empire. This period was also characterized by the democratization of aspirations to imperial power even to men of low status. As a consequence, in the fourth century usurpers were frequently disparaged by being labelled* tyranni *and bandits (*latrones*) and accused of recruiting criminals, always eager for* res novae, *for their ambitious projects. Studying provincial revolts in the fourth century therefore requires us to decode how they were related by ancient historians and to highlight the stereotyped explanations used to delegitimize them, either as usurpations or as bandit uprisings. Circumstantial detail often allows us to offer more complex explanations. This chapter will focus on three fourth-century historians writing in Latin or Greek: Aurelius Victor, Ammianus Marcellinus and Eunapius of Sardis. Especial attention will be given to the rebellion of Firmus in Mauretania Caesariensis and the numerous Isaurian uprisings in south-eastern Anatolia, both in mountainous and peripheral regions. The De Rebus Bellicis, which gives a particularly original interpretation of revolt and banditry, will also be discussed.*

In the early Empire, provincial revolts were generally interpreted as rebellions of peoples who were not fully integrated into *Romanitas* and who sought to recover their independence. Tacitus sometimes employs a more complex interpretative pattern by adducing specific causes, such as abuses committed by the Roman administration (Lavan 2017). Understandings of provincial unrest evolved in the third and the fourth century owing to changing political conditions. In particular, the diffusion of citizenship after the Antonine Constitution of 212 induced ancient historians to distinguish three types of revolts.

Some revolts were still seen as having an ethnic character, involving peoples who were not fully integrated, often dwelling in mountains. They were paradoxically viewed as barbarians inside the Empire, maintaining a way of life characterized by predation against their neighbours. By contrast, other provincial revolts could be interpreted as defending the principle of Roman *libertas* against a tyrant, especially if they were evacuated of any ethnic flavour. The proclamation of a usurper as the rightful rival to an alleged tyrant epitomizes the Roman character of this type of revolt. The African revolt against Maximinus Thrax in 238, which was recognized by the Roman Senate, provides the model of this legitimate form of revolt. At the same time, contemporary authors were clearly shocked by the multiplication of usurpations on a provincial or regional scale during the crisis of the third century, such as the so-called Gallic Empire between 260 and 274 and the complex adventure of Palmyra. These events elicited growing concern about the danger of separatist tendencies in some parts of the Empire. This period was also characterized by the democratization of aspirations to imperial power even to men of low status. As a consequence, in the fourth century usurpers were frequently disparaged by being labelled *tyranni* and bandits (*latrones*).[1] They were also accused of recruiting bandits and criminals, always eager for *res novae*, for their ambitious projects.[2]

Studying provincial revolts in the fourth century therefore requires us to decode how they were related by ancient historians and to highlight the stereotyped explanations used to delegitimize them, either as usurpations or as bandit uprisings. Circumstantial detail often allows us to offer more complex explanations. This chapter will focus on three fourth-century historians writing in Latin or Greek: Aurelius Victor, Ammianus Marcellinus and Eunapius of Sardis. An anonymous petition of the fourth century, the *De Rebus Bellicis*, which gives a particularly original interpretation of revolt and banditry, will also be discussed. Especial attention will be given to the rebellion of Firmus in Mauretania Caesariensis between 370 and 374 and the numer-

---

[1] MacMullen 1963, Barnes 1996, Neri 1997. Carausius was the first usurper to be labelled as a *latro* and a pirate: *Pan. Lat.* 8(5).6.12.
[2] Eunapius of Sardis states that Nepotianus, a member of the Constantinian dynasty, recruited bandits to take over the city of Rome in 350: Zos. 2.43.2.

ous Isaurian uprisings in south-eastern Anatolia, particularly in the work of Ammianus. Mauretania and Isauria were mountainous and peripheral regions whose inhabitants were accused of a strong tendency to banditry. It is however necessary to differentiate punctuated revolts from occasional banditry.

Provincial unrest in the historical work of Aurelius Victor

The historian Aurelius Victor, who wrote an epitome of Roman history in 360, is a good example of the tendency of late antique historians to emphasize the role of ambitious leaders, aspiring to become kings or emperors, in their presentation of provincial revolts. Aurelius Victor had a special interest in the third century crisis. He denounced the democratization of *adfectio regni* in this period, even to *ignobiles* without knowledge of liberal arts, like Maximinus Thrax in 235. He also denounced the subjection of the Orient to *latrones* under Gallienus, obviously alluding to Palmyrene leaders (*Caes.* 24.9–10, 33.3). The historical literary genre of the epitome gained a new importance in the fourth century and responded to the need of civil servants of lower status to have some knowledge of Roman history. However, abbreviation produced greatly simplified descriptions of provincial unrest, as can be illustrated by three case studies: the supposed usurpation of Calocerus in Cyprus, the Jewish revolt of 351–352 and the Gallic *Bagaudae* of the third century.

Aurelius Victor reports that Calocerus, master of herds of camels belonging to the imperial *res privata* (*magister pecoris camelorum*), decided in 326, during the reign of Constantine, to seize the island of Cyprus *specie regni*.[3] This could either refer to an attempt at usurpation or, less plausibly, to the establishment of a kingdom in Cyprus.[4] Constantine condemned Calocerus to be executed *servili aut more latronum*, by being burnt alive or crucified – punish-

---

3 Aur. Vict. *Caes.* 41.11–12: *Quorum cum natu grandior, incertum qua causa, patris iudicio occidisset, repente Calocerus magister pecoris camelorum Cyprum insulam specie regni demens capessiverat. Quo excruciato, ut fas erat, servili aut latronum more, condenda urbe formandisque religionibus ingentem animum avocavit, simul novando militiae ordine.* Aurelius Victor referred to the murder of Crispus by his father Constantine in 326. Cf. PLRE I, Calocaerus: 177, Salomon 1984.
4 Aurelius Victor often used the term *regnum* for imperial power: *Caes.* 27.6, 29.4, 33.9, 36.2, 37.6, 39.48, 41.16.

ment Aurelius Victor deemed justified. *Magistri* of imperial herds were often of servile status. They were frequently accused of cattle rustling like *latrones*, illustrative of their supposedly low morality.[5] To Aurelius Victor, Calocerus epitomized the democratization of *adfectatio regni* to persons of low status, which was seen as a form of madness.[6] He probably had very little information about Calocerus, but this did not prevent him from attributing clear motivations to him. By contrast, Orosius, Hieronymus of Strido and the *Anonymus Valesianus* are much more guarded, merely associating Calocerus with *res novae*.[7] This ambiguous term can signify a usurpation but also any other kind of unrest as *seditio* or *rebellio*. These two texts also depart from Aurelius Victor in dating the events to 334 or 335, which probably reveals an error on Aurelius Victor's part. Calocerus was probably executed by Dalmatius, half-brother of Constantine, in 334–335, and not by his homonymous son who became Caesar later (*PLRE* I, Flavius Dalmatius 6: 240–41). The Byzantine historian Theophanes mentions Calocerus as a would-be usurper and his execution by being burnt alive, events which he dates to 332–333 (43B, AM 5825). It is very unlikely that Calocerus, probably a freedman, aspired to become emperor, since all the usurpers known from the fourth century were generals or high-level civil servants, or that he intended to restore the Hellenistic kingdom of Cyprus, by this time long-abolished.[8] He was probably involved in some kind of social unrest with popular support. It may have been connected with the earthquake which devastated Cyprus in 331–332 and a food crisis in Syria and Cilicia between 331 and 333 (Theophanes 43A-43B, Jer. *Chron.* a. 333). Aurelius Victor limited himself to ascribing the revolt to the ambitions of its leader, which were particularly shocking given his low social status. No further explanation was needed.

Aurelius Victor states that Jews of Palestine launched a *seditio* in 351 or 352 with the aim, stigmatized as criminal, of making one of them, Patricius,

---

5 For example, in the inscription of Saepinum in southern Italy in 168 under Marcus Aurelius (*CIL* IX, 2438).
6 A law of 392 (*CTh* 1.29.8) condemned the habitual *insania* of the *latrones*.
7 Jer. *Chron.*, a. 334: *Calocerus in Cypro res novas molitus opprimitur*; Oros. 7.28.30: *Calocaerum quendam in Cypro adspirantem novis rebus oppressit. Tricennalibus suis Dalmatium Caesarem legit*; Anon. Vales. 6.35: *Calocaerum quendam in Cypro aspirantem novis rebus suppressit. Damatium, filium fratris sui Dalmatii, Caesarem fecit.*
8 Salomon 1984. However, Calocerus is defined as an usurper in most historical works on the fourth century, for example by Elton (2006: 337) in *The Cambridge Companion to Constantine*. His failure is explained by the lack of support from the army. No usurper is securely attested under Constantine.

a sort of king. Exactly the same vocabulary is used as for Calocerus (*in regni speciem*).⁹ Aurelius Victor does not suggest that this was a messianic attempt to restore the Jewish kingdom. It is however the first Jewish rebellion attested since that of Bar Kochba under Hadrian. Aurelius Victor seems to have supposed that this was an ethnic rebellion with obvious separatist aims. He is however the only source to mention Patricius and an attempt to restore a Jewish kingdom, as usurpation is particularly unlikely in this case. Hieronymus of Stridon, who wrote his *Chronicle* around 379, only mentions the murder of some Roman soldiers and the subsequent massacre of thousands of people and the destruction by fire of three cities (Diocaesarea, Tiberiade and Diospolis), by the Caesar Gallus, who had been put in charge of the Orient by Constantius II in May 351.¹⁰ Hieronymus is clearly critical of the severity of the repression. Later sources limit the unrest to Diocaesarea, thereby lessening its importance. The Byzantine historian Theophanes is the only source to record that the Jewish rebels killed many pagan Greeks and Samaritans.¹¹ Talmudic sources suggest social discontent among textile workers in some cities of Judea. They also show that most of the rabbinic elites supported the general sent by Gallus to suppress this unrest, Ursicinus. An attempt to restore a Jewish kingdom is therefore unlikely. The most likely explanation is that there were some serious riots in Judea in 351–352 that were limited to three cities and had complex social and religious motivations.¹² Aurelius Victor may have been responding to rumours attributing some role in these events to a man named Patricius. Despite writing relatively soon after these events, Aurelius Victor seems to have exaggerated them to accord with the traditional depiction of the Jewish people as being permanently opposed to the Empire and aspiring to an independent kingdom.¹³ His account also fits

---

9 Aur. Vict. *Caes.* 42.11: *Et interea Iudaeorum seditio, qui Patricium nefarie in regni speciem sustulerant, oppressa*. On this revolt see Geiger 1979, Stemberger 2000: 161–84.

10 Jer. *Chron.* a. 352: *Gallus Judaeos qui interfectis per noctem militibus arma ad rebellandum invaserant oppressit caesis multis hominum milibus usque ad innoxiam aetatem et civitates eorum Diocaesariam Tiberiadem et Diospolim plurimaque oppida igni tradidit*.

11 Sozom. *Hist. eccl.* 4.7, Socrates *Hist. eccl.* 2.33, Theophanes AM 5843. Ammianus does not mention this revolt.

12 Geiger 1979, Stemberger 2000: 162 and Bijovski 2007 play down the importance of this revolt, arguing that several urban riots were artificially connected by late antique historians, especially Aurelius Victor.

13 Aurelius Victor might have dramatized these events to place Patricius in parallel with the occidental usurper Magnentius in Gaul in 350–353 under the same emperor Constantius II. Aurelius Victor mentions this usurper in a previous section of his work: *Caes.* 42.8–10.

his favourite interpretative scheme, ascribing provincial to ambitious leaders characterized by their madness. He could have explained this revolt as a reaction to the cruelty of the Caesar Gallus, which he elsewhere denounces, but he preferred to dismiss it as a purely ethnic rebellion, needing no specific explanation (*Caes.* 42.12).

This pattern also explains Aurelius Victor's treatment of a long-debated problem earlier in the third century, the *Bagaudae* uprising in Gaul in 285–286. Eutropius, who dedicated his own *Epitome* to the emperor Valens circa 370, presents it as a peasant revolt. Gallic *rusticani*, gathered in a *factio*, took two leaders (*duces*), Amandus and Aelianus, and called themselves *Bagaudae*. Eutropius elected to describe these events using a deliberately vague and neutral term, *tumultus*, which could denote either a revolt or a military mobilization of Gallic peasants.[14] According to Aurelius Victor, by contrast, it was Amandus and Aelianus who gathered a force of *agrestes* and bandits and began plundering the countryside and attacking cities. They were called *Bagaudae* by the inhabitants (*incolae*) of Gaul[15]. Unlike Eutropius, Aurelius Victor denounces their actions as criminal. It was therefore for him not a peasant revolt, but rather the expression of the ambitions of two leaders, who recruited bandits and desperate *agrestes* for their personal projects.[16] He seemed to have interpreted these events as having some parallels with the Gallic usurpers of the Rhine region during the period 260–274.

The rhetor Mamertinus gave a more complex, though still ambiguous, interpretation of these events in a Latin panegyric dedicated to the emperor Maximian in the year 289. He attributes the revolt to the madness of some Gallic peasants and shepherds who wanted to become soldiers in order to win social status and prestige. Mamertinus praises Maximian for his clemency towards them. He clearly shows that *Bagaudae* were at the outset peasants

---

14 Eutr. 9.20.3: *Ita rerum Romanarum potitus, cum tumultum rusticani in Gallia concitassent et factioni suae Bacaudarum nomen imponerent, duces autem haberent Amandum et Aelianum, ad subigendos eos Maximianum Herculium Caesarem misit qui levibus proeliis agrestes domuit et pacem Galliae reformavit.*
15 Aur. Vict. *Caes.* 39.18–20: *Namque, ubi comperit Carini discessu Aelianum Amandumque per Galliam, excita manu agrestium ac latronum, quos Bagaudas incolae vocant, populatis late agris, plerasque urbium tentare, statim Maximianum, fidum amicitia, quanquam semiagrestem, militiae tamen atque ingenio bonum, imperatorem iubet.*
16 Raymond Van Dam followed the interpretation of Aurelius Victor, even stating without clear proof that Aelianus and Amandus were two landowners. See Van Dam 1985: 26–27, Pottier 2011: 439 n. 46.

who organized themselves to defend Gaul against barbarian invaders, even if they later got out of control.[17] This account is more credible than that of Aurelius Victor and should be preferred. Mamertinus suggested that this strange episode was best forgotten, implying that it could not be assigned to any familiar category of disorder.[18] Ancient writers often assumed that it was inappropriate to describe these shameful events in detail, which makes the study of these revolts more difficult. A later panegyric in 307 even presented the events of 285–286 as a rebellion of all Gaul, implicitly involving both cities and countryside, prompted by the damage done to the region in the past by barbarians or usurpers (*iniuriae priorum temporum*). Maximian's challenge was to convince the Gauls that they could benefit from submitting to the renovated Empire.[19] Aurelius Victor's interpretation should therefore be discarded, since he again resorts to over-simplification, blaming revolt on ambitious leaders.

The revolt of Firmus in Mauretania Caesariensis

Between 370 and 372, Firmus, born to a prominent local tribal family, instigated a revolt in Mauretania Caesariensis and gained control of most of the province. He was defeated in 374 by the general Theodosius the Elder, sent by the emperor Valentinian, who forced him to commit suicide.[20] The ancient sources offer various interpretations of his aims, presenting him either as a barbarian king or a Roman usurper, and of the nature of his revolt.

African Catholic authors, like Augustine of Hippo and his friend Orosius in the beginning of the fifth century, accused Firmus of being a *rex barbarus*.[21] Their purpose was polemical, since Firmus supported the Donatist Church. Augustine states that the Donatists in Mauretania Caesariensis were even denounced as *Firmiani*, as if had they participated in his revolt (*Ep.* 87.10).

---

17 Chauvot 1998: 28–31, Pottier 2011: 453.
18 *Pan. Lat.* 10(2).4.1–4: *cum militaris habitus ignari agricolae appetiverunt, cum arator peditem, cum pastor equitem.*
19 *Pan. Lat.* 6(7).8.3: *Hic est qui in ipso ortu numinis sui Gallias priorum temporum iniuriis efferatas rei publicae ad obsequium reddidit, sibi ipsas ad salutem.*
20 For the dating, Drijvers 2007: 143.
21 August. *C. Ep. Parm.* 1.10.16: *regem barbarum Firmum*; Oros. 7.33.5: *Interea in Africae partibus Firmus sese excitatis Maurorum gentibus regem constituens Africam Mauretaniamque vastavit.*

An abbreviated Roman imperial history of the beginning of fifth century states rather ambiguously that Firmus intended to reinstate the kingdom of Mauretania, which had been absorbed into the Empire in 40 AD.[22] This explanation presumed that Moorish tribes had a permanent tendency to revolt against Roman power. However, these accounts may over-emphasize the role of Firmus in these events. The senator Symmachus, who was present in Africa in 373–374 as *proconsul Africae*, merely notes that Mauretania had suffered from a *rebellio barbarica* and does not even mention Firmus (*Ep.* I.64).

Two other accounts explicitly describe Firmus as a usurper. An African document of the early fifth century, the *passio* of the martyr Salsa of the coastal Mauretanian city of Tipasa, represents that saint as having prevented Firmus from taking his city in a long siege. Firmus is denounced in this text as an *hostis publicus* and would-be usurper whose pretensions were ridiculous because he was a *gentilis* of tribal origin.[23] He relies on the aid of bandits (*praedones*) and barbarian kings. Thus, even contemporary African catholic sources give contradictory interpretations of Firmus' political aims, revealing divergence in local memory barely thirty years after the events. Eunapius of Sardis, a Greek historian who wrote at the end of fourth century, also presents Firmus as a usurper. According to Eunapius, the Africans, unable to endure the heavy burden of taxes imposed by the emperor Valentinian and the avarice of his generals in Mauretania, presented Firmus with a purple cloak and the imperial title.[24] Eunapius thus supposed that all Africa, and not only Mauretania, supported Firmus, which would give him more legitimacy. Eunapius, being of eastern origin, obviously had limited knowledge of these events.

The most detailed account of the revolt is to be found in Book 29 of Ammianus Marcellinus's history, although his main focus was the suppression of the revolt by Theodosius the Elder. Ammianus' account is ambiguous. He presents the revolt as a barbarian uprising of tribes poorly integrated into *romanitas*, but he also provides some details that hint at a usurpation. Am-

---

22 *Epitome de Caesaribus*, 45.7: *Huius tempore Firmus apud Mauritaniam regnum invadens exstinguitur*. The same formulation is used to report the usurpation of Procopius in Orient in 365, who is however described as a *tyrannus* (46, 4). The *Epitome* characterizes therefore Firmus either as a king or a usurper.
23 *Passio Sanctae Salsae* 13: *vellet (...) sibi imperii dominatum contra ius fasque degener vindicare gentilis*; dated by Piredda 2002: 37–42.
24 Zos. 4.16.3. For the date of the works of Eunapius, see Liebeschuetz 2003.

mianus traces the revolt to a kind of inheritance dispute triggered by the death of a tribal leader, Nubel, who is described as a *potentissimus regulus* of the *nationes Mauricae* (29.5.2). He was himself a member of the *Jubaleni* tribe, whose name recalls a former king of Mauretania before its annexation in 40 AD (29.5.44). Firmus, one of the sons of Nubel, killed his brother Sammac. Ammianus seems to have been influenced by the Sallustian account of the revolt of the Numidian king Jugurtha in 118–105 BC, which similarly originated from internal strife in a royal family after the death of a Roman client king (Drijvers 2007: 148). That revolt too posed a significant challenge to the Roman state. So Ammianus implicitly represents Firmus as having been motivated by a desire to inherit his father's position as some sort of client king in Mauretania. Ammianus implied that Firmus was not unjustified in murdering his brother. The *magister officiorum* Remigius prevented the emperor from hearing Firmus' arguments at the behest of his son, the count Romanus, who commanded the Roman army in Africa. Sammac was one of his clients. In Ammianus' account, Firmus makes a personal decision to rebel from the empire (*ab imperii dicione descivit*) because he was afraid of being executed without fair trial.[25] Surprisingly, Ammianus seems to lend the revolt some legitimacy by relating it to one of his favourite themes, the corruption of the central administration. Valentinian is presented as a *princeps clausus*, taking bad decisions because members of his court feed him false information about events in distant provinces.

Ammianus presents this revolt as a generic case of tribal rebellion, even if he never suggests that Firmus wanted to become king, which is therefore unlikely. He interprets it as a real *bellum*, as Caesarea, the provincial capital, was burned and plundered.[26] Firmus quickly gained the support of some tribes of Mauretania Caesariensis, which Ammianus assumed were always eager for *dissensio*.[27] This revolt did not require any further explanation because Am-

---

25 Amm. Marc. 29.5.2–3: *Nubel velut regulus per nationes Mauricas potentissimus vita digrediens, et legitimos et natos e concubinis reliquit filios, e quibus Zammac comiti nomine Romano acceptus, latenter a fratre Firmo peremptus discordias excitavit et bella. Quae cum ad obruendam defensionem suam agitari adverteret Maurus, ultimorum metu iam trepidans, ne amendatis, quae praetendebat, ut perniciosus et contumax condemnatus occideretur, ab imperii dicione descivit.*
26 Amm. Marc. 29.5.18, 42. Augustine of Hippo (*C. Ep. Petil.* 2.83.184) also mentions a *bellum* of Firmus.
27 Amm. Marc. 30.7.10: *Africam deinde malo repentino perturbatam discriminibus magnis exemit, cum voraces militarium fastus ferre nequiens Firmus, ad omnes dissensionum motus perflabiles gentes Mauricas concitasset.*

mianus assumes that these tribes had no proper political aims besides their inclination to plunder, explained by their poverty and mountainous territory.[28] The *Musones* tribe was supposedly devoted to murder and *rapinae* and joined Firmus merely to enjoy freedom to loot (29.5.27). Ammianus reports that Theodosius the Elder accused Firmus of being a bandit (*latro*, 29.5.46). He deployed the common literary *topos*, already illustrated by Aurelius Victor, of suggesting that an ambitious leader could easily gather bandits for a rebellion.[29] Ammianus may also have been inspired by the account of the revolt of Tacfarinas under Tiberius in Tacitus, whose history he aimed to continue. Tacitus presented Tacfarinas as a Roman deserter who had rallied bandits and then barbarian tribes against Roman rule in Africa (*Ann.* 2.52, 3.20–21, 3.73–74, 4.24–25). Tacitus reduced a revolt with complex socio-economical causes to the ambitions of an outsider. The revolt of Firmus similarly allowed Ammianus to illustrate a general principle: trivial events could accidentally cause serious problems for the Empire.

Ammianus probably insisted on the barbarian character of the revolt of Firmus in order to exalt the commander who supressed it, Theodosius the Elder. Ammianus was writing between 390 and 395 during the reign of Theodosius' son, the emperor Theodosius.[30] His narrative has panegyrical tones. Ammianus compares Theodosius the Elder with famous republican and imperial generals such as Fabius Cunctator and Corbulo.[31] As we have seen, he probably drew on the Sallustian account of the revolt of Jugurtha. He probably relied on a *relatio* of these campaigns sent by Theodosius the Elder to the imperial court (Sabbah 1978: 206–7, 238). Elsewhere in his work, Ammianus remarks on the difficulties and dangers of writing contemporary history (26.1.1). To enhance the prestige of Theodosius the Elder, Ammianus mentions his victories over tribes outside the Roman Empire such as the

---

28 Ammianus repeatedly remarks that the mountainous landscape of Mauretania prevented Theodosius from repressing the crimes committed by these tribes.
29 Ammianus (21.10.6) praised Aurelius Victor and probably knew his work well.
30 His entire work was published in 390 or 391 according to Matthews 1989: 24–27.
31 Amm. Marc. 29.5.4, 32. However, Ammianus also somewhat oddly compares Theodosius to Lusius Quietus, a general of Trajan who was, like Firmus, born in a tribe of Mauretania. This might be a paradoxical valorization of Firmus. Ammianus may have intended to show his readers that he refused to be bound by the conventions of panegyric. For Ammianus as an allusive historian, Kelly 2008.

Ethiopians and *Isaflenses*, who were supposedly led by a king.[32] Ammianus seems to have transformed the revolt of Firmus into another external war, as if Theodosius had subjugated unconquered tribes. This presentation also legitimized the extreme measures used in repressing the rebels by implying that this was the only solution because, like the Lernaean Hydra, they constantly gained new life.[33]

Ammianus' suggestion that the tribes of Mauretania were permanently inclined to banditry and rebellion must be criticized. No revolt or period of massive banditry is attested in Mauretania Caesariensis between the expedition of Maximian Herculius in 297–298 and the rebellion of Firmus. The latter cannot have originated from a dispute over the inheritance of Nubel, as if he was a king of a client kingdom. No kings were indeed allowed within Roman territory.[34] Only *principes* and *praefecti gentis* are attested in Mauretania Caesariensis in the fourth century (Leveau 1973). Moreover, Ammianus' Nubel is probably to be identified with Flavius Nuvel, a former *praepositus* of a regular military unit, the *equites armigeri iuniores*, who was the son of a *comes perfectissimus* with a Roman name, Saturninus (*CIL* VIII 9255, *ILCV* 1822). He was therefore part of the Roman administration. The notion of an alliance between an African rebel and kings of the *Mauri* was just a literary *topos* designed to accentuate the threat posed to the Roman order.[35] Ammianus, by giving the title of *regulus* to Nubel, gave a misleading interpretation of what

---

32 Amm. Marc. 29.5.13 (Ethiopians), 29.5.46 (Igmazen as king of *Isaflenses*). Claudian (*Gild.* 1.249–58, 351–57) stated that the Ethiopians supported Gildo, the count of Africa and brother of Firmus, during his revolt in 397–398; compare Modéran 1989: 827.
33 Some soldiers and municipal councillors who joined Firmus were burned alive or had their hands cut off (Amm. Marc. 29.5.22; 43), probably by application of a law of Constantine of 323 condemning those who participated in the plundering of barbarians to be burnt alive (*CTh* 7.1.1). Drijvers (2007: 154) supposed that Ammianus was implicitly denouncing the cruelty of Theodosius by describing in detail the sufferings of the deserters and accomplices of Firmus, despite the explicit praise elsewhere. This interpretation seems uncertain.
34 An inscription of the middle of the third century records the defeat of four kings of the *Bavari* in Mauretania Caesariensis (*AE* 1907, 159). Another inscription of same period and region mentions three kings without ethnic characterization (*AE* 2003, 2024). They may have come from outside the Empire. If they had been settled inside for a long time, these tribes may have given meaning to their rebellion by giving themselves kings. These titles could also have been invented by the generals who vanquished them to enhance their personal prestige.
35 It recalls the alliance of Jugurtha with the Moorish king Bocchus under the Republic. Gildo, brother of Firmus, was also accused of having allied with kings of Moorish tribes during his rebellion in 397–398 (Claud. *Cons. Stil.* I.248–58, 351–57).

can only have been informal influence over some tribes of Mauretania.[36] He implied a loss of imperial control over Mauretania, which is contradicted by other sources, and some kind of separatist project on Firmus's part.[37]

However, Ammianus was a conscientious historian and his account includes some details that reveal the Roman character of Firmus' revolt. Ammianus states that Firmus wore a red cloak (*sagus puniceus*)[38] and had been crowned with a necklace (*torquis*), as a substitute for diadem, by a tribune of a Roman regular unit.[39] The use of a *torquis* as diadem recalls the usurpation of the Caesar Julian in Gaul in 360 as narrated by Ammianus himself (20.4.18). However, Ammianus refers to Firmus only with the vague terms *rebellis* and *perduellis*, qualifying him simply as an enemy of the State, and never calls him a *tyrannus*, the unequivocal term for a usurper.[40] The *sagus puniceus* was not a purple cloak, an exclusive part of the imperial *regalia*, and could befit a Roman general. The *torquis* could have been given to Firmus as a reward for military valour and not as a diadem. It is therefore very unlikely that Firmus took the title of emperor. All known usurpers of the fourth century were generals or high-level civil servants. Moreover, Firmus three times attempted to negotiate with Theodosius with real hopes of being forgiven, which would have been impossible if he was either a usurper or a king (Amm. Marc. 29.5.8, 11, 15–16). In fact, the only reason Ammianus compares the revolt of Firmus to a usurpation was to emphasize his importance. It also permitted him to highlight one of his favourite themes, the danger of revolts or usurpation caused by the influence of bad court advisers, like the *magister officiorum* Remigius. In that sense, it was for him not dissimilar to the usurpation of Silvanus in Gaul in 355.[41]

---

36 For the use of the term *regulus* in fourth century, Fanning 2010.
37 This was notably the interpretation of Kotula 1970.
38 Amm. Marc. 29.5.48: *Paulo ante vesperam visus est Firmus, equo celsiori insidens, sago puniceo porrectius panso milites clamoribus magnis hortari, ut dedant Theodosium oportune, truculentum eum adpellans et dirum et suppliciorum saevum repertorem, si discriminibus eximi vellent, quae perferebant.*
39 Amm. Marc. 29.5.20: *Et Constantianorum peditum partem Tigavias venire iusserat cum tribunis, e quibus unus torquem pro diademate capiti inposuit Firmi.*
40 Amm. Marc. 29.5.36, 52, 55 (*perduellis*), 29.5.20 (*rebellis*). Theodosius the Elder denounces Firmus as a *latro* (29.5.46) but Ammianus does not use himself this stigmatizing term. He qualifies two usurpers, Julian (21.13.16) and Procopius (26.9.10), as *rebelles*. However, he also clearly described Procopius as *usurpator* (26.7.12), which was not the case for Firmus.
41 Amm. Marc. 15.5. The long narrative of the revolt of Firmus also suggests a parallel with the oriental usurpation of Procopius in 365 against Valens, the brother of Valentinian (Amm. Marc. 26.5–10).

In fact, Ammianus' narrative contains numerous clues showing that the revolt of Firmus was a provincial and military revolt, supported by local elites. Ammianus mentions that Firmus' recruits included a Roman officer charged with the administration of Mauretanian tribes (*praefectus gentis*), a leading decurion (*primatis*) and his son, and two regular military units.[42] Firmus seems to have had some influence on the soldiers of Theodosius the Elder even at the end of his military campaign.[43] He seems to have occupied Icosium without besieging or damaging it, unlike the case in Caesarea, the provincial capital, which was burned (Amm. Marc. 29.5.16). Augustine states that the city of Rusucurru opened its gates to Firmus (*Ep.* 87.10). On the other hand, the support he enjoyed from Mauretanian tribes was limited and he never attempted to engage Theodosius the Elder in open battle. The only tribes whose support Ammianus mentions are the *Mazices* and *Musones*, and they soon submitted to Theodosius and abandoned Firmus (Amm. Marc. 29.5.17, 25–27).

Ammianus himself even offered an alternative explanation of this revolt, but in a later chapter of his work. In the conclusion to his account of the reign of Valentinian, Ammianus explains the rebellion of Firmus as a reaction to the greed and cruelty of military officers, particularly Romanus the count of Africa, which Valentinian had failed to control (30.7.10). In this context, it was less necessary to eulogize Theodosius the Elder. This later account implies that Firmus had a large base of popular support in Africa. Moreover, Ammianus devotes a long section of Book 28 of his work to the persecution of local elites of Leptis Magna in Libya between 365 and 370 by the count Romanus, whom they accused of corruption. Ammianus accused his father, the *magister officiorum* Remigius, of having protected Romanus in this case as he did later against Firmus (28.6.8–29). Ammianus therefore offers two different explanations of the rebellion of Firmus: an uprising of barbarian Moorish tribes in a distant province and a legitimate revolt against the corruption of local and military administration. This inconsistency allowed him to insist on what were for him two major weaknesses of the Empire.

Eunapius of Sardis was therefore mistaken in stating that Firmus was a usurper. However, he gives the same explanation of his revolt as Ammianus in his second account, at approximately the same date. The Africans were

---

42 Amm. Marc. 29.5.24 (tribune of a cohort of mounted archers, a *princeps* and a *praefectus gentis* of the tribe of the *Mazices*), 29.5.43 (decurions), 29.5.20, 22 (military units).
43 Some of these soldiers deserted during a battle against Firmus: Amm. Marc. 29.5.48–49.

unable to endure the heavy burden of taxes imposed by the emperor Valentinian and the avarice of his generals in Mauretania.[44] This explanation gives the revolt a Roman character as a defence of *libertas* against the tyrannical rule of an emperor. Eunapius probably had in mind the usurpation of Gordianus in Africa Proconsularis against the cruelty and greed of emperor Maximinus Thrax in 238, which he had summarized in very similar terms at the beginning of his work.[45] That usurpation in 238 was supported by African local elites and the city of Carthage, and was legitimized by the Roman Senate. This shows that in the fourth century, a provincial rebellion could only have a positive reading if it was interpreted as a rightful usurpation with republican tones against the abuse committed by a tyrant and lacked any ethnic specificity. This suggests that Firmus' revolt was in reality a provincial rebellion supported some local elites and soldiers, and not an uprising of tribes never fully integrated into *Romanitas*.

Banditry and revolt in Isauria

The inhabitants of Isauria in the Taurus mountains in the south-east Anatolia caused much trouble between the third and fifth centuries.[46] Cilicia had been well known for banditry and piracy in the first century BC. Tacitus mentions two revolts in this region, both involving the tribe of the *Cietae*. In 36 AD, this tribe attempted to secede from the Empire to reject the newly imposed Roman fiscal system. The second revolt in 52 AD involved a siege of the city of Anemurium. Tacitus described the *Cietae* as barbarians, but not as bandits (*latrones*).[47] He therefore explained this revolt by the weak integration into the Empire of these mountain populations. However, no further uprisings are known until those, not very well documented, of the bandit leaders Trebellianus between 260 and 268 and Lydius during the reign of Probus. It was only from 354 that the Isaurians caused serious problems to the Empire. Three different sources written at the end of the fourth century or the beginning of the

---

44 Zos. 4.16.3. For the date of Eunapius' historical work, see Liebeschuetz 2003.
45 Zos. 1.13–14. Hdn. 7.10–24 provides a detailed narrative of the usurpation of 238, which was probably read by Eunapius.
46 On Isaurians in this period, see Shaw 1990, Lenski 1999, Pottier 2005.
47 Tac. *Ann*. 6.41, 12.55.1; see Lavan 2017: 26.

fifth – Eunapius of Sardis, Ammianus Marcellinus and the *Historia Augusta* – give different accounts of these Isaurian troubles. These events were usually explained by a traditional scheme linking residence in the mountains, a pastoral economy, poverty and banditry and also by a supposed ethnic propensity to banditry. However, these authors occasional suggest a more complex and original understanding of these troubles. Their character should also be questioned, as it is often difficult to differentiate massive banditry from revolt with political aims.

Ammianus Marcellinus, himself a native of Syria, devotes much attention to the Isaurian troubles from the beginning of the preserved part of his history. He states that, after infrequent and secret raids for the purpose of plunder (*latrocinia*), the Isaurians launched a real *bellum* in 354 by besieging the capital city of the province, Seleucia; though it was defended by no less than three legions, the Romans did not dare to confront them in a pitched battle.[48] For Ammianus, the year 354 represented a decisive change as latent banditry gave way to full scale revolt against the empire. A geographical work of the middle of the fourth century also remarks that the Isaurians had recently escalated from mere banditry to open hostility towards the Empire.[49] Yet Ammianus also emphasized the Isaurians' rebellious spirit and thereby made the *bellum* of 354 seem less exceptional. The Isaurians have an unstable disposition and oscillate between staying at peace and launching numerous raids for no reason. These bandits (*latrones*) periodically launch uprisings (*mota*) because of their rebellious (*perduellis*) spirit (14.2.1). He also assimilated them to wild beasts and to snakes which emerge from their lairs in spring to plunder the countryside (14.2.2, 19.13.1). Their raids were comparable to natural disasters inflicted on the Empire by Fortune or the Furies (28.2.11). He therefore does not really differentiate the *bellum* of 354 from other raids of lesser extent in 359 and 368 that he mentions. They were probably launched by individual Isaurian leaders without mobilization of the entire region.[50] In fact, Ammianus could not envisage a definitive solution to the problem. Only energetic leaders, such as the count and governor of Isauria in 359, Lauricius (19.13.2), and the *vicarius Asiae* in 368, Musonius (27.9.6), could prevent their expedi-

---

48 Amm. Marc. 14.2.1–20. He did not however use the terms *seditio* or *rebellio* to describe these events.
49 *Expositio totius mundi et gentium* 45: *iterum autem de Cilicia est et Isauria, quae viros fortes habere dicitur, et latrocinia aliquando facere conati sunt, magis vero ed adversarii Romanorum esse voleurunt*.
50 Amm. Marc. 14.2.1 (*perduellis*), 19.13 (raids of 359), 27.9.7 (raids of 368).

tions, and only temporarily.[51] The main import for Ammianus is to illustrate the weakness of the Empire, which even has to fight on an internal front.

Ammianus was, however, a conscientious historian. As for the rebellion of Firmus, he gives some clues which make it possible to better understand the distinctive nature of the *bellum* of 354. He states that Isaurians were exasperated by the execution of some of their *consortes* at Iconium by condemnation *ad bestias*, contrary to custom (*praeter morem*) – which would have been an unprecedented outrage. This passage provides crucial details. The Isaurians were probably outraged because the culprits were protected from such punishments by a privileged status. They probably belonged to the municipal elite.[52] However, Ammianus undermines his own explanation by stating that this was just a pretext for their natural savagery.[53] Moreover, Ammianus made no attempt to connect these executions with the cruelty of Caesar Gallus, who ruled the Orient at this time. Yet he had strongly denounced Gallus' illegitimate execution of members of the civic elite of Antioch in 354 in a chapter which precedes the narrative of the Isaurian revolt (14.1). Thus, as in Firmus' case, Ammianus refused to attribute this unrest to the cruelty of provincial administration and imperial rule in the fourth century, even though this is one of the main themes of his history. For Ammianus, only senators and municipal elites of civilized areas could be sympathetic victims of state violence. He seems not to have considered injustice towards persons in peripheral regions as sufficient grounds for revolt. In a parallel segment of his work, Ammianus links the rebellion in 365–369 of the *Austoriani*, a Libyan tribe on the desert fringes, to a desire to avenge the burning alive of one of their countrymen, who had been accused of being a spy. However, he describes the *Austoriani*, like the Isaurians, as wild beasts aroused by madness.

---

51 Lauricius garrisoned a fortified post previously occupied by *latrones* (*ILS* 740). An epitaph of Musonius, quoted by Eunapius (*frg*. 45), compared him to Homeric heroes.

52 Matthews 1989: 363 supported this interpretation. On the contrary, Shaw 1990: 246 and Hopwood 1999: 184 supposed that a treaty with the Empire was signed before 354 which gave a partial autonomy to Isauria. However, this treaty is not attested and it is rather unlikely that an emperor would have given such autonomy to a region within the Empire. The treaty of 368 mentioned by Ammianus (27.9.7) was probably limited to certain Isaurian leaders in mountainous area and did not concern the whole of Isauria.

53 Amm. Marc. 14.2.1–2: *ex latrociniis occultis et raris, alente inpunitate adulescentem in peius audaciam ad bella gravia proruperunt*.

He thereby implies that vengeance was only a pretext for this tribe to resume their periodic raids against Libyan cities.[54]

Ammianus gives other clues as to the nature of Isaurian uprisings. He states that the citizens of the city of Germanicopolis in Isauria played a role in the ratification in 368 of a truce between the Empire and some Isaurian chieftains who had to give hostages. He implies that the Isaurians listened to their *sententiae*. They were not just intermediaries between the Isaurians and the Empire. Ammianus even describes them as *signiferi*, standard bearers, of the rebellion, as if they played a leading role in the *bellum* of 354.[55] In other words, banditry and revolt in Isauria did not just involve some village leaders in the highest mountains but also local cities and some of their elite. Yet Ammianus, though he recounts military events with precision, fails to name a single Isaurian leader or to specify which parts of Isauria was involved in each uprising, showing even less interest than for the revolt of Firmus, though he was himself from nearby Syria.[56]

Ammianus gives some other socio-economic context to these uprisings. He twice remarks that the Isaurians were reduced to desperation by a famine at the time of the *bellum* of 354 (14.2.2, 13–14). He also explains the truce of 368 by noting that the Roman army had blockaded some strongholds in the mountains and thereby condemned their inhabitants to hunger (27.9.7). There is evidence that there was indeed a famine in Cappadocia, near Isauria, in 368.[57] The *bellum* of 354 could therefore be interpreted as a concerted reaction, involving local city elites, to a serious food shortage. The populations of this remote rural region could not have benefitted from food distributions, since they were reserved for the cities. Ammianus denounces the Caesar Gallus for executing several municipal councillors of Antioch in 354 to satisfy the *plebs* of this city who had accused them of exacerbating the

---

54 Amm. Marc. 28.6.4: *Huius necem ulcisci, ut propinqui damnatique iniuste causantes, ferarum similes rabie concitarum exsiluere sedibus suis.* Ammianus (27.9.1–7) notably groups together the uprisings of Isaurians in 368 and those of the *Austoriani* to put them in parallel. He mentions cases of massive banditry in Gaul and Syria in 369 in a later chapter (28.2.10–14) to give a similar impression.

55 Amm. Marc. 27.9.7: *Ubi cum is nec quiescendi nec inveniendi ad victum utilia copia laxaretur, per indutias pacem sibi tribui poposcerunt, Germanicopolitanis auctoribus, quorum apud eos ut signiferae manus semper valuere sententiae, obsidibusque datis (ut imperatum est), immobiles diu mansere, nihil audentes hostile.*

56 As remarked by Matthews 1989: 365. For example, Ioh. Mal. 13.38 (Dindorf 345.8–11) mentions Balbinus, an Isaurian leader who was executed under the reign of Theodosius. He therefore gave audacious leaders a larger role in Isaurian banditry than did Ammianus.

57 According to Gregory of Nazianzus and his friend Basil of Caesarea, the Cappadocian famine of 368 was particularly serious (Basil. *Ep.* 27.31; Greg. Nyss. *Or.* 43.34–35). See Holman 1999.

famine by their speculations. He also let the *consularis Syriae* Theophilus be lynched by the *plebs* (14.7.2–6). The populations of nearby rural districts did not have the same possibility of influencing emperors or high-level officials as the urban *plebs*. It is likely that the food shortage of 354 gave birth to a growing feeling of unity among the Isaurians, who may have gathered around natural elites such as the municipal councillors. There was therefore a real provincial revolt against the rule of the Caesar Gallus in 354 in Isauria.

Eunapius of Sardis, who lived in Asia Minor, was very concerned about the Isaurian menace. Indeed, the Isaurians launched long-distance raids into Cappadocia and Syria in 403–406, approximately when Eunapius was writing his history.[58] Yet he showed surprisingly little interest in the Isaurian uprisings of the fourth century, which were recorded by Ammianus for the years 354, 359 and 368. Eunapius only mentions a revolt in 377 which was not reported by Ammianus and involved sieges of cities of Lycia and Pamphylia. In this passage, however, he refers to the Isaurians as Solymes, Pisidians or Cilicians of the mountains (Zos. 4.20.1–2). This suggests that many acts of banditry or revolts committed by inhabitants of other mountainous districts in Asia Minor were attributed falsely to the Isaurians, owing to their bad reputation. For example, the rhetorician Himerios mentions operations in the 340s against bandits in Pisidia, a distinct region west of Isauria.[59]

In fact, Eunapius develops the theme of banditry in Isauria in a different way to Ammianus. Eunapius preferred to develop at length a fictional anecdote related to the deeds of some Isaurians in the third century rather than relating the fourth century uprisings in detail. He focuses on the actions of the Isaurian bandit leader Lydios who is supposed to have taken the city of Cremna in Pisidia under the reign of emperor Probus (276–282) and fiercely defended the city against Roman forces which besieged it. However, his cruelty caused him to be betrayed by one of his men, which indicates that Eunapius did not see him as a rightful ruler but as a kind of tyrant.[60] In fact, Eunapius used these events as a pretext to introduce a traditional bandit story, inspired by popular Greek novels, for which Eunapius had a particular appre-

---

58 Zos. 5.15.4–16; 5.25.2; Eunap. *frgm*. 84.
59 Himer. *Or.* 25.10, describing the actions of the proconsul and former *vicarius* of Asia, Skylakios.
60 Zos. 1.69. Lydios is not otherwise known. His name denotes a non-Isaurian origin. It is probably not possible to identify him with Palfuerius, an Isaurian bandit leader who was submitted by Probus and was mentioned at SHA *Prob*. 16.4–17.1.

ciation,[61] like Herodian, a Greek historian of the first part of third century.[62] These stories introduced a moral discourse about the righteous ruler, which disparaged new leaders from regions not fully integrated into civilization. Eunapius also reuses the theme, familiar from the history of Aurelius Victor, of the ambitious leader who recruits bandits as followers. However, Stephen Mitchell has used using archaeological and epigraphical data to show that Eunapius misrepresented an actual rebellion of the city of Cremna in Pisidia in 278, probably due to fiscal pressures, by attributing the unrest to a wandering gang of bandits from distant Isauria.[63] Eunapius preferred to use the scheme of the bandit leader rather than narrate the unthinkable rebellion of cities, like the Roman colony of Cremna and perhaps Germanicopolis in the fourth century. Unlike Ammianus, Eunapius explained Isaurian banditry by the personal ambitions of some of their leaders, who had no difficulties gathering followers in this poor and mountainous region.

Surprisingly, the Roman senatorial author of the *Historia Augusta*, a Latin collection of imperial biographies written in the beginning of the fifth century, offers a more comprehensive analysis of unrest in Isauria.[64] He invents an Isaurian rebellion against the tyrannical and cruel emperor Gallienus between 260 and 268, probably to give his interpretation of the Isaurian uprisings of the fourth century. The Isaurians give themselves an emperor, Trebellianus, with the sole purpose of protecting themselves from Gallienus. The author of the *Historia Augusta* dismissed those who devalued Trebellianus as an *archipirata* by saying that he minted coins and built a *palatium* for himself in Isauria. Even if his aspirations were ridiculous, they testified to his Roman identity. Trebellianus was not intrinsically different from the numerous other usurpers who challenged Gallienus. The author of the *Historia Augusta* therefore challenged conventional interpretations of the Isaurians. He also insisted on the personal role of ambitious leaders, as Eunapius did. After Gallienus sent a general who killed Trebellianus, the Isaurians, fearing strong reprisals, decided to secede. They were from this point considered barbar-

---

61 He develops the story of the bandit Charietto rallying to the Caesar Julian in Gaul in 358 (Zos. 3.7.1–7). He states that the emperor Theodosius himself, with some soldiers, went to various inns to investigate crimes committed by barbarian bandits in Macedonia in 391 (Zos. 4.48). This is very doubtful.
62 See for example the story of the deserter Maternus in the reign of Commodus: Hdn. 1.30–33.
63 Mitchell 1999; see also Zimmerman 1996.
64 For the date, see Rohrbacher 2016: 165–66, Savino 2017: 148–49.

ians and an internal *limes* was created to separate them from the Empire.[65] The author of the *Historia Augusta* implied that a policy of clemency could have prevented this failure (SHA *Tyr. Trig.* 26.1–6). Trebellianus is probably a fiction.[66] His narrative is therefore an allusion to the Isaurian problem of the fourth century, perhaps specifically the *bellum* of 354. The tyrant Gallienus could stand for Constantius II and his Caesar Gallus, in charge of the east in 354. The author of the *Historia Augusta* considered the Isaurian problem insoluble, a view more relevant to the period after 354. The sole way to prevent uprisings by the Isaurians was to deport them in the Cilician plains and settle army veterans in their mountains, as the good emperors Claudius II and Probus are supposed to have done (SHA *Tyr. Trig.* 26.7, *Prob.* 16.5–6). Ancient historians were generally inclined to give simplified analyses of banditry, attributing it to a distinct, barbarian ethnic identity as Ammianus does, or to the role of ambitious leaders as Eunapius and the author of the *Historia Augusta* do. However, historians like Ammianus and the author of the *Historia Augusta* leave enough clues to inform more complex interpretations and permit us to understand these uprisings as provincial revolts.

A socio-economic interpretation of banditry in the anonymous *De Rebus Bellicis*

An anonymous proposal for reforms addressed to an unknown fourth-century emperor, the *De Rebus bellicis*, offers a more original and complex analysis of provincial unrest. The fiscal and monetary policy of Constantine is condemned as having favoured the wealthy *potentes*, the only ones who could possess gold. The humblest (*tenuiores*) were also violently oppressed by taxation officials. The *afflicta paupertas*, heated by *odium*, began to commit robberies (*latrocinia*) in the countryside, mainly directed at the beautiful houses of the *potentes*, causing destruction in both halves of the Empire. Many *pauperes* then became professional criminals and supported *tyranni* who were in

---

65 A distinct *limes* sector is not attested in Isauria in the fourth and fifth centuries. However, the governors of Isauria gained increased military power with the title of count from the reign of Constantius II.
66 He is not recorded in another source. His name seems to be derived from the supposed author of this biography, Trebellius Pollio, which highlights his Roman identity.

turn supressed by the emperor to whom the treatise was dedicated.[67] Though the language is vague, it suggests that the *pauperes* created those usurpers. The author of this treatise thus offered a social, economic and also moral explanation of provincial unrest which it saw as endemic since the reign of Constantine. Banditry is identified as a low-level rebellion with a distinct aim: social vengeance against *potentes* who had no respect for laws or *pietas*. Banditry is not related to any ethnic identity or particular geographic setting, but only to poverty.[68] The anonymous author seems to have linked banditry and usurpation in order to accentuate the political threat to the addressee of his treatise and thereby convince him of the need to implement the proposed reforms. It was with the same purpose that he exaggerated his analysis by suggesting that most *pauperes* became bandits and supporters of usurpers. He drew on the common *topos*, illustrated by Ammianus in his treatment of the revolt of Firmus, that usurpers could easily mobilize bandits who were by nature always eager to support *res novae*. However, in his case, the bandits are supposed to have proper political aims: *odium* of the *potentes* and the state. This author also seems to draw on one of the main models for explaining internal Roman strife, Sallust's account of the Catilinarian conspiracy. This supposed that, during a period characterized by the elite corruption, ambitious leaders could gather criminals and people eager for *res novae* to foment a revolution (Sall. *Cat*. 5.10–13). In the *De Rebus Bellicis*, however, these people were morally justified. The corruption and *avaritia* of the elites excused the *impietas* of the *pauperes*.

This petition was probably sent in 368 or 369 to Valentinian or his brother Valens who ruled the eastern part of the Empire.[69] Its author, seeking employment in the administration, was probably inspired by the numerous

---

67 Anon. *de rebus bell.* 2.1.4–6: *Constantini temporibus profusa largitio aurum pro aere, quod antea magni pretii habebatur, vilibus commerciis assignavit; sed huius avaritiae origo hinc creditur emanasse. ... Ex hac auri copia privatae potentium repletae domus in perniciem pauperum clariores effectae, tenuioribus videlicet violentia oppressit. Sed afflicta paupertas, in varios scelerum conatus accensa, nullam reverentiam iuris aut pietatis affectum prae oculis habens, vindictam suam malis artibus commendavit. Nam saepe gravissimis damnis affecit imperia populando agros, quietem latrociniis persequendo, inflammando odia; et per gradus criminum fovit tyrannos, quos ad gloriam virtutis tuae produxit magis quam succendit audacia.*

68 Cassius Dio (75.1–2) already linked banditry and poverty in the third century. He states that, when Septimius Severus ended the recruitment of Italians in the Praetorian cohorts, they were forced to become bandits or gladiators to earn a living. However, the interpretations of the author of the *De Rebus Bellicis* are unique in ancient literature because of their complexity.

69 According to Mazzarino 1951: 73–74 and Giardina 1989: xxxvii-lii, the treatise was addressed to Constantius II between 353 and 360. Another interpretation more convincingly defended by

laws enacted by these emperors to prevent the oppression of the *rustici* by the *potentes*, especially the creation or reformation of the function of *defensor plebis*.⁷⁰ The next chapter of the work proposes measures against the habitual corruption of provincial governors. Thus, social unrest dating back to the reign of Constantine is only supposed to have acquired political significance relatively recently. The author may have been thinking of the usurpation of Procopius and Marcellus in 365 against Valens, which Ammianus Marcellinus claimed was supported by criminals and persons of low status (26.7, 26.10.3), or of Firmus himself, who was sometimes assimilated to a usurper as already seen. However, the author of the *De Rebus Bellicis* might not have had a particular *tyrannus* in mind. He may just have been warning the emperor of a risk of future usurpations if the socio-economic problems were not solved. He may also have been inspired by the usurpation of Magnentius in 350 against the emperor Constans at *Augustodonum* in Gaul. According to Eunapius, Magnentius was supported by the inhabitants of this city but also by the peasants of the countryside.⁷¹ The *De Rebus Bellicis* shows that administrative officials of the fourth century could propose more complex interpretations of provincial unrest than those of contemporary historians, who were more bound to traditional *topoi*, or the simplifying schemes of panegyrics. Its criticisms of the *impietas* of *potentes* are surprisingly close to those developed by some Christian writers, such as Salvian of Marseille, writing in the middle of the fifth century.⁷²

Conclusions

In general, provincial uprisings were only recorded by ancient historians if their intensity was sufficient to assimilate them to full-fledged wars (*bella*),

---

Thompson 1952 proposes a redaction between 366 and 369 under Valentinian. For Cameron 1979, the pamphlet was sent to Valens between 368 and 369.

70 Between 364 and 373 Valentinian profoundly transformed the office of the *defensor civitatis* which had existed at least since Constantine (*CTh* 1.29.1–5).

71 Zos. 2.42.4. Magnentius accused Constans of being a tyrant in front of his troops (2.47).

72 According to Salvian, the fiscal tyranny of the municipal elites over *pauperes* explained why many of them joined the *Bagaudae* (*Gub.* 5.24). However, Salvian refused to describe them as *latrones*. The author of the *De Rebus Bellicis*, who deplored Constantine's confiscation of temple properties, was himself a pagan.

characterized by the assault of cities, or if they could provide colourful anecdotes involving strange and ridiculous usurpers or bandit leaders. These anecdotes allowed them to highlight by contrast the qualities of good emperors or generals, such as Theodosius the Elder, who suppressed the revolt of Firmus.

Two schemes of interpretation were used to demean the rebels as criminals. Many uprisings were condemned, especially by Ammianus Marcellinus, as ethnic banditry, the work of internal barbarians such as Isaurian and Mauretanian tribes. No further explanation was needed. They were indeed inevitable. Other narratives of provincial unrest emphasized the role of leaders motivated by desire to become kings of newly created states or usurpers because of their *audacia* and ambitions. This implied a democratization of the imperial office, such that even men of the lowest status could aspire to it. This was perceived as a growing threat to the stability of the Empire and was often explained by the weakness of the ruling emperor. Yet some usurpations could be valorized as a defence of Roman *libertas* against abuses committed by emperors who were regarded as tyrants, if they had no particular ethnic identity and if some elements of the social elite were involved. As the legitimacy of any usurpation was always opened to debate, as Eunapius suggests for Firmus and the *Historia Augusta* for Trebellianus, some clemency had to be shown towards these rebels.

Ammianus in particular rarely attributed rebellions to the wrongdoings of provincial administration, as Tacitus often did, because he did not want to legitimize them. As Myles Lavan has noted, Tacitus rarely dismissed provincial rebels as mere bandits (2017: 24, 30). On the contrary, even if Ammianus gave some hints of a deeper comprehension of the nature of provincial unrest, he preferred to offer simpler explanations more in line with his conception of the weakness of an Empire that was threatened by internal and external barbarians. He thus chose to give more attention to these uprisings than other contemporary historians but without offering any more complex an analysis of their causes. The contrast with Tacitus, whose historical work he aimed to continue, could probably be explained by the fact that Tacitus was more confident in the resilience of the Empire against internal dissent (Woolf 2011: 43, Lavan 2017: 34). Ammianus' narratives of provincial uprisings must therefore be challenged and deconstructed.[73] The use of these stereo-

---

73 The methodology defined by Kelly 2008 for the study of the historical work of Ammianus should therefore be applied to these events.

types exemplifies the difficulty late antique historians had in recognizing the existence of provincial revolts possibly supported by cities and their elites in an Empire which was supposed to be ever more integrated. It also exemplifies their reluctance to attribute these rebellions to socio-economic causes, as the *De Rebus Bellicis* did exceptionally.

Works cited

Barnes, Timothy. 1996. 'Oppressor, persecutor, usurper: the meaning of tyrannus in the fourth century', in Giorgio Bonamente and Marc Mayer, *Historiae Augustae Colloquium Barcinonense*, n. s. 4. Bari, 55–65.

Bijovski, Gabriela. 2007. 'Numismatic evidence for the Gallus revolt: the hoard from Lod'. *Israel Exploration Journal* 57(2): 187–203.

Cameron, Alan. 1979. 'The date of the Anonymous *De Rebus bellicis*', in M. W. C. Hassal, ed., *Aspects of the De Rebus Bellicis. Papers Presented to Professor E. A. Thompson*, BAR International series, LXIII. Oxford, 2–14.

Chauvot, Alain. 1998. *Opinions romaines face aux barbares au IVe siècle ap. J. C.* Paris.

Drijvers, Jan Willem. 2007. 'Ammianus and the revolt of Firmus', in Jan den Boeft, Jan W. Drijvers, Daniel den Hengst and Hans Teitler, eds., *Ammianus after Julian. The Reign of Valentinian and Valens in Books 26–31 of the Res Gestae*. Leiden, 129–55.

Elton, Hugh. 2006. 'Warfare and the military', in Noel Lenski, ed., *The Cambridge Companion to the Age of Constantine*. Cambridge, 325–346.

Fanning, Steven. 2010. '*Reguli* in the Roman Empire, Late Antiquity, and the Early Germanic Kingdoms', in Ralph Mathisen and Danuta Shanzer, eds., *Romans, Barbarians and the Transformation of the Roman World*. Farnham, 43–53.

Geiger, Joseph. 1979. 'The last Jewish revolt against Rome: a reconsideration'. *Scripta Classica Israelica* 5: 250–57.

Giardina, Andrea. 1989. *Le cose della Guerra*. Rome.

Holman, Susan. 1999, 'The hungry body: famine, poverty, and identity in Basil's Hom. 8'. *Journal of Early Christian Studies* 7: 337–63.

Hopwood, Keith. 1999. 'Bandits between grandees and the state: the structure of order in Roman Rough Cilicia', in Keith Hopwood, ed., *Organised Crime in Antiquity*. London, 177–206.

Kelly, Gavin. 2008. *Ammianus Marcellinus. The Allusive Historian*. Cambridge.

Kotula, Tadeuz. 1970. 'Firmus, fils de Nubel, était-il usurpateur ou roi des maures'. *Acta Antiqua Academiae Scientiarum Hungaricae* 18: 138–40.

Lavan, Myles. 2017. 'Writing revolt in the early Roman Empire', in Justine Firnhaber-Baker and Dirk Schoenaers, eds., *The Routledge History Handbook of Medieval Revolt*. Oxford, 19–38.

Leveau, Philippe. 1973. 'L'aile II des Thraces, la tribu des *Mazices* et les *praefecti gentis* en Afrique du Nord'. *Antiquités Africaines* 7: 153–92.

Lenski, Noel. 1999. 'Assimilation and revolt in the territory of Isauria from the 1st Century B. C. to the 6th Century A. D.'. *Journal of the Economic and Social History of the Orient* 42: 413–65.

Liebeschuetz, Wolfgang. 2003. 'Pagan historiography and the decline of the Empire', in Marasco Gabriele, ed., *Greek and Roman Historiography in Late Antiquity. Fourth to Sixth Century A. D.* Leiden, 177–218.

MacMullen, Ramsay. 1963. 'The Roman concept robber-pretender'. *Revue Internationale des droits de l'antiquité* 10: 221–25.

Matthews, John. 1989. *The Roman Empire of Ammianus*. Ann Arbor.

Mazzarino, Santo. 1951. *Aspetti sociali del quarto secolo. Ricerche di storia tardo-romana*. Rome.

Mitchell, Stephen. 1999. 'Native rebellion in the Pisidian Taurus', in Keith Hopwood, ed., *Organised Crime in Antiquity*. London, 155–76.

Modéran, Yves. 1989. 'Gildon, les Maures et l'Afrique'. *Mélanges de l'École française de Rome* 101: 821–72.

Neri, Valerio. 1997. 'L'usurpatore come tiranno nel lessico politico della tarda antichità', in François Paschoud and Joachim Szidat, eds., *Usurpationen in der Spätantike*. Stuttgart, 71–86.

Piredda, Anna Maria. 2002. *Passio Sanctae Salsae: testo critico con introduzione e traduzione italiana*. Sassari.

Pottier, Bruno. 2005. 'Banditisme et révolte en Isaurie aux IVe et Ve siècles vus par les Isauriens eux-mêmes: la Vie de saint Conon'. *Mediterraneo Antico* 8: 443–74.

–. 2011.'Peut-on parler de révoltes populaires dans l'Antiquité tardive ? Bagaudes et histoire sociale de la Gaule des IVe et Ve siècles'. *Mélanges de l'École française de Rome* 123: 433–65.

Rohrbacher, David. 2016. *The play of Allusion in the Historia Augusta*. London.

Sabbah, Guy. 1978. *La méthode d'Ammien Marcellin. Recherches sur la construction du discours historique dans les Res Gestae*. Paris.

Salomon, Maciej. 1984. 'Calocaerus, *magister pecoris camelorum* e l'indole della sua rivolta in Cipro nel 334'. *Studi in onore Arbaldo Biscardi* V: 78–85.

Savino, Eliodoro. 2017. *Ricerche sull'Historia Augusta*. Napoli.

Shaw, Brent. 1990. 'Bandit highlands and lowland peace: the mountains of Isauria-Cilicia'. *Journal of the Economic and Social History of the Orient* 32: 199–233 and 237–70.

Stemberger, Gunther. 2000. *Jews and Christians in the Holy Land: Palestine in the Fourth Century*. Edinburgh.

Thompson, Edward. 1952. 'Peasants revolts in late Roman Gaul and Spain' *Past & Present* 2: 11–23.

Van Dam, Raymond. 1985. *Leadership and Community in Late Antique Gaul*. Berkeley.

Wiedemann, Thomas. 1979. 'Petitioning a fourth-century emperor: the *De Rebus Bellicis*'. *Florilegium* 1: 140–50.

Woolf, Greg. 2011. 'Provincial revolts in the early Roman empire', in Mladen Popović, ed., *The Jewish Revolt against Rome: Interdisciplinary perspectives*. Leiden, 27–44.

Zimmerman, Martin. 1996. 'Probus, Carus und die Räuber im Gebiet des pisidischen Termessos'. *Zeitschrift für Papyrologie und Epigraphik* 110: 265–77.

10. Towards a Discursive History of Christian Persecution

James Corke-Webster

Abstract: *This chapter begins to excavate the evolution of literary accounts of Christian persecution in the first three centuries. It treats the texts of the New Testament, the apologetic writings of Justin and Tertullian, and the historiographical narratives of Eusebius and Lactantius, focusing on the imagined agency of persecution, and the conceptual frameworks and related lexicons employed. It explores the increasing focus on the figure of the emperor, as well as the varying use of judicial and martial models. And it suggests that these evolutions were due less to changing historical circumstances, and more to wider social shifts in the culture of imperial society and the literary oeuvre of early Christianity.*

In Mervyn LeRoy's 1951 film *Quo Vadis*, the plot centres on the Roman emperor Nero's brutal persecution of Christians. In one prolonged scene, the camera flicks from the huddled mass of Christians singing on the floor of the Colosseum as lions are released around them, to Peter Ustinov's deranged Nero becoming increasingly agitated as he watches from the stands. This blockbuster's melodramatic imagination typifies – indeed, helped create – the now classic image of the persecution of Christians under the Roman empire, whether it be the setting, the period, or the means of execution.

The film's title comes from words spoken in the apocryphal *Acts of Peter* by the resurrected Jesus to Peter as he flees Nero's Rome. That is rather appropriate, since, the film's historical authenticity is, like that of Christian apocrypha, problematic. There is no good evidence for Neronian execution of Christians either in the Colosseum or by throwing them to lions. The best ancient sources note that 'Nero had offered his Gardens for the spectacle, and gave an exhibition in his Circus' (Tac. *Ann.* 15.44.9) and that 'they were covered with wild beasts' skins and torn to death by dogs; or they were fastened on crosses, and, when daylight failed were burned to serve as lamps by night' (Tac. *Ann.* 15.44.8).[1] In fact, the entire historicity of Nero's persecution has been recently questioned.[2]

The film's inaccuracy prompts a further question, however, namely whence this traditional picture arose? In cinematographic terms, this is easy to answer. *Quo Vadis*, like much of Hollywood's so-called 'swords and sandals' genre, was inspired by a late nineteenth-century painting, Jean-Léon Gérôme's *The Christian Martyrs' Last Prayer* (Fig. 1).[3] The debt is most obvious in the arena scene from the film highlighted in Figure 2, since it has clearly been constructed to echo the painting's frame – the three-pronged nature of the turning point in a kind of Colosseum/Circus Maximus hybrid, for example, or the relative positioning of lions and Christians.[4] In literary terms, we can trace the influence on Henryk Sienkiewicz's 1895 novel *Quo Vadis*, the film's source material, of Frederic Farrar's 1891 *Darkness and Dawn, or Scenes in the Days of Nero: A Historic Tale* (Malik 2020: 3, 184).

LeRoy's debt to Gérôme, and Sienkiewicz's to Farrar, are two small links in a mimetic chain that has constructed an image of Christian persecution very different from its reality.[5] In this chapter, I piece together some of the earliest elements of that chain, via writings produced in the first three centuries after the supposed events.[6] I treat in turn the texts of the New Testa-

---

1 Translations from Jackson 1937.
2 Shaw 2015 (critiqued in Jones 2017, with response in Shaw 2018; further critique in Van Der Lans and Bremmer 2017, Cook 2020), anticipated in brief in Moss 2013: 138–39. See too more radically but with a similar result Carrier 2014.
3 Wyke 1997, and more recently Rich 2019 on the material practice of Hollywood research departments that facilitated such inspiration, though Rich discusses only the influence on *Quo Vadis* of another of Gérôme's paintings, *Pollice Verso*. Both authors also identify multiple other fascinating stimuli.
4 Discussed, though without detail, in Wyke 1997: 122–23. There are multiple such parallels; an earlier still (2.16.44) preserves Gérôme's image of one lion emerged and the heads of two further large cats coming through the trapdoor. The film's depiction of Christians praying and its stylisation of Peter also echo the painting. Gérôme himself knew the setting should be the Circus, but elements of what he painted resemble the Colosseum; see viewing notes at https://art.thewalters.org/detail/36782/the-christian-martyrs-last-prayer/ – though these in fact err due to ignorance of Tacitus.
5 *Quo Vadis* itself stood (and stands) in a self-referential Hollywood mimetic chain; see Rich 2019: 166–70, and more generally Tashiro 1996: 19.
6 This is a prolegomenon to a wider research project. These 'links' should not be conceived as linear; multiple such ties could be drawn between the extant texts, and plenty more with those not extant. The most glaring omissions here are Christian martyr *acta* and *passiones*, which mobilise by turns the imagery of both cosmic warfare and judicial state – though not often imperial – agency (for affirmation of the former but a different take on the latter, see Middleton 2012: 169–70). These

Towards a Discursive History of Christian Persecution 221

Fig. 1: Oil painting by Jean-Léon Gérôme entitled *The Christian Martyrs' Last Prayer* (1863–1883). *The Walters Art Museum, Baltimore*

Fig. 2: Still from the motion picture *Quo Vadis* showing Christians awaiting their death in the arena. *Mervyn LeRoy and Mann 1951: 2.16.47*

ment (products of the second half of the first and earliest part of the second centuries), the apologetic writings of Justin and Tertullian (dated to the end of the second and start of the third centuries) and the historiographical narratives of Eusebius and Lactantius (written in the late third and early fourth centuries).[7] Though each discursive 'layer' is necessarily varied, being made up of multiple authors writing in their own distinctive circumstances, and necessitating caution about being overly schematic, nevertheless it is possible, I suggest, to trace a clear literary development in the presentation of the persecution of Christians. I focus here on two elements – first, the imagined agency of persecution, and second the conceptual frameworks and related lexicons employed.

For the first, I am interested in the central conception that it was Roman emperors who persecuted Christians, using Nero as a convenient focus. Nero is only the most famous of the many emperors often treated as having targeted Christians. Over the last century scholars have become increasingly cautious about attributing the Christian persecution to direct imperial agency, Neronian, or otherwise.[8] I argue here that in fact emperors only gradually became the main focus of Christian discourse about persecution in the first three centuries. So while they are almost entirely absent in the New Testament – with the debatable exception of *Revelation* – emperors as individuals become the prime focus in the apologetic writings of the late-second and early-third centuries, while the attitudes of successive emperors as a whole are a key structural principle to fourth-century imperial historiography.

For the second, I argue that while the majority of the New Testament presents persecution within a judicial context, *Revelation* introduced to the canon an alternative overarching framework, namely that of cosmic warfare. These two conceptual models were mobilised in different ways and in different combinations in later Christian writings. The apologists in both content and form take the former to its natural conclusion (though the latter is not entirely absent, in Tertullian in particular). But the latter became important again in the historical writings of both Eusebius and Lactantius. These evolu-

---

are omitted here in part for reasons of space, but also those of dating. The texts selected allow us to isolate three 'moments' in early Christian literary history. The martyr *acta*, on the other hand, cannot be easily fixed even by century; see for example, Moss 2010, Muehlberger 2022.

7 I am not investigating the attitudes to empire evidenced in these texts, a bigger and more well-trodden topic.

8 For an introduction, see Corke-Webster 2020.

tions, I argue, were due less to changing historical circumstances, and more to wider social shifts in the culture of imperial society and the literary oeuvre of early Christianity.

Prophecy and the Canon

I begin with a brief survey of the origins of the idea of Christian persecution in the texts that would ultimately make up the New Testament canon – the four Gospels, *Acts*, the Pauline, Pseudo-Pauline and assorted other letters, and the book of *Revelation*. In these texts, I suggest, the greatest weight is placed on Jewish agency. When we do encounter Gentile antagonism – in general in later texts of the canon – it is almost exclusively at the level of the local elites who ran the cities of the eastern empire. The Romans, when they do appear, do so more often as figures in fact offering protection. The emperor himself is a distant figure, barely in focus, except arguably in the contested case of *Revelation*. Moreover, the suffering of the earliest followers of Christ, both actual and anticipated, is described and imagined via two modes of discourse – the judicial and the martial. Via both aspects – agency and model – the New Testament establishes the baseline for the literary treatment of the persecution of Christians.

In the earliest gospel, that of Mark, Jesus warns his followers to anticipate trouble. After predicting the destruction of the Jerusalem Temple (*Mark* 13:2), he foreshadows the events that will precede 'the end' (*Mark* 13:7).[9] Included is a prediction of the disciples' suffering:

As for yourselves, beware; for they will hand you over to councils (παραδώσουσιν ὑμᾶς εἰς συνέδρια); and you will be beaten in synagogues (εἰς συναγωγὰς δαρήσεσθε); and you will stand before governors and kings (ἐπὶ ἡγεμόνων καὶ βασιλέων σταθήσεσθε) because of me, as a testimony to them. ... When they bring you to trial and hand you over (καὶ ὅταν ἄγωσιν ὑμᾶς παραδιδόντες), do not worry beforehand about what you are to say; but say whatever is given you at that time, for it is not you who speak, but the Holy Spirit. Brother will betray brother to death, and a father his child, and children will rise against parents and have them put to death; and you will be hated by all (ἔσεσθε μισούμενοι ὑπὸ πάντων) because of my name. But the one who endures to the end will be saved. (*Mark* 13:9–13)

---

9 Translations of all New Testament texts from the NRSV.

This represents the Ur-text for Christian expectations of suffering (part of a generic belief that salvation requires suffering and death; e.g. *Mark* 8:35).[10] It reflects a parochial provincial perspective. The 'councils' are *synedria*, local Jewish courts that echoed the Jerusalem Sanhedrin (Hooker 2001: 309). The 'governors' are Roman magistrates, and the 'kings' likely Roman client kings.[11] This passage seems designed to echo the supposed experience of Jesus, and possibly John the Baptist too; *paradidōmi* is used throughout Mark's passion narrative, and Jesus appears in sequence before the Sanhedrin and the governor Pilate, as John appears before Herod Antipas).[12] While there is a sense of universal antagonism, then, the primary focus seems to be Jewish agency.[13]

The other synoptic gospels repeat this prediction. *Matthew* includes it in the same context: 'Then they will hand you over to be tortured (παραδώσουσιν ὑμᾶς εἰς θλῖψιν) and will put you to death (καὶ ἀποκτενοῦσιν ὑμᾶς), and you will be hated by all nations (ἔσεσθε μισούμενοι ὑπὸ πάντων τῶν ἐθνῶν) because of my name' (*Matthew* 24:9). This is simultaneously more explicit about the expected result, and vaguer on those responsible, with no mention of judges or executioners.[14] Matthew also reuses verses 9, 11, and 12 of the Markan material in Jesus' instructions to the disciples about their impending mission (*Matthew* 10:17–23). Here the context again is clearly local, and Jewish. The verses gloss the initial instruction to 'go rather to the lost sheep of the house of Israel' (*Matthew* 10:5). And this section closes: 'When they persecute (διώκωσιν) you in one town, flee to the next; for truly I tell you, you will not have gone through all the towns of Israel before the Son of Man

---

10 There is a huge bibliography here. In fact, suffering and death represent the essence of Christian identity in Mark; see most recently Middleton 2014. On suffering and early Christian identity more broadly see Perkins 1995.
11 By the time the gospels were likely written, the Jewish ethnarchs were no longer a feature of the political landscape. But they were in the historical context in which the gospels are set, and Mark uses this language for one of them, Herod Antipas, calling him 'King Herod (ὁ βασιλεὺς Ἡρῴδης)' (*Mark* 6:14). This prediction of the disciples likely deliberately echoes Jesus' experience; see Middleton 2006: 154; I am also grateful to Ben Kolbeck for discussion of this point.
12 Hooker 2001: 309–10, citing Lightfoot 1950: 51–52. Hooker also notes prophetic echoes from the Hebrew Bible here, further confirming the Jewish frame of reference; see e.g. Micah 7:6, 4 *Ezra* 6:25 and 7:27.
13 Hengel 1985: 28 and van Kooten 2014: 439–45 suggest that Nero is intended by a subsequent reference in the same chapter to 'the desolating sacrilege' (*Mark* 13:14). This is based upon linguistic similarities with other New Testament texts, including *Revelation*, and is dismissed by Malik 2020: 65 as part of her wider argument; see further on pp. 234–35 below.
14 Filson 1971: 253 on the universal referents of this phrase.

comes' (Matthew 10:23). That is not to say that Matthew envisages nothing beyond that Jewish context; his gospel ends with the so-called 'Great Commission', when Jesus directs his disciples 'Go therefore and make disciples of all nations (πάντα τὰ ἔθνη)' (Matthew 28:19).[15] But suffering is not discussed at that point, nor is there the same degree of contextual detail.[16] Even more so than in Mark, then, the anticipated suffering of Christians seems to occur overwhelmingly in a provincial Jewish setting.[17]

Matthew also here employed what would become the most common term for persecution in Greek, the verb *diōkō* and its cognate forms. This classical term was well-familiar from the earliest Greek texts, regularly mobilised in diverse contexts, and meaning by turns to pursue, drive or prosecute, applied to people, animals, plants, objects, winds, and even arguments (Liddell and Scott 1883: 380). Mark had used the noun *diogmos* only in the abstract. In the parable of the sower, the seed sown on rocky ground corresponds to those who 'when trouble or persecution (θλίψεως ἢ διωγμοῦ) arises on account of the word, immediately fall away' (Mark 4:17; see too 10:30 and cf. Matthew 13:21). Matthew uses it more frequently, and his usage again usually points to suffering at the hands of Jewish agents. At the end of the Beatitudes Matthew says 'Blessed are you when people revile you and persecute you (ὀνειδίσωσιν ὑμᾶς καὶ διώξωσιν) ... for in the same way they persecuted (ἐδίωξαν) the prophets who were before you' (Matthew 5:11–12; see too 5:44). Even clearer, the evangelist rails against Jewish leaders – 'Woe to you, scribes and Pharisees, hypocrites' (Matthew 23:29) – refers to the earlier deaths of the prophets, and continues 'I send you prophets, sages, and scribes, some of whom you will kill and crucify (ἀποκτενεῖτε καὶ σταυρώσετε), and some you will flog (μαστιγώσετε) in your synagogues and pursue (διώξετε) from town to town' (Matthew 23:34). The language of the earlier prediction is thus repeated here in a clear Jewish context, connecting the persecution of the disciples to that of the Jewish prophets.

It is Luke who introduces *diōkō* into Mark's original prediction: 'they will arrest you and persecute you (ἐπιβαλοῦσιν ἐφ' ὑμᾶς τὰς χεῖρας αὐτῶν καὶ διώξουσιν); they will hand you over to synagogues and prisons (παρα-

---

15 With thanks to Sarah Parkhouse.
16 Nor, given the existence of the Jewish diaspora, would a universal mission in and of itself necessitate suffering from Gentile agents, let alone emperors.
17 This is not to ignore theological explanations of Matthew's focus on Israel, merely to note that one consequence is that it contributes to the absence of the person of the emperor in the anticipation of persecution.

διδόντες εἰς τὰς συναγωγὰς καὶ φυλακάς), and you will be brought before kings and governors (ἀπαγομένους ἐπὶ βασιλεῖς καὶ ἡγεμόνας) because of my name' (*Luke* 21:12). This is the only time Luke uses *diōkō* in this context (and only once otherwise; *Luke* 17:23). Like Matthew, though, Luke repeats the sentiment elsewhere too, when Jesus teaches: 'When they bring you before the synagogues, the rulers, and the authorities (εἰσφέρωσιν ὑμᾶς ἐπὶ τὰς συναγωγὰς καὶ τὰς ἀρχὰς καὶ τὰς ἐξουσίας)' (*Luke* 12:11). Luke, the latest of the gospels, is known for its more elite, urban, Hellenistic framing. Here, in the language of ἐξουσία, the author may have the structures of Roman power in view.[18] But his focus is on the scale of those he calls the *archai* – the local rulers of the Greek east of the Roman empire – as we will see more clearly in the treatment of *Acts* below.

In John's gospel we do not find repetition of these exact sayings. But we do find a comparison between the experience of Jesus and that foreseen for the disciples using the same language: 'If they persecuted me, they will persecute you (εἰ ἐμὲ ἐδίωξαν, καὶ ὑμᾶς διώξουσιν)' (*John* 15:20; see too 17:14). He summarises: 'I have said these things to you to keep you from stumbling. They will put you out of the synagogues (ἀποσυναγώγους)' (*John* 16:1–2). When speaking elsewhere of Jesus' experience, John says that 'the *Ioudaioi* started persecuting (ἐδίωκον) Jesus' (*John* 5:16).[19] John therefore presents a consistent picture of persecution due to Jewish agency.[20]

In Luke's sequel to his gospel, the *Acts of the Apostles*, Jesus' prophecies come to fruition. In describing the ensuing events Luke works to systematically exculpate the Romans, which means again highlighting the agency of the Jews.[21] Initial resistance to the apostles arises in *Acts* from the same Jewish authorities that targeted Jesus. Peter and John are first to suffer; 'the priests, the captain of the temple, and the Sadducees ... arrested them (ἐπέβαλον αὐτοῖς τὰς χεῖρας) and put them in custody (ἔθεντο εἰς τήρησιν)' (*Acts* 4:1–3; an interrogation follows at 4:5–22). The experience is explicitly tied by Luke to that of Jesus (*Acts* 4:23–30). Events repeat later (*Acts* 5:17–42); this time the apostles are 'flogged (δείραντες)' (*Acts* 5:40). The supposed first martyr,

---

18 It is interesting in this regard that *Luke-Acts*, one of the latest texts in the canon, has been read alongside the apologists, as in e.g. Nasrallah 2010.
19 Sanders and Mastin 1968: 163 suggest reading the imperfect as conative – i.e. that the Jews tried to persecute Jesus, but without success on this occasion.
20 Sanders and Mastin 1968: 343 assume Jewish agency in *John* 15:20.
21 Oft-noted; see e.g. Williams 1964: 224: 'Luke loses no opportunity of stressing the friendliness of the authorities to St. Paul or the Gospel' and then at 250: 'a certain anti-Jewish tendency in Luke'.

Stephen, is stoned to death by Jewish actors (*Acts* 7:58-9) after '[t]hey stirred up the people as well as the elders and the scribes; then they suddenly confronted him, seized him, and brought him before the council (ἐπιστάντες συνήρπασαν αὐτὸν καὶ ἤγαγον εἰς τὸ συνέδριον)' (*Acts* 6:12), a sequence that directly echoes Jesus' predictions. This again explicitly references the treatment of the prophets (*Acts* 7:9; 7:35-39; 7:51-53),[22] where the verb *diōkō* recurs: 'Which of the prophets did your ancestors not persecute? (τίνα τῶν προφητῶν οὐκ ἐδίωξαν οἱ πατέρες ὑμῶν)' (*Acts* 7:52).

Stephen's death is usually considered the narrative hinge in *Acts*, serving to introduce Paul - on whom the book will subsequently focus - who is present as a bystander. Luke narrates how 'That day a severe persecution (διωγμὸς μέγας) began against the church in Jerusalem' (*Acts* 8:1; see too 11:19, using τῆς θλίψεως). We read 'Saul was ravaging (ἐλυμαίνετο)[23] the church by entering house after house; dragging off (σύρων) both men and women, he committed them to prison (παρεδίδου εἰς φυλακήν)' (*Acts* 8:3; see too the accounts of Paul's own conversion at 9:4-5; 22:4; 22:7-8; 26:11; 26:14-15), where the mention of prison echoes Luke's adaptation of the original saying, discussed above. We read too how Paul was 'breathing threats and murder (ἀπειλῆς καὶ φόνου) against the disciples of the Lord' (*Acts* 9:1) and attempts to 'bring them bound (δεδεμένους ἀγάγῃ) to Jerusalem' (*Acts* 9:2; see too 9:21-22).[24] Here again, then, Luke focuses exclusively on Jewish agency.

Luke's focus then shifts to Paul's own experience, but he too suffers in a Jewish context. First, in Damascus, 'the Jews plotted to kill him (συνεβουλεύσαντο οἱ Ἰουδαῖοι ἀνελεῖν αὐτόν)' (*Acts* 9:23); then again in Jerusalem (*Acts* 9:29-30; see too 20:3). In Pisidian Antioch, 'the Jews incited the devout women of high standing and the leading men of the city, and stirred up persecution (ἐπήγειραν διωγμὸν) against Paul and Barnabas, and drove them out (ἐξέβαλον αὐτοὺς) of their region' (*Acts* 13:50; echoing *Luke* 9:5). Next, '[t]he same thing occurred in Iconium ... the unbelieving Jews stirred up (ἐπήγειραν) the Gentiles and poisoned their minds (ἐκάκωσαν τὰς ψυχὰς) against the brothers' (*Acts* 14:1-2). Luke then tells how 'an attempt was made (ἐγένετο ὁρμὴ) by both Gentiles and Jews, with their rulers (τοῖς ἄρχουσιν αὐτῶν), to maltreat them and to stone them (ὑβρίσαι καὶ λιθοβολῆσαι α-

---

22 It may also have been assimilated to the evangelists' accounts of Jesus; see Williams 1964: 111-12.
23 Williams 1964: 114 notes the animalistic connotations of this term.
24 Williams 1964: 125 notes in 'the man who made havoc (ὁ πορθήσας)' (*Acts* 9:21) a possible Lukan echoing of Paul's language in *Gal*. 1:13 and 1:23.

ύτούς)' (*Acts* 14:5). That the punishment was stoning suggests that for Luke this was an internal Jewish affair. History repeats itself in Lystra: 'Jews came there from Antioch and Iconium and won over the crowds. Then they stoned (λιθάσαντες) Paul and dragged (ἔσυρον) him out of the city' (*Acts* 14:19). Throughout the first half of *Acts*, then, the author clearly envisages Jews as the prime driving force behind persecution, even when they work with or through Gentile actors.[25]

In *Acts*' second half, Paul increasingly interacts with Gentiles and thus comes onto the radar of the magistrates of Greek cities of the eastern provinces.[26] But Luke still systematically shifts attention back to Jewish agents. Often the authorities' interest is catalysed by Jewish agitation. So, for example, the Jews in Thessalonica mobilise a crowd that declares to the local authorities – 'τοὺς πολιτάρχας' (*Acts* 17:6) – that '[t]hey [Paul, Silas, and their ilk] are all acting contrary to the decrees of the emperor (τῶν δογμάτων Καίσαρος)' (*Acts* 17:7). In response, 'after they had taken bail from Jason and the others, they let them go' (*Acts* 17:9). At this first mention of the emperor, then, Luke minimises conflict. And at the end of *Acts*, when the Jews hatch a secret plot to kill Paul (*Acts* 23:12–14), the Romans are used as pawns, since the plotters suggest that the Jewish authorities call for the Roman tribune who has Paul 'to bring him down to you, on the pretext that you want to make a more thorough examination (ὡς μέλλοντας διαγινώσκειν ἀκριβέστερον) of his case. And we are ready to do away with him before he arrives' (*Acts* 23:15; see too 23:20–21; 23:30).

In fact, Rome serves almost as a guarantor of protection for Christians. In Philippi, when Paul and Silas are seized and taken 'into the marketplace before the authorities (ἐπὶ τοὺς ἄρχοντας)' (*Acts* 16:19), 'the magistrates (οἱ στρατηγοὶ) had them stripped of their clothing and ordered them to be beaten with rods (ῥαβδίζειν),[27] and after 'a severe flogging (πληγὰς), they threw them into prison (ἔβαλον εἰς φυλακήν)' (*Acts* 16:22–23). But when the next morning these magistrates order their release (*Acts* 16:35), Paul accuses them of beating Roman citizens without trial (*Acts* 16:37), and Luke reports that 'they

---

25 The client king Herod Agrippa I makes a brief cameo persecutory appearance when he 'laid violent hands (ἐπέβαλεν ... τὰς χεῖρας κακῶσαί) upon some who belonged to the church. He had James, the brother of John, killed with the sword (ἀνεῖλεν ... μαχαίρῃ). After he saw that it pleased the Jews, he proceeded to arrest (προσέθετο συλλαβεῖν) Peter also' (*Acts* 12:1–3; see too 12:11). Here again Luke is sure to attribute even royal actions to the Jews more generally.
26 For an introduction to these, see Roselaar 2016.
27 The authorities here would likely be *duoviri* or *quattuorviri* and *aediles*; see Williams 1964: 194.

were afraid (ἐφοβήθησαν) ... so they came and apologized (παρεκάλεσαν) to them' (*Acts* 16:38–39). In Ephesus, fear of Roman retribution dissipates brewing discontent amongst Paul's opponents (*Acts* 19:23–41). When a military officer arrests Paul in Jerusalem, Luke presents it as protection from a Jewish-inspired mob (*Acts* 21:27–36). And again, after learning that Paul is a Roman citizen, even this officer is worried about having bound and almost flogged him (*Acts* 22:29). At *Acts*' denouement, when the Jewish authorities are arguing about Paul, a Roman tribune arrests him 'fearing that they would tear Paul to pieces (μὴ διασπασθῇ ὁ Παῦλος ὑπ' αὐτῶν)' (*Acts* 23:10). And when he sends Paul on to the governor, the accompanying note says that 'This man was seized by the Jews and was about to be killed by them (συλλημφθέντα ὑπὸ τῶν Ἰουδαίων καὶ μέλλοντα ἀναιρεῖσθαι ὑπ' αὐτῶν), but when I had learned that he was a Roman citizen, I came with the guard and rescued (ἐξειλάμην) him' (*Acts* 23:27).

When governors finally appear on the stage of *Acts* this picture continues. The first, Gallio (of Achaia), simply refuses to hear the Jewish case against Paul (*Acts* 18:12–17). When Paul is eventually arraigned before the governors Felix and Festus, both are notably passive. In the former case, the Jews are the driving agents (*Acts* 24.1; 24.9); Felix delays (*Acts* 24.22), then leaves Paul in prison 'since he wanted to grant the Jews a favour' (*Acts* 24:27; see too 25:9). When Festus replaces Felix, again, the Jews push for sentencing (*Acts* 25:1–3; 25:7) but Festus demurs (*Acts* 25: 4–5). This same dynamic prompts the most famous appearance of the emperor in *Acts*. When Festus attempts to pass Paul over to internal Jewish judicial procedure in Jerusalem, Paul replies 'I am appealing to the emperor's tribunal (τοῦ βήματος Καίσαρός); this is where I should be tried ... I appeal to the emperor (Καίσαρα)' (*Acts* 25:10–11). The emperor appears only then in the vaguest of senses, as the core symbol of Rome's role as a guarantor of justice – in other words, in the role entirely integral to the conception of the 'emperor' from its origins.[28]

When we shift attention to the New Testament epistles, the emperor barely features in the repeated references to the present and future sufferings of Christians. When Paul is explicit about agency, he always has the Jews in his sights. He speaks of himself as 'formerly a blasphemer, a persecutor (διώκτην), and a man of violence' (*1 Tim*. 1:13) – *diōktēs* is found neither in non-Christian writings nor elsewhere in the New Testament.

---

28 On the emperor as 'ever-present protector', illustrated by Lucius' (abortive) appeal to the emperor in Apuleius' *Golden Ass*, see Millar 1981: 66.

Of his own experiences, he recalls how 'Five times I have received from the Jews the forty lashes minus one (τεσσεράκοντα παρὰ μίαν). Three times I was beaten with rods (ἐρραβδίσθην). Once I received a stoning (ἐλιθάσθην)' (*2 Cor.* 11:24–25). Elsewhere he speaks of 'the Jews, who killed both the Lord Jesus and the prophets, and drove us out (ἐκδιωξάντων)' (*1 Thess.* 2:15). And when he asks, 'why am I still being persecuted (τί ἔτι διώκομαι) if I am still preaching circumcision?' (*Gal.* 5:11), he implies that the persecution is perpetrated by those who would have no need to do so if he were advocating this symbol of Jewish identity.

Often Paul does not explicitly assign agency, as, for example, when he discusses the apostles' missionary experience: 'We are afflicted (θλιβόμενοι) in every way, but not crushed; perplexed (ἀπορούμενοι), but not driven to despair; persecuted (διωκόμενοι), but not forsaken; struck down (καταβαλλόμενοι), but not destroyed' (*2 Cor.* 4:8–9; cf. *1 Cor.* 4:12; *2 Cor.* 6:4–9, 12:10; *1 Thess.* 1:6, 3:5; *2 Thess.* 1:4; *Gal.* 6:12; *Rom.* 8:35–6, 12:14, 16:3–4; *Phil.* 1:7; *Phlm.* 1:13).[29] But Jewish agency is often implied, because Paul uses the same language for his own pre-conversion persecution (*1 Cor.* 15:9; *Gal.* 1:13; 1:23; *Phil.* 3.6; see too *1 Thess.* 4.13 which echoes the language used of Stephen at *Acts* 7.60).[30] That he uses the same language while mobilising a Hebrew Bible metaphor is telling: 'But just as at that time the child who was born according to the flesh persecuted (ἐδίωκεν) the child who was born according to the Spirit, so it is now also' (*Gal.* 4:28–29). Since Paul explicitly associated the mother of the former child with 'the present Jerusalem' (*Gal.* 4:25), persecution seems to be attributed primarily again to Jewish agents (see too e.g. *Rom.* 8:35; citing *Ps.* 44:22). Where Paul does clearly envisage Gentile persecution, as in his comment to the Thessalonians, 'For you, brothers and sisters, became imitators of the churches of God in Christ Jesus that are in Judea, for you suffered (ἐπάθετε) the same things from your own compatriots as they did from the Jews' (*1 Thess.* 2:16; see too 1.6; 3.3–4),[31] the framework remains local rather than imperial.

In the Pseudo-Pauline epistles, the unknown authors followed Paul's usage. When the author of *2 Timothy* predicts that 'all who want to live a godly

---

29 There is a huge bibliography on these passages; see recently e.g. Middleton 2009.
30 On the last see Donfried 1985: 349 and Bruce 1990. *Gal.* 1.13 and 1:23 also use 'was trying to destroy (ἐπόρθουν) it' and 'tried to destroy (ἐπόρθει)' respectively; see above n. 19.
31 Barclay 1993: 514 (though I would demur from his ready explanation of the causes of that antagonism being intra-religious tension).

life in Christ Jesus will be persecuted (διωχθήσονται)' (2 Tim. 3:12), it comes immediately after 'Paul' speaks of 'my persecutions, and my suffering (τοῖς διωγμοῖς, τοῖς παθήμασιν) the things that happened to me in Antioch, Iconium, and Lystra ... What persecutions I endured (οἵους διωγμοὺς ὑπήνεγκα)' (2 Tim. 3:11). That list of locations makes clear that the author has in mind Paul's experiences as described in Acts (Acts 13:50; 14:1–2; 14:5; 14:19), where agency was firmly placed on the Jews. In the same text 'Paul' says that he 'was rescued from the lion's mouth (ἐκ στόματος λέοντος)' (2 Tim. 4:17). Later authors interpreted this to be about Nero,[32] but this is not present in the original text; rather the reference is inherited, being both a generic metaphor common for antagonists (see e.g. Ps. 7.3, which in the LXX also calls the latter 'my pursuers (τῶν διωκόντων)') and a specific reference to God closing 'the lions' mouths (τὰ στόματα τῶν λεόντων)' (Dan. 6:22; cf. 1 Macc. 2:60; Bassler 2011: 120).

Finally, we turn our attention to Revelation. Here again, anticipated Christian suffering is at the heart of the letter. So, the author's message to the church in Smyrna reads.

I know your affliction and your poverty (τὴν θλῖψιν καὶ τὴν πτωχείαν), even though you are rich. I know the slander on the part of those who say that they are Jews and are not, but are a synagogue of Satan (τῶν λεγόντων Ἰουδαίους εἶναι ἑαυτούς, καὶ οὐκ εἰσὶν ἀλλὰ συναγωγὴ τοῦ Σατανᾶ). Do not fear what you are about to suffer. Beware, the devil is about to throw some of you into prison so that you may be tested (μέλλει βάλλειν ὁ διάβολος ἐξ ὑμῶν εἰς φυλακὴν ἵνα πειρασθῆτε), and for ten days you will have affliction (θλῖψιν). Be faithful until death, and I will give you the crown of life. Let anyone who has an ear listen to what the Spirit is saying to the churches. Whoever conquers (ὁ νικῶν) will not be harmed by the second death. (Rev. 2:9–11)

This passage again connects present and anticipated suffering with Jewish agency. But this is also, as in Paul, given a cosmic dimension here, since Jewish and Satanic agency are elided. What is more, the passage ends with military language (the verb nikaō is characteristic of Revelation) signalling that a cosmic martial framework is overlaid above the anticipated mundane incarceration (Middleton 2006: 161–63).

In addition to Jewish agency, however, traditional interpretations suggest that Rome, its emperors, and Nero specifically, are all also blamed for

---

32 On Eusebius' imaginative reuse of this passage, which depended on earlier martyr narratives, see below on p. 254.

Christian suffering here.³³ The crux is the sequence of 'beasts'. The first beast, 'like a leopard, its feet were like a bear's, and its mouth was like a lion's mouth' (*Rev.* 13:2), had Satan's 'power and his throne and great authority', and a death-blow on its head, now apparently healed; 'In amazement the whole earth followed the beast' (*Rev.* 13:3). It 'was allowed to make war on the saints and to conquer them (ποιῆσαι πόλεμον μετὰ τῶν ἁγίων καὶ νικῆσαι αὐτούς)' (*Rev.* 13:7). This is usually read as a cipher for Roman imperial power, and a prediction of persecution from an (apocalyptically-returned) Roman emperor, usually seen as Nero.³⁴ This beast recurs later, 'full of blasphemous names' (*Rev.* 17:3), with 'seven heads and ten horns', and bearing a woman. This is glossed as referring to seven mountains and seven kings, and since the woman is explicitly called 'the great city that rules over the kings of the earth' (*Rev.* 17:18), this is again read as Rome (with her seven hills) and the Julio-Claudian and (possibly) Flavian emperors.³⁵ The author then speaks of how 'they will make war (πολεμήσουσιν) on the Lamb, and the Lamb will conquer them (νικήσει)' (*Rev.* 17:14). This apocalyptic language is certainly the nearest we find to an association between Christian suffering and imperial – and specifically Neronian – agency in the New Testament.

It is not entirely clear, however, that *Revelation* had either Nero, or even Roman emperors, in view. First, Shushma Malik has comprehensively demonstrated that the Antichrist-Nero tradition was created in late antiquity.³⁶ The tyrannical reputation of Nero was neither so systematic in the first century, nor so prevalent in the east where *Revelation* was composed,

---

33 The non-Pauline epistles contain only very general references to persecution, repeating biblical language, and with no obvious agents in view; e.g. 'Yet if any of you suffers (πασχέτω – from previous verse) as a Christian, do not consider it a disgrace, but glorify God because you bear this name' (*1 Pet.* 4:16).
34 E.g. Caird 1984: 162 suggesting that the first monster's appearance from the sea echoes the annual maritime arrival of the proconsul of Ephesus; the association with Nero is at 164. For a recent statement of this traditional view, with bibliography see Middleton 2012: 165–66.
35 E.g. Caird 1984: 211–62, highlighting the presence of temples to the goddess Roma in the first three cities to whom *Revelation* was addressed; see too 216–19. At 36–38 Caird links the author's statement that Satan resides in Pergamum to the construction there of the first imperial cult temple to Roma and Augustus (*Rev.* 2.12.13). And at 137–38 the reference to the bodies of the martyrs lying 'in the streets of the great city' (*Rev.* 11.8) is taken to refer to Rome. In all these examples there is nothing explicitly imperial.
36 Malik 2020, refuting an assumption repeated from Bousset 1895 to Van Kooten 2007 (a bibliographic survey at 17–28 notes examples of earlier scepticism). *Revelation* was the prime biblical text used for this re-imagining, with *2 Thess.* 2:3, *Daniel*, and *1 John* (and the non-canonical *Sibylline Oracles* and *Ascension of Isaiah*).

as to be useful as an easily recognised reference.[37] The details used to tie the first beast to Nero – in particular the mortal wound, and the sequence of seven kings with one returning as the eighth – do not unproblematically point to Nero. And in fact, a clear link was made only in the late third century, by Victorinus of Pettau.[38]

Second, the imagery and numbering are dependent on *Daniel* (7:2–7), creating one beast out of the four there described (Caird 1984: 162). Such language need not therefore necessarily refer to Rome and its emperor, but could simply be a generic symbol of worldly rule.[39] The number seven, for example, might not refer to Rome's hills, since such imagery was more widespread in ancient Canaanite and Jewish tradition.[40] Moreover, the imagery of seven heads and ten horns was applied not just to the first beast but to *Revelation*'s original dragon (*Rev.* 12:3). The author then calls the dragon 'that ancient serpent, who is called the Devil and Satan' (*Rev.* 12:8), a participant in the cosmic war in heaven.[41] He also speaks of Christian suffering as part of this battle with Satan: 'they have conquered (ἐνίκησαν) him by the blood of the Lamb and by the word of their testimony (τὸν λόγον τῆς μαρτυρίας αὐτῶν)' (*Rev.* 12:11).[42] This is also the only time that *Revelation* uses cognates of *diōkō*: 'when the dragon saw that he had been thrown down to the earth, he pursued (ἐδίωξεν) the woman who had given birth to the male child' (*Rev.* 12:13). In addition, *Revelation* is less concretely historical even than other apocalyptic texts employing similar language, problematising whether a definitive identification was intended (Malik 2020: 50–51, 78).

---

37 Malik 2020: 28–50.
38 Malik 2020: 65–78; among the extensive earlier literature see in particular Minear 1953. Further, the number 666, often used to link the beast to Nero, is in fact the number of the second monster (*Rev.* 13:11–18; at 18), the other descriptors of which do not fit Nero.
39 Malik 2020: 72 and 74; Caird 1984: 164 appears to hedge his bets (*contra* 218): 'It is thus misleading to say that the monster *is* Rome, for it is both more and less: more because Rome is only its latest embodiment; and less, because Rome is also, even among all the corruptions of idolatry, "God's agent of punishment, for retribution on the offender" (*Rom.* xiii.4)'; see too later at 214 on *Rev.* 17:1–6.
40 E.g. *1 Enoch* 60:88; 6:13; 7:32–33; 7:54. Caird 1984: 150 and 161; see too at 218 on the symbolic power of seven for this author.
41 See too Caird 1984: 159 on how the 'water like a river' (*Rev.* 13:15) that comes from the serpent's mouth must refer to Christian-Jewish conflict. Caird subsequently attributes the dragon's later move 'to make war on the rest of her children' (*Rev.* 12:17) to state persecution, without evidence or discussion.
42 Caird 1984: 220 affirming the view that this must refer to persecution.

Third, the actual persecution is predicated of the ten kings 'who have not yet received a kingdom, but they are to receive authority as kings for one hour, together with the beast' (*Rev.* 17:12). These ten kings echo the ten horns of *Daniel*, which represented ten Seleucid kings that preceded Antiochus VI Epiphanes. They have no obvious direct point of reference in the Roman world (Caird 1984: 163, 219–20). Since we also read that 'the ten horns that you saw, they and the beast will hate the whore', it is difficult to draw simple equations with Rome and its emperors.

With the possible exception of *Revelation*, then, the figure of the emperor does not appear in the literary landscape of the New Testament as the figure responsible for persecution. And while his governors do feature, they are the instruments rather than the agents of persecution; the latter role is overwhelmingly taken by the Jews, sometimes as provokers of Gentile agents. Roman agents more often appear as symbols of protection. So while the language of *Revelation* might have brought Rome and the emperors to mind for some readers, and indeed it is possible that this was intended, that would represent an outlier in the New Testament.

This survey also demonstrates that there are two broad conceptual frameworks for understanding persecution at work in the New Testament. Because much of the canon's interest – catalysed, among other things, by the prophetic tradition of the Hebrew Bible – was in public witness, the first, and most important, was judicial. But we also see an alternative martial framework come to fruition in *Revelation*.[43] This warfare was cosmic – the natural end point of cosmic imagery in the gospels – with Christians' suffering conceived as part of the ongoing battle between God and Satan. The boundary between these judicial and martial frameworks is porous, since Satan was the ultimate 'accuser' (the literal meaning of *satan* in Hebrew) and was habitually depicted as the prosecutor of the heavenly law court in the Hebrew Bible, rabbinic writings, and New Testament (e.g. Caird 1984: 154–56). These two conceptual models, and their philological matrices, establish the groundwork for subsequent treatment of Christian persecution.

---

[43] On this cosmic dimension, see especially Middleton 2006, on its basis in the New Testament at 135–71 (with Middleton 2014). The language of cosmic contest and martial language is certainly found in Paul (e.g. *Eph.* 6:10–17; *1 Thess.* 5:8) but often metaphorically, without explicit connection to imagined this-worldly suffering of Christians (see debate at 143). Danielic imagery is also found there, but not in a martial nexus, and without clear imperial referent (as suggested by Barclay 1993: 529 n. 60 without evidence). I respectfully demur from Middleton's position that Mark's language (for example ἐπιτιμᾶ-) is martial.

Justice and Apology

As part of his predictions of their future suffering in the synoptic gospels, Jesus reassures the disciples: 'When they bring you to trial and hand you over, do not worry beforehand about what you are to say (τί λαλήσητε); but say whatever is given you at that time, for it is not you who speak, but the Holy Spirit' (*Mark* 13:11). Matthew also uses the verb *laleō* (*Matthew* 10:19) but Luke makes an important change: 'do not worry about how you are to defend yourselves (ἀπολογήσησθε) or what you are to say' (*Luke* 12:11). In his use of *apologeomai*, Luke introduces more formal judicial language appropriate to his Hellenistic urban context. His vision of formal Christian 'defence' came to fruition in the writings of the second and third century apologists. Most important among this umbrella of diverse Christian writers, and anchoring their eastern and western traditions respectively, were Justin, writing in Rome in the mid-second century, and Tertullian, writing in Carthage in the early third.

Both Justin and Tertullian wrote *Apologies* (in Justin's case two survive), 'defences' of Christians against their apparent mistreatment by the populace and Roman authorities alike, that may or may not have envisaged the latter as their real-life audience.[44] Both are conscious of their debts to texts of the New Testament.[45] Justin says that 'only the things which we say and which we learnt from Christ and the prophets who came before him are true' (*1 Apol.* 23.1).[46] An entire section of the *First Apology* consists of summary and discussion of Jesus' teaching, including direct citation of the gospels (*1 Apol.* 14.4–17.4). When Justin speaks of 'the powerful word which his apostles, going out from Jerusalem, proclaimed everywhere, though death had been decreed against those who taught or simply confessed the name of Christ which we everywhere both embrace and teach' (*1 Apol.* 45.5) we are hearing echoes of Jesus' own warnings. Tertullian, writing in Latin, knew both the evolving

---

44 I consider here only Tertullian's *Apology* and Justin's so-called *First Apology* for reasons of space. The relationship between Justin's two apologetic texts is fraught; for a good summary of the problem and possible solutions, see Parvis 2008: 57. I eschew here the much-masticated question of their audience; put simply, I consider an internal Christian audience more likely; see especially Young 1999 and Cameron 2002.
45 I have argued elsewhere that the idea of suffering 'for the Christian name', found throughout the apologists, is also dependent on the New Testament; see Corke-Webster 2017: 404. Nasrallah 2010: 138 n. 57 also nods to this.
46 Greek text and translation taken from Minns and Parvis 2009.

canon, and Justin. He too makes repeated references to 'this more modern literature of ours (*nostrum hanc novitiolam paraturam*)' (*Apol.* 47.9; see too 31.1 and 37.1). Again, when he says that 'the school is in fact hated for the name of its founder' (*Apol.* 3.6), we see his debts to New Testament texts. Both apologists are thus familiar with the depiction of the persecution of Christians in the New Testament. And they adopt its judicial framework. But they put emperors front and centre. This is clear from both form and content. Justin's *First Apology* resembles a petition and appeals for justice 'To the emperor Titus Aelius Hadrian Antoninus Pius Augustus Caesar, and to Verissimus his son, philosopher, and to Lucius, the son of Caesar by nature and of Pius by adoption, lover of learning' (*1 Apol.* 1.1).[47] This imperial focus runs like a vein through the text; his choice of scriptural proof-text, for example, is determined by his imperial addressees, namely *Psalm* 2 from the Septuagint: 'And now, O kings (βασιλεῖς); understand, be instructed all judges (οἱ κρίνοντες) of the earth' (*1 Apol.* 40.16; Nasrallah 2010: 143).

More than this, however, Justin envisages these emperors as directly involved in the judicial processes against Christians, both preventing and perpetrating violence. The former builds on the sense in the New Testament that Rome and its actors could serve as a source of protection for Christians. So, for example, he suggests that an imperial investigation will inevitably produce 'a verdict (τὴν ... ψῆφον) which would actually be against yourselves' (*1 Apol.* 2.3–4; see too 5.1; 8.5; 31.5; 68.1–2). And he appends an apparent rescript of Hadrian to the end of the *First Apology* that tends to limit the persecution of Christians (*1 Apol.* 68.5–10; via which he claims imperial precedent to support his petition).[48]

But his imperial addressees are also explicitly spoken of as persecutors themselves. Again, building on but expanding the New Testament precedent, he follows the passage discussed above about the apostles' mission with a message to his imperial addressees: 'But even if you read these words with hostile intent (ὡς ἐχθροὶ), you can do nothing further, as we said before, than kill, which bears no harm to us (*1 Apol.* 45.6). The reader thus moves directly from apostolic precedent to imperial persecution. Justin also uses the lexi-

---

[47] There is some disagreement over which emperors were originally included, but the debate is not important for our purposes; see Minns and Parvis 2009: 34–41. Some have removed Lucius, most recently Marcovich 1994.

[48] On its likely inauthenticity see Nesselhauf 1976 (still largely ignored by more recent commentators).

con of the New Testament, but of emperors. For example, when he speaks of his addressees' failure to persecute 'heretics' such as Simon, Meander, and Marcion, he states: 'after the ascension of Christ to heaven the demons were putting up certain people who asserted that they were gods, who were not only not persecuted (ἐδιώχθησαν) by you, but were even deemed worthy of honours' (1 Apol. 26.1; see too 26.7).

We find the same focus on imperial agency in Tertullian's *Apology*. This was addressed not to emperors but to their appointees, 'the magistrates of the Roman Empire (*Romani imperii antistites*)' (*Apol.* 1.1; *passim*).[49] But the emperors' imagined responsibility for persecution still shines through. Tertullian speaks of magistrates 'not allowed openly to investigate' (*Apol.* 1.1; see too 1.7), thus indirectly putting emperors – the only higher authority – in his crosshairs. Later, he explicitly calls them out:

You, sir, then, who fancy we care nothing for Caesar's safety, look into the words of God, into our books (*litteras nostras*), which we do not hide, and which many a chance throws into the hands of outsiders. Learn from them, that the precept is given us (to the point of overflow of kindness) to pray to God even for our enemies (*inimicis*), to beseech his blessings for our persecutors (*persecutoribus nostris*). Who are more the enemies and the persecutors of Christians (*inimici et persecutores Christianorum*) than those against whose majesty we are accused of treason? But here it is explicitly named and in plain terms. 'Pray,' he says, 'for kings, and for princes and powers (*pro regibus et pro principibus et potestatibus*), that all things may be tranquil for you.' (*Apol.* 31.1–2, see too 37.1)

Here Tertullian jumps from Christians persecuted because of perceived slights against emperors to emperors themselves being persecutors. Equally important, we can see Tertullian, like Justin, working to tie this imperial agency to precedents found in 'our books', referencing a Pauline passage (*1 Tim.* 2.2) which in its original context had nothing to do with persecution. Here we see the apologetic switch in persecutory agency in action, as Tertullian appropriates a New Testament passage in service of painting the emperors as persecutions.

Tertullian, in fact, goes beyond Justin because he explicitly names and shames individual emperors as persecutors. Nero is his first candidate: 'Consult your histories. There you will find that Nero was the first to rage with the imperial sword (*Caesariano gladio ferocisse*) against this school in the very hour of its rise in Rome' (*Apol.* 5.3; see too 5.8). As the opening clause shows, Tertullian was riffing off the binary schema of 'good' and 'bad' emperors found

---

49 Latin text and translation from Glover and Rendall 1931.

in earlier Graeco-Roman historiography. In this he was dependant on another apologist, Melito of Sardis, who wrote an *Apology* addressed to Marcus Aurelius, extant only in fragments (Eus. *Hist. eccl.* 4.13.8, 4.26.1, 4.26.5–11). Melito wrote that 'Nero and Domitian alone of all ... desired to bring our doctrine into ill repute' (*apud Hist. eccl.* 4.26.9).[50] Both were suggesting that only Rome's imperial tyrants had persecuted Christians (*Apol.* 5.4) while better emperors had not (*Apol.* 5.5; see too 5.6–8). This further solidifies for Tertullian's readers the link between persecution and imperial agency: 'Such are ever our persecutors (*insecutores*) – men unjust, impious, foul' (*Apol.* 5.4). We see the jump from the New Testament conceptual framework to that of the apologists clearest when Tertullian says: 'His disciples, also, were scattered through the world, in obedience to the precept of God their teacher; they suffered much from Jewish persecution (*a Iudaeis insequentibus*) ... finally, at Rome, through the cruelty of Nero (*per Neronis saevitiam*), they sowed the seed of Christian blood' (*Apol.* 21.25). It is this latter imperial agency that forms these apologists' almost exclusive focus.

Moreover, Tertullian also 'imperialised' the second persecutory idiom of the New Testament, cosmic warfare. He used military language of the cosmic contest of which Christians were part akin to that of *Revelation* (e.g. *Apol.* 27.4; *Scorp.* 4.4). But he also called out his gubernatorial addresses because 'you wage war (*debellatis*)' (*Apol.* 29.5) against Christians. And he declared '[l]et the Emperor, as a last test, make war on heaven (*caelum denique debellet imperator*), carry heaven captive in his triumph, set a guard on heaven, lay taxes on heaven. He cannot' (*Apol.* 30.2). In line with the schema of good/bad emperors, he challenges the reader: 'from among so many emperors down to today, men wise in things divine and human, pick me out one who warred against the Christians (*edite aliquem debellatorem Christianorum*)' (*Apol.* 5.5). This interwove imperial agency into both models of New Testament persecution.

The apologists' picture of the agency behind Christian suffering thus had a different focus from that they inherited from the New Testament. Emperors take centre-stage – not just as sources of protection, as was implicit in the New Testament, but of persecution itself. That reflects, I suggest, not a change in the nature of historical persecution but a discursive shift, one catalysed by the judicial zeitgeist of the Antonine period.[51] Recent

---

50 Translations from Lawlor and Oulton 1927; Greek text from Bardy 1952–58.

51 The former point is controversial (and goes against the consensus established by de Ste Croix 1963 and Barnes 1968), and I simply state rather than prove it here. I refer the interested reader

innovative work has explored this already. Maud Gleason (1999), in a typically pioneering piece, noted the obsession with the Roman courtroom shared by Christian authors and their non-Christian contemporaries; Brent Shaw (2003) demonstrated the degree to which this permeated into the early Christian (sub)consciousness. Laura Nasrallah's work has argued that the apologists' writings must be read alongside the discursive and monumental landscapes of their world (2010). For Justin, that manifests in his focus on the nexus between justice, piety and philosophy, all ideals foregrounded in the ideological programmes of the Antonine emperors he addressed (Nasrallah 2010: 119–68). Similarly, Ari Bryen (2012) has suggested that Justin's quotation of legal precedents can be seen as part of a wider development of such provincial agency in the metaphorical arena of the courtroom. Such precedent-gathering was one aspect of a wider provincial attempt to harness state mechanisms to their advantage (which necessarily involved accepting and working with those mechanisms, e.g. Bryen 2014).[52] Most recently – and most pertinently – Carly Daniel-Hughes and Maia Kotrosits (2020) have persuasively argued that Tertullian's depictions of Christianstate interactions are not representations of his Carthaginian reality but one more manifestation of a broader tendency for contemporary provincials to fantasise about Roman judicial power. But it seems to me that the very focus on the emperors' role in the provincial experience of justice – or perhaps better, the assumption that suffering and punishment under the empire are ultimately traceable to the emperor – is itself also a product of this context.

The idea that all provincials had a link to the emperor goes back to Augustus and the foundation of the imperial system – we have already seen it implicit in the New Testament, as it can be found throughout all imperial literature (cf. Ando 2000: e.g. 336–405). But it was with the Nerva-Antonine dynasty that, with the Republican façade entirely stripped away, the idea that the experience of the empire's denizens was directly dependent on the character of the man resident in the Palatine reached its zenith. The Antonine emperors encouraged this association via an increased focus on character in their ideological programmes.[53] It is no coincidence that the glut

---

to Corke-Webster 2023 – a prolegomenon to a fuller future study of the Christian experience of persecution – which emphasises the continuity of agency behind persecution throughout the first three centuries (delation from an eclectic mix of community agents united not by inter-religious antagonism but by their intimacy with Christians).
52 I have profited here greatly from conversations with Ben Kolbeck; see further Kolbeck 2022.
53 See e.g. on character and coinage Noreña 2011.

of texts that judged first-century emperors on their character (most familiar now via the Tacitus-Suetonius-Pliny triptych) began to be produced in the early second century. Suffering provincials in this period were implicitly encouraged, I suggest, to look to the emperor's character as both ultimate cause of and potential source of relief for their experience. Since by far the most common means of interaction with the Roman imperial project in this (relatively non-martial) period was via the Roman judicial system,[54] and emperors themselves prioritised this in their ideological programmes,[55] it is entirely predictable that provincial musings upon their judicial experiences should increasingly focus on the emperors as individuals. The prominence of the nexus between emperors and justice in this period is perhaps best demonstrated by the unprecedented centrality of a building dedicated to justice – the Basilica Ulpia – in Trajan's Forum, where the emperor's person was symbolically ever-present.[56] The apologists' discursive escalation of the canonical predictions of suffering onto the imperial scale was thus part of a wider tendency prompted by changing imperial ideology.

War and Historiography

Justin demonstrates an occasional interest in the just retribution imperial persecutors could expect.[57] We read, for example,

> And if you will take no heed of our praying and putting everything in the open we will not be harmed at all; but rather we believe and have been convinced that each of you will pay penalties in eternal fire according to the worth of his actions; and in proportion to the capabilities which he received from God an account will be required, as Christ indicated, saying 'To whom God gave more, more also will be required of him' [referencing *Luke* 12:48].

---

[54] See on petitions especially Connolly 2010 and Kelly 2011.
[55] Noreña 2011: 60 on the dominance of *aequitas* on coinage; see discussion in Kolbeck 2022: 57–58, 71–78.
[56] The basilica's significance is highlighted by Nasrallah 2010: 154–61, building on Packer 1997 and 2001.
[57] Tertullian also touches on the deaths of emperors, but only in the context of apotheosis (*Apol.* 13.8).

Consider what happened to each of the kings that have been. They died just like everybody else. (1 *Apol*. 17.4–18.1, see too 21.3–6, 45.6 and 55.7)[58] Justin here sowed a seed that flowered in the early fourth century. Most famously, in *On the Deaths of the Persecutors* (*De mort. pers.*), the Latin writer Lactantius systematically describes in graphic detail the gruesome ends of those emperors he considered persecutors – Nero, Domitian, Decius, Valerian, Aurelian, Diocletian, Maximian, Galerius, and Maximinus Daia.[59] His contemporary in Greek, Eusebius of Caesarea, displays a similar but less systematic delight in the downfalls of persecutors in his *Ecclesiastical History*. It is to these two fourth-century writers,[60] their big-picture historiographical perspectives, and their distinctive inheritance of the canonical and apologetic tradition, we now turn.[61]

Both Eusebius and Lactantius knew the developing canon (Eusebius lists the four gospels, *Acts*, the letters of Paul and one apiece for John and Peter, as well as *Revelation*, at *Hist. eccl.* 3.25.1–2; Lactantius employs few quotations, in line with his general methodology – see *Div. inst.* 4.5.3, but knew and was influenced by *Revelation* in particular).[62] Eusebius knew two *Apologies* by Justin (e.g. *Hist. eccl.* 4.18.1–2), and had access to a Greek translation of Tertullian's *Apology* of dubious accuracy (e.g. *Hist. eccl.* 2.2.4).[63] Lactantius speaks of Tertullian with respect, though laments his complex Latin (e.g. *Div. inst.*

---

58 Cf. too Tertullian's gloating at the prospect of emperors brought low and persecuting magistrates' punished posthumously (*De spect.* 30.3).
59 The deaths of the tetrarchs Severus, Constantius, and Maxentius are also related, but none are described as persecutors, and their deaths are accordingly recorded as happening 'gently (*leniter*)' (*De mort. pers.* 26.11) and quietly while asleep (*De mort. pers.* 24.8), in the first two instances, while Lactantius records Maxentius' drowning without further comment (*De mort. pers.* 44.9). Translations and Latin text from Creed 1984.
60 Eusebius' (self-made) claim to the title is obvious; on the long-running debate over the genre of Lactantius' *On the Deaths of the Persecutors*, see most recently Castro Hernández 2017 who labels it 'una narrativa histórica con finalidad apologética' (at 40), words that would equally well fit Eusebius' *Ecclesiastical History*.
61 For Eusebius' biography see Corke-Webster 2019: 1–53; for the dating and editions of the *Ecclesiastical History* (between 313/4 and 326), Corke-Webster 2019: 57–62. For Lactantius' biography see Bowen and Garnsey 2003: 1–6; for the dating of *On the Deaths of the Persecutors* (between 313/4 and 316), Winkelmann 2003: 11–12.
62 For Eusebius, see Carriker 2003: 232–24; for Lactantius, Ogilvie 1978: 96–108. On Lactantius' use of *Revelation* see Creed 1984: 82 (mentioning *De mort. pers.* 2.6 – discussed below – *Div. inst.* 7.14–20 and 24–26, as well as *Epit.* 66–67).
63 For Eusebius, see further Carriker 2003: 220–23 on Justin and 261–62 on Tertullian.

5.1.23–27; 5.4.3; 7.1.26), and knew the *Apology* and perhaps also *To Scapula*.[64] Both writers' treatment of persecution was, I argue, built upon, but developed in new directions, an inheritance from both sources.

Nero can again serve as our example. In Eusebius' *Ecclesiastical History*, we first meet him in Book 2 as the appointer of Festus, before whom Paul appeared in Caesarea and by whom he was sent to Rome. Eusebius quotes: 'I was delivered out of the mouth of the lion' (*Hist. eccl.* 2.22.3; quoting 2 *Tim.* 4.17, and see too *Rev.* 13.2). As we saw above, this had no imperial connotation. But Eusebius gave it one: 'giving this name, it seems, to Nero, on account of his cruel nature (διὰ τὸ ὠμόθυμον)' (*Hist. eccl.* 2.22.4). He then links Paul's actual martyrdom to the emperor, using exactly the type of canonical prediction we considered above: 'this also he foretells still more clearly in the same writing, when he says: "For I am already being offered, and the time of my departure is come"' (*Hist. eccl.* 2.22.5; quoting 2 *Tim.* 4.18).

This use of Paul lays the groundwork for Eusebius' subsequent treatment of Nero's persecution. Chapter 25 is entitled 'Concerning the persecution under Nero (Περὶ τοῦ κατὰ Νέρωνα διωγμοῦ) during which Paul and Peter were adorned with martyrdoms at Rome on account of piety'.[65] Eusebius refers to Nero's other crimes – 'he plunged into vile habits' (*Hist. eccl.* 2.25.1) – but refers readers to non-Christian historiography for details: 'many have given us the facts about him in most accurate accounts' (*Hist. eccl.* 2.25.2). He thus highlights that Graeco-Roman schema of 'good' and 'bad' emperors to which he was indebted. He goes on to make clear that Nero is being introduced not just for what he did but because he introduces a pattern: 'he was the first emperor (πρῶτος αὐτοκρατόρων) to be proclaimed as the foe of piety towards the Deity' (*Hist. eccl.* 2.25.3). He acknowledges his apologetic predecessors here: 'it is the Roman Tertullian who mentions this' (*Hist. eccl.* 2.25.4). Lactantius shares the debt; he too calls Nero 'first persecutor (*primus omnium persecutus*) of the servants of God' (*De mort. pers.* 2.6; see too 2.8), and later describes him as 'so evil a beast (*tam malae bestiae*)' (*De mort. pers.* 2.7). In both we therefore find the New Testament tradition of prophetic suffering and the apologists' model of imperial injustice. But what is latent in Tertullian's reference

---

64 See Ogilvie 1978: 90–92 (though not positing close or extensive dependence), and more recently Freund 2015 and Colot 2015. Lactantius also knew Minucius Felix's *Octavius*, which made use of Tertullian; see Ogilvie 1978: 92–95. Creed 1984: xxxix n. 133 also finds precedent for Lactantius' delight in the suffering of Christians' enemies in Tertullian's *On Spectacles* and *Revelation*.
65 My translation; the Neronian attribution is elided in the translation in Lawlor and Oulton 1927: 59.

to Nero as the first persecutor has become a fully realised schema – Eusebius speaks of twelve antagonistic Roman emperors; Lactantius of nine.[66] In part, this was because the genres in which they wrote necessitated a longer chronological interest. But it was also due to their particular literary-political projects. I have argued elsewhere that Eusebius used the schema of good and bad emperors as one of the struts on which to build his work.[67] By suggesting that mistreatment of Christians was part and parcel of tyranny, as made famous in the Roman literary imagination by Nero and Domitian, and that Rome's best emperors, the Nerva-Antonine dynasty, had protected Christians, Eusebius worked to tarnish the image of the recent tetrarchs, whose legacy was still in flux.[68] Lactantius' project was not dissimilar.[69] Initial treatment of the persecutions of Nero and Domitian in chapters 2 and 3 is a prolegomenon to the tetrarchic persecutions that occupy chapters 7 to 51. Indeed, his stated focus is the recent sufferings of his addressee Donatus due to 'the wicked and bloodthirsty commands of the tyrants (*tyrannorum nefaria et cruenta imperia*)' (*De mort. pers.* 1.3), but he says he will treat 'from the beginning, since the Church's foundation, who were its persecutors (*qui fuerint persecutores*)' (*De mort. pers.* 1.8). Both projects were thus concerned to mobilise the first three centuries as rhetorical tools to speak about the fourth.[70]

Eusebius and Lactantius also appropriate the non-judicial model of persecution from the New Testament, namely warfare.[71] When Eusebius first describes Nero's persecution, he says in martial language that the emperor 'armed (ὡπλίζετο) himself even against piety towards the God of the universe' (*Hist. eccl.* 2.25.1); he subsequently describes Nero as 'the foe (πολέμιος) of

---

66 This is noted for Lactantius by Baynes 1955: 351.
67 Corke-Webster 2019: 249–79; on Nero at 252–56, and the tetrarchic 'pay off' at 266–71. See too DeVore 2013: 115–16.
68 On the evolution of the *topos* of the tyrant, see Dunkle 1967, 1971, and more recently Kalyvas 2007.
69 I accept, with the majority of scholars, Lactantius' authorship. For bibliography see Winkelmann 2003: 11 n. 36 and more recently Gordon 2010 (refuting Rossi 1961 and De Decker 1984 specifically). My own take on *On the Deaths of the Persecutors* can be found in Corke-Webster 2022.
70 Almost all scholarship that has considered these texts together has focused on issues of source criticism and reliability. Meinking 2013 briefly considers their interests and purposes (though limited to Book 8 of Eusebius' *History*) with a focus on divine anger, arguing that their intellectual worlds were built on different foundations (philosophical, for Eusebius, in line with Greek tradition; rhetorical, for Lactantius, in line with Latin tradition).
71 Harrison 1936: 83 noted the appearance of the nexus between persecution and warfare in Eusebius (as well as the interesting use of *eirēnē* for the period after persecution in Hegesippus, *apud* Euseb. *Hist. eccl.* 3.20.6, 3.32.6). Moss 2013: 220–22, linking it to internal attacks on heretics – certainly present, but not Eusebius' only referents for such language, as demonstrated here.

piety towards the Deity' (*Hist. eccl.* 2.25.3). Both terms are associated above all with soldiers and war (Liddell and Scott 1883: 1062–63, 1239). He built here on Tertullian's comment that Nero 'was the first to rage with the imperial sword' (*Apol.* 5.3) but made the language more explicitly martial. Indeed, Eusebius made war a key conceptual and structural model for his entire project. This is most obvious in the so-called second preface of the *History*, at its central point:

> Other writers, indeed, of historical narratives would have transmitted in writing, to the exclusion of all else, victories won in war (πολέμων νίκας) and conquests over enemies (τρόπαια κατ' ἐχθρῶν), the prowess of generals (στρατηγῶν τε ἀριστείας) and brave deeds of warriors (ὁπλιτῶν ἀνδραγαθία) defiled with blood of myriads whom they slew for the sake of children and fatherland and other possessions; but our narrative of God's commonwealth will inscribe on everlasting monuments the record of most peaceful wars (τοὺς ... εἰρηνικωτάτους πολέμους) fought for the very peace of the soul, and of those who therein contended valiantly (ἀνδρισαμένους) for truth rather than fatherland, for religion rather than their dearest: it will proclaim for everlasting remembrance the steadfastness of the champions of religion, their deeds of bravery and much endurance, the conquests (τρόπαιά), too, over devils, and victories (νίκας) won over invisible adversaries (ἀοράτων ἀντιπάλων), and the crowns (τοὺς ... στεφάνους) gained when all was done. (*Hist. eccl.* 5.pr.3–4, see too 1.1.2, 8.4.2)

David DeVore has demonstrated how Eusebius foregrounded both the physical violence in martyrdom tales and the scale of their suffering to present Christian experience as a war.[72] He argues that Eusebius sought to emphasise the metaphysical theatre of this war. This is certainly present; Eusebius built here on the cosmic precedent that went back to *Revelation*. But he was also very deliberately, I suggest, picking up Tertullian's use of warfare language to speak of imperial treatment of Christians.[73] This was part of a conscious attempt to shift attention from the courtroom to the battlefield, one

---

[72] DeVore 2013: 128–33.
[73] We perhaps find another example at *Hist. eccl.* 8.13.9. The Greek reads 'Τὰ μὲν οὖν πρὸ τοῦ καθ' ἡμῶν πολέμου τῆς Ῥωμαίων ἡγεμονίας'. Lawlor and Oulton 1927: 270 translate this: 'Now as concerns the state of the Roman government before the war against us'. But it could also be translated: 'Now as concerns the state of things before the war of the Roman government against us'. This is discussed by DeVore 2013: 116[n720]. I note in addition that Τὰ ... τῆς Ῥωμαίων ἡγεμονίας meaning 'the state of the Roman government' does not occur elsewhere in the Eusebian corpus (though see Euseb. *martyr. Pal.* 3.7 [SR] for 'τὰ κοινὰ τῆς Ῥωμαίων ἡγεμονίας').

element of Eusebius' attempt to mute the charismatic but unstable power of martyrs.[74]

Lactantius also mobilised the concept and language of warfare.[75] He says of Nero that he 'leapt into action to overturn (*ad excidendum*) the heavenly temple and to abolish righteousness (*delendamque iustitiam*)' (*De mort. pers.* 2.6). *Excido* bears the lexical connotations of siege warfare. Such military language recurs throughout. The opening crows that Christianity has 'all its opponents (*adversariis*) removed' (*De mort. pers.* 1.2; see too 5.1 and 43.1). Though *adversarius* need not exclusively refer to enemies in war, it was increasingly used by imperial historians in that sense,[76] and Lactantius' own meaning is clear from a parallel application describing Licinius' battle with Maximinus Daia: 'the Licinians launched an attack and penetrated the lines of their opponents (*adversarios*)' (*De mort. pers.* 47.1). Elsewhere Lactantius describes Galerius as making God 'his enemy (*infestum*)' (*De mort. pers.* 20.5), a term again most familiar from military contexts (and again, Lactantius' only other use concerns the Carpi, at *De mort. pers.* 9.2).[77] In a direct appeal to the work's addressee, Donatus, Lactantius explicitly merges imperial aggression and cosmic warfare:

Nine times you were subjected to various torments and agonies; nine times you defeated the adversary (*adversarium ... vicisti*) by gloriously bearing witness; in nine battles you overcame the devil with his minions (*proeliis diabolum cum satellitibus suis debellasti*); with nine victories you triumphed (*victoriis ... triumphasti*) over this world with its terrors. How pleasing was the spectacle to God, when He saw you victoriously bringing under the yoke of your chariot not gleaming white horses or enormous elephants, but rather the very men who celebrate the triumphs (*ipsos potissimum triumpatores*)! This is the true triumph, when the masters are mastered (*Hic est verus triumphus, cum dominatores dominantur*). They were conquered and subdued (*Victi ... ac subiugati sunt*) by your virtue when, despising their wrongful command (*nefanda iussione*), you routed all the terrifying apparatus of their tyrannical power (*omnes apparatus ac terriculas tyrannicae potestatis ... profligasti*) by your steadfast faith and strength of mind. ... This it is to be a disciple of God, a soldier of Christ such that no enemy can ensnare you (*militem Christi, quem nullus hostis expugnet*), no pain conquer (*vincat*)

---

74 On Eusebius' consistent shift away from dialogue in martyr narratives, see DeVore 2013: 108–9 and 114; and Corke-Webster 2019: 179–81, with more on his ambivalence towards martyrs at 175–211.

75 Baynes 1955: 349 noted the importance of *Revelation* for Lactantius: 'under the stress of the Galerian persecution Apocalyptic was reborn'.

76 Lewis and Short 1969: 49.

77 Lewis and Short 1969: 945. The overall metaphor is perhaps also apparent in Lactantius' focus on the eventual deaths of the persecuting emperors.

or torture afflict you. In the end, after those nine most glorious fights (*pugnas*) in which the devil was overcome (*diabolus victus est*) by you, he did not dare to pit himself (*congredi*) against you further; he had found out that he could not conquer you in battle (*proeliis ... superare*). (*De mort. pers.* 16.5–10)

In fact, this martial schema underpins the entire work. Lactantius writes at its conclusion: 'Let us then celebrate the triumph (*triumphum*) of God with exultation. Let us throng the victory (*victoriam*) of the Lord with praises, let us celebrate it with prayers day and night, let us celebrate it so that He may confirm for ever (*in saeculum*) the peace (*pacem*) which He granted to His people after ten years' (*De mort. pers.* 52.4). A martial lexicon and conceptual model are fundamental to both Eusebius' and Lactantius' projects.

This shift was in part demanded by the new mode of discourse with which these Christians were experimenting. David DeVore has demonstrated how Eusebius was here participating in the 'traditional game of historiographical one-upmanship' (DeVore 2013: 105–40, quote from 106). His use of this conceptual model provides his work with the conflict theme, pre-battle panorama, set-piece speeches, bloody battle scenes, and triumphal monuments required by the genre of historiography. But beyond this, the very use of this mode of discourse – the invention of Christian historiography – is indicative of a wider shift, namely that Christianity was emerging onto, and beginning to see itself acting at, the level of state affairs. Genuine imperial interest in Christians, at the level of policy if not more generally, came only with Valerian's measures in the late third century, and crystallised in the tetrarchic 'Great Persecution' (see above n. 8). Both Lactantius and Eusebius wrote after and in response to these events; two consequences, I suggest, were a shift in their conception of the relation between Christians and Rome's representatives, and a corresponding desire to write grand narratives. It is also pertinent that both authors grew up in the second half of the third century, the age of the so-called 'soldier emperors'. Military imagery had always, of course, been a key dimension of imperial ideology. But in the balance with the other key aspects of the imperial image – in particular, civic and religious – the military dimension became of almost overwhelming importance in this period – certainly in comparison with the civic focus of the Antonines.[78] These fourth century historians, then, taking, combining, and upscaling the *lexica* of both the prophetic and cosmic persecution of the

---

78 See especially now on the changing image of the emperor Hekster 2023.

New Testament, and the imperial, courtroom focus of the apologists, forged a new conceptual model of Christian suffering – as a clash of states.[79]

Conclusion

In the final scenes of *Quo Vadis*, Nero dies a humiliating and cowardly death, assisted in suicide by his freedwoman and mistress Acte, his power and authority drained away. The morality of Hollywood demands the villain's comeuppance – Lactantius would have approved. We have come full circle. The cinema of the mid-twentieth century represents a popular and enduring vision of Christian suffering under the Roman empire. Its imagery has become so commonplace as to appear inevitable. But close study of its discursive history reminds us that it represents a complex that evolved slowly, over time, and in dialogue with both context and genre. Sinking a series of exploratory trenches into texts from successive centuries reveals the continuities and discontinuities in the evolution of Christian thought.

The centrality, and the expectation, of suffering is one of the – if not the – core message of early Christianities. We find it laced throughout those texts that became the New Testament canon. Since the latter encompasses an eclecticism of genres, authors, and dates, it unsurprisingly speaks in diverse voices. But taken as a whole, it established twin conceptual models for the expectation and experience of violence – judicial and martial. The former was primarily local in scope; the latter cosmic. That reflects Christianity's historical status in the first and early second centuries as a provincial cult still intimately connected to Judaism and its inheritance of cosmic imagery from the Hebrew Bible.

Later authors inherited and experimented with these models. The apologists, writing between the mid-second and early third centuries, took the judicial impetus and transferred it to the imperial stage. Here emperors appear front and centre as those primarily responsible for persecution. This was a shift of both focus and form, since the apologists employed the discur-

---

79 It is interesting, in this regard, that Shushma Malik traces the emergence of the association between Nero and the Antichrist to the same historical moment, in Commodian (mid-third century or later), Victorinus of Pettau (late third century), and Lactantius himself (early fourth). See Malik 2020: 81–82.

sive judicial mechanisms of empire – petitions and rescripts. This rhetorical move was a response to evolving imperial ideology and the provincial reactions that provoked. In the early fourth century, Christian authors began to experiment with a different form of discourse – historiography. Heirs to both the canon and apologetic, they catalysed a new picture of Christian suffering under Rome as catalysed by the clash between warring states. In that they were influenced both by the literary expectations of the genre, and by the historical circumstances in which they wrote, when Christianity had erupted onto the landscape of government. As Christianity grew, and Christian self-conceptions evolved, emperors in turn underwent a literary metamorphosis – from having either no role in the drama of persecution or an ill-defined one as potential protectors, through being the prime agents of persecution in judicial settings, to finally being its drivers in fully-fledged war.

In their Introduction to this volume, Lisa Eberle and Myles Lavan speak of their desire to both map the lexicon of unrest, the conceptual models used to understand it, and the wider discourses in which both were employed, as well as to explore and explain their evolution.[80] Christian discussion of their experience of suffering – encompassing both prediction and memory – provides an apposite case study for such a venture. Nevertheless, astute readers may have noticed that the lexicon familiar from many of the volume's other papers is not repeated here. In fact, however, it was perfectly possible for contemporary actors to view the early Christians in such terms – it was simply not the framing Christian self-conceptions privileged.

This is easily demonstrated. In Minucius Felix's *Octavius*, the imagined critic of Christianity accuses Christians of being 'a gang ... of discredited and proscribed desperadoes (*deploratae, inlicitae ac desperatae factionis*)' (*Oct.* 8.3) and 'a rabble of profane conspirators (*plebem profanae coniurationis*)' (*Oct.* 8.4).[81] Celsus seems to have described Jesus as 'the author of their sedition (αὐτοῖς τῆς στάσεως ἀρχηγέτης)' (Origen, *C. Cels.* 8.14; see too 3.14–15), responsible for the 'rebellious utterance (στάσεως ... φωνὴν)' (*C. Cels.* 8.2; see too 3.5; 8.17) that a man cannot serve two masters.[82] Christians are thus said to 'suffer from the disease of sedition (τῇ στάσει συννοσοῦντες)' (*C. Cels.* 8.49),

---

80 See this pp. 15–19 above.
81 Translation and Latin text from Glover 1931. Huebner 2019 suggests that the earliest surviving account of a trial of Christians presents them arraigned on a charge of *coniuratio*; this has been contested on both historical and papyrological grounds by Dolganov and Rebillard 2021.
82 Translation from Chadwick 1953; Greek text from Borret 1967–69.

and Celsus speaks of 'the common law' (*C. Cels.* 1.1) which 'the associations of the Christians violate'. Porphyry speaks of Christianity leading to 'barbarian recklessness (τὸ βάρβαρον... τόλμημα)' and 'contrary to the law (παρανόμως)' (apud Euseb. *Hist. eccl.* 6.19.7).[83] Any swift and violent response to groups described in this language – those, in sum, responsible for social unrest – would to the Roman authorities, and to most inhabitants of the empire, have seemed unremarkable.[84]

This chasm in perspective – sometimes expressed as the difference between prosecution and persecution – is well known.[85] Why the difference? It is not that those other perspectives are elite, and that of Christians not, because the authors of our texts are also 'elite' – not least because they were literate enough to produce such sophisticated writings. An alternative explanation might be that these Christian texts express an 'outsider' perspective. That is true to the extent that they were members of a minority group who suffered via the state apparatus. But such a view relies upon ungainly and outdated conceptions of the relationship between 'Christianity' and 'Rome' in binary, antagonistic terms. Numerous Christians were 'brought into' the imperial project, and were as invested in its stability as those that executed them. And that is to say nothing of the inherent complexity of identity that means that individuals can display different attitudes at different times and in different situations.[86]

What we are in fact seeing is simply, in my view, one 'subaltern' perspective among the plethora of those developed by the multiplicity of groups living, thriving, struggling, and dying under the Roman empire. The difference in the case of the Christians is that their perspective has determined the historical narrative, in the case of their persecution as elsewhere. It is for that reason that the fine-grained details of exactly how that perspective evolved in literary terms are so important. The limited study offered here should therefore serve first and foremost as a reminder that a full account of how the memory of Christian persecution evolved remains to be written.

---

83 Roman conceptions of Christianity are well-trodden ground; see most famously Benko 1980, 1984, Wilken 2003.
84 For a detailed account of the most famous judicial treatment of Christians, that of Pliny in Bithynia-Pontus, which suggests that Pliny was motivated by concerns of social unrest, see Corke-Webster 2017. On wider considerations of Christianity as a *coniuratio*, see Nagy 2002.
85 Most recently in Middleton 2021.
86 See especially Rebillard 2012.

Acknowledgements

I am grateful to the editors for their invitation to contribute and plentiful suggestions for improvement, as well as to Ben Kolbeck and Sarah Parkhouse for their insightful comments on written drafts.

Works cited

Ando, Clifford. 2000. *Imperial Ideology and Provincial Loyalty in the Roman Empire*. Classics and Contemporary Thought 6. Berkeley.
Barclay John M. G. 1993. 'Conflict in Thessalonica.' *Catholic Biblical Quarterly* 55: 512–30.
Bardy, Gustave. 1952–8. *Eusèbe de Césarée, Histoire ecclésiastique*. Paris.
Barnes, Timothy D. 1968. 'Legislation against the Christians'. *Journal of Roman Studies* 58: 32–50.
Bassler, Jouette M. 2011. *Abingdon New Testament Commentaries: 1 & 2 Timothy and Titus*. Abingdon.
Baynes, Norman H. 1955. *Byzantine Studies and Other Essays*. London.
Benko, Stephen. 1980. 'Pagan criticism of Christianity during the first two centuries A.D.'. *Aufstieg und Niedergang der römischen Welt (ANRW)* II.23/2: 1055–118
–. 1984. *Pagan Rome and the Early Christians*. London.
Borret, Marcel. 1967–69. *Origène. Contre Celse. Introduction, texte critique, traduction et notes*, 5 vols. Sources chrétiennes 132, 136, 147, 150, 227. Paris.
Bousset, Wilhelm. 1895. *Der Antichrist in der Überlieferung des Judentums, des neuen Testaments und der alten Kirche: ein Beitrag zur Auslegung der Apocalypse*. Göttingen.
Bowen, Anthony and Peter Garnsey. 2003. *Lactantius: Divine Institutes*. Translated Texts for Historians. Liverpool.
Bruce, F. F. 1990. *The Acts of the Apostles*. Grand Rapids.
Bryen, Ari Z. 2012. 'Judging empire: courts and culture in Rome's eastern provinces'. *Law and History Review* 30: 771–811.
–. 2014. 'Martyrdom, rhetoric, and the politics of procedure'. *Classical Antiquity* 33(2): 243–80.
Caird, George B. 1984. *A Commentary on the Revelation of St John the Divine*. London.
Cameron, Averil. 2002. 'Apologetics in the Roman empire – a genre of intolerance?', in Jean-Michel Carrié and Rita Lizzi Testa, eds, *Humana Sapit: Études d'Antiquité Tardive offertes a Lellia Cracco Ruggini*. Turnhout, 219–27.
Carrier, Richard. 2014. 'The prospect of a Christian interpolation in Tacitus, Annals 15.44'. *Vigiliae Christianae* 68: 264–83.
Carriker, Andrew. 2003. *The Library of Eusebius of Caesarea*. Leiden.

Chadwick, Henry. 1953. *Origen: Contra Celsum: Translated with an Introduction and Notes*. Cambridge.
Colot, Blandine. 2015. 'Africain, romain et chrétien: l'engagement religieux de Tertullien et de Lactance, chacun en son époque', in Jérôme Lagouanère and Sabine Fialon, eds., *Tertullianus Afer: Tertullien et la littérature chrétienne d'Afrique (IIe-VIe siècles)*. Instrumenta patristica et mediaevalia 70. Turnhout, 167–84.
Connolly, Serena. 2010. *Lives Behind the Laws: The World of the Codex Hermogenianus*. Bloomington.
Cook, John Granger. 2020. 'Chrestiani, Christiani, Χριστιανοί: a second century anachronism?', *Vigiliae Christianae* 74.3: 237–64.
Corke-Webster, James. 2017. 'Trouble in Pontus: The Pliny-Trajan correspondence on the Christians reconsidered'. *TAPA* 147(2): 371–411.
–. 2019. *Eusebius and Empire: Constructing Church and Empire in the Ecclesiastical History*. Cambridge.
–. 2020. 'The Roman persecutions', in Paul Middleton, ed., *The Wiley-Blackwell Companion to Martyrdom*. Chichester, 33–50.
–. 2022. 'Lactantius and empire: Political theology in *On the Deaths of the Persecutors*'. *Journal of Late Antiquity* 15(2): 333–66.
–. 2023. 'By whom were early Christians persecuted?'. *Past & Present* 261(1): 3–46.
Creed, John L. 1984. *Lactantius: De Mortibus Persecutorum*. Oxford.
Daniel-Hughes, Carly and Maia Kotrosits, 2020. 'Tertullian of Carthage and the fantasy life of power: on martyrs, Christians, and other attachments to juridical scenes', *Journal of Early Christian Studies* 28.1: 1–31.
De Decker, Daniel. 1984. 'Lactance: L'apport d'une concordance automatique appliquée aux études patristiques'. *SP* 15: 71–72.
de Ste Croix, Geoffrey E.M. 1963. 'Why were the early Christians persecuted?'. *Past & Present* 26: 6–38.
DeVore, David. 2013. 'Greek historiography, Roman society, Christian empire: The *Ecclesiastical History* of Eusebius of Caesarea'. PhD. Dissertation. Berkeley, CA.
Dolganov Anna and Éric Rebillard. 2021. 'Not a Roman Trial of Christians: a reassessment of P.Mil.Vogl. VI 287'. *Journal of Late Antiquity* 14(2): 177–212.
Donfried, Karl P. 1985. 'The cults of Thessalonica and the Thessalonian correspondence'. *New Testament Studies* 31: 336–56.
Dunkle, J. Roger. 1967. 'The Greek ryrant and Roman political invective of the late republic'. *Transactions of the American Philological Association* 98: 151–71.
–. 1971. 'The rhetorical tyrant in Roman historiography: Sallust, Livy and Tacitus'. *Classical World* 65(1): 12–20.
Gleason, Maud. 1999. 'Truth contests and talking corpses', in James Porter, ed., *Constructions of the Classical Body*. Ann Arbor, 287–313.
Filson, Floyd V. 1971. *A Commentary on the Gospel According to St. Matthew*. London.
Freund, Stefan. 2015. 'Tertullian bei Laktanz', in Jérôme Lagouanère and Sabine Fialon, eds., *Tertullianus Afer: Tertullien et la littérature chrétienne d'Afrique (IIe-VIe siècles)*. Instrumenta patristica et mediaevalia 70. Turnhout, 185–203.

Jackson, John. 1937. *Tacitus. Annals: Books 13–16*. Cambridge, MA.
Jones, Christopher P. 2017. 'The Historicity of the Neronian Persecution: A Response to Brent Shaw'. *New Testament Studies* 63: 146–52
Glover, Terrot R. and Gerald H. Rendall. 1931. *Tertullian: Apology; De Spectaculis. Minucius Felix: Octavius*. Cambridge, MA.
Gordon, Octavian G. 2010. 'Is *De mortibus persecutorum* an orphan indeed?'. *Studia Patristica* 46: 27–31.
Harrison, P. N. 1936. *Polycarp's Two Epistles to the Philippians*. Cambridge.
Hekster, Olivier. 2023. *Caesar Rules. The Emperor in the Changing Roman World c. 50 BC–AD 565*. Cambridge.
Hengel, Martin. 1985. *Studies in the Gospel of Mark*. Philadelphia.
Hernández, Pablo Castro. 2017. 'La construcción narrativa de Lactancio: una aproximación a la intención historiográfica en «De mortibus persecutorum» (s. IV d.C.)'. *Talia Dixit* 12: 39–66.
Hooker, Morna D. 2001. *A Commentary on the Gospel According to St Mark*. London.
Huebner, Sabine. 2019. 'Soter, Sotas, and Dioscorus before the Governor: The first authentic court record of a Roman trial of Christians?'. *Journal of Late Antiquity* 12(1): 2–24.
Kalyvas, Andreas. 2007. 'The tyranny of dictatorship: when the Greek tyrant met the Roman dictator'. *Political Theory* 35(4): 412–42.
Kelly, Benjamin. 2011. *Petitions, Litigation, and Social Control in Roman Egypt*. Oxford.
Kolbeck, Ben. 2022. 'Doing Justice? Christians, Courts, and Constructions of Empire'. PhD diss. King's College London.
Lawlor, Hugh J. and John E. L. Oulton. 1927. *Eusebius. The Ecclesiastical History and the Martyrs of Palestine*. Vol. 1. London.
LeRoy, Mervyn and Anthony Mann. 1951. *Quo Vadis*. Metro-Goldwyn-Mayer (MGM).
Lewis, Charleton T. and Charles Short. 1969 [orig. 1879]. *A Latin Dictionary*. Oxford.
Liddell, Henry G. and Robert Scott. 1888 [orig. 1843]. *Greek–English Lexicon*. 7th edn. Oxford.
Lightfoot, Robert H. 1950. *The Gospel Message of St. Mark*. Oxford.
Malik, Shushma. 2020. *The Nero-Antichrist: Founding and Fashioning a Paradigm*. Cambridge.
Marcovich, Miroslav. 1994. *Iustini Marturis Apologiae Pro Christianis*. Berlin.
Meinking, Kristina A. 2013. 'Eusebius and Lactantius: rhetoric, philosophy, and Christian theology', in Aaron P. Johnson and Jeremy M. Schott, eds., *Eusebius of Caesarea: Tradition and Innovations*. Washington DC, 325–50.
Middleton, Paul. 2006. *Radical Martyrdom and Cosmic Conflict in Early Christianity*. London.
–. 2009. '"Dying We Live" (2 Cor 6.9): discipleship and martyrdom in Paul', in Paul Middleton, Angus Paddison and Karen Wenell, eds., *Paul, Grace and Freedom: Essays in Honour of John K. Riches*. London, 82–93.
–. 2012. 'Enemies of the (church and) state: martyrdom as a Problem for early Christianity'. *Annali di Storia dell'Esegesi* 29(2): 161–81.
–. 2014. 'Suffering and the creation of Christian identity in the Gospel of Mark', in Brian Tucker and Coleman Baker, eds., *The T&T Clark Handbook to Social Identity in the New Testament*. London, 173–89.

–. 2021. 'Were the early Christians really persecuted?', in Outi Lehtipuu and Michael Labahn, eds., *Tolerance, Intolerance and Recognition in Early Christianity and Early Judaism*. Amsterdam, 229–50.

Muehlberger, Ellen. 2022. 'Perpetual adjustment: the Passion of Perpetua and Felicity and the entailments of authenticity'. *Journal of Early Christian Studies* 30(3): 313–42.

Millar, Fergus. 1981. 'The world of the Golden Ass', *Journal of Roman Studies* 71: 63–75.

Minear, Paul S. 1953. 'The wounded beast'. *Journal of Biblical Literature* 72: 93–101.

Minns, Denis and Paul Parvis. 2009. *Justin, Philosopher and Martyr: Apologies*. Oxford.

Moss, Candida. 2010. 'On the dating of Polycarp: rethinking the place of the Martyrdom of Polycarp in the history of Christianity'. *Early Christianity* 1(4): 539–74.

–. 2013. *The Myth of Persecution: How Early Christians Invented a Story of Martyrdom*. San Francisco.

Nagy, Àgnes A. 2002. 'Superstitio et Coniuratio'. *Numen* 49(2): 178–92.

Nasrallah, Laura. 2010. *Christian Responses to Roman Art and Architecture: The Second-Century Church amid the Spaces of Empire*. Cambridge, MA.

Nesselhauf, Herbert. 1976. 'Hadrians Reskript an Minicius Fundanus', *Hermes* 104: 348–61.

Noreña, Carlos F. 2011. *Imperial Ideals in the Roman West: Representation, Circulation, Power*. Cambridge.

Ogilvie, Robert M. 1978. *The Library of Lactantius*. Oxford.

Packer, James. 1997. *The Forum of Trajan in Rome: A Study of the Monuments*. 2 vols. Berkeley.

–. 2001. *The Forum of Trajan in Rome: A Study of the Monuments in Brief*. Berkeley.

Parvis, Paul. 2008. 'Justin Martyr'. *Expository Times* 120(2): 53–61.

Perkins, Judith. 1995. *The Suffering Self: Pain and Narrative Representation in the Early Christian Era*. London.

Rebillard, Éric. 2012. *Christians and Their Many Identities in Late Antiquity, North Africa, 200–450 CE*. Ithaca.

Rich, Aaron. 2019. 'The accent of truth: the Hollywood research bible and the republic of images'. *Representations* 145(1): 152–73.

Roselaar, Saskia T. 2016. 'Local Administration', in Paul J du Plessis, Clifford Ando, and Kaius Tuori, eds., *The Oxford Handbook of Roman Law and Society*. Oxford, 124–36.

Rossi, Sante. 1961. 'Il concetto di storia e la prassi storiografica di Lattanzio e del De mortibus persecutorum'. *Giornale Italiano di Filologia* 14: 193–213.

Sanders, Joseph N. and Mastin Brian A. 1968. *A Commentary on the Gospel According to St. John*. London.

Shaw, Brent. 2003. 'Judicial Nightmares and Christian Memory', *Journal of Early Christian Studies* 11.4: 533–63.

–. 2015. 'The Myth of the Neronian Persecution'. *Journal of Roman Studies* 105: 73–100.

–. 2018. 'Response to Christopher Jones: The Historicity of the Neronian Persecution'. *New Testament Studies* 64: 231–42.

Tashiro, Charles. 1996. 'When history films (try to) become paintings'. *Cinema Journal* 35(3): 19–33.

Van Der Lans, Birgit and Jan Bremmer. 2017. 'Tacitus and the persecution of the Christians: an invention of tradition?', *Eirene* 53: 299–331.

Van Kooten, George. 2007. 'The year of the four emperors and the Revelation of John: The "pro-Neronian" emperors Otho and Vitellius, and the images and Colossus of Nero in Rome'. *Journal for the Study of the New Testament* 30: 205–48.

–. 2014. 'The Jewish War and the Roman Civil War of 68–69 C.E.: Jewish, pagan, and Christian perspectives', in Mladen Popović, ed., *The Jewish Revolt against Rome: Interdisciplinary Perspectives*. Leiden, 419–50.

Wyke, Maria. 1997. *Projecting the Past: Ancient Rome, Cinema, and History*. New York.

Wilken, Robert L. 2003. *The Christians as the Romans Saw Them*. 2nd edn. New Haven.

Williams, Charles S.C. 1964. *The Acts of the Apostles*. 2nd edn. London.

Winkelmann, Friedhelm. 2003. 'Historiography and the age of Constantine', in Gabriele Marasco, ed., *Greek and Roman Historiography in Late Antiquity: Fourth to the Sixth Century A.D.* Leiden, 1–41.

Young, Frances. 1999. 'Greek apologists of the second century', in Mark Edwards, Martin Goodman, and Simon Price, eds., *Apologetics in the Roman Empire: Pagans, Jews, and Christians*. Oxford, 81–104.

11. Violent Histories: Women and Unrest from Roman to Late Roman Historiography

Ulriika Vihervalli

Abstract: *This chapter examines gendered unrest in Roman historiography, with a focus on narrative histories. It identifies dominant models of how women were portrayed in narratives of unrest, firstly surveying Livy and Tacitus, who offered women roles in the forms of instigation, mitigation, and suffering, placing women into the background of unrest with occasional standout moments. The reception and vitality of these models is then examined in the first two major Christian histories, Eusebius of Caesarea's* Historia ecclesiastica *and Orosius of Braga's* Historiae adversus paganos. *Both authors manipulated the dominant historiographical models of gendered unrest to emphasise different aspects of civic upheaval in their own accounts of a more Christian past. Eusebius downplayed any historic intervention by women at such events while still conceptualising unrest through female suffering. Orosius conversely made much use of Livian and Tacitean ideas, but his insistence on a new bloodless Christian era led to an implausible separation of unrest and women's suffering. These different approaches suggest that gendered unrest was a powerful rhetorical device for Roman and late Roman historians, reflected in its perseverance in records of unrest and its flexibility to centre different aspects of unrest.*

Roman society was susceptible to gendered violence. Situations of societal unrest were no exception.[1] Most often unrest took the form of politically or religiously motivated conflict, leading to succession crises, usurpation attempts, riots, revolts, persecutions, sieges, sacks, and other violent phenomena that undermined stability around women who relied on patriarchal structures for protection. Sources that record women's involvement in episodes of unrest are largely disinterested in the female experience. At the same time, male-authored narrative histories present a substantial archive

---

1 For ancient Rome, see Witzke 2016; for the late Roman period, see Vihervalli and Leonard 2023.

of roles that women might have played in such contexts. For instance, the involvement of elite women is better detailed than that of non-elite women. However, whether high or lowborn, women carried a gendered role in the rhetoric of unrest embedded in Roman and late Roman historiography.

While evidence for upheaval and disaster in Roman historiography is considerable, an understanding of how far societal unrest exacerbated hostile environments for women is still being developed.[2] Similarly, gendered perspectives on violence in the Roman world have attracted limited discussion.[3] Inevitably, a focus on female roles in the rhetoric of unrest in Roman historiography will distort the character of gendered violence at this time: Serena Witzke has critiqued Roman mytho-histories for depicting 'public, ideological, and unrealistic violence that was far removed from the violence that was most likely to be suffered by actual women in Rome' (2016: 254). A study on civic upheaval will contribute to the problem wherein domestic and private violence remains unrecorded and out of sight.[4] Historical narratives of unrest, therefore, simultaneously provide examples of women participating in unrest and the dangers this created for them, while also showcasing how discourses of unrest had gendered dimensions that authors used to portray a certain interpretation of the past and present. These two forces must be balanced to examine historical female vulnerability in unrest as well as the rhetorical endurance and value of such a *topos*. Given the concerns of this volume, this contribution focuses on the latter.

Tumultuous events formed the building blocks of works written in the ancient historiographical tradition. These gave visibility to female participation, yet the men writing in that tradition utilised instances of such participation to highlight different understandings of events. To examine the many roles that women played in episodes of unrest, and the rhetorical ends to which women were used in such accounts, this study examines the works of four historians: Livy, Tacitus, Eusebius, and Orosius. In the first part, I survey the foundational works of Livy and Tacitus for the roles they gave women

---

2 Important work has been done in related areas, especially in shifting the androcentric views of ancient warfare to include women – see Gaca 2011, 2016. Cam Grey has shared a methodological approach for violence with historians of gender and women, advocating that we must 'read into the silences and gaps of ... texts, to focus upon what authors do not say as much as upon what they do' (2013: 216).
3 Ando 1996, Cameron 2002, Gaddis 2005, Drake 2006, Cameron 2008, Stanton and Stroumsa 2008, Sizgorich 2009, Drake 2011, Shaw 2011, Kahlos 2013, Hahn 2014.
4 For domestic violence, see Dossey 2008, Hillner 2013.

in narratives of unrest. Both Livy and Tacitus outlined risks and opportunities that unrest created for women, firmly linking unrest with gendered violence in particular.

Crucially, these ways of figuring women in narratives of unrest were not set in stone; they could be negotiated and modified. The first two major Christian histories – by Eusebius and Orosius respectively – show shifts in how female vulnerability and suffering was utilised. Eusebius of Caesarea's *Historia ecclesiastica*, written in the early fourth century CE, shunned away from examples of exceptional female intervention and instigation, but still centred female suffering (Part 2). Orosius of Braga's *Historiae adversus paganos*, written in the early fifth century CE, attempted a return to classical historiography but pushed for a new bloodless image of genderless unrest (Part 3). Both, therefore, made use of and rejected earlier models, as informed by Christian priorities, demonstrating the flexibility and endurance of gender as a rhetorical lens through which unrest could be characterised. These gendered models of unrest at different points in history set the boundaries against which more historically informed female experiences must be examined.

Classical Models of Female Unrest

Ancient authors who boldly took on the task of history-writing did not lack examples of tumultuous times. In recording these, Livy's *Ab urbe condita* and Tacitus's *Historiae* and *Annales* placed women in various and at times exceptional roles during male-led unrest.[5] It is now well understood that the women implicated by unrest in foundational Roman historiography functioned as moral *exempla* for men to measure themselves against, which has rightfully attracted critique of women's limited lot as tropes instead of fully actualised people.[6] Women had important yet subjugated roles in how unrest was understood and perceived, showing up to deliver evocative

---

[5] Livy's and Tacitus's lexicon of unrest has been examined elsewhere in this volume in greater detail. For Livy's lexicon of unrest, see contributions of Hjort Lange and Kopp in this volume. For Tacitus, see those of Berthelot and Lavan.

[6] Smethurst described Livy's women as 'puppets' in Smethurst 1950: 80. See objections to this in Stevenson 2011: 188–89.

speeches to men caught up in political or military upheaval, either goading them on or begging them to stop, and perhaps teaching the (male) reader a moral lesson or two that was made more impactful when coming from the weaker sex.

The examples from Livy's account of Rome's early history are well known: the rape of the Sabines has women stage an emotional intervention between their husbands and fathers, while the killing of Verginia in the Roman Forum by her father makes up another dramatic moment.[7] Where civic upheaval occurred, Livian women could be starring figures in conflicts that were nevertheless led by men – more instances of this will be examined in what follows. Usually such cameos were reserved solely for elite women, while the lower class women who populate Livy's history were of lesser importance, becoming 'passive and inarticulate' (Smethurst 1950: 81). The occasional stand-out women in Livy's writing were nevertheless intrinsically interlinked with historical change (Claassen 1998, Stevenson 2011). Indeed, women gave narratives of unrest a moralistic dimension, evoking pity or pinpointing blame.

Tacitus likewise balanced the inclusion of women in male-driven accounts of upheaval. In an important study on Tacitean women, Anthony Marshall argued that no woman in Tacitus's historical works is included at random but rather women's inclusion bears heavy narrative significance in each case (1984: 170). When writing of more recent events, Tacitus placed imperial women firmly at the heart of the chaotic reigns of first century emperors.[8] Galleria, the wife of Emperor Vitellius, Tacitus tells us, intervened in the political chaos of 69 CE, protecting the senator Trachalus when alliances shifted after the suicide of Otho (*Hist.* 2.60). In another episode, Sulpicia Praetextata, the wife of Crassus Frugi, went to the senate with her children to demand justice for her late husband, who had been executed under Nero's tumultuous reign (*Hist.* 4.42). This display of matronly loyalty and maternity, in the words of Marshall, 'becomes tragic', as Sulpicia's interference did not result in punishment for the accused Aquilius Regulus (1984, 182). Such examples place female participation in male-driven upheaval, while underlining women's limited ability to off-set these larger events. Livy's and Tacitus's purposeful deployment of female characters for their own

---

[7] For Livy's women, see Smethurst 1950, Moore 1993, Brown 1995, Claassen 1998, Joshel 2002, Stevenson 2011.

[8] For the women in Tacitus' *Histories* and *Annals*, see Rutland 1978, Marshall 1984, Santoro L'Hoir 1994, Foubert 2010.

narrative ends is thus well established. What has received less attention, however, are the precise ways in which these women figured in narratives of unrest. In what follows, I suggest that three different functions can be identified: instigation, mitigation, and victimisation.

The first dominant model is that of instigation. In Livy, Tarquinius Superbus's rape of Lucretia resulted in a rebellion against him. After the assault, Lucretia's dying words before committing suicide were a demand that she be avenged, bringing about the end of Roman kings.[9] Livy vividly describes Brutus and his companions marching on Rome after Lucretia's call to arms, with citizens flocking the streets in confusion and awe – the king's attempts to quell this *motus* failed (1.59–60). While it was Tarquinius's abuse of Lucretia that had led to this *motus*, she emerged from her plight to demand male action and usurpation of power. Tacitus's examples of women stirring unrest are less historically impactful, but he too shows women encouraging men to act in certain ways. The wicked Calvia Crispinilla goaded Clodius Macer into rebellion in Africa in the late 60s (*ad instigandum in arma*; *Hist.* 1.73). In Britain, the queen Boudica beseeched her people to rise up against Roman rule (*Ann.* 14.35), thus spearheading one of the most famous revolts in the empire (*defectio*; *Ann.* 14.30). Women could also instigate unrest less directly by angering others, as did Queen Cartimandua whose private affairs led to her subjects revolting against her (*defectio*; *Hist.* 3.45). Women were more able to instigate unrest if they wielded political power, as Boudica and Cartimandua did, or if they had significant connections, as Lucretia and Calvia Crispinilla did. In these ways Livy and Tacitus placed morally outstanding and morally deplorable women alike, both Roman and non-Roman, as instigators of unrest. For them, the woman's character indicated whether the cause had been just or not.[10]

A second model has women trying to mitigate the dangers of unrest. In Livy, the Sabine women intervening on behalf of their new husbands prevented further conflict (1.13).[11] Tacitus offered short anecdotes of women attempting to minimise the damage caused by male-led tensions: He credited Agrippina the Elder for preventing mutiny (*seditione*) amongst soldiers stuck at the Rhine frontier. Rather than being presented in a positive light, how-

---

9 Livy, 1.58: '*uos*' inquit '*uideritis, quid illi debeatur.*' For Lucretia, see Donaldson 1982, Joshel 2002.
10 Importantly, Tacitus places Boudica in a positive light to undermine the moral failures of Roman men. See Gillespie 2015.
11 See Brown 1995 for discussion.

ever, Agrippina's intervention signalled the failure of men in charge of the situation.[12] Such female mitigation could also occur post-conflict, as when Eppopina hid her husband Julius Sabinus after his botched revolt in 69 CE, which led him to fake his own death – here she is an *insigne ... exemplum* for hiding her husband (*Hist.* 4.67), underlining that a woman's duty was to endure the consequences of male actions.

Finally, a third dominant rhetorical model centres upon female suffering, portrayed both through individual fates and in formulaic phrases evoking nameless groups of women. At different points in their respective narratives, Livy and Tacitus honed in on the victimisation of individual women. Verginia's death at the hands of her father is a good illustration of this phenomenon in Livy's myth-historical account of Rome's origins. In Tacitus, we might point to his portrayal of Vitia, mother of Rufus Geminus – after her son was executed for treason, she was killed for mourning him.[13] Tacitus plainly explained that 'even women were not exempt from danger' (*Ann.* 6.10), an astute reminder that end of conflict by no means meant that implicated women were now safe. He added: 'Where [women] could not be accused of grasping at political power, their tears were made a crime'. Tacitus thus underlined that female experiences of unrest were without exception centred around suffering. The peril that unrest posed for women is pervasive in these histories, fully acknowledged and utilised by the authors. Societal unrest placed women in unsafe situations, and women mitigated such hostilities with little control of the situation themselves, often in extremely tense political situations. The increased vulnerability of women was used to underline the unpredictability and danger of unrest.

Much more frequently, however, both authors charted unrest through the suffering of mass female groups. This model is fundamentally formulaic yet disturbing – such are Livy's *feminae et pueri* who cry out in Nesactium in 177 BCE when the city's men start killing their own rather than surrender (41.11.4–6). Elsewhere Livy linked women's cries and laments to bodily harm, with the anguish of the children in their care adding to a gendered experience (38.22.8). Tacitus likewise strengthened crises with women's despair,

---

12 Tac. *Ann.* 1.69: *conpressam a muliere seditionem, cui nomen principis obsistere non quiuerit.* Tacitus' depiction of Agrippina has been studied in McHugh 2012 and Gillespie 2020; for the mutiny, see Malloch 2004.

13 For the risk of women being executed after the downfall of their male relations, see Vihervalli and Leonard 2023.

as with the great fire of Rome that Nero was rumoured to have started, with 'the wailings of terror-stricken women' filling the air (*Ann.* 15.38). Such suffering female masses may be widespread in ancient historiographical writings, but this should not lead us to regard them as devoid of meaning. As Caryn A. Reeder has argued in relation to this *topos* in the works of Tacitus's contemporary Josephus, 'the rhetoric of suffering women and children is empowered by the actual experiences of women and children' (2013: 176). Mass groups of women suffering psychological or physical harm due to crises resonated with Roman readers because they reflected the unrest with which they were familiar. As such, female suffering was an effective way to describe societal disruptions, evoking severity and the uncontrolled, chaotic nature of unrest.

However, this final rhetorical model was not only made up of passive or bewailing victims. Women are also shown as defending themselves, although this did not curb violence. In Livy, the women of Veii threw rocks at invaders (alongside slaves), although these efforts too ended in their helpless cries (5.21.10–11). In Tacitus, the women of Cremona intervened in the violent chaos of their city with fatal results (*Hist.* 3.32). Caitlin Gillespie has recently studied this kind of collective female action during political or public crises in Tacitus. Gillespie argues that incidents of female groups claiming space in patriarchal spaces made their voices heard, seeking to evoke pity from male audiences, lamenting the upheavals taking place, and in some cases even echoing funerary rituals (2023: 104). The display of female despair helped authors emphasise the chaotic and brutal nature of male aggressions. Furthermore, whether in war or in peace, such female groups looked on as men concluded their disruptive affairs, as they did in Tacitus's narration of Vitellius resigning his powers in 69 CE, with women as part of the crowd, mutely observing as yet another perilous episode concluded.[14]

In sum, we may conclude that the presence of women in accounts of unrest served several rhetorical objectives. Women made up the fabric of unrest before, during, and after violent upheaval, and their presence provided a contrast to male agency and dominance. Women might be compelled to pick up rocks from time to time, but most often their inclusion was framed by their physical and emotional suffering, which allowed authors to emphasise the treacherous, fickle, and often violent nature of unrest. Notably, whether

---

14 Tac. *Hist.* 3.68: *in sua contione Vitellius, inter suos milites, prospectantibus etiam feminis, pauca et praesenti maestitiae congruentia locutus.* For the scene, see Galtier 2010.

a wicked woman instigated unrest, an implicated woman sought to mitigate unrest, a good woman was tragically harmed in unrest, or nameless mass groups of women were abused, the women involved were worse off, whether the incident was their doing or not (and it rarely was). These dominant models show that, for Livy and Tacitus, female experiences of unrest held rhetorical power through which unrest was conceptualised. This gendered perspective added to a sense of suffering and tragedy, as well as painting unrest as reckless and dangerous. In these situations, individual women could gain heightened importance, but most women became depicted as nameless masses. These models of gendered unrest were not, however, fixed – rather gendered understandings of unrest continued to evolve, not least in the earliest works of Christian historiography, which I examine in this paper's remaining two parts.

Female Suffering in Eusebius

Eusebius of Caesarea, credited as the inventor of church history, wrote his *Historia ecclesiastica* between c. 311 and 325 CE.[15] Eusebius's ten-book history spanned from the dawn of man to Eusebius's own age when Christianity had triumphed under Constantine. The work's genre and Eusebius's authorial decisions have all been scrutinised but his approach to history-writing was, for better or worse, original (DeVore 2013, Grafton 2020). He had witnessed Christian persecution in the Eastern provinces and also viewed the Christian past as one of upheaval: he recorded 'countless' Jewish revolts (2.6), Roman military campaigns, and earlier persecutions in his work.[16] Set against this pervasive unrest, Eusebius focused in particular on female suffering, with female instigation and mitigation being generally absent. The Christian influence that informed Eusebius's writing also put a new spin on female suffering, as unrest was now most notably centred around the experiences of female martyrs.

---

15 For the competing theories on the composition of Euseb. *Hist. eccl.*, see Corke-Webster 2019: 57–65.
16 See also the revolt of Judas the Galilean in Euseb. *Hist. eccl.* 1.5; the revolt during Passover in 2.19; the Jewish revolts in Egypt in 4.2, 4.5.

Eusebius's shift in focus becomes apparent in his account of events before Christ, which feature hardly any women. Eusebius did not allow individual women to intervene in narratives of unrest, neither to instigate them nor to prevent or mitigate their consequences. He disregarded the heroines of the Roman past, and thus we find no Lucretia or Verginia here. Interested in the history of the church, the women who made it into his narrative were involved in the life of Christ and his disciples.[17] The one exception to this pattern comes from his account of the siege of Jerusalem in 70 CE, which includes gruesome details of starving and dead women in the city (3.6). In a harrowing anecdote, a famine-struck woman called Mary eats her own son, and upon being discovered she demands: 'Wretched child, for what do I protect you in war, famine, and rebellion (*stasis*)? Even if we live among them as slaves to the Romans, famine anticipates slavery, and the rioters (*hoi stasiastai*) are worse than both'.[18] Mary's inclusion in the work echoes the women in Livy and Tacitus who could enter a crisis to deliver a moralising speech condemning the events around them – Boudica's oration to her troops is perhaps the most notable example.

However, Mary's story was not Eusebius's original work, but taken directly from the account of Josephus, who utilised stories of women's suffering to interpret the horrors of war.[19] Using female experiences in this way added to the pitiful and desperate depiction of the upheaval at hand – here, a horrific siege that left countless dead. Eusebius quoted Josephus at great length for this siege, showing that he wished to show the full breadth of misery and devastation. In this, Mary was instrumental – but also coincidental.

As noted by Elizabeth Clark, Eusebius's inclusion of women reflects the sources that he used rather than his own enthusiasm for women's experiences – nearly all accounts involving women come from the many citations that he put into the history from other authors and are not his original contributions (1992: 256–7). Indeed, we cannot find another story like Mary's, where a woman caught up in unrest emerges to reflect on it. The

---

17 Herod the Great's mother and wife (1.6, 1.8); Salome and Herodias (1.8, 1.11); Nero's mother and wife (2.25). For Nero in Euseb. *Hist. eccl.*, see Corke-Webster 2019: 252–56. The first woman mentioned in the work is Cleopatra (*Hist. eccl.* 1.5) to note her and Mark Antony's deaths.
18 Euseb. *Hist. eccl.* 3.6: 'βρέφος,' εἶπεν, 'ἄθλιον, ἐν πολέμῳ καὶ λιμῷ καὶ στάσει, τίνι σε τηρῶ; τὰ μὲν παρὰ Ῥωμαίοις δουλεία κἂν ζήσωμεν ἐπ᾽ αὐτούς, φθάνει δὲ καὶ δουλείαν ὁ λιμός, οἱ στασιασταὶ δὲ ἀμφοτέρων χαλεπώτεροι' (trans. Deferrari 1953: 151).
19 Joseph. *BJ* 6.193–213. See Reeder 2013; and for Eusebius's use of Josephus, see Carriker 2003: 157–61.

only other individual women involved with urban upheavals that Eusebius recorded were martyrs, and unlike Mary's fate in Jerusalem, for Eusebius their suffering had not been pitiful.

Christian women endured significant episodes of unrest in the form of persecutions. Eusebius's depictions of early martyrdom scenes in Lyon in 177 CE (5.1) and in Alexandria c. 245–251 CE (6.41) foreground the torture of women, whose bravery was all the more laudable due to their weaker sex.[20] The anecdotes are brutal: a woman called Quinta was dragged 'through the entire city over the rough pavement', getting flogged, with her feet bound, before the mob stoned her to death (6.41.4, transl. Deferrari 1969: 71). As with Mary, Eusebius was quoting someone else when including the story of Quinta – in this case, Dionysius of Alexandria. Quinta did not, however, seek to reflect the horrors of unrest, nor was she to be bewailed as an unfortunate outcome of civic upheaval. Women like Quinta were admirable examples of Christian piety, and her suffering only amplified her heavenly victory. In this way, Eusebius radically reinterpreted the suffering of (certain) women in violent episodes, as did martyrologies more widely: a violent death paved the way to heaven. The rhetoric of female suffering could, therefore, carry a positive message for Christian audiences in the exceptional context of martyrdom.

Beyond this specific context, Eusebius's gendered models of unrest cleaved quite closely to Livy and Tacitus. Eusebius, drawing again on Josephus on Jewish revolts in Syria, wrote of the dead, naked bodies of women and children to showcase the horrors of revolts and uprisings (2.26). Quoting from earlier sources in this way, Eusebius reaffirmed that unrest and female suffering had historically gone hand in hand. This assertion comes to the fore especially towards the end of his history when he recorded the events of the early fourth century that he himself had witnessed. Here he heavily relied on gendered unrest to conceptualise the tyranny the world had suffered prior to the ascension of Constantine.

In Books 8 to 10, Eusebius used his own knowledge and experience to cover the end of the tetrarchy and the civil wars fought by Constantine between 306 and 324 CE. This had been a violent and restless time throughout the Roman Empire, and many had been implicated and harmed – especially, it seems, women. Indeed, nearly every woman included in these final three

---

20 For female martyrs in *Hist. eccl.*, see Hall 1993: 10–15.

books is impacted or victimised by religious or political violence.[21] The victimisation of women was central to Eusebius's representation of recent unrest, interwoven into his depiction of tyranny in a way that finds echoes in the works of Livy and Tacitus.

These accounts of female suffering centre around Constantine's rivals Maxentius and Maximinus Daia. Maxentius's time in Rome between 308 and 312 is the most elaborate, featuring the mindless killing of citizens during an oppressive regime: '[Maxentius] used to separate lawfully wedded wives from their husbands, insult them most disgracefully, and send them back again to their husbands.'[22] Maximinus Daia, on the other hand, sexually abused women and virgins in the Eastern provinces, while some women chose death over sexual violation (8.14).[23] Here, political upheaval is articulated through gendered violence targeted at mass groups of women – a familiar model that clearly remained as vibrant and timely in the early fourth century as before and was the model Eusebius most relied on. He also gave some more detailed examples that bear comparison to Livy and Tacitus: one cannot help but think of Lucretia when Eusebius records the unnamed wife of a prefect killing herself in order to avoid sexual abuse at the hands of Maxentius, thus evoking self-inflicted female deaths when tyrants took sexual interest in them – this woman, however, ended her life before violation like a good Christian.[24] The scale of unjust unrest, therefore, was measured through female experience, but the women concerned had become far more nameless and, ultimately, abstract than their pagan predecessors.

For Eusebius, women continued to characterise unrest, but they had morphed into an indistinct mass of sufferers rather than being individuals in their own right – unless a female martyr was in question, in which case Eusebius was able to interpret her suffering in a positive light. Beyond the context of martyrdom, however, unrest was even more male than it had

---

21 Euseb. *Hist. eccl.* 8.9, 8.12, 9.5 include female martyrs in the East. The only woman in Books 8 to 10 not physically abused or threatened with violence is Constantine's half-sister Constantia (10.8), noted for her marriage to Licinius. However, Constantine was now waging war against Licinius, once more drawing Constantia into male-led unrest.
22 Euseb. *Hist. eccl.* 8.14: διαζευγνὺς γέ τοι τῶν ἀνδρῶν τὰς κατὰ νόμον γαμετάς, ταύταις ἐνυβρίζων ἀτιμότατα, τοῖς ἀνδράσιν αὖθις ἀπέπεμπεν, translated in Deferrari 1969: 193–94. Maxentius is also accused of cutting up pregnant women for magic, and Eusebius also included accusations of Licinius raping the wives of senators in his later work on Constantine, in Euseb. *Vit. Const.* 1.55.
23 One Christian woman whom Maximinus especially desired was exiled for her refusal of him (8.14).
24 This story is repeated in Euseb. *Vit. Const.* 1.34.

been, but its severity could still be evaluated through female pain. In this way, women complete the picture of unrest amongst Jews, early Christians, and the people of Eusebius's own day. The civic unrest of the early fourth century, in particular, was conceptualised through the sexual and physical abuse of women – this was the wont of tyrants, and Eusebius used these rhetorical models to emphasise the brutality of regimes. Gendered models, then, both shifted and endured, linking unrest with violence against women. This literary tradition could, however, present a problem (and an opportunity) for a historian like Orosius who wished to present a more favourable vision of the past.

Orosius's Bloodless Unrest

Around 418 CE, the Hispanic presbyter Orosius of Braga composed a universal history from the creation Adam up to the fifth century.[25] This was the first major Christian history written since Eusebius.[26] His *Historiae adversus paganos* were written in seven books, in which Orosius sought to counteract the instability of his time by arguing that historically the world had had it worse – since the arrival of Christ, world matters had improved, as signalled by the prosperity and peace of Augustus's reign.[27] Despite this novel interpretation, Orosius drew on earlier Roman historians to 'return to the grand tradition of classical historiography,'[28] which allows us to question how Orosius repeated earlier gendered models of unrest, and how women were centred in these, especially after Eusebius had utilised women as a more anonymous group upon whom unrest was inflicted upon. Crucially, Orosius wished to show that the fifth century was more divinely favoured than the

---

25 The term 'universal' is misleading here, as discussed in Van Nuffelen 2012: 170–76. For an overview of Orosius, see also Zecchini 2003: 319–29.
26 As argued by Van Nuffelen 2020, chronicles were the *modus operandi* in the fourth century, despite the publication of Euseb. *Hist. eccl.* Before Orosius wrote his work, the most notable contribution to a Christian narrative history was the 401/2 CE translation of Eusebius into Latin by Rufinus of Aquileia, who added two books of his own to continue the work; see Humphries 2008.
27 This central thesis is argued at 3.8.3–7 and 6.20.4–7.
28 Zecchini 2003: 321. For Orosius's use and engagement of classical historiography, see Van Nuffelen 2012: 76–92.

pagan past, and arguably, this complicated his deployment of gendered models of unrest.

Orosius's lexicon of unrest echoes that of earlier historiography: *motus* and *seditio* are the most common, designating mutinies, urban riots, civil wars, and revolts by subjugated peoples; *rebellio* and *defectio* also occur, while the piracy that Pompey sought to combat is labelled as *latrocinium*.[29] Orosius made much use of Roman history-writing, but he was not a blind follower of earlier writers, as his interpretation of heavenly intent and the place of Rome within a divine plan cannot be reconciled with the views of Livy and Tacitus.[30] Nevertheless, as Orosius accounted for historic unrest, he added his own interpretation of the models we have examined: instigation, mitigation, and suffering.

When Orosius recounted historic upheaval, he readily recorded Livy's famed women: the Sabine women, Lucretia, and Verginia are all included, albeit in abbreviated form – the Sabine women do not step in to prevent bloodshed; nor does Lucretia deliver her dying words.[31] The exceptional roles these women played in their contexts of unrest is lost, both as instigators and mitigators – their fame may have preceded them, but Orosius nevertheless minimised their roles in unrest. Orosius did upon occasion add his own remarks to such women, as when he discussed the Gracchi who were infamous for *impias seditiones* (5.10.10) – and, like Livy, Orosius credited one of the family, Sempronia, with instigating her husband's death; however, the account differs as Livy noted Sempronia was not charged for this (*Per.* 59), whereas Orosius recorded that she was. This may be Orosius's attempt to demonstrate the wickedness of the past, thus adding to Livy's version the immorality of such pagan women. Indeed, Orosius was fascinated by the motif of violent women, especially when non-Roman, detailing their brutal natures (van Nuffelen 2012: 127–28) – for instance, he recorded the suicides of Gallic women who started with their own children before killing themselves (5.16.21). Overall, we find much more female presence in the turbulent past here than in Eusebius, with some indication of women acting as instigators and mitigators of unrest, even if in abridged forms. Orosius

---

29 *motus* at 2.19.4, 3.2.10, 3.16.1, 3.23.44, 5.9.5, 6.6.7, 6.11.15, 6.12.1, 6.21.23; *seditio* at 4.6.32, 4.8.4, 5.8.1–2, 5.9.1–3, 5.10.10, 5.12.3–4, 5.17.2, 5.17.10, 6.22.2, 7.5.6–8, 7.6.14, 7.12.7, 7.23.5, 7.28.25, 7.29.6; *defectio* at 5.18.8, 5.22.9–10, 7.17.7; *rebellio* at 7.9.2; *latrocinium* at 6.18.19.
30 Walter 2020: 211–12.
31 For Sabine women, see 2.4.2–5; for Lucretia 2.4.12, where her rape is mentioned – Orosius says nothing of her suicide or call to arms; Verginia receives the longest treatment at 2.13.6.

further seems to have added a fourth gendered model of unrest: the savage and violent woman who lacked self-control, both as woman and, in most cases, as a barbarian.

Book 7, the final book of Orosius's work, covers history from the birth of Christ to 416/7. This four-hundred-year period is an overwhelming itemisation of unrest: usurpations, revolts, civil wars, and mutinies mark all corners of the empire. Much of this was taken from an earlier chronicle by Jerome, but Orosius also made much use of Tacitus. Amidst all this unrest, women are largely absent,[32] despite Orosius having recorded many of the key women in Livy's history. Some echoes of female vulnerability during unrest are discernible, however, as when Orosius noted the deaths of Elagabalus and his mother in a military uprising in Rome (*tumultu ... militari*, 7.18.5). The role of women in conflict is noted when Constantine's wife Fausta sided with her husband against her father Maximian (7.28.10), and when Constantine waged civil war against his half-sister's husband (7.28.19) and later ordered her son to be executed (7.28.26). Whereas Eusebius had been keen to show Constantine as a pious ruler, Orosius was more forthright about the considerable upheaval that this era of civil war and consolidation of power caused, especially for implicated elite women.

However, Orosius's recording of unrest hinged upon his insistence that, ever since the reigns of Theodosius I in the East and Honorius in the West, conflict in the Roman world had been resolved without bloodshed: 'almost all of these [recent conflicts], right down to the present day, have ended with the fruit of a clear-cut and holy victory, and with very little, or no, shedding of blood.'[33] This perspective required Orosius to consider the slaughter of 10,000 Gothic soldiers as 'little' – and, indeed, numerous political players continue to perish violently as his history draws to a close (7.35.19). Far-fetched as this claim therefore was, it nevertheless meant that Orosius did not use gendered models of female suffering as crutches for his conceptu-

---

32 Orosius records several bad emperors having sexual liaisons with female relatives: Caligula (7.5.9), Nero (7.7.2 and 7.7.9), Caracalla (7.18.2). Other women of note are Helena of Adiabene who provided grain to the people of Jerusalem (7.6.12), Hadrian's unnamed wife (Vibia Sabina, 7.13.3), Severus Alexander's mother Mamea for her Christian studies (7.18.7 and 7.19.2), Queen Zenobia's wars with Aurelian (17.23.4), Constantius Chlorus's marriage to Theodora (7.25.5), Constantine's mother Helena (7.25.16), and Constantine's half-sister Eutropia (7.29.11).

33 Oros. 7.35.9: *et tamen omnia paene usque in hodiernum diem et quidem cum fructu simplicis sanctaeque uictoriae uel nullo uel minimo sanguine quieuerunt*, trans. Fear 2010: 389. Orosius also makes similar arguments at 7.34.8, 7.35.5, 7.37.14.

alisation of unrest – and this is precisely how he proceeded, by writing out women altogether in the civic upheavals from Theodosius I onwards, with the exception of two: an unnamed elderly virgin and Galla Placidia, both discussed below, who Orosius included to showcase that unrest no longer harmed women.

Orosius's version of imperial history thus discarded the most enduring *topos* of gendered unrest: female suffering. This is especially striking as he used this model frequently to describe unrest in the more distant past.[34] After the coming of Christ, however, Orosius describes unrest only in genderless terms, referring to the deaths and abuse of a *populus* or of *accolae* (7.8.10, 7.12.8). Women are no longer singled out in these broader descriptions of unrest – Orosius did not use the model of female suffering for the Christian era that he had previously used to underline the vivacity, brutality, or the unjust or chaotic nature of unrest. This omission of generic female suffering (and the limited number of instances of individual female suffering) in the final book of his *Historiae* supported the work's central thesis that the new Christian era was more blessed than earlier times – emphasising the brutal abuse of women did not fit into this motif and as such was written out. The closest Orosius comes to any such 'women and children' *topos* is when Galerius defeated Narseus's army in 298 CE, for which Orosius drew on Jerome to note the capture of Persian women and children – but Orosius gave this detail only a brief acknowledgement, with the lack of sympathy he was liable to show these foreigners (7.25.11). The omission of gendered unrest is made even more obvious by accounts of martyrdoms. Where Eusebius had given disturbing details of torture for several female martyrs, Orosius gave none, even as he listed the ten persecutions Christians had faced. Persecutions were not bloodless in his version of the past, but they were genderless.[35] This should not be regarded as editorial brevity from Orosius, but as a conscious effort to gloss over and decentre gendered models of unrest.

However, women making dramatic appearances still held narrative power, as is shown by the single female-centred anecdote of Book 7: when

---

34 Orosius has many examples of gendered suffering in Books 1 to 6, most from military contexts, but the most evocative of these is the slaughter of children and subsequent suicide by Gallic women after their men had been defeated by Romans who now refused to spare the women of rape (5.16.13–21; cf. 6.21.17).
35 For Orosius's persecutions, see Walter 2020: 220–24. This genderless language is seen in 7.15.4 (*multique sanctorum martyrio coronati sunt*), and similarly at 7.17.4 (*plurimique sanctorum per diuersas prouincias martyrio coronati sunt*).

a Gothic soldier ran into an elderly virgin amidst the sack of Rome in August of 410 (7.39.3–10). The virgin warned the soldier against plundering church goods, appearing as a moral *exemplum* that could easily be plucked from classical historiographies, with Christian gloss. The soldier was so impressed by the woman's piety that he and a whole troop of Gothic soldiers helped her carry the holy vessels to St Peter's Basilica, in a holy procession orchestrated by the Gothic leader Alaric himself (for alternative, less flattering versions of the encounter, see Vihervalli 2022). Orosius thus knew how dramatic heroines could still embellish unrest, and how this gendered perspective could provide a moral analysis of the men involved. This time women implicated by unrest luckily both lived to tell the tale and retained their bodily inviolability – an intentional juxtaposition with past models of unrest.

It is perhaps fitting, then, to end this survey with the last woman recorded in Orosius's history: the imperial princess Galla Placidia (7.40.2, 7.43.2, 7). Abducted by Alaric and forcefully married to Gothic ruler Athaulf, her experience is treated by Orosius as a harmonious and opportune development. Athaulf is painted as a ruler who 'strove to avoid war, and ... strove to love peace', and in this the intelligent and skilled Galla Placidia helped her husband, advising him in good rulership – an ideal match by all accounts (7.43.7). Yet we would be remiss to believe this depiction of their marriage: Galla Placidia had been abducted by Alaric's men and forcibly married. Her lack of consent underlines that unrest curbed female freedom from lowest to highest social orders and placed women in grave danger (cf. Leonard 2019). This is ignored by Orosius, in an attempt to remove women's suffering from his account of an improved Christian era. Orosius's insistence on Galla Placidia's good fortune laboriously attempted to reject the humiliation that her abduction constituted for imperial power. Instead, he depicted an era in which, finally, unrest was no longer tied to female misfortunes – if only that were plausible.

Orosius manipulated gendered models of unrest by defying the expectations of female suffering that the historiographical tradition had set up. As such, the unrest in the post-Augustan era was largely gender-neutral, and in the post-Theodosian era supposedly free of bloodshed and completely void of female suffering. This is a remarkably different way of depicting unrest from the tradition in which Orosius situated his work. By avoiding the pervasive model of women's suffering for his own time, Orosius was able to communicate his vision of a more brutal Roman past and a more peaceful Christian present, demonstrating, yet again, that gender was a powerful rhetorical tool for making sense of unrest in the Roman world.

Conclusions

Roman and late Roman historians gave episodes of unrest gendered dimensions, using these to make different judgements of unfolding events. While all authors depicted unrest as overwhelmingly male in its instigation and development, their pictures of unrest were textured by background and secondary female participation. This female presence illuminated the nature of unrest: how intense, reckless, unwise, unpredictable, or cruel it had been. We find dominant models that place women as instigators, mitigators, or sufferers, and of these three the last was the most enduring and all encompassing.

These models were evoked across centuries, shifting focus onto different aspects of unrest, reflecting authorial intent and priorities. Livy and Tacitus relished dramatic female interventions by mytho-historical and historical women, depicting their actions sympathetically if the woman was respectable, or as offensive, if the woman was immoral. Most of all, women's presence in unrest could be used to convey the scale of disaster and horror, with masses of violated, killed, or bewailing women reflecting the extent of societal breakdown in a culture of gendered violence.

Christian authors continued these models in different ways: Eusebius had no space for standout heroines but included abused women to convey the civic unrest of the early fourth century, which he sought to condemn in an effort to demarcate the winning and losing sides. Female martyrs also gained a more central position, with their horrific suffering as a part of mob violence depicted as divinely guided and desirable. Even so, the depiction of these women's experiences is not comparable to the prominence of individual women in episodes of unrest in classical historiography. Orosius, on the other hand, shows authorial manipulation of gendered unrest most clearly of all writers examined here: he denied that female suffering took place in his own time by writing out women in episodes of unrest, despite recording this for the more distant Roman past, while the two women he included in episodes of recent unrest, as luck would have it, overturned the *topos* by having a pleasant experience.

Gendered unrest was a powerful device through which upheaval could be perceived, measured, and conceptualised in Roman and late Roman historiography. The different uses reveal authorial intent and priorities. Women may well have been secondary to male-led aggressions and strife, but unrest was incomplete without their presence and subsequent suffering – at least until Orosius wished to argue for a world free of this. Gendered depictions of unrest emphasise that authors knew well that women lived in hostile environments where abuse or assault was always a possibility, and especially so when chaos erupted. Authors could use gendered unrest to conceptualise the upheaval according to their own interests, placing female models into their narratives. Though they lurked in the background, therefore, the women in Roman historiography show that unrest was not an exclusively masculine exercise – without them, its depiction remained incomplete.

Works cited

Ando, Clifford. 1996. 'Pagan apologetics and Christian intolerance in the ages of Themistius and Augustine'. *Journal of Early Christian Studies* 4(2): 171–207.
Brown, Robert. 1995. 'Livy's Sabine women and the ideal of "concordia"'. *Transactions of the American Philological Association* 125: 291–319.
Cameron, Averil. 2002. 'Apologetics in the Roman empire – a genre of intolerance?', in J. M. Carrie and R. Lizzi Testa, eds., *Humana Sapit: Études d'Antiquité Tardive offertes à Lellia Cracco Ruggini*. Turnhout, 219–27.
–. 2008. 'The violence of orthodoxy', in Eduard Iricinschi and Holger M Zellentin, eds., *Heresy and Identity in Late Antiquity*. Tübingen, 102–14.
Carriker, Andrew. 2003. The Library of Eusebius of Caesarea. Leiden.
Claassen, Jo-Marie. 1998. 'The familiar other: the pivotal role of women in Livy's narrative of political development in early Rome'. *Acta Classica* 41: 71–103.
Clark, Elizabeth. 1992. 'Eusebius on women in early church history', in Harold W. Attridge and Gohei Hata, eds., *Eusebius, Christianity and Judaism*. Detroit, MI, 256–69.
Corke-Webster, James. 2019. *Eusebius and Empire: Constructing Church and Rome in the Ecclesiastical History*. Cambridge.
DeVore, David. 2013. 'Genre and Eusebius's Ecclesiastical History: prolegomena for a focused debate', in Aaron Johnson and Jeremy Schott, eds., *Eusebius of Caesarea: Traditions and Innovations*. Cambridge, MA, 19–50.
Donaldson, Ian. 1982. *The Rapes of Lucretia: A Myth and Its Transformations*. Oxford.
Dossey, Leslie. 2008. 'Wife beating and manliness in Late Antiquity'. *Past & Present* 199(1): 3–40.

Drake, H.A., ed. 2006. *Violence in Late Antiquity: Perceptions and Practices*. Aldershot.
—. 2011. 'Intolerance, religious violence, and political legitimacy in Late Antiquity'. *Journal of the American Academy of Religion* 79(1): 193–235.
Foubert, Lien. 2010. 'Literary constructions of female identities: the parallel lives of Julio-Claudian women in Tacitus's Annals'. *Studies in Latin Literature and Roman History* 323: 344–65.
Gaca, Kathy L. 2011. 'Girls, women, and the significance of sexual violence in ancient warfare', in Elizabeth D. Heineman, ed., *Sexual Violence in Conflict Zones: From the Ancient World to the Era of Human Rights*. Philadelphia, 73–88.
—. 2016. 'Continuities in rape and tyranny in martial societies from antiquity onward', in Stephanie Lynn Budin and Jean MacIntosh Turfa, eds., *Women in Antiquity: Real Women Across the Ancient World*. London, 1041–56.
Gaddis, Michael. 2005. *There Is No Crime for Those Who Have Christ: Religious Violence in the Christian Roman Empire*. Berkeley, CA.
Galtier, Fabrice. 2010. 'La chute de Vitellius dans les Histoires de Tacite'. *Dialogues d' Histoire Ancienne Supplément* 4(2): 479–91.
Gillespie, Caitlin. 2015. 'The wolf and the hare: Boudica's political bodies in Tacitus and Dio'. *Classical World* 108(3): 403–29.
—. 2020. 'Agrippina the Elder and the memory of Augustus in Tacitus' Annals'. *Classical World* 114(1): 59–84.
—. 2023. 'Women's collective action in Tacitus' Annals'. *Classical World* 117(1): 83–108.
Grafton, Anthony. 2020. 'Mixed messages: the early modern reception of Eusebius as a church historian'. *International Journal of the Classical Tradition* 27(3): 332–60.
Hahn, Johannes. 2014. *Gewalt und religiöser Konflikt: Studien zu den Auseinandersetzungen zwischen Christen, Heiden und Juden im Osten des Römischen Reiches (von Konstantin bis Theodosius II.)*. Berlin.
Hall, Stuart G. 1993. 'Women among the early martyrs'. *Studies in Church History* 30: 1–21.
Hillner, Julia. 2013. 'Family violence: punishment and abuse in the late Roman Household', in Leslie Brubaker and Shaun Tougher, eds., *Approaches to the Byzantine Family*. Aldershot, 21–45.
Humphries, Mark. 2008. 'Rufinus's Eusebius: translation, continuation, and edition in the Latin *Ecclesiastical History*'. *Journal of Early Christian Studies* 16(2): 143–64.
Joshel, Sandra R. 2002. 'The body female and the pody politic: Livy's Lucretia and Verginia', in Laura McClure, ed., *Sexuality and Gender in the Classical World: Readings and Sources*. Oxford, 163–90.
Kahlos, Maijastina. 2013. *Forbearance and Compulsion: The Rhetoric of Religious Tolerance and Intolerance in Late Antiquity*. London.
Leonard, Victoria. 2019. 'Galla Placidia as "human gold": consent and autonomy in the sack of Rome, CE 410'. *Gender and History* 31(2): 334–52.
Malloch, S.J.V. 2004. 'The end of the Rhine mutiny in Tacitus, Suetonius, and Dio'. *Classical Quarterly* 54(1): 198–210.
Marshall, Anthony J. 1984. 'Ladies in waiting: the role of women in Tacitus' Histories'. *Ancient Society* 15: 167–84.

McHugh, Mary R. 2012. '*Ferox Femina*: Agrippina Maior in Tacitus's *Annales*'. *Helios* 39(1): 73–96.
Moore, Timothy J. 1993. 'Morality, history, and Livy's wronged women'. *Eranos* 91: 38–46.
Reeder, Caryn A. 2013. 'Pity the women and children: punishment by siege in Josephus's *Jewish War*'. *Journal for the Study of Judaism* 44: 174–94.
Rutland, Linda W. 1978. 'Women as makers of kings in Tacitus' Annals'. *Classical World* 72(1): 15–29.
Santoro L'Hoir, Francesca. 1994. 'Tacitus and women's usurpation of power'. *Classical World* 88(1): 5–25.
Shaw, Brent D. 2011. *Sacred Violence: African Christians and Sectarian Hatred in the Age of Augustine*. Cambridge.
Sizgorich, Thomas. 2009. *Violence and Belief in Late Antiquity: Militant Devotion in Christianity and Islam*. Philadelphia, PA.
Smethurst, S. E. 1950. 'Women in Livy's "History"'. *Greece & Rome* 19(56): 80–7.
Stanton, Graham N. and Guy G. Stroumsa, eds. 2008. *Tolerance and Intolerance in Early Judaism and Christianity*. Cambridge.
Stevenson, Tom. 2011. 'Women of early Rome as *exempla* in Livy, *Ab Urbe Condita*, book 1'. *Classical World* 104(2): 175–89.
Van Nuffelen, Peter. 2012. *Orosius and the Rhetoric of History*. Oxford.
–. 2020. 'What happened after Eusebius? Chronicles and narrative identities in the fourth century', in Richard Flower and Morwenna Ludlow, eds., *Rhetoric and Religious Identity in Late Antiquity*. Oxford, 160–79.
Vihervalli, Ulriika. 2022. 'Wartime rape in late antiquity: consecrated virgins and victim bias in fifth century west'. *Early Medieval Europe* 30(1): 3–19.
Vihervalli, Ulriika, and Victoria Leonard. 2023. 'Elite women and gendered violence in late Roman Italy', in Jeroen W. P. Wijnendaele, ed., *Late Roman Italy – Imperium to Regnum (c. 250–500 CE)*. Edinburgh, 201–222.
Walter, Anke. 2020. *Time in Ancient Stories of Origin*. Oxford.
Witzke, Serena S. 2016. 'Violence against women in ancient Rome: ideology versus reality', in Werner Riess and Garrett G. Fagan, eds., *The Topography of Violence in the Greco-Roman World*. Ann Arbor, MI, 248–74.
Zecchini, G. 2003. 'Latin historiography: Jerome, Orosius, and the western chronicles', in Gabriele Marasco, ed., *Greek and Roman Historiography in Late Antiquity: Fourth to Sixth Century A.D.* Leiden, 317–45.

12. Roman War, Rabbinic Law, and Provincial Sovereigntism

Natalie B. Dohrmann

Abstract: *This essay traces the smouldering aftermath of unrest against Rome on one provincial population: the tannaitic rabbis. It reflects on the meaning and motivations behind the rabbinic resistance to civil strife, connecting it to their commitment to the rule of law. In this essay I explore how law is not only anathema to social unrest, but both anchors and animates a rabbinic machinery that works actively to prevent it. The rabbis pursue a number of avenues to short-circuit the traditional catalysts of Jewish unrest/rebellion, and a selection of culturally volatile topics, seen together, create a network in which the rabbis' own stated aims can come to pass. In suppressing unrest, the rabbis are not only defending themselves bodily from Roman intervention (though they do that too) but also creating inner Jewish conditions necessary for the establishment of their audacious nomos. The essay concludes by defining as 'sovereigntist' a form of provincial politics baked into both the tannaitic and imperial endeavors.*

The appointment of just judges is to be effective in restoring Israel and resettling them on their land, and in preventing them being felled by the sword. (Sifre *Deuteronomy* § 144)

One well-known origin myth for the rabbinic movement begins atop the walls of a besieged Jerusalem sometime in the early part of the Jewish war against Rome. There we find Rabban Yohanan ben Zakkai trying in vain to quell the resistance of his compatriots in the face of Vespasian's seige; Yohanan and Vespasian, in this telling, share in common a desire to save the temple from Jewish zealots, whose savage impiety threatens to activate overwhelming Roman force. Having failed to bring the rebels to reason, Yohanan arranges to escape the city, masquerading as a dead man. His students manage to deposit before the Roman general his coffin, from which the sage arises. Vespasian, recognizing Yohanan as an ally, immediately grants him favors: 'I ask nothing of you' the sage replies, 'save Yavneh, where I might go and teach my disciples and there establish a house of prayer and perform all the commandments' (Avot de Rabbi Natan A, chapter 4). 'Go' says Vespasian, but before he can return to the work of crushing the revolt, Yohanan ben Zakkai interprets biblical prooftexts to augur Vespasian's ascension to emperor.

The metaphorics of the tale could not be more heavy-handed: Judaism is raised from the dead by the hands of a great scholar and his disciples, to thrive in a peaceful vineyard far from the devastated landscape of Jerusalem and the burning embers of the temple – protected by an empire better left unprovoked. The rabbinic ideal imagined here is a collective of philosopher pietists who won't cause any trouble – indeed their founding patron is Vespasian himself!

It is a myth of course (and a late one), a literary set piece familiar from Josephus's almost identical exhumation from the well at Jotapata, complete with his recognition as a friend by Vespasian, his prophecy of Vespasian's emperorship, and his securing of favored prisoner status (Joseph. *BJ* 3.340–92). Nonetheless, this late antique tale has served, *mutatis mutandis*, as a paradigm for understanding the rabbinic orientation toward the Roman empire (Neusner 1962: 112–22). From this 'Yavneh' emerges a set of rabbinic scholarly works exploring divine law and lore that, according to the standard reading, will translate the Jew from member of doomed polity to successful subject citizen who has traded a holy land for a holy text, obdurate nationalism for obedience to Torah's law, so long as it doesn't get in Rome's way. This imagined Jew can thrive more or less unbothered by the empire.

Given the brutality with which the Romans put down a series of high-profile Jewish rebellions in the late first and second centuries, such retreat seems reasonable. Seth Schwartz, most poignantly, paints a picture of the ferocity, dislocation, enslavement, loss of land, and death, that striate the major Jewish uprisings in 66–73, 115–117, and 132–135 CE. Schwartz reads the peaceful and extensive Romanization of the eastern cities of the Galilee in the second and third centuries as evidence of the traumatized exhaustion of the Jewish populace. The rabbis, whose first works are dated to the turn of the third century, arose in this scenario not to fight with fists but to resist the obliteration of Judaism, and redefine and reanimate the religion for a new era.

This is likely to be an uninviting start to an essay on unrest in the rabbinic imagination. Indeed the rabbis do not merely keep their heads down regarding empire, but invest heavily in the prevention of future unrest. This essay is interested in the meaning of this effort.

The Rule of Law

The central achievement of the early rabbis (the tannaim) was the Mishnah – a legal document produced in the late second and early third century CE. In the Mishnah we encounter a form of Judaism, grown from seeds of older Torah theology and a tradition of communal god-given law but representing something new altogether in scope, depth, and focus (see e.g., Halbertal 2013, Schwartz 2020, Rosen Zvi 2017). The Mishnah and the other tannaitic sources perform and communicate a legalism that, for the rabbis, eclipses other forms of religiosity and religious expertise and sets the divine law at the center of a reorientation of Jewish life and practice (Dohrmann 2013). Its concern is not limited to the sort of pragmatic legal topics that might have been the expected purview of a provincial ethnic judge – status, family, contract, and tort law, say. On the contrary, while it includes plenty of law that could offer practical guidance for judges/courts, the Mishnah also covers swaths of law that were off limits according to the empire such as criminal law, or obviated by history such as laws governing the long-destroyed temple and sacrificial cult, or law so arcane, or private as to be functionally useless to any imaginable court situation.

Because it had no mechanism for enforcement, and because the rabbis were few and lacked institutional authority, the tannaitic corpus has often been treated as a sort of religious literature (*contra* which Schwartz 2016). And yet, a host of genres better suited to moral exhortation, theological and philosophical reflection, or identity formation abound in the rabbis' ambit. If rabbinic halakhah was meant to communicate such content, and not to act 'as law', then why do they write so very much very technical law? Why do they set legal expertise above all other forms of religious expertise? Law is not only the form in which rabbinic thought happened to be cast, but is a choice that – even divorced from the particulars of its content – carries with it its own conceptual logics and imperatives that have been too easily subsumed to ideas of religion (Dohrmann 2015). Just as a recipe demands one read it with one eye to the kitchen and to eating, so being essentially legal, the tannaitic corpus asks one to inhabit law's inherent conceptions of and claims to jurisdiction. Of interest for the present purposes, moreover, it is to be underscored that law is concerned with the stuff of the everyday, and it structures, furnishes, and inhabits a functioning polity; the rule of law stands, in short, opposed essentially to the state of war – be it against Rome or, as this essay argues, between Jews. The law requires a baseline of social and political stability (Baumgarten 2017). With this in mind, in this essay I'd like to explore how law is not only anathema to social unrest of all sorts, but both anchors and catalyzes a rabbinic machinery that works actively to prevent it.

The standard narrative found in traditional Jewish jurisprudential sources tells us that the proper working of the law is what *creates* peace (Leviticus 26; Deuteronomy 28; see also Flatto 2020); indeed, this is the explicit promise of the covenant at Sinai. However, this narrative shows little interest in the conditions preparatory to the institution of law.[1] In wartorn landscapes that have lost all civic and institutional rudders, such as that inhabited by the tannaim, the creation of stability is an indispensable imperative that must precede and accompany the establishment of the rule of law. Creating an environment that will support the success of such an undertaking requires the most delicate cultural negotiations, to wit: building faith in institutions, managing disruptive narratives of the past, soothing sectarian difference, and, in several culturally specific ways, turning down the heat on existing sociocultural triggers to unrest.

My thinking here is inspired by contemporary studies on how to prevent the recurrence of disorder and foster the establishment of the rule of law in the aftermath of violence. When civil wars, brutal dictators, foreign imperial assault, or other disruptions cease, how does a people (re)build a just society out of the wreckage? Modern theorists and policy makers study this question in relationship to global trouble spots such as Rwanda, Kosovo, East Timor, and Afghanistan. The material is modern, statist, and in a hundred other ways anachronistic, and yet it offers a new way to think about a series of apparently loosely connected rabbinic innovations and priorities as cohesive extensions of the legal program, grounded in a specific Roman context. This literature sees the rule of law as the most durable bulwark against future social breakdown. (Not coincidentally, the Roman Empire similarly imbricates Pax Romana with legal justice.[2]) However, in work such as that of Jane Stromseth and Pablo de Greiff, and in reports such as the World Bank's World Development Reports on Conflict, Security, and Development,[3] what stands out to me is precisely their focus on the conditions necessary for the establishment of rule of law in the first place. These works uniformly insist

---

1 This is not to say that there is none. See for example the midrashic treatment of Exodus 18, in Mekilta de-Rabbi Ishmael, *Nezikin* 1.
2 On which more below, also Ando 2000, 2017, Lavan 2017.
3 E.g., World Bank 2011, Stromseth, Wippman, and Brooks 2006, de Greiff and Cronin 2002.

that this requires broad cultural investment 'outside the legal frame' (Walzer 2015: xxiv) – prior and adjacent to law – as vital buttresses to the writing of a constitution and court-based application of justice.

Theorists of the rule of law draw our attention to a fragile interstitial space: the gap between war/unrest and the institution of justice. Recognizing the rabbinic landscape as such a space adds to our understanding of a range of rabbinic gestures that do not seem, on first blush, to be directly tied to the legal project. By looking at a selection of culturally volatile topics and how the rabbis attempt to manage them, I will draw attention to a network whose shared effect is to create the conditions in which their own stated aims – the establishment of the rule of divine law – can come to pass. The rabbinic treatment of topics as disparate (and often nonlegal) as bathhouse culture, authorship, eschatology, dialogue, heresiology, and the temple may be seen as strategies sharing in common the effect of preventing material resistance. Underscoring the political coherence of this material, in which the primacy of legal logic serves to create communal stability and prevent unrest *despite* anti-Roman sentiment, pushes beyond the typical treatment of resistance. Rather than stopping at questions merely of culture, or some terminal notion of legitimation, identity, or self-fashioning, I posit that even peace-keeping is in itself a political goal that contains seeds of unrest.

It is a mostly tacit presumption in the field that the rabbis were able to thrive in part because of the Pax Romana in the East in the centuries following the end of the Bar Kokhbah revolt, and that the rabbis resisted less the material extractions and humiliations of submission to foreign power than the competition and seductions of rival modes of belonging, being, and belief, extending from the Roman empire and Christianity to rival Jews.

The proximate threat of imperial violence that subtended the provincial life of Jews in the early centuries of the Common Era ought not overshadow the Jewish legacy of rebellion and agita so prevalent in the same centuries. A Jewish commitment to unrest itself – even and especially when deployed in defense of threatened Jewish ideals and beliefs, property, and institutions – did not vanished overnight from Jewish self-understanding, even with the rise of the accomodationist rabbis. The number of avenues the rabbis used to short-circuit traditional catalysts of Jewish conflict suggest the perduring potency of the pugnacious Jew in the Jewish imagination. And further that, in suppressing unrest, the rabbis were not defending themselves bodily from Roman intervention as such (though they did that too), but were creating inner Jewish conditions for the establishment of the rabbis' rule of law. Though the enmeshed dynamics of peacekeeping and justice echo imperial strategies (Bryen 2021), the rabbinic work, I suggest, is not operating with an eye toward the imperial center: rather it is an internally focused operation to make a common cultural ground from which their objectives can be achieved.

Accommodation and Resistance

The biblical covenant outlined in the Pentateuch is predicated on the existence of an autonomous nation, with its own laws and mores: observing those laws brings peace, the failure to do so causes military defeat. Leviticus makes the stakes of law for sovereignty clear:

> if you will not obey me (God) and do not observe all these commandments (v.14) ... I will set my face against you and you shall be struck down by your enemies; your foes shall rule over you (v. 17) ... 'I will bring the sword against your cities, I will send pestilence among you, and you shall be delivered into enemy hands'. (v. 25) (Leviticus 26, vv. 14–25)

Failure to keep the law brings on assault by and submission to foreign powers. However, the perilous geopolitical reality of Judea and Israel meant that Jews were subject to imperial dominators throughout their history. As a simple biblical economy of sin and punishment was often unsatisfactorily explanatory, the covenant was theologized to keep pace. Since the time of the Babylonian Exile and then Persia, Judaism has found ways to massage a covenantal tradition that is ostensibly built on national sovereignty (primarily as monarchy) into a system that could function more or less comfortably under imperial domination. In this way rabbinic thought represents an extension of a long tradition of Jewish accommodation to external powers.

The Second Temple cult and priestly aristocracy, for example, spent nearly their entire history working with and under imperial rule from the Persian through Hasmonean and Roman eras: think of the success of the Oniads under the Ptolemies, the comfortable social position of Ben Sira, the Herodians, and, most vocally, Josephus (especially as he ventriloquizes through Agrippa II at *BJ* 2.345–-402). For each, working easily *with* empires was the way to thrive, finding internal theological rationale for *realpolitik* pragmatism.[4] We should not be surprised that the rabbis claim Ezra – a pious and ethnically proud political and legal leader who was on the payroll of the Persian administration – as a prominent forbearer. Though the rabbis are certainly heirs to this Jewish legacy of getting along with empires, to see rabbinic accommodation as *un*remarkable is to underestimate not only the brutal lived reality of Judea as the soil from which the early rabbis grew (Eck 1999), but to presume without evidence that Judaism's rebellious side, one both ideal and real, went quietly moribund as well.

Josephus spends a great deal of time describing the heedless bravery of the Jewish fighter, noting the 'national characteristics: boldness, dash ... the refusal to acknowledge defeat' – traits he contrasts with the 'disciplined and serried ranks' of the Romans (*BJ* 6.17, trans. Williamson). This dash is made manifest in battle-scene depictions of outsized Jewish courage that proffer a more positive version of Tacitus's derisive remark that the Jews 'think nothing of facing death' (*Hist.* 5.5). Indeed, in choosing to end the *War* with the scene at Masada, Josephus expresses indisputable pride in Jewish mettle. A Roman perception of Jewish fearlessness in war is not confined to Tacitus, and may have reverberated in the Jewish psyche as well. Tens of thousands of Jews were enslaved in the aftermath of the war, and many would have lived in or passed through Rome. Indeed, many rabbis too travelled to Rome (e.g. Sifre Deuteronomy § 43). Beyond the still standing arch of Titus and its images of handsome Jewish rebels being marched in triumph, the Circus Maximus contained a second arch reporting that Titus 'tamed the Jewish people and destroyed the city of Jerusalem, [a thing] either sought in vain by all generals, kings, and peoples, before him or untried entirely' (Granino 2017, as treated in Barron 2021). The two arches were unmissable in the city, and the colosseum and Templum Pacis were yet other monuments to the scale of the Judean rebellion. Regardless of its exaggeration and its function in Flavian legitimation[5], even the now-tamed and humiliated Jew could well have been

---

4 I have not listed Alexandrian Jewish sources here since they are in Greek so less clearly in the rabbinic literary ambit, but they obviously exhibit a parallel exegetical tradition, deftly theorizing a Judaism more or less comfortably subservient to foreign rule.
5 On the arch inscription, see Barron 2021; cf. Goodman 2007. On Jewish martial savagery: Cass. Dio 68.31 (of the Jewish revolt in Cyrene): 'They would eat the flesh of their victims, make belts for themselves of their entrails, anoint themselves with their blood and wear their skins for clothing; many they sawed in two, from the head downwards.'

flattered by this attention. Romans in short may not have been the only ones for whom this Judean reputation for ruthlessly fighting was significant.

Josephus does not deign to grant meaningful ideologies to the Jewish rebels of his history, but through his scorn we can clearly discern religiously animated actors, using a discourse of freedom, zeal, and commitment to divine sovereignty, ideas often run through with some forms of messianic eschatology (e.g. Joseph. *BJ* 2.118; 2.517–18, 2.254–62, *AJ* 18.23). Many of the rebel groups hailed from the same Galilean hills where the rabbis lived and worked some generations later. A Judaism that sanctions shedding blood for the God of Israel appears throughout Jewish history: its exemplars run from biblical Moses, Joshua, Phineas, and David to the Maccabees, the Sicarii and Zealots, through those joining the Bar Kokhbah uprising, and several local skirmishers along the way. While the rabbis may have been a model minority, Jews in the aggregate were not.

Recurrent eruptions of violence cannot be explained solely by ad hoc external provocation. If we take seriously not only the martial glory of the biblical epic, but the frequency of Jewish unrest in the centuries leading up to the earliest rabbinic literature (the Mishnah ca 200 CE) and in concentrated form in the generations before and in which the rabbinic movement was birthed, we might see an impulse to fight for one's beliefs to be deeply consistent with Jewish cultural expectations and ideals. Despite the extremis of the past three revolts, history tells us that such national personality traits rarely disappear completely (Isaacs 1990: 80–89; cf. Sizgorich 2009). Imagine trying to convince the Spartans that they are a nation of poets or the Scythians that they are heirs of Ghandi, or my Irish relatives that they're not the sort of people who'd throw a punch if slighted. This to say that even if we grant that the quiet of the late second and early third centuries was a product of national depletion, armed resistance was still part of Judean self-understanding, and managing this tradition to prevent its recurrence may well have required concerted effort. There is plenty of evidence suggesting that the rabbis attempted just that.[6] The process was not linear, nor does every bit of the evidence work in the same direction, but there is no denying that the preponderance of the legal-cultural project is focused on, indeed is pred-

---

6 Greg Woolf (2011: 32) writes: 'Rebels might be expected to emerge from those who subscribed least to the ideologies formed at the centre of empire, and among those peoples who participated least in civic and imperial culture and cult. Regions at the geographical margins of empire ... Judaea.' The rabbis seem in this regard a counter-example.

icated on, the successful taming of the fighting Jew, past present and future. Without peace there can be no rule of law.

Deescalation and Cultural Inoculation

The early rabbis prepared a many-fronted bulwark against both the reality and the spectre of recurrent violence.[7] The symbolic and conceptual landscape drawn by the rabbis in a range of extra-legal arenas seems bound by a shared aversion to creating martial conflict, an investment in the reinscription both of potent cultural symbols and historical memory. The tannaim imagine a big tent of Jewish belonging, write galvanizing patriots and patriotism out of history, and prioritize the this-worldly regime of law. Things that threaten to catalyze action against empire are defanged, recast, or sidelined altogether.

A wide array of rabbinic positions may be seen collectively to do the work of inoculating the culture against unrest. The phenomena that I will touch on below have not however to my knowledge been read collectively as logical extensions of, or in service of, the legal project per se. Rather they have been studied individually in a range of contexts – theology, history, philology and exegesis, Christian polemic, philosophical thought, rhetoric, and post-colonial studies. Stepping back and seeing them all together allows us to appreciate their collective effect of creating the preconditions necessary for the establishment of the rabbis' capacious new legal regime in the aftermath of bloody violence.[8] If we take seriously that the Mishnah envisions a Jewish polity built on divine law, then we can see how they also would have needed to create the social stability necessary for its success. They would have

---

7 See Bryen 2021 on the pervasive and mercurial nature of Roman violence against provincials in the first centuries CE and attempts to control it from the center by means of increasing imperial nomicization. He writes: 'One of the results of the reaction to the processes of domination and exploitation that took place in the republic and into the first century was the eventual *juridification* of the provincial landscape ...' (65). The phenomenon I am chronicling is an attempt to manage that same violence from below, using law too, though in a markedly different way.
8 Jerusalem Talmud, *Rosh Hashanah* 4.8.2 tells why the time in which one blows the shofar as part of the ritual for Rosh ha-Shanah was formally moved from early morning service to later in the day: since once in the past the Romans mistook the morning blast as a call to war and came and attacked and killed several Jews.

been motivated to neutralize things that had in the past, and threatened in the present and future, to cause Jews to raise arms – against each other no less than against external enemies. I have chosen religiously potent exemplars, and not economic ones (such as taxation, status, or the annexation of land), because, as John Collins notes: economic factors, however important 'were not always the factors that directly motivated rebels ... the problems that motivated rebels to *act* were cultural and symbolic', things, in other words, 'profoundly integrated with ethnic identity' (Collins 2016: 201; note though Honigman 2014, Andrade 2010). Aligning these topoi, each of course with its own discrete sources, concepts, and scholarly literature, allows one to discern among them a coherence as interdependent stabilizing gestures.

The contemporary literature cited above, which maps the best way to build a just polity in the aftermath of war or imperialist domination, all begins from a base line prerequisite of instilling faith in legal institutions, and much can and has been said about how the rabbis align with those priorities. The halakhah sells its justice as divine, capacious, and unbiased. It minimizes the legal import of social hierarchy (no *honestiores* or *humiliores*; Hayes 2021); similarly access to justice does not rely on heredity, assuming, naturally, that you are Jewish, and male (Libson 2021; compare Connolly 2010). The material regularly underscores the wisdom, learning, and moral purity of the rabbinic judge and jurist and the fairness and moderation of its punitive regimes, it polemicizes against corruption and bribery, and other more or less expected commitments to justice 'shielded from power' (Flatto 2020: 110) and backed by a program of paideia and an embedded notion of divine sanction. All standard issue. Still, as the modern literature on non-recurrence of violence and the rule of law underscores, all this is necessary *but insufficient* if the culture is inclined to fall back into habits, ideologies, and narratives that result in violence. In the examples below we find the tannaim working to mold the culture in ways that prevent the ascendance of incendiary habits, narratives, and ideologies.

Sectarianism and individual authority

Given the rampant factionalism and sectarianism of the previous centuries, from Pharisees and Sadducees, to the Dead Sea collective, to the murderous militias devouring each other in the besieged Jerusalem with which we opened, it is notable that the rabbinic nomos chooses not to prioritize one

Jewish group over another. 'Do not split yourself into several factions, but rather be one faction', says one tannaitic commentary (Sifre Deuteronomy § 96). Rhetorically at least, all of Israel is the law's imagined constituency. 'The major goal of the ... rabbis seems to have been not the expulsion of those with whom they disagreed but the cessation of sectarianism', writes Shaye Cohen (1984: 27), and the tannaim, 'for the first time, "agreed to disagree"' (1984: 30).[9] Formally, tannaitic resistance to internal schism manifests in discourse that is dialogical and polyvocal. Competing positions are commonly left side by side. The decentralized sprawling interconnection of the laws combined with what Vered Noam described in a recent lecture as a 'tendency to lenience' and flexibility (especially as compared to Qumran's sectarian law), all serve to minimize rigid legal dogmatism, rhetorically, formally, and institutionally.[10]

Form and content again converge on the topic of individual power, which the rabbis take pains to undermine. Tannaitic literature is unauthored. Authority, both literary and social, is depicted as dispersed, and, outside of the disciple circles accrued to individual rabbis, the meritocratic collective has almost no ex-officio hierarchical stemma.[11] Additionally, though the law/Torah is presumed to have been given by God, the rabbis assert that its interpretation and application now rests in human hands.[12] Vesting legal authority with the rabbinic majority diminishes the sway of any one of them, further softening the risk of schism.

Prophetic authority poses another threat to institutional authority. Charismatics, many making prophetic claims, are known to have electrified and divided the Judean populace in the prerabbinic era, most recently

---

9 See though Goodman 2011. Even the most exclusionary rhetorics of heresy may have served to define a broad nation of Israel, papering over difference as much as reifying it, see Ophir and Rosen-Zvi 2018, Goodman 2003: 128. It is important to note that divisions and hierarchies existed within the movement and between the movement and its 'others'—which makes even more stark the general obfuscation of such conflicts and hierarchies on the rhetorical level.
10 Though far from lax, tens of studies might be adduced here demonstrating cases in which the rabbis softened laws so as to adjust to communal or political obstacles.
11 Hezser 1997. On the way anonymity may engage empire in a different way see Portier-Young 2011. On individual power and the rule of law, see Flatto 2020: 93, and 145–48 on resistance to the individual power of judges.
12 *lo' ba-shamayin hi'* (it is not in heaven) (Dt 30:12), most famously depicted in Babylonian Talmud, *Bava Metsia* 59a-b.

surrounding Bar Kokhbah.[13] Josephus describes many such characters, in addition to whom we can count Jesus of Nazareth, Qumran's Teacher of Righteousness, John the Baptist, and other messianic and prophetic claimants. The rabbis are singularly resistant to authority claims based on revelation unmediated through Torah – the rabbis of course are its brokers, themselves encircled by a rigorous culture of moderating paideia. Even the Ur-prophet himself, Moses, is met with deep ambivalence in tannaitic sources, and aggadic texts cleverly stamp out the possibility of extra-rabbinic prophetic authority claims going forward using a range of strategies.[14] This too is consistent with legalism: not only do prophets claim unmediated and often antinomian authority, but 'one of law's usual functions', writes Robert Cover, 'is to hold off the Messiah' (1992: 194).

An adjacent concept, the eschaton with its next-worldly justice, is similarly incompatible with the rabbis' immanentist legal now. The early rabbis hold the world-to-come, like the messiah, at a safe distance; both ideas appear in tannaitic sources but drained of political urgency. In general, apocalyptic traditions that enjoyed wide circulation in the Second Temple era, are attenuated by the tannaim, where not expunged altogether. Biblical Enoch, a major figure in prerabbinic apocalyptic Judaism (Reed and Reeves 2018), for example, is notably absent from the tannaitic imagination. Epistemological regimes similarly commit to the realm of the this-worldly: esoteric and other-worldly gnosis is sidelined (cf. Mishnah, *Avot* 3.1). Eschatology (with its own implicit antinomianism) falls to law's countervening temporality (Dohrmann 2016).

Of course each of these rabbinic stances has multiple functions and etiologies. We know, for example, that early 'Christians' (Jesus followers) embraced Jewish eschatological traditions, and part of the rabbinic retreat from this form of thought may well have had to do with the defining of cultural boundaries in reaction to the emergent Christian movement (Reed 2023). But it is also true that (1) legal regimes do not coexist easily with either messianism or eschatology, and (2) that these ideas, especially the former, drove

---

13 Whether or not Shimon Ben Kosibah (a.k.a. Bar Kokhbah) was a charismatic leader or 'an irascible ineffective micromanager,' he bore the mythic mantle of messiah. Schwartz 2016: 246–48.
14 For an elegant excursus on this topic, see Mekilta de-Rabbi Ishmael, *Pisha* 1. Also Mekilta de-Rabbi Ishmael, *Amalek* 2 and 3; Sifre Numbers 157. Another form of the cooptation and management of revelation by the rabbinic legal project appears in Mishnah, *Avot* 3.2. Moses cuts a different, more heroic figure in a range of Second Temple sources, from Jubilees, to Artapanus, even amulets such as Pap.Colon. XXII/1 32. See also Najman 2003, Furstenberg 2012.

Jews into the carnage of the Bar Kohkbah revolt. In other words, fear of unrest is at least as plausible an explanation for the rabbis' 'soft' messianism as is nascent Christianity. All to acknowledge that while topics as complex as heresy, prophecy, and apocalypticism are deeply embedded in a range of cultural and historical discourses, one shared effect of their rabbinic packaging is that their political immanence is dulled. The rabbis are not looking for a fight.

History and Time

Charting successful transitions between violent past regimes and more stable and just future ones means being attentive to the ways the memory of the past may impede progress. 'Persuading stakeholders to work collaboratively requires signals of a real break with the past ... as well as mechanisms to "lock-in" these changes' (The World Bank 2011: 13). Analogous to the ways that the Roman civil wars permitted Augustus's dramatic construction of an empire-cum-republic, the late second-century caesura following a century and half of intermittent conflict between Rome and the Jews offered a special opportunity to recraft the past.[15] The way that past was remembered (or forgotten) would have important repercussions for the rabbinic present. We find that both history and the idea of time are manipulated by the earliest rabbis in ways that serve their legal agenda. The genre of law itself is an effective buffer against history in that laws cover general situations and ideal cases, and as such are formally disengaged from the specificity of any particular political moment or memory. In other words, the nomistic temporality of the Mishnah operates in a time-space that lies just outside of – and so to an extent is disengaged from – the potentially destabilizing realia of the present. The paradigmatic nowhere of the legal code is also manifest in the nonlegal material. The content of the tannaitic (nonlegal) aggadah is similarly marked by a lack of historical specificity, blurring not only the Roman present but also the Second Temple past. Reliable historical detail is desperately rare in the corpus – to the extent that names, years, events and places do exist, they are diffused through didactic, folk, and typological habits, sapping the past of its perhaps triggering specificity and altering collective memories.

---

15 Indeed, on the rabbinic retreat from history there is a sea of ink, most thoughtfully in a recent essay by Reed 2023; also Tropper 2004.

But formal impediments to historical memory were only part of the equation. Another element of the management of the past is the elision of depictions of glorious past battles – and their opportunities for memorialization – both from the Second Temple era, and even the biblical past. This cannot have been an easy feat. During the Roman era, the Jews fought several full-fledged wars and participated in an unknown number of smaller skirmishes. Major literary fodder might have been mined concerning the dramatic counter-imperial victories of the Maccabees (whose success was not unconnected to the machinations in the East by an ambitious Roman republic). Yet the Hasmoneans moulder in the wings of the tannaitic imagination. The more recent dramatic successes and noble failures of heroic Judeans in the revolts of 66 and 132 are rendered similarly quiescent in the tannaitic corpus.[16]

While the Second Temple past might be usefully ignored, the rabbis make the Bible the center of their literary world; and in the Bible military glory is an apparently inescapable theme; military victory a premier indicator of divine favor (Wright 2020). Yet the early rabbis deftly defuse the themes of both external war and stasis. They build extensive exegetical traditions around biblical heroes but even then they are rarely figured as martial – celebrated instead as rabbi-like pietists and scholars. David is perhaps the most obvious example: the mighty collector of foreskins and slayer of Goliath in the Bible, he emerges in midrash as Psalmist and student of Torah.[17] Israelite victories led by Israelite generals largely disappear from sight. Beyond God as warrior, military heroes such as Joab have only bit parts in early midrash. Sifre Deuteronomy § 357, another example, describes Moses gazing over all the regions of the land of Israel, each, according to the passage, 'inhabited in peace', but destined in the future to be overthrown by enemies. Amazingly the successful conquest of the Canaanites by Israelite armies does not merit mention. I could go on. The reappearance of much of this history in later rabbinic works argues for its likely conscious suppression by these early formative, and more fragile generations.[18] These retellings materially alter, or attempt

---

16 See Noam 2018, D. R. Schwartz 2008, Gafni 2019.
17 In a cognate gesture, the tannaim radically curtail the Jewish library, censoring or simply removing from view all Jewish and non-Jewish literatures except the Bible, further blunting the survival of Second Temple traditions that may have, among other things, celebrated or inspired unrest.
18 Noam 2018. Much has been written about the rabbinic erasure of the Second Temple past by the rabbis (see esp. Reed 2023) and it makes sense that the centrality of unrest to that story is a key factor.

to do so, the Jewish past, rendering rabbinic space one at its origin 'inhabited by peace'.

Temple and Priesthood

The rabbis' insertion of their own authority into the workings of the temple cult has been explored by many, commonly focusing on rabbinic claims to legitimacy and the denigration of what is presumed to be a rival authority posed by the remnant of the priesthood.[19] The rabbis do certainly assert their meritocratic legal expertise above that of the hereditary priests; however to say this is solely meant to write themselves a Second Temple past or to quiet rival authorities as an end in itself feels incomplete. If I might borrow a thought David Flatto applied to Josephus's polemic against monarchy: at issue is the threat of the priest to the concept of the law, not the denigration of priests to the benefit of the rabbi (2020: 87). There evidence suggests that the rabbis may be, again, pushing down a potential center of discord. Certain priests in the past were themselves opponents of the imperial status quo, from the Hasmoneans to the Dead Sea sect leadership, as well as several prominent leaders of the war in 66 CE, Josephus ironically among them (e.g. BJ 2.562–64). Aaron, by contrast, the tannaitic paragon of the high priest, is repeatedly celebrated as a peace keeper by the rabbis.[20] More significant, the Jerusalem temple itself was a lightning rod for sectarianism and violence in the Second Temple era. The tannaim, however, do not populate it with Maccabean guerrillas or Hellenized Hasmoneans, fill it with rioting pilgrims or surround it with Roman centurions.[21] The Mishnah's temple is politically boring real estate, a sanctified space showing little trace of its actual history as a stage on which Jews of many ilks, in ink and in body, dramatically negotiated empire, law, and identity.

---

19 Mishnah, *Yoma* 1 and passim, Cohn 2013; cf. Joseph. *Ap.* 2.187.
20 Mishnah, *Avot* 1.12, Sifra, *Millu'im* 1.2 (Weiss ed., 45d), Tosefta, *Sanhedrin* 1.2–3.
21 Cf. Joseph. *BJ* 2.10–13, 2.411, Joseph. *AJ* 17.23 for a just a very few examples. See also Noam 2018, Weitzman 1999, Chilton 1992, McClelland 1989.

Idolatry

My last example is idolatry. Idols peppered the Roman cities that the rabbis plied (Schwartz 2001a), from pagan temples to pleasure palaces, and no one needs to be persuaded that idolatry was a line in the sand for Jews. It was often depicted as the rallying cry for upheaval not only in the biblical narratives but throughout Second Temple (and Roman) sources as well.[22] The Maccabean revolt is famously sparked when Seleucid forces insist Jews worship an idol:

> a Jew came forward in the sight of all to offer sacrifice on the altar in Modein, according to the king's command. When Mattathias saw it, he burned with zeal and his heart was stirred. He gave vent to righteous anger; he ran and killed him on the altar. At the same time he killed the king's officer who was forcing them to sacrifice, and he tore down the altar. Thus he burned with zeal for the law, just as Phineas did against Zimri son of Salu. (1 Macc 2:23–26)

And so begins the Maccabean rebellion. Phineas is the Bible's poster boy for religious zeal, having slain fornicating idolaters in Numbers 25 by impaling them *in flagrante* before the altar. His fiery righteousness earns his family the priesthood, and for this he becomes the chosen forefather of the Hasmoneans themselves, who not coincidentally claim (usurp) the hereditary high priesthood on the power of their Phineas-like zeal. In the tannaitic midrash on Phineas however, his vigilante piety is met with some qualms: not only is the act of the idolaters broken down into a legally legible set of transgressions – Phineas is thus not a man driven by rage but rather an agent of just punishment – but Phineas's agency is erased behind the assertion a miracle of animating the violent execution of the fornicators – divine agency in other words (Sifre Numbers 131, Mack 2013, Halbertal 2013). No self-help here except through the halakhah.

Another well-known example of the prohibition of idolatry sparking and justifying unrest comes from Josephus:

> Now the king [Herod] had put up a golden eagle over the great gate of the temple, which these learned men exhorted them to cut down; and told them, that if there should arise any danger, it was a glorious thing to die for the laws of their country; because the soul

---

[22] From the manifesto in Deuteronomy 12, to such high-profile examples as Phineas and the Moabites (Num 25), folk traditions of Abraham in the house of idolatry (*Jubilees* 11), the threat of Caligula's image in the temple (Joseph. *AJ* 18.262–309, Tac. *Hist.* 5.9; cf. *Hist.* 5.5); and see the sources in Furstenberg 2010.

was immortal, and that an eternal enjoyment of happiness did await such as died on that account; while the mean-spirited, and those that were not wise enough to show a right love of their souls, preferred a death by a disease, to that which is the result of a virtuous behavior. (Joseph. *BJ* 1.648–50)

Offended by the eagle icon, several Jews in Jerusalem of Herod's time followed some Second Temple 'learned men', 'most skillful in the laws', into the fray.[23] Though these sages are in many ways forerunners of the rabbis, the tannaim eschew their bellicose methods of confronting idols in their own cities. Indeed, though their treatment of idolatry is extensive, the rabbis measurably lower the heat surrounding idolatry by domesticating plastic images of gods. Yair Furstenberg comprehensively catalogs the apparently counterintuitive strategies the rabbis used to allow Jews to coexist with idols and idolaters, despite not only the Bible's clear stance, but even rabbinic demands that one must give up one's life before engaging in idolatry.[24] The rabbis define what counts as an idol or as idol worship so narrowly and flexibly as to render prohibitions against them difficult to transgress. Many excellent studies have been devoted to these sophisticated legal and rhetorical feints. The easing of the category allows even the most pious Jew to participate in a few significant, if circumscribed, parts of urban life, from marketplace to bath house, despite the profusion of pagan idols (Halbertal 1993, Schwartz 2001b, Furstenberg 2010, Gvaryahu 2021). The imperial cult would have been beyond the pale however, and so too holding local municipal office.[25] Laws concerning idols walk a line between drawing clear communal lines and avoiding incitement.

There is no doubt that minimizing the threat of idolatry would have in theory removed Jewish incentives to act out against the state and so incite

---

23 'There were two men of learning in the city [Jerusalem,] who were thought the most skillful in the laws of their country and were on that account had in very great esteem all over the nation; they were, the one Judas, the son of Sepphoris, and the other Matthias, the son of Margalus. There was a great concourse of the young men to these men when they expounded the laws, and there got together every day a kind of an army of such as were growing up to be men' (Joseph. *BJ* 1.648). These learned sages are mustering an army; no tanna, to put it mildly, musters an army; cf. Joseph. *AJ* 4.309–10.

24 E.g., Tosefta, *Shabbat* 16.14; cf. Sifre Numbers 111; In some ways this writes large the approach found in Simcha Gross's (2018) notion of the Babylonian Talmud's 'anti-martyr act'. Cf. Kahana 2012.

25 Schwartz in an email correspondence notes that 'Tertullian at least considers the problems of being a Christian *decurio* or legionary, the Mishnah never does, presumably because it wanted these options to be unthinkable.'

Roman wrath. But this is not all it does: we see now that this pacifying outcome also serves the rabbis' own ends and in its own terms. If Jews are incited to smash idols everywhere, and the city is a place of ongoing strife, rabbinic law becomes moot.[26]

Conclusion

Provincialization

The survival of Judaism, according to Rabban Yohanan ben Zakkai, wanted only three things – prayer, teaching, and the performance of 'all the commandments' – each of which was presumed to fall outside of Rome's political concern. Laws however are not anodyne, they claim subjects and presume authority. To what extent, then, were 'all of the commandments' meant to be unobjectionable to Rome? Jewish history makes clear that rabbinic law operated, such that it did, at the mercy of foreign law. And so the tannaim worked unobtrusively in the Roman landscapes of the second- and third-century Galilee to develop and interpret a divine law code, arbitrating cases when the occasion allowed, but no more (Lapin 2012, Furstenberg 2021). This historical reality, compounded by the post-Roman legacy of the halakhah, often lulls us into treating their wholly novel legal system as a largely academic operation.[27] Yet by making law and legalism the predominant modalities of Judaism, the rabbis claim implicitly that they are playing (or at a minimum are asserting their right to play) on the field of power.

And yet the rule of law demands peace. Political theorists of late twentieth- and twenty-first- century conflict zones sharpen certain elements helpful for the analysis of antiquity by drawing attention to the fragility and volatility of post-war landscapes. This helps us recognize a new salience for actual Jewish rebellion in the early rabbinic work of 'reconstruction.'[28] In

---

26 Though it is dangerous to use later evidence to make claims for what precedes, I do think the trend in the Yerushalmi and beyond to increasingly soften the prohibitions against idolatry might suggest that the tannaim mark an early, and novel, foray in that direction.
27 Particular laws receive scholarly attention, but less so the claims of the system as a whole in distinctly legal terms distinct from the history of halakhah.
28 In his insistence on the significance Rome's devastation of the Jews for the history of post-war Judaism, I am also indebted to the work of Seth Schwartz; cf. Schwartz 2016: esp. at 234–38.

addition, this scholarship frames the Mishnah's vast Jewish nomosphere in a war-riven world as a very particular form of Romanization animated by a logic and demands of its own.[29] This is to say that while rabbinic legalism certainly borrows Roman vocabularies and logics, the legal world the rabbis construct has a strong internal coherence that energizes all corners of the corpus, legal and nonlegal. Since legal regimes require social stability, rabbinic quiescence and pacifism then may not simply describe the pragmatic survival strategy of a small group of bookish religious conservatives. Nuanced by the tacit demands of a legal code, unrest threatens the rabbis uniquely.

It may seem that the rabbinic work of quelling unrest is more a Roman story than a Jewish one. The Romans, after all, are still in charge. The rabbis imbibe Roman provincial ideology: they think, in part at least, in Roman terms and categories—even figuring Rome as Israel's estranged twin (Berthelot 2016)—and in this way become, for all practical purposes, model citizens of the empire (Ando 2000, Woolf 2009, Lapin 2012, Dohrmann 2013). So this rabbinic suppression of ideas they deem destabilizing not only reechoes a Roman paradigm by which law and peace are part of the same breath, but serves imperial ends. Rabbi Hanina says:

pray for the welfare of the government, for were it not for the fear it inspires, every man would swallow his neighbour alive. (Mishnah, Avot 3.2)

Yet one misreads the material if one does not take seriously some measure of rage and protest. If Pablo de Greiff and Ciaran Cronin are right, moreover, successful state building under these conditions demands some sort of reckoning with the violence of the past (de Greiff and Cronin 2002). Can we find truth and reconciliation in our rabbinic imaginary? Only in small doses. Theology steps in in many cases to rationalize suffering and Roman domination as the just will of the God of Israel, though this thinking does not always satisfy. The Mishnah peevishly permits the murder of a non-Jewish Roman, for example, and the payment to him of only half damages in certain tort cases (Tosefta, 'Avodah Zarah 8(9): 4–5; Mishnah, Bava Kamma 4.3). In the lore, foreign kings are subjected to gruesomely poetic deaths.[30] These

---

29 We ought not take for granted that the community would center law in religious identity; we see nothing like it in the the parallel emergence of Christianity.
30 Mekilta de Rabbi Ishmael, Shirata; Babylonian Talmud, Gittin 56b. More on rabbinic anti-Romanness see Rosen-Zvi 2017.

and many other cultural steam valves nest within an oral tradition inaccessible to the Romans. I have argued in this essay that what keeps this anger and pain from erupting into civic disruption is the foundational priority of law – *rabbinic law not Roman*. Even if parts of the rabbinic legal corpus develop in ways that adjust to Roman grants of autonomy and mimic legal categories in ways that may allow for enfranchisement in some legal venues,[31] others emphatically do not. Given its scope, it is clear that tannaitic law cannot be fully comprehended as opportunistic, mimetic, or careerist vis-à-vis Rome. The question is how to read the law in a way that encompasses that which exceeds the bounds of pragmatism.

We find in the tannaitic corpus one provincial workshop where the Roman imperial experiment is played out in the voice of the provincials themselves. This evidence insists that provincial history not be monolithic, and recalls Calgacus's cry that the after-effects of Roman devastation need to be carefully disentangled from the underside of the Pax Romana.[32]

Rabbinic Sovereigntism

Empires extract: dignity, resources, power. The Mishnah represents a theoretical reappropriation in slow motion, facing off against the Jewish past and the Roman present alike. In contemplating the ways that rabbinic resistance to unrest apparently partners in the Roman spread of peace in the provinces, I want to close by asking, counterintuitively, how rabbinic peacekeeping might in itself be a facet of a different form of unrest – a provincial mindset hard to see from the Roman center. 'Cultural resistance', writes Seth Schwartz, may in theory be 'politicized at the first sign of a crack in Roman power'.[33] Schwartz asks us to find hard edge beneath an apparently harmless and inward-looking cultural enterprise. About the apparent folly of anyone rebelling against Rome, Greg Woolf writes: 'it is difficult for us to understand the incidence of provincial uprisings, unless at least some of the rebels had

---

31 For exemplary case studies along these lines see Furstenberg 2021, Hezser 2021, Malka 2019, Malka and Paz 2019, Hayes 2019.
32 Lavan 2017; also Ando 2017 on the claims implicit in the Roman ideas of peace.
33 Schwartz 2020: 410. In this I am playing with a sort of provincial echo of Lavan's sense that the Roman peace enfolds within *itself* a threat, an action, and a promise as much as a state of being (Lavan 2017: 105). Might this be a way to think about the work of internal pacification exerted by the rabbis?

a very different assessment of the situation'.[34] If they are themselves rebels, the rabbis seem to be playing a long game indeed, but not so long that is it eschatological, and not so misty as to be merely utopian. The tannaim may represent more think tank, in other words, than department of theology and philosophy.

Despite lacking power, recent work of Naiweld and Flatto argues, the rabbis nonetheless circumscribe what I will label a distinctly Jewish 'sovereigntism': 'a political model in which the sovereign de facto was a judicial institution'.[35] I'd like to extend these theoretical observations, once again taking my inspiration from modern political theory. Sovereigntist declarations in medieval and early modern thought describe less *facts* of power than *claims* to it; they do not happen in a vacuum but always arise in dialogue with some other competing authority.[36] According to Alles and Badie, such claims are by nature dialectical and inevitably impact the stronger as well as the weaker claimant. Sovereigntist discourse demands 'emancipation from what is perceived as an external or illegitimate authority' (2016: 6), and that demand, even when unfulfilled, becomes a political fact on the ground.

The term sovereigntism is primarily at home in modern contexts where subordinated populations assert their rights to various degrees of self-determination. I am drawn to it as a descriptive tool for the tannaim for a number of reasons. One, it centers the political demands of law *qua law*. Secondly, sovereigntism is a framework for reading the complex political interplay between the dominant and the subordinate, and it refuses a zero-sum assessment of power. Indeed, theorists insist that even (and in our case especially) when not realized, sovereigntist claims, such as Quebec's, have an impact on the real political landscape of Canada no less than Quebec (Alles and Badie 2016: 7). In defining the Mishnah as sovereigntist, we are seeing it as a legal and cultural stance taken against encroaching imperial power that is political and dialectical *ab ovo*. The same theorists note the double-edged aims of all sovereigntist claims, embodying 'a principle of order and conservatism

---

34 Woolf 2014: 44. See in this the important essay by Kahana 2012.
35 And here each is charting the ascendance of the court in distinction to monarchy or priestly theocracy, in other words they are making internalist jurisprudential arguments. Naiweld 2021: 412, and Flatto 2020 for a look at later Jewish engagement with the idea.
36 It is a concept originating in the struggle between western European monarchs and papal authority. Alles and Badie 2016: 6, 8.

as well as a principle of contestation'.[37] As a descriptor of the aims of the Mishnah, the language of sovereigntism acknowledges the inextricably imperially-embedded nature of tannaitic legalism, *without discounting the political potential of the subaltern*. The rabbinic claim to sovereignty that is implicit in the halakhic project is in some ways always-already enmeshed in, and, I suggest, is unimaginable without, the imperial status quo (and vice versa). This dialectical approach may even nuance standard perspectives on the politics of the Romanized provincial more broadly.

Acknowledgements

I am grateful to Clifford Ando, Yair Furstenberg, Seth Schwartz, Anne O. Albert, Elsie Stern, and Peter Struck for their valuable input. A short excerpt of this essay appeared as 'Pax Tannaitica', *Jewish Quarterly Review* 112.4 (2022).

Works Cited

Alles, Delphine and Bertrand Badie. 2016. 'Sovereigntism in the international system'. *European Review of International Studies* 3(2): 5–19.

Ando, Clifford. 2000. *Imperial Ideology and Provincial Loyalty in the Roman Empire*. Berkeley.

–. 2012. 'The Roman city in the Roman period', in Stéphane Benoist, ed., *Rome, une cité impériale en jeu*. Leiden, 109–24.

–. 2017. 'Pax romana: peace, pacification and the ethics of empire'. *c4ejournal*. https://c4ejournal.net/2017/05/22/clifford-ando-pax-romana-peace-pacification-and-the-ethics-of-empire-1-c4ej-1-2017/

Andrade, Nathanael. 2010. 'Ambiguity, violence, and community in the cities of Judaea and Syria'. *Historia* 59(3): 342–70.

Barron, Caroline. 2021. 'The (lost) arch of Titus: the visibility and prominence of victory in Flavian Rome', in Katell Berthelot, ed., *Reconsidering Roman Power: Roman, Greek, Jewish and Christian Perceptions and Reactions*. Rome, 157–77.

---

37 Alles and Badie 2016: 6. Rosen-Zvi 2017 notes the conjoined antagonism and quiescence of the Mishnah regarding Rome. Also Ando 2012 for a nuanced look at overlapping and constructed sovereignties of peripheral urban spaces and peoples, from conflicting but simultaneous Greek and Roman perspective.

Baumgarten, Albert I. 2017. '"Sages increase peace in the world": reconciliation and power', in Christine Hayes, Tzvi Novick and Michal Bar-Asher Siegal, eds., *The Faces of Torah: Studies in the Texts and Contexts of Ancient Judaism in Honor of Steven Fraade*. Bristol, Conn., 221–237.

Berthelot, Katell. 2016. 'The rabbis write back! L'enjeu de la "parenté" entre Israël et Rome-Ésaü-Édom', *Revue de l'histoire des religions* 233(2): 165–92.

Bryen, Ari Z. 2021. 'Citizenship and its alternatives,' in Myles Lavan and Clifford Ando, eds., *Roman and Local Citizenship in the Long Second Century CE*. Oxford, 41–68.

Chilton, Bruce.1992. *The Temple of Jesus*. University Park, 97–136.

Cohen, Shaye J. D. 1984. 'The significance of Yavneh: pharisees, rabbis, and the end of Jewish sectarianism'. *Hebrew Union College Annual* 55: 27–53.

Cohn, Naftali. 2013. *The Memory of the Temple and the Making of the Rabbis*. Philadelphia.

Collins, John J. 2016. 'Temple or taxes? What sparked the Maccabean revolt?', in John Collins and J. G. Manning, eds., *Revolt and Resistance in the Ancient Classical World and the Near East: In the Crucible of Empire*. Leiden, 189–201.

Connolly, Serena. 2010. *Lives behind the Laws: The World of the Codex Hermogenianus*. Bloomington.

Cover, Robert. 1992. 'Folktales of justice', in Martha Minow, Michael Ryan and Austin Sarat, eds., *Narrative, Violence, and the Law: The Essays of Robert Cover*. Ann Arbor.

De Greiff, Pablo and Ciaran Cronin. 2002. *Global Justice and Transnational Politics: Essays on the Moral and Political Challenges of Globalization*. Cambridge, Mass.

Dohrmann, Natalie. 2013. 'Law and imperial idioms: genre and the hegemony of Jewish law', in Natalie Dohrmann and Annette Yoshiko Reed, eds., *Jews, Christians and the Roman Empire: The Poetics of Power in Late Antiquity*. Philadelphia, 63–78.

–. 2015. 'Can "law" be private? The mixed message of rabbinic oral law', in Clifford Ando and Jörg Rüpke, eds., *Public and Private in Ancient Mediterranean Law and Religion*. Berlin, 187–216.

Eck, Werner. 1999. 'The Bar Kokhba Revolt: the Roman point of view'. *Journal of Roman Studies* 89: 76–89.

Flatto, David C. 2020. *The Crown and the Courts*. Cambridge, Mass.

Furstenberg, Yair. 2010. 'The rabbinic view of idolatry and the Roman political conception of divinity'. *Journal of Religion* 90(3): 335–66.

–. 2012. 'The agon with Moses and Homer: rabbinic midrash and the Second Sophistic', in Maren R. Niehoff, ed., *Homer and the Bible in the Eyes of Ancient Interpreters*. Leiden. 299–328.

–. 2021. 'Imperialism and the creation of local law: the case of rabbinic law', in Katell Berthelot, Natalie Dohrmann, and Capucine Nemo-Pekelman, eds., *Legal Engagement. The Reception of Roman Law and Tribunals by Jews and Other Inhabitants of the Empire*. Rome.

Gafni, Isaiah. 2019. 'The Hasmoneans in rabbinic literature', in *Jews and Judaism in the Rabbinic Era: History and Historiography*. Tübingen, 59–75.

Goodman, Martin. 2003. 'Thinking about the early separation of Judaism and Christianity in pictures', in Annette Reed and Adam Becker, eds., *The Ways that Never Parted*. Tübingen, 121–28.

–. 2007. *Rome and Jerusalem*. New York.

–. 2011. 'Religious variety and the temple in the late second temple period and its aftermath', in Sacha Stern, ed., *Sects and Sectarianism in Jewish History*. Leiden, 21–37.

Granino, M. G. 2017. *L'iscrizione dell'arco e l'Anonimo di Einsiedeln*, in *Bullettino della Commissione Archeologica Comunale di Roma*, CXVIII, 2017, 229–36.

Gross, Simcha. 2018. 'A Persian anti-martyr act: the death of Rabba bar Nahmani in light of the Syriac Persian martyr acts', in Geoffrey Herman and Jeffrey Rubenstein, eds., *The Aggada of the Bavli and Its Cultural World*. Providence, 211–42.

Gvaryahu, Amit. 2021. 'Roman coinage and its early rabbinic users: a reappraisal'. *Jewish Quarterly Review* 111(4): 529–54.

Halbertal, Moshe. 1993. 'Coexisting with the enemy: Jews and pagans in the Mishnah', in Graham N. Stanton and Guy G. Stroumsa, eds., *Tolerance and Intolerance in Early Judaism and Christianity*. Cambridge, 159–72.

–. 2013. 'The history of halakhah and the emergence of halakhah'. *Dine Yisrael* 9: 1–23. [Hebrew]

Hayes, Christine. 2019. 'Roman and Jewish law: looking for interaction in all the right places'. *Law and History Review* 37(4).

–. 2021. "Barbarians" judge the law: the rabbis on the uncivil law of Rome', in Katell Berthelot, Natalie Dohrmann, and Capucine Nemo-Pekelman, eds., *Legal Engagement. The Reception of Roman Law and Tribunals by Jews and Other Inhabitants of the Empire*. Rome.

Hezser, Catherine. 1997. *The Social Structure of the Rabbinic Movement in Roman Palestine*. Tübingen.

–. 2021. 'Did Palestinian rabbis know Roman law? methodological considerations and case studies', in Katell Berthelot, Natalie Dohrmann, and Capucine Nemo-Pekelman, eds., *Legal Engagement. The Reception of Roman Law and Tribunals by Jews and Other Inhabitants of the Empire*. Rome.

Honigman, Sylvie. 2014. *Tales of the High Priest and Taxes: The Books of the Maccabees and the Judean Rebellion against Antiochus IV*. Berkeley, CA.

Isaac, Benjamin. 1990. *The Limits of Empire: The Roman Army in the East*. Oxford.

Kahana, Menahem. 2012. '"When you enter the land": a tannaitic controversy and its realistic meaning'. *Tarbiz* 81: 143–64. [Hebrew]

Lapin, Hayim. 2012. *Rabbis as Romans: The Rabbinic Movement in Palestine, 100–400 CE*. Oxford.

Lavan, Myles. 2017. 'Peace and empire: *pacare, pacatus*, and the language of Roman imperialism', in E. P. Moloney and Michael Stuart Williams, eds., *Peace and Reconciliation in the Classical World*. London, 102–14.

Libson, Ayelet Hoffman. 2021. 'Commandments and the community of law in Tosefta Berakhot'. *Jewish Quarterly Review* 111(2): 155–84.

Mack, Hananel. 2013. 'The zealousness of Phinehas the son of Elazar the son of Aaron the Priest'. *Mahanaim* 5: 122–29. [Hebrew]

Malka, Orit. 2019. 'Disqualified witnesses between tannaitic halakha and Roman law: the archeology of a legal institution'. *Law and History Review* 37(4): 903–36.

Malka, Orit and Yakir Paz. 2019. '*Ab hostibus captus et a latronibus captus*: the impact of the Roman model of citizenship on rabbinic law'. *Jewish Quarterly Review* 109(2): 141–72.

McClelland, J. 1989. *The Crowd and the Mob*. London, 34–59.

Naiweld, Ron. 2021. 'The rabbinic model of sovereignty in its biblical and imperial context', in Katell Berthelot, Natalie Dohrmann, and Capucine Nemo-Pekelman, eds., *Legal Engagement. The Reception of Roman Law and Tribunals by Jews and Other Inhabitants of the Empire*. Rome.

Najman, Hindy. 2003. *Seconding Sinai: The Development of Mosaic Discourse in Second Temple Judaism*. Leiden.

Neusner, Jacob. 1962. *A Life of Rabban Yohanan ben Zakkai, ca. 1–80 C.E.* Leiden.

Noam, Vered. 2018. *Shifting Images of the Hasmoneans: Second Temple Legends and Their Reception in Josephus and Rabbinic literature*. Transl. Dena Ordan. Oxford.

Ophir, Adi and Ishay Rosen-Zvi. 2018. *Goy: Israel's Multiple Others and the Birth of the Gentile*. Oxford.

Portier-Young, Anathea E. 2011. *Apocalypse against Empire: Theologies of Resistance in Early Judaism*. Grand Rapids, Mich.

Reed, Annette Yoshiko. 2023. 'The rabbinic retreat from history and the forgetting of the second temple past'. *Jewish Studies Quarterly* 30: 367–90.

Reed, Annette Yoshiko and John C. Reeves. 2018. *Enoch from Antiquity to the Middle Ages*. Oxford.

Rosen-Zvi, Ishay. 2017. 'Is the Mishnah a Roman composition?' in Christine Hayes, Tzvi Novick and Michal Bar-Asher Siegal, eds., *The Faces of Torah: Studies in the Texts and Contexts of Ancient Judaism in Honor of Steven Fraade*. Göttingen, 487–508.

Schwartz, Daniel R. 2008. 'Remembering the second temple period: Josephus and the rabbis, apologetics and rabbinical training', in Verena Lenzen, ed., *Erinnerung als Herkunft der Zukunft*. Bern, 63–83.

Schwartz, Seth. 2001a. *Imperialism and Jewish Society, 200 BCE–640 CE*. Princeton.

–. 2001b. 'The rabbi in Aphrodite's bath: Palestinian society and Jewish identity in the high Roman empire', in Simon Goldhill, ed., *Being Greek under Rome. Cultural Identity, the Second Sophistic and the Development of Empire*. Cambridge, 335–61.

–. 2016. 'The impact of the Jewish rebellions, 66–135 CE: destruction or provincialization?' in John C. Collins and Josephs Gilbert Mannins, eds., *Revolt and Resistance in the Ancient Classical World and the Near East: In the Crucible of Empire*. Leiden, 234–52.

–. 2020. 'The Mishnah and the limits of Roman power', in Katell Berthelot, ed., *Reconsidering Roman Power: Roman, Greek, Jewish and Christian Perceptions and Reactions*. Rome, 387–416.

Sizgorich, Thomas. 2009. *Violence and Belief in Late Antiquity: Militant Devotion in Christianity and Islam*. Philadelphia.

Stromseth, Jane, David Wippman and Rosa Brooks. 2006. *Can Might Make Rights? Building the Rule of Law after Military Interventions*. New York.

Tropper, Amram. 2004. 'The fate of Jewish historiography after the Bible'. *History & Theory* 43: 179–97.

Walzer, Michael et al. 2015. *The Jewish Political Tradition*, Vol. 1: *Authority*. New Haven, Conn.

Weitzman, Steven. 1999. 'From feasts into mourning: the violence of early Jewish festivals'. *Journal of Religion* 79(4): 545–65.
Woolf, Greg. 2009. *Becoming Roman: The Origins of Provincial Civilization in Gaul*. Cambridge.
–. 2011. 'Provincial revolts in the early Roman empire', in Mladen Popović, ed., *The Jewish Revolt against Rome: Interdisciplinary Perspectives*. Leiden, 27–44.
World Bank. 2011. *World Development Report 2011: Conflict, Security, and Development*. World Bank. https://openknowledge.worldbank.org/handle/10986/4389 License: CC BY 3.0 IGO.
Wright, Jacob L. 2020. *War, Memory, and National Identity in the Hebrew Bible*. Cambridge.

Index

A
Aaron, 289
Abdera, 92 n. 41
accommodation, to imperial rule, 280–83
Acts of Peter, 219
Acts of the Apostles, see New Testament
Aemilius Sura, 44
Aeneas Tacticus, 161–62
agency
    in Christian persecution narratives, 222–40
    in unrest, 12, 13
    in unrest narratives, 12, 13, 15, 25
        of soldiers/plebeians, 132–39
        of women, 27
    of indigenous people in the face of imperial violence, 34–35
Aggadah, 287
Alles, Delphine, 295
American Civil War, 64–65
Ammianus Marcellinus, 200–5, 207–10
ananke, 155, 161
animal metaphors in narratives of unrest, 87, 207, 208
Antiochus IV Epiphanes, 38, 47, 234
Antonine Constitution, 194
Antoninus Pius, 164, 167–68
apocalypse, 46, 47, 286
apocalyptic literature, 39
apology, Christian, 235–40, 247–48
aporia, meaning of, 154

apostasis, 104, 152, 162
Appian
    representation of military unrest, 134, 139 n. 40
    representation of unrest in the provinces, 18, 21–22, 23, 25, 70, 151–59, 161, 163–69
Apuleius, *Golden Ass*, 229 n. 28
Aramaic Levi Document, 40–41
arch of Titus, 281
Aristonicus, revolt of, see slave revolts
Aristotle, 80, 83 n. 20
asphaleia, 94
Athenaeus, 78
Athenion, 78
Athenodorus of Tarsus, 89–91
Athens
    Classical, 75–76, 92 n. 40, 94–95
    Roman period, 78–81
    unrest in 88 BCE, see urban unrest
Augustus, 163–64, 179–80
Aurelius Victor, 195–99
authis polemein, 185–86
automatic response to external stimuli as trope in unrest narratives, 12, 15–16, 87, 107, 165
Avot, see Mishnah
Avot de Rabbi Batan, see Talmud

B
Babylonian Dynastic Prophecy, 44

Badie, Bertrand, 295
Bagaudae, 198–99
bandit stories, 210–11
banditry, 11 n. 9
  in Iberia, 155
  reconceptualised in the *De rebus bellicis*, 213
  trope of, in unrest narratives, 108, 180–81
  see also latrocinium; latrones
Bar Kochba revolt, *see* Judea, unrest in
barbarism, trope in unrest narratives, 12, 26, 87; *see also* ethnicity; geography; race
Batavian Revolt, 69–70 CE, *see* provincial revolts
Bava Kamma, see Mishnah
bellum, 16, 174, 179, 181–82, 214–15
bellum civile, 16–17, 19, 24, 55–57, 66–67, 71, 142 n. 49, 178
bellum intestinum, 60
Beyerle, Stefan, 46
Bible, in the world of the tannaitic rabbis, 288
Boethos of Tarsos, 88
Boudica, 259, 263
boukoloi, 14
Breviarium totius imperii, 163–64
Bryen, Ari, 239

C

Calocerus, revolt of, 195–98
Capua, Roman troops in, *see* military unrest
Carthage, 35–36, 156, 166
Cartimandua, 259
Cassius Dio, 18, 19, 70–71, 139 n. 40, 185–87
categorisation, in discourses of unrest, 16–17
Celsus, 248–49
Chaldaeans, 39, 43
Christian discourses, as a frame for discourse of unrest, 18–19

Christian persecution, 21, 22, 26–27, 219–50
Cicero, 36, 56–57, 61–63, 109
  categorisation of unrest 60, 126, 178–79
Civil Wars, Roman, 24, 60, 70, 165
Clark, Elizabeth, 263
class, in unrest narratives, 22, 26, 158
class bias, of unrest narratives, 85–86, 162
Cleon, 79
Clitomachus, 35–36
Clodius Macer, 259
Cohen, Shaye, 285
coins, Roman imperial, 164, 167
collective action, 10
Collins, John, 284
comedy, as frame for discourses of unrest, 78–79
concordia, 93
coniuratio, 130–31
Corcyra, *stasis* at, *see* Thucydides
Corinthians, Epistles to, see New Testament
Coriolanus, 161
Cover, Robert, 286
criminality, trope in unrest narratives, 12, 16, 22, 26
Cronin, Ciaran, 293

D

Daniel-Hughes, Carly, 239
Daniel, Book of, see Hebrew Bible
David (king), 288
De Greiff, Pablo, 278, 293
De rebus bellicis, 18, 23, 212–14
defectio, 15, 25, 61, 128–30, 174, 179, 267
demagogues, stereotypes of in unrest narratives, 78–79, 81
depoliticisation, in unrest narratives, 77, 82, 91, 94, 165
Deuteronomy, see Hebrew Bible
Devore, David, 244, 246
Diaspora Revolt, in Alexandria, 115–17 CE, 167
Didius, Titus, 155, 158

INDEX

Dio Chrysostom, 77, 85, 94, 97–98
Diodorus Siculus, 87–88, 91 n. 35, 160
diogmos, 21, 26, 225
diōkō, 224–26, 233
diōktēs, 229
Dionysius of Halicarnassus, 36, 160 n. 26, 161
discursive history, 15–23, 124, 153, 247
disease metaphors in narratives of unrest, 89, 111
dream interpretation, 43–45
duBois, Page, 47

E
eirēnarch, 93
eirēnē, 93, 243; *see also* peace (*pax*), rhetoric of
elites,
 Christian, 249
 Greek civic,
  involvement in unrest, 75–98
  understandings of unrest, 24, 75–98
 provincial,
  eager to delegitimise unrest, 24, 27–28, 119–20
  involvement in unrest, 14
  understandings of unrest, 17–18, 20, 24–25, 27–28, 105, 119–20
 Roman imperial,
  involvement in unrest, 175, 204–6
  understandings of unrest, 15–16, 17, 20, 24, 25–26, 158–59
 see also rabbis, tannaitic
Ephesians, Epistle to, *see* New Testament
Ephesos, unrest in, *see* urban unrest
epistemic violence, 18, 24, 34–35
epistemicide, 42–43, 49
emperors, in unrest narratives, 22, 27, 89, 167, 222, 229, 231–34, 236–40, 248
emphylios polemos, 59–61, 66–67
empire, conceptions of, 21–22, 25, 26, 163–64, 166, 169, 174–75, 189, 193–94

Enoch, 286
Enoch, Book of, 233 n. 40
environment, in unrest narratives, 162; *see also* geography; landscapes
Ephesos, unrest in, *see* urban unrest
eschatology, 286
essentialising accounts of character, in unrest narratives, 15–16, 17, 19, 157, 159, 201–2, 207, 215
ethnicity, in unrest narratives, 17, 26, 78, 86, 157, 194, 197–98, 206–7; *see also* barbarism; geography; race
ethnography, as a frame for discourse of unrest, 18
ethnosuicide, 34, 42
Eunapius of Sardis, 200, 205–6, 210–11
Eusebius of Caesarea, 27, 241, 242, 243–44, 262–66
exemplarity, 47
externalising models of unrest, 22, 25–26, 173–89; *see also* internalising models of unrest
Ezra, 281
Ezra, Book of, see Hebrew Bible

F
Falerii (Falisci), revolt of, 22, 24, 59–61
Farrar, Frederic, 220
Fernoux, Henri, 96
Firmus, revolt of, 199–206
fiscality, in unrest narratives, 18, 26, 186–87, 212–14
Flatto, David, 289, 295
Flavius Josephus, *see* Josephus
Florus-Sacrovir revolt of 21 CE, *see* provincial revolts
food insecurity and unrest, 14, 160–61, 209–10
Fox, Matthew, 36
freedom (*libertas*), rhetoric of, 16, 17, 94–95, 106–7
Freeman, Joanne, 64
Fregellae, revolt of, 56, 61–64

fremere, 140

G
Gabriel, archangel, 45
Gaius Gracchus, 156
Galatians, Epistle to, see New Testament
Galla Placidia, 270
Gauthier, Philippe, 89
gender, in unrest narratives, 27; *see also* women
geography, in unrest narratives, 157, 158, 162; *see also* environment; landscapes
Gérôme, Jean-Léon, 220
Gillespie, Caitlin, 261
Gleason, Maud, 239
Golden Ass, see Apuleius
Gospels, *see* New Testament
governors, Roman, *see* magistrates
Grunewald, Thomas, 181
Guha, Ranajit, 12, 13–14, 28, 112

H
Hadrian, 163, 166, 167
Hahn, István, 166
Hasdrubal, 166
Hebrew Bible
    Book of Daniel, 18, 23–24, 33–50, 231, 232, 233
    Book of Ezra, 224 n. 12
    Book of Micah, 224 n. 12
    Book of Psalms, 46, 230, 231, 236
    Deuteronomy, 278, 290 n. 22
    Leviticus, 278, 280
    Numbers, 290
Hegesippus, 243
Hellenisation, Judaean, 39
Heller, Anna, 96
Herennius Modestinus, 142–44
Herodotus, 44, 92 n. 40
Hippolytus, 37 n. 12
Historia Augusta, 211–12
historiography, as a frame for discourses of unrest, 18, 141–42

Homer, 83 n. 19
homonoia, 76, 93
hostis publicus, 56
Huqoq Mosaics, 39

I
idolatry, in the Jewish tradition, 18, 290–92
immorality, trope in unrest narratives, 12, 15, 17, 19, 20, 157
internalising models of unrest, 22, 25–26, 187–89; *see also* externalising models of unrest
irrationality, trope in unrest narratives, 12, 25
Isauria, unrest in, 206–12
Iulius Civilis, 182–85
iusta seditio, 128, 143

J
January 6th 2021, 9
Jerusalem, 167, 275–76, 281
Jerusalem Talmud, *Rosh Hashanah*, 283 n. 8
Jesus of Nazareth, 224, 286
John, Epistles of, see New Testament
John, Gospel of, see New Testament
John the Baptist, 224, 286
Josephus, 41, 276, 280, 281–80
    representation of unrest in the *Jewish Antiquities*, 290 n. 22, 291 n. 23
    representation of unrest in the *Jewish War*, 17, 20, 24–25, 103–20, 263, 290–91
Jubilees, Book of, 290 n. 22
Judea, unrest in, 12, 14–15, 18, 282, 284, 285–86
    in 167–60 BCE, 38, 290
    in second century BCE, 33–50
    in 66–70 CE, 103–20, 181–82, 183, 263, 275–76
    in 132–36 CE, 279, 285–86, 286–87
    in 351/1 CE, 196–98
    see also Diaspora Revolt
jurisprudence, 22, 26

as a frame for discourses of unrest, 18, 142–43, 177–78, 187–89
jurists, Roman, 17, 25, 142–44, 173–78, 187–89
Justice, Stephen, 12, 13–14
justice, value in unrest narratives, 84, 86
Justin, 235, 236–37, 240–41

K
Kalymna, 36
Kelly, Benjamin, 184
kinēma, 104 n. 5
Kosmin, Paul, 38, 45
Kotrosits, Maia, 41, 239

L
Lactantius, 241–43, 245–46
land, theme in unrest narratives, 18, 25, 153–59, 162–63, 165
landscapes, in which unrest is seen as natural, 157, 183, 201–2, 206–7
Lantschner, Patrick, 13
latrocinium, 180–81, 188, 108, 267
latrones, 26, 194
lawfulness, rhetoric of, 84–85
legati Augusti pro praetore, 164
legalism, 277, 286, 296
legitimacy, in unrest narratives, 19, 20, 21–22, 24, 82, 83 167; *see also* unrest, delegitimisation of
Lendon, Jon, 123
LeRoy, Mervyn, 219–21
lēstai, 20, 107, 108, 152
lēsteia, 19
Leviticus, see Hebrew Bible
Livy, 25, 27, 161 n. 31, 125–31, 257–62
Lucretia, 259, 265
Luiselli, Valeria, 35
Luke, Gospel of, see New Testament
Lusitanian War, 155
Lusitanians, slaughter of, 158, 166, 167
Lycia, unrest in, 81–83, 85

M
Maccabean Revolt, *see* Judea, unrest in
Maccabees,
 First Book of, 42, 231
 First and Second Books of, 37
MacRae, Duncan, 46
Mader, Gottfried, 111, 115
magistrates, Roman, in unrest narratives, 15, 17, 157–58, 158–59, 167, 229
Malik, Shushma, 232
Manesas of Termessos, 91–93
Marius, 70
Mark, Gospel of, see New Testament
Marshall, Anthony, 258
Mason, Steve, 105
martyrdom narratives, 219–21, 222 n. 6, 264
Marx, Karl, 151–52, 168
materialism, in unrest narratives, 151–53, 168, 186–87
Matthew, Gospel of, see New Testament
Melian Dialogue, 161
Melito of Sardis, 238
Mercenary Revolt against Carthage, 22, 60–61
messianism, 286–87
Micah, Book of, see Hebrew Bible
migration narratives, 162
minoritisation, 37, 249
Minucius Felix, 248
military unrest, 16, 25, 123–45
 among Roman troops in Capua in 342 BCE, 125–31
 on Rhine frontier in 14 CE, 135–39, 259–60
Mishnah, 46, 277, 287, 296
 Avot, 286, 293
 Bava Kamma, 293
Mithridates VI Eupator, 14, 78, 153–54, 157–58
moral character, in unrest narratives, 17, 17–18, 19, 81, 84, 87–88, 89, 157, 167
Moses, 286

motus, 12, 267
murmuring,
    strategy in military unrest, 139–40
    trope of in narratives of unrest, 140–42
    see also soundscapes
mutiny,
    no separate term for in latin, 16, 123–24 n. 1, 126
    see also military unrest; *seditio*
Mylasa, unrest in, *see* urban unrest

N

Naiweld, Ron, 295
Nasrallah, Laura, 239
New Testament
    Acts of the Apostles, 226–29, 231
    Book of Revelation, 224 n. 13, 231–34, 241, 244–45
    Epistle of John 1, 232 n. 36, 241
    Epistle of Peter 1, 232 n. 33, 241
    Epistle to Philemon, 230
    Epistle to the Corinthians 1, 230
    Epistle to the Corinthians 2, 230
    Epistle to the Ephesians, 234 n. 43
    Epistle to the Galatians, 227 n. 24, 230
    Epistle to the Philippians, 230
    Epistle to the Romans, 230, 233 n. 39
    Epistle to the Thessalians 1, 230
    Epistle to the Thessalians 2, 230, 232 n. 36, 234 n. 43
    Epistle to Timothy 1, 229
    Epistle to Timothy 2, 230–31
    Gospel of John, 226, 241
    Gospel of Luke, 225–26, 235, 240, 241
    Gospel of Mark, 223–24, 225, 235, 241
    Gospel of Matthew, 224–25, 235, 241
Nebuchadnezzar, 39, 41–43, 44
necessity, in unrest narratives, 154–56, 161–62, 166
neōterismos, 104, 113
Nero, 220–22, 231–33, 237–38, 242, 243–44, 247
New Comedy, 47

Noam, Vered, 285
non-state spaces, 11 n. 9
Numantia, destruction of, 166–67
Numbers, *see* Hebrew Bible

O

O'Gorman, Ellen, 182
Opimius, Lucius, 61–63, 69–70
Orosius of Braga, 22, 27, 266–71
Osgood, Josiah, 68, 163–64
Ouliades, in Mylasa, 90–91

P

Patara, *see stadiasmos Patarensis*
Parsard, Kaneesha Cherelle, 48
paternalism, in unrest narratives, 88
Paul (apostle), 227–29
peace (*pax*), rhetoric of, 10, 13, 24, 77, 81–82, 86, 90, 280, 288–89; *see also eirēnē*
peiratai, 152
Pékary, Thomas, 11
Pericles, 85
Peter, Epistles of, *see* New Testament
philantrōpia, 87–88
Philemon, Epistle to, *see* New Testament
Philippians, Epistle to, *see* New Testament
philosophy, as a frame for discourses of unrest, 78, 92, 154
philotimia, 92–93
Phineas, 290
piracy
    after the First Mithridatic War, 153–54, 157–58
    from Cilicia, 157
    in Roman law, 176–77
Plato, 79, 162 n. 31
plēthos, 82
Plutarch, 85 n. 24, 94–95
poetry and unrest, 88–89
polemos, 19, 27
politeia, 76

political thought, as a frame for discourses
    of unrest, 18, 80
Polybius, 2, 36, 45 n. 27, 58–61, 80 n. 11, 83
    n. 19, 86–87
Pompey, 157, 167
Pomponius, Sextus, 173, 175–76
Portier-Young, Anathea, 34, 38, 47
Porphyry, 249
post-conflict reconstruction, 278–79
potentes, in unrest narratives, 18–19
Posidonios of Apamea, 78–81, 159–60
Price, Jonathan, 59
prophecy, 45–46, 49, 285–86
prose of counter-insurgency, 12–13, 15–16,
    20, 112
provincial revolts, 11 n. 9, 13, 14, 23, 25, 26,
    173–89
  Batavian Revolt, 69–70 CE, 182–84,
    260
  Gaul, 21 CE, 181, 183
  Mauretania, 370–74 CE, 199–206
  see also Diaspora Revolt; Judea; Isauria
Psalms, Book of,
Pseudo-Daniel, 44
Punic War, First, 58–59, 156
Punic War, Second, 56
Purcell, Nicholas, 35–36

Q
Qumran community, 50, 286
Quo Vadis, 219–22, 247

R
rabbis, tannaitic, 18, 20, 27–28, 283–93
Rabasa, José, 34, 36, 42, 49
race, in unrest narratives, 158; *see also*
    barbarism; ethnicity; geography
Rajak, Tessa, 42
rationality in narratives of unrest, *see*
    irrationality
rebellare, 186
rebellio, 15–17, 19, 174, 179, 184–85, 267
Reeder, Caryn A., 261

religion, in unrest narratives, 115–18
res novae, 196
resistance, 10, 11 n. 9, 13 n. 11, 21, 23, 34, 37,
    279, 280–83
Revelation, Book of, see New Testament
rhetoric, as a frame for discourses of
    unrest, 18, 25, 78, 161
Rhine frontier, *see* military unrest
Romans, Epistle to, see New Testament
rule of law, 277–80
rural unrest, 11 n. 9, 198–9

S
Sabine women, 259–60
Sallust, 68–70, 213
Sagalassos, unrest in, *see* urban unrest
Samos, 91 n. 36
Satan, 234–35
SC de Cn. Pisone patre, 142 n. 49
Schwartz, Seth, 39, 276, 294
Scipio Aemilianus, 166–67
Segal, Michael, 41
secessio (plebis), 127–28
Secession of the Plebs, 161
sectarianism, rabbinic discussions of, 18,
    27
securitas, 181
seditio, 16, 17, 19, 126–27, 131, 178, 184, 267;
    see also iusta seditio
Servilius Caepio, Quintus, 155, 158
Shaw, Brent, 239
Sibylline Oracle, Fourth, 44
Sicilian Slave War, First and Second, *see*
    slave revolts
Sienkiewicz, Henryk, 220
Sifre Deuteronomy, 275, 281, 285, 288
Sifre Numbers, 290, 291
sikarioi, 20, 109
slave revolts, 10, 11 n. 9, 14
  Aristonicus, revolt of, 14, 47
  First Sicilian Slave War, 160–61
  Second Sicilian Slave War, 87–88

social order, conceptions of, 86–95; *see also* peace (*pax*), rhetoric of
Social War, 66, 69–70
soundscapes of unrest, 139–44
sovereigntism, 294–96
spontaneity, trope in unrest narratives, 12, 13, 17, 183, 185–86
stadiasmos Patarensis, 46 BCE, 81–86
statues, destruction of, 44–45
stasis
    changes in meaning, 17, 20
    in Thucydides, 57, 58, 59, 77, 81, 86
    representation of arbitrators, 90–94
    representation of factions, 78–85, 87–90
    threat to cultured civility and peace, 86–95
    traditional and/or classicising discourses, 77–86, 89, 93–98
    usage in Josephus, 19, 104, 111–15
Stephen (martyr), 226–27
stoning, 10, 227–28
Strabo, 180, 88–91, 162
Stromseth, Jane, 278
subalternity, 48, 249, 296
Suetonius, 46 n. 32, 163 n. 33, 180–81
Sulla, 24, 66–67, 70
Sulpicius Galba, Servius, 155, 158, 167
survivance, 24, 34
Susannah and the Elders, 49

T
Tacfarinas, 108, 180–81, 202
Tacitus
    representation of unrest, 15–16, 17, 20, 25, 27, 158–59, 180–81, 182–85
        female involvement, 257–62
        military unrest, 135–39
        unrest in Judaea, 281, 290 n. 22
    thematisation of unrest in the *Histories*, 11, 182
Talmud, 46
    Avot de Rabbi Batan, 275–76

see also Mishnah
tannaim, *see* rabbis, tannaitic
Tarquinius Superbus, 44, 259
Tarsos, unrest in, *see* urban unrest
taxation, *see* fiscality
Telos, 91 n. 36
Temple, in Jerusalem, 289
terrorism, 174
Tertullian, 235–36, 237–38, 240 n. 57, 241–43
textualisation, as response to imperial violence, 34–36, 46–47, 49–50
Thessalians, Epistles to, *see* New Testament
Thucydides, 57–58, 68, 77, 81, 82 n. 17, 84 n. 20, 86, 160 n. 26, 161
Tiberius, 180–81
Timothy, Epistles to, *see* New Testament
Titus, 281
tlacuilo, 35
Torah, 46, 285; *see also* Hebrew Bible
Tosefta
    Shabbat, 291 n. 24
    '*Avodah Zarah*, 293
tragedy, as frame for discourses of unrest, 166
Trajan, 164, 167
translatio imperii, 43
triumph, 62
tumultus, 15, 56, 179, 198
turnips, 10
tyrannus, 194, 204
tyranny, in unrest narratives, 22, 26, 80

U
Ulpian, 173–76, 187–88
urban unrest, 11 n. 9, 13, 14, 15
    in Athens, 88 BCE, 77–81
    in Corcyra, *see* Thucydides
    in Ephesos, 14
    in Mylasa, 90–91
    in Sagalassos, 91–93
    in Tarsos, 88–91
unrest,

attitudes to, 19–20, 165
boundary-work performed by the term in ordinary usage, 13
defined, 10, 12, 13
delegitimisation of, 20, 21, 82, 108–15; *see also* legitimacy, in unrest narratives
female experience of, 255–56
frequency of in the Roman empire, 11, 124 n. 2
observers of, 28
poetry in, 88–89
politics of, 13–15
relationship to Roman rule, 13
responses to, 158, 166–67
see also banditry; Christian persecution; Civil Wars, Roman; Judea, unrest in; military unrest; mutiny; provincial revolts; slave revolts; urban unrest; usurpation
unrest, discourses of, 15–19
categorisation in, 16–17
contestation over, 77–98
explanation in, 17–18, 19
framing in, 18–19, 159–63
histories of, 22–23
influences between Greek and Latin, 19
influence of Roman context on, 76, 93–94, 96
innovation in, 19, 21, 22–23, 25
modern, 9, 28
politics of, 19–23
relationship to conceptions of empire, 21–22, 163–69, 174–75, 193–94, 238–40
relationship to conceptions of social order, 24
responsibility in, 24–25, 26–27
subject positions in, 19, 21
see also agency; animal metaphors; automatic response; barbarism; class; class bias; criminality; demagogues; stereotypes of; depoliticisation; disease metaphors; environment; ethnicity; food; gender; geography; immorality; irrationality; land; landscapes; legitimacy; moral character; murmuring; paternalism; poetry; race; spontaneity
unrest, lexicon of, 16–17, 19, 20, 21, 246, 248; *see also apostasis; authis polemein; bellum; bellum civile; bellum intestinum; coniuratio; defectio; diogmos; emphylios polemos; kinēma; latrocinium; lēsteia; motus; neōterismos; polemos; rebellio; res novae; secessio; seditio; sikarioi; tumultus*
usurpation, 11 n. 9, 22, 193–216

V
Velleius Paterculus, 69–70, 136, 180–81
Verginia, 260
Vespasian, 167, 275–76
Victorinus of Pettau, 233
Viriatus, 108, 158
Vizenor, Gerald, 34
vociferatio, 140–44

W
war, horrors of, 167
wisdom literature, 40–41
Weitzman, Steven, 39, 41
Witzke, Serena, 256
Woolf, Greg, 138–39, 294
women, in unrest narratives, 18, 21, 22, 27, 255–72
World Bank, World Development Report on Conflict, Security, and Development, 278

X
Xenophon, 80–81, 83 n. 21

Y
Yohanan ben Zakkai, 275–76, 292

Contributors

Katell Berthelot is CNRS professor affiliated with the Centre Paul-Albert Février, Aix-Marseille University. Her field is the history of Judaism in the Greco-Roman world, with a particular focus on Jewish literature in Greek, the Dead Sea Scrolls and rabbinic literature.

James Corke-Webster is Reader in Classics, History and Liberal Arts at King's College London. His research focuses on early Christian and late antique history and literature, focussing on Christian historiography and martyr narratives.

Natalie B. Dohrmann is the Associate Director of the Katz Center for Advanced Judaic Studies at the University of Pennsylvania and the co-editor of the *Jewish Quarterly Review*. She specializes in rabbinic Judaism, with a special interest in ancient Jewish law and its Greco-Roman context.

Lisa Pilar Eberle is Assistant Professor in the Institute for Ancient History at the University of Tübingen. She is a historian of the Roman republic and empire, with a particular interest in legal culture, settler colonialism, and the relationship between rule and resistance.

Benjamin Gray is Senior Lecturer in the School of Historical Studies at Birkbeck, University of London. His research focuses on ancient Greek city-states, their ethical and political debates, and the implications of those debates for the later history of citizenship, democracy and political theory.

Hans Kopp is Assistant Professor in the Institute of History at the University of Cologne. His research examines Greek historiography and concepts of 'rule over the sea' (*thalassokratia*), Roman discourses and practices of disobedience, and the reception of classical antiquity in later periods.

Carsten Hjort Lange is Associate Professor of History at Aalborg University. He is a Roman historian with an emphasis on republican history, focusing on civil war, political and military history as well as ancient historiography.

Myles Lavan is Professor of Classics at the University of St. Andrews. His research draws on comparative and quantitative methods to investigate slavery, citizenship, and the ideology and language of empire in the Roman world.

Dan-el Padilla Peralta is Associate Professor of Classics at Princeton University. He works on the religions and politics of the Roman republic and empire, shuttling between literary and material sources and social-scientific approaches.

Bruno Pottier is Professor of History at Aix-Marseille University. He is a historian of Late Antiquity with a focus on historiography, religious movements, and cultures of violence, especially in Gaul and North Africa.

Ulriika Vihervalli is based at the National Library of Finland and is an Honorary Research Fellow at the University of Liverpool. She is a late Roman historian specialising in societal and cultural change between the fourth to sixth centuries CE with a focus on gender and sexual norms and behaviours in patristic thought.